Dogs Hate Crates:

How Abusive Crate Training Hurts Dog Families & Society

A scientific and emotional expose on the most widespread abuse of dogs in society today, and one of the last taboos that dog lovers still fear to confront. Dogs Hate Crates *reveals how America's acceptance of excessively crating/caging dogs- both in puppy mills and private homes- contributes to a variety of extremely serious problems that increasingly affect all of us. What you read will shock you.*

by
Ray & Emma Lincoln
Authors of *The Cure for Useless Dog Syndrome*

Dogs Hate Crates: How Abusive Crate Training Hurts Dog Families & Society

By Ray & Emma Lincoln

Copyright @ 2011 by Ray & Emma Lincoln

Published by: Awesome Book Publishing
P.O. Box 1157
Roseland, FL 32957

First Edition

ISBN: 978-0-9840538-5-8

Disclaimer: This book is intended to provide general information about the negative effects of excessively crating/caging dogs and general advice about positive alternatives for training and housing. The authors and the publisher do not offer any specific advice or treatment plans in this book for individual cases, and this book is not intended as a substitute for the advice of a veterinarian, qualified behaviorist, etc. for the care, training or treatment of readers' dogs. **DANGER: It's not safe to suddenly open a crate or cage without a safe plan and allow a dog (or especially a young puppy) out if the animal is in immediate danger of injuring or killing itself** for example, by chewing on exposed electric wires or ingesting chemicals. First, make appropriate plans and arrangements to protect the dog, which could include "dog-proofing" (removing hazards); proper supervision & behavior training; and keeping young pups in safe areas. **CAUTION: There is danger of death or extreme physical injury if people release crated dogs that are behaving aggressively without first taking appropriate safety precautions.** The authors advise readers to evaluate each situation carefully before they act to keep humans (especially children) and animals safe and to consult local experts and make decisions based on their best judgment. This book doesn't offer specific advice for individual cases, since safety precautions differ depending upon many factors. Owners should make decisions for housing and training their dogs based on the safest alternatives; and/or consult qualified local professionals. The authors and Publisher waive any liability in cases of injury to humans, animals or property.

This book is lovingly dedicated: by Ray to the memories of Alfie & Killer and by Emma to the memories of Lola, Boss & Baby- our beloved canine relatives who raised us.

Table of Contents

Prologue: Dawn at a Suspected Puppy Mill; The Case of "Boxy"

Our vigil starts at dawn. But even though we may witness animals' suffering, we probably can't rescue any dogs today. Cruelty to dogs is a particularly difficult crime to prove because of the way it hides behind locked doors and the veil of rural and suburban secrecy. And, even though reports of what we expect to find inside deeply sadden us, all we can do today is gather evidence. The dogs will likely sleep again tonight as they did last night, until the law can make a judgment.

Currently, laws are insufficient to do much about the particular shades of gray behind the shingles and the thick landscaping. For now we have to wonder what the neighbors would think as they woke up and brewed their coffee this morning if they knew of the pain hiding behind the weathered privacy fence and the screen of trees. We watch a polished black pickup truck back quickly out of the driveway with a whispered hush. It isn't even 7:00 in the morning, it's still dark, and already, from deep within the bowels of the structure, we hear a puppy screaming.

The sound explodes as we step into a completely darkened anteroom with unclear purpose. The excited shrillness of the animals' cries rise in intensity as we step in from outdoors. Sharp yelps that feel like rusted implements jabbing at our ears seem to bounce from all directions, alternating with frenzied bouts of low labored panting that sound more like a little freight train than a little dog. Then we're assailed by another scream like the one we heard from outside.

The sound seems to crash through every nerve in our bodies, like a lighting rod drawing a bolt. Meanwhile we try to fight disorientation in the small, darkened space. The smell of feces assails our noses, a sick diarrhea smell, reminiscent of the lingering smell in those animal shelters that still euthanize dogs. It's a unique smell that can never be covered up by ammonia- the smell of generations of dogs' terror. As I pull the outer door fully shut behind us, more waves of odor assail us in the space of unknown dimensions, which feels stuffy and suffocating like a trap.

The time I've spent in the space can be measured in seconds, but it's already oppressive. Philosophically, I struggle with the feeling of losing my identity as a successful career woman and even losing a part of my soul in this moment. In this place I feel completely removed from the orderly schedule on my Blackberry, the messages on my voicemail and the unopened packet of exotic coffee blend waiting beside the mug my editor gave me last Christmas. Here it's easy to forget the striking city backdrop that can usually jumpstart my inspiration before deadlines; easy to forget the time of day, the season of year and my priorities and ideologies from just a few moments ago when I could still breathe.

In this space just drawing a deep breath seems like a priority. All I crave this second is air and light and a reprieve from the sound of the animal's screaming that threatens to tear apart my civilized brain. Along with the vocalizations, we hear a constant rattling and pattering sound- also frenzied- that sounds as if ten dogs are caged in here. As we advance the jangle of metal becomes even louder, and the huffing and the screaming increase, along with the waves of sickly fecal odor. Truly, in my pounding heart, I don't really know if I wish to see what is contained in the cage.

Now my partner switches on his flashlight. A single bronze beam cuts across the deep shadows in the direction of the animal's cries and I have my first view of the reality. Two green, almost phosphorescent, eyes shine from the darkness, staring at us. The screaming, clawing and rattling stops for a second and this gives me time for my first deep breath.

Then all the noises resume, seemingly ten times more vigorously than before. In the split second of pause, I've seen inside the cage. Now I just have to make sense of the different pieces of my observation to put them together. The wide glowing eyes, the white foam-decorated huffing jowls, the twisted unnatural posture of bent skinny back-they are all nothing more than ugly manifestations of the animal being cramped in the too-small cage. What we're actually looking at is a puppy. He appears to be a purebred brindle-colored Boxer pup, about 9 months old, with a white mask around a funny face that, in other settings, might be considered endearingly cute. But here, his somewhat exaggerated features seem to represent no more than a stylized mask of pathos.

In perfect health, this animal could be valuable, selling for up to $1,200-$2,500 in the retail market. But observing him in this context, it is hard to see. It's hard to process everything I know with journalistic objectivity. Although I love dogs, it's hard not to take an instinctive step back just to regain my own bearings. And it's hard not to want to escape outside to recharge on the power of life lived in freedom, where one can judge the time of day from the position of sun in sky.

I blink as the animal in the cage again goes crazy. He spins in tight circles, causing his small cage to rock on itself, and we notice loose feces squeeze out onto a towel folded under the cage, apparently anticipating this mess.

After a bit more rattling, the animal gives a frenzied yelp, even more shrill and pained than the other cries.

I look to my partner. "I think he might have hurt himself".

Cautiously, I step closer to the cage. It's strange how this environment has made even a confirmed dog lover like me recoil with what I guess is some atavistic fear of something so unnatural. As my partner holds the small flashlight beam up to help me, I immediately see the problem. The animal, shaking so hard now that his forty-pound body hitting the cage also creates a rattling, has caught his paw in the wire.

It's hard to make sense of his position, his unnaturally twisted back, his pouting clownish face and his jowls and snuffling nose smeared with feces pressed into the bars, distorting their shape. It's hard to tell if the puppy is really deformed or just shoved into a much too small cage that he cannot stand in without crouching.

The wire cage is just big enough for him to turn around in, but not quite tall enough for him to comfortably stand, hence the bent back. I try to assess his predicament as accurately as possible, but it's hard as the puppy trembles and claws, rocking the cage. One paw is free, and he lifts it repeatedly in frenzy, splaying his toes as he hits at one wire wall. The other paw, which is brindle colored with a little white mitten soiled now with feces and what seems like rivulets of red blood, has been caught above him within the bars of the cage. His little clownlike face gyrates under the trapped paw, biting at it attempting to free it. As he huffs, it sounds almost like he's laughing.

I bend to get close, pushing my camera out of the way on one hip and attempt to push on the trapped paw from the outside. The puppy gives another sudden scream, which feels like a knife cutting through me. The paw is slick with feces and blood and the puppy's thin hot drool; the scream frightens me and I lose my tenuous grip, failing him as his sounds settle back to whimpers and he squints shut those imploring big brown eyes.

"Oh, screw," I let slip in frustration. Deeper in the structure, I suddenly hear, unmistakably, the frenzied barking of more dogs- multiple small dogs, it sounds like. I know my partner must hear it, too. "God," I say. "What are we going to do?"

"Just try to free this one's paw."

I go back to the cage and grasp the splayed white mitten harder, this time ignoring if I cause pain as I wrestle several of the plump toe pads around the deeply pressed in wire that hurts my hand, too. "Be calm, little Boxy," I tell the animal, almost ashamed that I have christened him with a name. "It's all right. It will be all right," I lie.

The puppy struggles so that I feel his hot teeth and tongue on my fingers, but he doesn't bite. As his freed paw falls from the wire with a thump, his body hits the side of the cage. Ungainly, he fills almost the entire space as he slumps in a silly approximation of lying down, but without enough room to stretch out his gangling growing legs.

Simultaneously, my partner breathes, "Be careful". His warning is unnecessary, for now I can only see this Boxer as the puppy he is. Something has snapped in me after I pushed past my irrational barrier of fear of the unknown and touched him.

The dog seems to sense that I've come over more to his side. He pushes his face in a corner, making silly sounds of breathing and trying to lick at me through the bars. He tries to dance with his paws but cannot get balance. He moans deep in his chest with frustrated love.

Despite the stench of his sick feces that darken his white stockings and slick every inch of his purebred brindle body, I am also in love. I know I'm a professional, come here to expose these conditions for the greater good, but if I were seeing this dog in a pet store right now, I would take him. It would be hard to remove him from the cage without being hit by flailing body parts, too-long claws that now won't stop their digging motion even for an instant and the ever-present mess of diarrhea. But I still crave to cuddle the flailing animal up against my chest just long enough to take him out of here.

I look up to a nearby surface and make out the shape of a thick white towel, part of a pile that is perhaps used to clean up the dogs.

"Can I take him out of the cage?" I ask, "Just to clean him up?"

There's just enough light for me to see my partner frown as he shakes his head. He steps around, looking for a source of light, finds a tiny window behind a washing machine piled high with soiled white linens and cranks a dusty fake wood mini-blind that's probably rarely opened. A little misty light filters in and we see it would have been futile to search for a light switch in here, since the pebbled ceiling has no overhead fixture. The room is cramped, and filled- with more filthy linens from the dogs awaiting washing, with tools and utility items whose function is not immediately clear, and stacked cardboard bankers' boxes stuffed with what must be years of financial records. All is dwarfed by a super-sized washer and dryer, probably an investment of thousands of dollars proving that, whatever these people are, they certainly aren't hurting for money.

My partner breaks my reverie by sliding the camera from off my shoulder so that he can start angling around the cage, snapping photos. I remember to take out my handheld pad and I start scribbling some notes.

Although the whimpering pup is now firmly established in my mind as "Boxy", I describe him in as clinical and dispassionate shorthand as possible. "Purebred Boxer- undersized for his age- yellow diarrhea- excessive tearing/panting. Abnormal vocalizations." (Boxy's voice is raw, raspy and hollow from what may have been months of daily screaming. Now that we're near and I've touched him, his sharp shrieks have stopped. Now he whimpers, alternating with an odd rumbling sound- not growling, but more like a sound the earth might make before an earthquake or some natural eruption. I've never heard a dog make quite this sound before.)

"Come on," my partner says as he reaches toward the window, ready to crank the blind closed again. "We better photograph the other dogs while we can."

I touch his shoulder to stop him, while I quickly glance around and down and then back up at the ceiling. "There's no air conditioning vent in this area, is there?"

"It doesn't look like it," he says.

Right now, this side of the building is completely shaded and even with the early hour and sun just rising, we are already sweating and finding it hard to breathe in here. I calculate the sun's movement for later in the day and I imagine that this tiny room with no ventilation will start to bake in a few more hours. I scrawl more notes, leaning the pad on my leg so I can also bend and examine the inside of the cage, looking for something specific.

I am met with two deep brown eyes, questioning and full of pathos. The puppy licks his nose in a hopeful expectation of getting out to greet me that has no basis in reality, or former experience, but everything to do with the unique faith of a dog. And just so I'll notice him in case I haven't, he dances on his mittens even harder and lets rip with a drawn-out yodel-like cry that's almost amusing.

I find myself smiling and apologizing. "No, not you, Boxy. You can't go with us."

My soft mushy voice hardens to a more serious tone as I report to my partner over my shoulder. "They left nothing in this cage for him. No toys. Nothing... He's an intelligent animal... How can he just sit here all day every day?"

My partner just adjusts his long lens to take more pictures of the 9-month old puppy. I can't even be sure Boxy will be alive when the people who own this property return. Yet I must wait, and reason that Boxy's lived so many days like this already and he'll probably continue to live for as long as we have to struggle with legal channels to get him help.

How the animal suffers is another story, one we can only hope to bring to the world by continuing to act dispassionately while we follow proper procedure. Since I am a woman of reason, information and scientific facts, I cannot break the law on a whim of my heart and just steal this puppy away from here. My priority must be to protect the good of the many, including those dogs we hear whimpering deeper in this structure, and all those others being bought, sold, bred and housed like this, all across America, day after day, year after year until the end of their lives.

If there's going to be a change, just like with other important social movements in the recent past, we must trust that facts will do it, and our larger efforts would only be hampered by the impulsive protectiveness of a woman's motherly heart.

But still my voice cracks as I exclaim, "But there's no water dish in his cage! And this room is going to bake. The sun probably hit this wall at one or two in the afternoon, and it won't go down until after seven. How may hours until they get back to give this dog water? Eight hours? Ten? *Twelve?*"

At first the only answer is the Boxer pup's now thready whimpers as he settles with his face splayed on a paw and his nose pressed through a little square of feces-soiled wire. My partner snaps the camera's lens cap back on, and cranks the plastic mini-blind to again shroud the anteroom in dimness. I can make out enough to see his lips tighten as he tells me, "That's exactly what we're here to find out..."

The story of "Boxy" is fiction but, unfortunately, it's based on real cases we've encountered, with nothing exaggerated. And the particular horror of this case is not just the suffering of this dog, but the scale on which the same conditions are repeated, every day, in communities across America. The story above also asks you to think a bit. As you read it, you may have perceived something uniquely disquieting, something that brought an instinctive chill as you found yourself more than just disturbed, but sensing something that scared and shook you in an even deeper sense.

Now, if you're ready to step out of your comfort zone, we'll ask you to venture into a philosophical and moral area where perception changes everything. The exact same scenario, as written above, a story that any compassionate dog lover would feel disturbed reading, can be recast. The real abuse the story characterizes is *so* extreme and *so* prevalent that dog lovers will feel compelled to do something to stop it as soon as they see the truth. But, in order to see the truth, we must be ready to believe it, and to never see our world quite the same way... Because the real horrors of crating dogs go far beyond puppy mills.

Chapter 1: Introduction- The Worst Abuse of Dogs Today

Part A: Excessive Crating- The Worst Abuse of Dogs Today

It's easy to assume the story of "Boxy" is the story of a "puppy mill", where mass numbers of dogs intended for breeding and sale to pet shops are caged year after year in inhumane conditions.

Boxy is an innocent young dog suffering in a cramped wire cage, and in the confines of his yearning and frustrated mind, for 12 hours of hell every day, followed by 8 or more hours of the same each evening. If we believe that an animal has the ability to feel emotional pain, then this pup feels it daily, in addition to all his physical discomfort. If we believe he has either a mind, a heart or a soul, it will disturb us to perceive the hours of distress he suffers, knowing he'll likely live like this for the rest of his life.

But what if you knew that the way Boxy, and millions of other dogs like him, are living is a story of love; of the deepest, most spiritual love for a family member? What if the people who put this young dog in the cage he lived in all day believed their motives were the highest? And what if they were told to cage him by experts? The truth is, in America today, the people who sentence dogs like Boxy to life in cages may be your friends. They may be your next-door neighbors or your relatives. Or they may even be you.

The truth is, the "puppy mill" described in the preceding chapter- the stifling little room where a screaming young dog is left in his own filth in a tiny cage for 12 hours at a stretch and up to 23 hours total on weekdays- exists in a well-kept suburban home right next to yours. And most families that house their dogs like this are otherwise average law-abiding people who may have been convinced by professionals and online propaganda that it's the right thing.

Right now, you probably know people who crate their pet dogs, for life, under similar conditions for up to 12 hours at a stretch and up to 18-23 hours total per day. These people may be otherwise nice, reasonable folks that you turn to for financial advice, education, medical care or even spiritual guidance. They may identify themselves as devoted dog lovers, and they may not even realize how little freedom they allow their dogs.

In recent decades, special interests throughout the dog industry have deliberately "spun" the concept of locking pet dogs in cramped cages in suburban homes as something positive to make families accept the fiction that dogs actually *enjoy* living locked in cramped wire cages 18-23 hours total per day- because a crate resembles a dog's "home" or "den". And people you know may have already told you to cage *your* dog or puppy...

DEFINITIONS:

1. Definition of a Dog Crate:

A small wire or plastic cage that locks, used to contain a pet dog so that he cannot move around freely or escape until released by a human. Today, crates are increasingly being used for housetraining, behavioral training and for housing pet dogs whenever owners are away from home. There are many sizes and "experts" advise using a crate size small enough that the dog has no more room to move than to stand up and turn around. Crates are commonly used inside houses. But there're also frequently used outdoors (sometimes stacked) by large-scale puppy mill breeders or breeders of dogs used for fighting. And some shelters and rescues are now stacking small crates to make room for many more dogs than they could if they continued to use traditional kennels.

People who recommend crates for pet dogs never refer to them as cages (even though this is exactly what they are). Instead "experts" strongly encourage dog owners to use

euphemistic terms including: "house", "bed", "home", "room" or, misuse of the word "kennel". (True kennels are actually full-size wire indoor and/or outdoor enclosures that are many times larger and leave dogs room to walk, pace and play.)

Popular dimensions for home dog crates vary from as small as 22 in. x 13 in. x 16 in; to "extra-large". The medium large size, used for dogs like Boxers, Golden Retrievers, Labrador Retrievers or Pit Bulls is 36x24x28. Dog behavior expert Diane Jessup's website, workingpitbull.com explains in detail that these dimensions are smaller than the dimensions allowed by law for cages for laboratory dogs. The area in a crate is also significantly smaller than the average square footage a tethered dog has to wander in.

2. Definition of Excessive Home Dog Crating: **Crating or caging a pet dog for a period of time that produces immediate or long-term physical pain, emotional distress or negative behavioral changes in the dog; and/or any negative consequences or risk of danger to the owners.**

Each situation is completely different depending upon the effect upon the individual dog and thus the definition of "excessive crating" must always be subjective.

Some people consider any amount of caging a dog cruel, while others become disturbed when daily crating goes beyond a certain number of hours. Most people who care about dogs would probably agree that crating a pet dog at home every weekday for the rest of his life for 18 to 22 or 23 total hours each day is excessive, yet this practice is currently common among "normal, average" Americans who provide loving and legal care to their dogs in every other aspect.

Note that 18 hours a day total crating a dog or pup is no more than 8 hours overnight, plus an eight-hour workday with hour-long commutes to work and back.

Many people forget to include overnight hours when calculating total hours per day that their dogs are crated. Including these night hours, 18 hours per day seems to be a typical amount of weekday crating for approximately half the owners who currently crate. If the family also sends the dog to his crate so he won't "act crazy" as they try to prepare for school, eat dinner or watch television, and if they then crate him for several more hours if they leave for any nighttime activities, the dog may spend up to 22 or 23 hours in the crate during that 24-hour period! This is an amount of caging most people would immediately react to as unconscionable in theory. Yet once families consider the crate an acceptable manner of containing a dog in their home, it's surprisingly easy to slip into numbers like this in the midst of the stressful demands of a busy family schedule.

3. Definition of a "Puppy Mill"- Another name for inhumane large-scale puppy breeders (many with hundreds of dogs on premises) whose operations are characterized by:

-dogs never released from tiny wire cages or crates. (Breeding bitches commonly reside in cages for life.)

-dogs and puppies that receive no human interaction (unless they're grabbed roughly).

-dogs overcrowded in painfully hot, cold, dark and/or filthy conditions.

-diseased dogs and pups often denied veterinary care or compassionate treatment

-deliberately criminal violations of the law, or abusing "loopholes" in the law

-selling pups to pet stores, or directly to customers over the Internet, and misrepresenting pertinent facts about the kennel

The Humane Society of the United States estimates that there are currently about 10,000 puppy mills in the country, which, combined, produce 2-4 million dogs per year. These pups are traditionally sold to pet shops or directly to consumers over the Internet. So, if you obtained your puppy through these sources, he almost certainly endured horrific stress and was denied proper husbandry and socialization by his breeder before he came to your home.

How crates are now being used

Once used primarily for travel, dog shows or housing laboratory animals, small wire cages commonly known as dog "crates" are now becoming increasingly popular with private dog owners for use in their homes as a convenience. This trend has been spurred by a large number of dog professionals- possibly the majority- who now recommend crates for housetraining and containing dogs of every age whenever owners are away or cannot supervise. Because of these recommendations, many adult dogs are being locked in crates barely big enough for them to turn around in every night, every workday and every time the owners leave the home for the rest of their lives.

For housetraining, advocates of crating prescribe locking puppies in cages so small that if the pups have bowel or bladder accidents they'll be forced to suffer the discomfort of lying in their own filth for hours. The idea is that a puppy with an immature body will instead choose to endure the pain of full bowels or bladder trying to "hold it in". And, surprisingly, thousands of popular dog trainers and other experts who advertise themselves as "positive" or "gentle" have no problem heartily recommending this practice.

Many dog people also advise owners to completely withhold water whenever a puppy (or dog) is crated so he'll stay "empty" and not mess on himself. And, because of this advice, and long work shifts, many owners now leave young puppies crated for up to 14 hours at a stretch without water.

Without Crating, You Can Housetrain a Puppy in Just Days: Do you know anybody who's been lucky enough to housetrain their puppy in less than a week, without cruelty? We do. We've personally done it with our dogs. Quite a few of our customers have done it. And we know many people who've housetrained dogs in days in the past. None of the people we've known who've housetrained their dogs this quickly used crates, and none used cruel corrections. For dogs to be housetrained this quickly they must, however, start with perfect health, sound breeding/genetic background and proper care and behavioral shaping for their age prior to coming into the home. While a normal healthy pup can be housetrained in days or weeks, for those with pre-existing issues or illness (such as many pups from "puppy-mills, or pet-shops) it can take exponentially longer. But attempting to crate-train pups with serious problems won't speed up housetraining. In fact, it can make it take much longer. See Chapter 13 and our comprehensive book *Awesome Puppy* for detailed instructions on housetraining without crates.

Crate-training is a destructive method of housetraining

Despite the fact that soiling the area where the animal lives goes against canine instinct and feels deeply unpleasant to a dog, many puppies with undeveloped bowels and bladder can't physically help soiling in their crates. They then have to sit in their own mess for as many as 8, 10 or 12 hours and their owners routinely hose down both the cages and the pups down every day when they come home from work.

Often repeated bowel or bladder accidents are the first sign that a puppy is suffering from a painful bladder infection, intestinal worms or parasites or other disease. But, because of crate training, sick pups, especially those originating from pet stores and puppy mill breeding facilities rife with disease, often endure weeks or months lying in their own waste in tiny cages in their new owners' homes before their medical conditions are diagnosed.

Unfortunately, the timing of this everyday trauma often coincides with a natural "fear stage" in puppy development (the timid period sometime between 8 to 12 weeks, as explained by scientists and researchers in Chapter 3). At this time, even a single exposure to undue stress, if it feels too intense, tends to cause young dogs lifelong emotional damage.

Trying to "crate train" properly, many owners that work feel caught in a tough situation. They can't afford to leave work early or hire someone to come in, yet "experts", including many of today's professional dog trainers, give them no alternative to crating. So, rather than allowing their pup the run of a single "dog-proofed" room like a kitchen, with papers (or wee-wee pads) left on the floor like most families used to do, instead they leave the young pup in a tiny crate where he can barely turn around for 8, 10 or 12 hours at a stretch. Then, also on advice of "experts", they leave him crated for another eight or more hours overnight.

Even if the owner lets their pup out for fifteen minutes after four or five consecutive hours, if they promptly return him to his crate after each short bathroom break, **the pup may be living 18 or more hours a day total locked up and hardly moving.**

All this confinement, without adequate stimuli to aid pups' development, can lead to more than just immediate distress. Excessive crating has been documented to cause a wide array of serious physical and behavioral symptoms in dogs including fear, aggression and loss of ability to bond with people. See the list of 115 symptoms below:

Probable ill effects of excessive crating.

Excessive Crating causes a wide array of physical, psychological and behavioral symptoms in dogs, which vary depending upon the sensitivity of the individual dog and

other factors. **Some symptoms caused by Excessive Crating occur immediately. Others may result over periods of time ranging from days, to months, to years.** Which side effects a dog suffers also depends upon the period in its life the dog is crated and prevented from encountering stimuli in the outside world, and whether the excessive crating occurs during critical weeks of puppy development (as described in Chapter 3).

Some of the side effects we list below are obvious results of crating. Others are documented physiological reactions where Excessive Crating and lack of stimuli can impair social development (as described in the research studies in Chapter 3). And other symptoms, such as hyperactivity or uncontrolled jumping on people, can mix neurological and behavioral components. These behaviors can become part of a vicious cycle if, each time the dog shows the hyperactive tendencies, rather than training more healthy alternative behaviors, the owners react by simply crating him more.

Some owners may not know how existing behavior problems in their dogs started. But **many problems that involve inappropriate reactions to novel stimuli (like lunging at dogs or people on walks) often have some connection to Excessive Crating and isolation from proper stimuli in the dog's past.**

Throughout the book, we discuss evidence of how Excessive Crating contributes to many of the problems listed, which range from simply annoying to highly serious. (The connection between excessive crating and some other problems listed is still hypothetical, so we hope listing them here may spark further interest and scientific inquiry.)

Anecdotally, in our practice of working with dogs with serious emotional problems, we have observed a strong correlation between excessive crating and ALL of the problems that follow. It's difficult to scientifically isolate the variable of excessive crating after we work with dogs, since when excessive crate time stops, dogs also start enjoying a more healthy life in other aspects- such as increased physical movement and exposure to novel stimuli. **But the fact that so many other variables tend to improve once Excessive Crating stops is evidence in itself of how crating deprives dogs.** The true clinical case studies in this book demonstrate different combinations of these symptoms of excessive crating and kennelosis, or kennel syndrome. We also portray the etiology of many of the symptoms in the reconstructed cases of Boxy in the Prologue, Bouncy in Chapter 6 and Champ, the unique hour-by-hour scenario in Chapter 4 that follows a young German Shepherd Dog on a typical workday contrasting whether he is crated or free in the home.

Note that the starred items below have been proven or observed to occur in cases of dogs that have been rescued from puppy mills, hoarders and other extreme crating

situations. Some of the starred items have also been documented in veterinary literature as symptoms of "kennelosis" or "kennel syndrome" often seen in dogs caged long-term without adequate stimuli in shelter situations. You will read more scientific information about causes of specific physiological and psychological effects in Chapter 3 and Chapter 5. And **owners who observe a large number of the symptoms and categories below in a new dog of unknown origin would have good reason to suspect that their new dog originated in a puppy mill and/or suffered Excessive Crating at some point in its development**).

Probable ill-effects of excessive crating:

Aggression:
People aggression *
Children aggression *
Cage aggression (aggressive displays towards people while the dog is caged) *
Fear aggression*
Fighting*
Attacking/killing of other family pets *
Growling*
Snapping*
Food Aggression*
Possession Aggression*
Serious/abnormal aggression on people by young puppies*
Attacking/Killing/Consuming Siblings or Cagemates*

Reactivity:
Lunging at other dogs*
Responding badly to outside animals*
Chasing shadows*
Responding badly at veterinarian's office*
Responding badly at groomers'
Lunging at bikes and strollers*
Problems with dealing with large numbers of people*
Touch sensitivity*
Excessive reactions to strangers

Phobias:

Fear of people*
Fear of people of a certain gender
Fear of light*
Fears of anything unknown*
Fear of other dogs*
Fear of moving objects*
Fear of being removed from crate*
Fear of the world outside the crate*
Fear of travel (in car)
Fear of noise

Illness:

Bone growth abnormalities*
Problems with thermal regulating*
Dogs not reaching full size*
Obesity
Poor physical fitness*
Physically abnormal appearance*
Dull, lifeless eyes with abnormal responsiveness*
Skin ailments*
Slower reflexes
Poor coat*
Eating disorders
Back problems*
Urinary infections*
Fever*
Hot Spots/ skin ulcers*
Ingrown nails*
Matted coat*
Abnormal odor*
Early "Senility"
Untimely death*

Lower Intelligence:

Taking longer to learn name
Not able to figure out new problems as quickly as uncrated dogs
Dulled senses*
Impaired judgment
Tendency to act before thinking*
Wildness*
Inability to "read" people*
Inability to notice pain in people
Personality out of line with the norm for the breed*
Problems recognizing social signals in dogs*

Mental illness:

Autistic (withdrawn) symptoms*
Self-mutilation*
Compulsions
Panic*
Anxiety*
Depression*
Lethargy*
Fear*
Phobias
PICA behavior- swallowing inedible objects like pins or gravel
Abnormal sexual acting out on dogs and people
Stereotyped (repetitive) behaviors*
Separation anxiety
Uncontrolled drooling
Shivering/Trembling
Sudden Incontinence
Submissive urination
Sideways walking*

Hyperactivity:

Spinning*
Running frantically in house
Excessive barking

Jumping without reason
Movement never ceasing
Tail chasing

Behavior problems:
Counter surfing, garbage raiding
Jumping on people
Pulling on lead
Nipping
Chasing kids
Clawing people
Knocking people over
Harder chewing; nervous chewing
Taking treats too hard
Playing too hard with people
Destroying possessions
Eating furniture and wood

Injury:
Loss of teeth, or cracked teeth*
Loss of eyes from wire*
Cuts from wire*
Toe and foot injury
Head injury from banging head on crate sides*
Scarring from rubbing face on crate*
Lose of smell from nose trauma*
Spine problems from small crates*

Personality changes:
Shyness*
Timidity*
Lack of trust for humans*
Loss of protection drive for owners
Lack of play drive with humans*
Dislike of touch*
Dislike of coming to people

Feral dog behaviors*
Defiance towards humans*
Disinterest in humans*
Lack of loving behavior towards humans

Elimination problems:
Lifetime indoor soiling*
Soiling on humans' beds
Soiling themselves*
Eating feces*
Diarrhea accidents when stressed

The connection between excessive crating, lack of stimuli and physical, emotional and mental problems in development is confirmed by veterinary and also human psychology journals. For example, *Blackwell's Five-Minute Veterinary Consult Clinical Companion* mentions lack of exposure to a variety of locations and objects during the sensitive socialization period as a likely causative factor in fears, including fears of people, places and things (particularly in dogs absolutely deprived of social and environmental exposure before 14wks of age.) According to this veterinary manual, fear responses "encompass emotional, psychological and physiologic... (and)... interfere with quality of life". Fear responses include "freezing, fighting or fidgeting" and can involve multiple body systems including behavioral (including hypervigilance, avoidance behaviors and possible aggression): cardiovascular, endocrine/metabolic (including increased circulating cortisol); musculoskeletal, nervous (including increased motor activity, repetitive activity and self-injury): skin/exocrine (usually secondary to self-injury).

Patricia McConnell discusses crating laboratory dogs without adequate stimuli

Patricia McConnell, Ph.D., a professor and certified applied animal behaviorist, is currently one of the country's most respected and beloved experts on dogs' emotions and aberrant behavior. In her book *For the Love of a Dog* she describes how she was one of the first to persuade her colleagues to enrich environments for dogs being raised in cages in laboratory conditions. "Ironically," McConnell says, "the general public is often less aware of enrichment's importance. My associates and I often see dogs who were raised in conditions designed to handicap the development of their minds, not encourage it.

"These poor dogs can't handle change of any kind and depending on their genetics, they either slink... in terror or roar in like freight trains off the tracks... There's always a lot that can be done to help this... if you have the time and patience- but just like a house built on a shaky foundation, the result is never as it would be if you'd started out right from the beginning."

Just like laboratory dogs, young pups that are excessively crated in the home are also deprived of simple stimuli such as feeling the texture of different flooring on their paws, running and learning to balance, watching leaves move in the wind outside the windows or birds suddenly fly by or scenting the paths of their owners in different parts of the house- even feeling the difference between lying in a cool shadow or a warm beam of sun. **In a crate, a pup is not even able to stretch out fully to experience the sensations of moving his own body!**

Ms. McConnell continues, **"If dogs grow up with little environmental stimulation they can turn into adults who are lacking in the ability to handle even minor stress.** Stress is just change after all, and if a pup has matured in an environment that never changes, she doesn't develop a brain that is wired to cope with it. Numerous studies on rats and non-human primates show that barren environments create individuals who are unable to cope with stress as adults because the stress-related pathways in their brains aren't able to develop normally."

Pressure and Propaganda; how supporters of crating/caging dogs "spin" information in their favor:

Despite the fact that many dog owners instinctively consider caging pet dogs for life cruel, very many trainers and dog professionals strongly support crating not just for housetraining, but as a way of life for all adult dogs.

If you surf the Internet, you'll find endless optimized sites featuring opinionated pro-crate instructions and opinions including sarcastic jabs at people who want dogs to be free alternating with "facts" about how dogs are "den animals" that "love crates". This pro-crate information is rarely backed by standard scientific method and often relies on circular or twisted logic. Yet pro-crating logic already dominates Internet searches and bookstore shelves. And many pet stores, shelters and even some veterinary offices now hand out free literature featuring crate-training instructions with no alternatives.

As home dog training and psychology specialists, we encountered many owners who start out reluctant to crate their dogs and are then pressured by peers or harassed by dog industry professionals until they finally try it.

Supporters of crating, including many authors of currently popular dog books, vaguely cite "wolf studies" in their favor, even though any study of wolves reveals that wolves are intelligent and highly energetic hunters that migrate vast distances as a group in search of prey. Studies also reveal that wolf pups do *not* remain in the den after weaning at about 8 weeks. (See details of wolf and puppy development in Chapter 3.)

As evidence in their favor, crating supporters sometimes use the observation that traumatized dogs that have never seen the world will often fearfully run back to their crates whenever they encounter any new situation. Some behaviorists point to displays of anxiety like this as proof that dogs love spending the majority of their time in these small cages while, in reality, excessive crate time and lack of healthy stimulation in formative early weeks can produce dogs that run back to their crates because they are afraid of the world.

Today sales people aggressively attempt to sell crates to every puppy buyer. Meanwhile crating supporters often refer to crates as "beds" or "houses" rather than "cages", so those unfamiliar with the items may not even know what they are referring to. **A good number of "traditional" or "old-fashioned" families (like ours before we were exposed to the truth about crating through our work) have never owned, used or even heard of a dog crate and would never guess that their peers and neighbors cage their beloved pet dogs.** In "traditional" homes like ours, adult dogs still comfortably co-exist with their families in every part of the home, even when the people go out. So there's a communication gap. People who've never crated can easily make the mistake of assuming that their friends' dogs also live free in their homes. Co-workers or friends often converse at length, sharing cute dog stories. And yet they rarely discuss the one vital difference of whether their otherwise pampered dog spends the majority of his day free in the house or locked up in cramped conditions that many of us would find inhumane for any animal.

Home crating can produce similar problems as puppy mills

In Chapter 11, we detail some of the most terrible cases of overcrating that have made the headlines- animal hoarders, puppy mill breeders and even worse. But dogs suffering in these environments that violate the law aren't the only dogs suffering symptoms of kennel-craze today. People increasingly observe these extreme and baffling symptoms in their living rooms. And despite the magic that dogs can do to help humans, and the life many of us recall enjoying with them (as eloquently described by canine experts in Chapter 11), our expectation for quality of life with dogs seems to be unraveling on a societal basis in certain vital ways.

Some extremely troubled dogs and pups come to new owners already damaged from excessive crating (for example from puppy mills and pet stores) and they may require a special effort in rehabilitation. But sometimes it's the new owners who follow the wrong advice and start excessive crating. And this can immediately compromise their pup's behavior and possibly lead to lifelong personality and behavior flaws.

Diane Jessup, a highly respected author and expert on canine aggression who has appeared on *48 Hours, The Oprah Show* and numerous other news programs, points out on her website workingpitbull.com, *"Crates are (only) designed for short term housing while a dog is in transport. They are not meant to house a dog all day, every day, while you are at work. Housing a dog in a crate- even a large one-does not meet the (very) minimum USDA standards of living space for dogs kept in research laboratories."*

Private pet owners are able to skirt space requirements for enclosures because of the wording of the law. This is because, for a family dog, the house, rather than the crate would be considered a "primary enclosure" even though, in reality, the animal might spend more than 90% of his time crated. **Certain types of containment, along with the absence of appropriate exercise and stimulation are known to encourage violent behavior in dogs. One well-known example is tethering**, a staple for making dogs intended for fighting more aggressive. **Many individuals who prepare dogs for the fight ring also crate their dogs- deliberately isolating them from a normal life and normal stimulation**. And, in parts of Africa, people who wish to make their dogs more protective are known to lock the dogs in overheated darkened wooden packing crates, with no real contact with the outside world, for the formative first year of their lives.

Most people would agree that tethering dogs long-term or imprisoning them in boxes to make them vicious is cruel. Yet, ironically, many dog trainers who push owners to crate proudly call themselves "positive" and assert that crate training in private homes is a *gentle* training method.

The Dog Crating Conspiracy

In Chapters 8, 9 and 10, we explore large-scale motives behind America's recent love affair with Excessive Dog Crating, including the fervent push by many "professionals" to make every suburban dog owner crate their dogs at home, along with continued reluctance of our nation to completely abolish puppy mills. **If puppy mills continue producing millions of dogs a year, and if more Americans crate dogs inappropriately in** homes, the negative (and sometimes even dangerous) consequences will affect more families and start impacting our quality of life as a society. But we reveal why certain individuals and powerful private interests- including many that dog lovers would not suspect, are so strongly motivated to make Americans embrace excessive crating as a way of life for dogs.

We'll also advance theories as to why proponents of Home Dog Crating often defend the practice so vehemently. **The idea that we should cage beloved pet dogs every day for life may seem ridiculous to many people on a gut level. But this propaganda, stated as absolute fact and often accessed through online links to otherwise reliable sources, has recently spread throughout the Internet and written literature at epidemic speed.**

Even searches for topics like "abusive crating" and "dogs dying in crates" bring up thousands of *pro*-crating writings. And dog owners must wade through these to finally read important scientific information on the dangers or drawbacks of crating. One example is information on the well-documented and highly serious syndrome called kennelosis, or "kennel craze", known to be brought on by excessive caging and information on how this syndrome can manifest in pet dogs, as well as dogs in institutional settings.

In this chapter we list hundreds of symptoms, including those associated with "kennel craze" that are known, or suspected to be, results of excessive crating. But a casual Internet search by a novice dog owner may never reveal that the troubling constellation of symptoms they observe in their family dog is consistent with a syndrome known to be caused by excessive cage time.

These days a majority of new dog owners are commonly given advice, instructions and literature from pet professionals that tell them to cage their dogs or puppies, with no other alternatives mentioned for housetraining or teaching manners.

From a few interesting facts in an otherwise heartwarming article in *"O", The Oprah Magazine*, we suspect that some dog "expert" even tried to push crating propaganda on Oprah Winfrey, a famous person who's known for helping dogs and crusading against puppy mills. In the article, Oprah describes adopting a sweet rescue puppy and helping her battle a terrible illness. Then Oprah happens to mention that she pitied the puppy when the tiny animal cried after being crated, so she unlocked the door and let the pup sleep in her bed.

We don't know Oprah's current stance on crating (although by making a public statement on the dangers of Excessive Crating, she could influence many people and help many dogs). But, interestingly, in the article, Oprah referred to crating as something she knew she *had* to do, even though eventually she stopped when the puppy's distress upset her too much.

Based on how she reacted, it certainly doesn't seem that Oprah thought up the idea of crate- training her puppy on her own. Rather Oprah Winfrey, one of the most powerful people in America, with access to many high-level experts in every field, likely followed the advice of some well-known dog trainer or behavioral "expert" who convinced her, for a short while, to cage her pup and ignore her own feelings.

We encountered a similar example of crating doctrine disguised as expert information in one well-promoted Southern shelter where standardized cards clipped to each kennel with individual dogs' descriptions all included a space for a yes or no answer to the question, "is crating good for this dog?" Even though the dogs present on the day we visited were all very different and many other facts on their cage cards varied, the behavioral training staff at the shelter had filled in the cards for *every single dog present in the shelter* to say "yes". And we have since found out that many shelters are now routinely sending cages home to families along with their adopted dogs.

We believe "information" like this about crating, with no mention of problems or discussion of alternatives, assumes that dog lovers and potential adopters shouldn't think for themselves. (For example, in this same facility with its lovely climate controlled public spaces and every cage card advocating crating, dogs still live indoors without air conditioning in the worst Southern heat, and the shelter routinely takes public money to kill strays although it's not mentioned anywhere in the heartwarming literature.)

We believe crate training doctrine tends to go hand in hand with intentionally depriving the public of all the facts. Instead, we believe dog owners should receive as much information as possible, and then form their own opinions about canine husbandry. Even while individuals involved in the daily management of dogs devote much of their resources to spreading one-sided information in favor of crate training, research studies described in this book (especially chapters 3 and 5) prove that excessive crating during a puppy's formative months, in the absence of sufficient stimuli, exercise and socialization, can profoundly impair his future behavior and ability to bond with people.

We believe, because of this, many families who follow "expert" advice to crate their dogs may miss out completely on the healthy, almost spiritual, dog/owner bonding they were hoping for, or the healing benefits of pets (as described eloquently by the experts in Chapter 12.) And a generation of children may grow up without knowing the full joy of life with a family dog.

Stopping Excessive Crating May Be the Most Important Dog Cause Today

Something needs to be done, right now, to help the millions of dogs and puppies still suffering unimaginable horrors in puppy mills and also the dogs- possibly millions-suffering Excessive Crating in private homes.

There's plentiful evidence to indicate that Excessive Crating is likely the single largest causative factor underlying most serious canine behavioral problems today. This in turn leads to more dogs being surrendered/abandoned and more dogs euthanized in shelters.

Every day, when people speak out personally against excessive crating, more vocal opponents on the pro-crate side of what's lately being labeled the "great crate debate" argue their feelings away. And the Internet makes it easy for private interests to benefit by popularizing crating. But we believe the scientific and behavioral facts in this book will immediately resonate with many readers. We believe dog owners will no longer tolerate being pressured or deceived simply to profit certain individuals in the dog industry, and that they will no longer wish to participate in a practice that never felt right to them in the first place.

There are many things we can do right now to stop the needless pain of the hundreds of thousands, or even millions, of dogs that are caged right now. The past two decades in America have brought about the rise of Excessive Home Dog Crating. **But now it's time to deconstruct the myth that "crates are great", and restore dogs as well-behaved "family members" who live full-time in our homes rather than living with them as slavering strangers in cages that make us feel alienated and a little afraid.**

Many people who care about helping dogs have already leant financial and volunteer support to well-publicized causes like spaying and neutering, prosecuting animal cruelty and promoting adoptions. And these causes also involve education- spreading progressive thinking about the kindness dogs deserve. So does the cause of protecting dogs from excessive caging.

Who needs to read this book?

Your dog may already be showing symptoms of Excessive Crating. *Dogs Hate Crates* is written for those people who already perceive a problem, and also for every dog owner who want to know how crating can affect their dogs and their families. This includes owners who currently crate, and owners who are concerned that their dog may have been excessively crated (or tethered) in a puppy mill, pet shop or former home.

Many of our readers may already have concerns about caging the dogs they love. And dog owners who have read this far may wonder whether some of *their* dogs' problem behaviors could be symptoms of kennelosis, kennel craze or kennel syndrome.

The truth is that **normal dogs should not show any of the negative symptoms or behaviors listed earlier in this chapter.**

These are all signs of a dog out of balance. In addition to physical symptoms, a dog that has been excessively crated may slowly change in personality, making him difficult to control, neurotic, mentally damaged and unresponsive to humans to the degree he should have been. Dogs are wonderfully resilient. So in most cases, safely integrating the excessively crated dog back into the home can heal many of the ill effects. But in some extreme cases, where cumulative effects of Excessive Crating combine with other factors, dogs may develop incapacitating fears or show aggression that makes rehabilitation difficult.

We detail the specific changes in dogs caused by excessive confinement throughout the book, citing true case studies and scientific and scholarly evidence. We also detail a dog's hour-by-hour reactions to a day crated vs. uncrated in Chapter 4. And, in Chapter 3, we detail normal dog and wolf puppy development week by week and contrast normal intelligence, sensory and social development in pups during critical weeks with dogs deprived of socialization and stimuli, as they are when excessively crated.

Chapter 5 details information about the effects of excessive caging from experts and veterinarians and Chapter 11 describes puppy mills and some of the most terrible abuses of dogs. Chapter 11 also includes the case study of Patton, the "Whirling Dog". Another disturbing case study- the story of Smoky, "the Dog in a Dumpster" appears in Chapter 12- following animal experts' discussion on all the ways dogs help people and ways the dog/owner bond can be lost if the trend of crating continues.

It is easier to live with dogs without crating! And in Chapters 13 and 14 we describe alternatives for housetraining and behavior shaping without crates, including highly effective hints that are not covered in other books. There is hope. Chapter 15 tells the true story of Bridget, a lovely young dog rehabilitated following 22 hours a day caged in a dim hallway- a dog that finally learned not to be afraid of light and Chapter 16 lists easy ways every dog lover can improve the problem of overcrating society-wide,

Chapter 2: The Dark Side of the Dog Utopia

The societal extent of the tragedy of Excessive Dog Crating

Historically, Americans have refused to give in to special interests. Rather, throughout the history of our nation, we've found striking ways to rise above difficulties by relying on our unique strengths and keeping our values intact. For example, when so many of our pets died because of tainted pet food imported from China, many owners made our outrage known to the industry by completely changing the way we feed our pets and demanding an overall higher standard. Likewise we can also assert our personal right to decide how to house and train our dogs!

The experts quoted in Chapter 12 eloquently detail the ways dogs benefit our physical and emotional health- including helping us fight disease and live longer. And the love we share with our dogs can transcend words, yet it's something all of us that still live with dogs as our best friends immediately recognize.

But meanwhile, **many branches of an increasingly sophisticated 50 billion dollar industry and beyond lately encourage the fiction that locking dogs up can substitute for the essential bond of an ideal dog-owner relationship. And, because of major societal shifts in lifestyle increasing numbers of dog owners have been embracing this fiction.** In a country where some estimates count 77.5 million dogs, a huge number of these- perhaps the majority- now spend significant time crated in their families' homes. Many dog lovers used to feel strongly that it was wrong for dogs to live in kennel runs. And yet so many dogs today- in rescues, at boarding facilities and at groomers', as well as those in private homes, are now housed in cages a tiny fraction of that size most of every day and night for life.

Millions of dogs are also still suffering in tiny cages at "puppy mill" breeders. The pups that survive the stress of their initial weeks of life are shipped to pet stores or directly to customers via the Internet. And it's a sad irony that, while all of these pups will be welcomed into new private homes, only some of them will ever live freely with their human families. Others will simply arrive at another environment where they'll be caged the majority of each day for the rest of their lives, near, but yet critically separated from, their owners. Meanwhile owners' relationship with these dogs can shrink down at times to just spying on two eyes glowing out at them from a cage as they return from a twelve-hour workday.

Easy Self-Help: If you currently crate your dog, you can start making his days better right now with this simple exercise: First place a notepad and pen near your dog's crate and have all family members record for each day the exact times they released the dog or puppy from the crate and then the exact times they put him back in, including the overnight hours. After a week, add up each day's time the dog spent in the crate. Next compare the total number of hours per day you'd *ideally* want to crate your dog with the number of hours each day he *actually* spent crated during that week. If you never intended to crate your dog as many hours each day as you actually did, you can now easily make small changes.

Brainstorm alternate plans with family members and/or try the training suggestions in Chapters 13 and 14. Then keep records one more time and see if you're able to reduce the number of hours your dog spends in the crate next week. Most dog owners can easily make small changes like this, and reducing the number of hours the dog spends in the crate makes most people feel better and really improves their dogs' quality of life!

Unfortunately, even if you do not personally crate, you may face problems with a dog that has already come to you from a background of overcrating in a puppy mill or with former owners. These adjustment issues, in individual cases and on a societal scale, now affect how many dogs are surrendered to shelters, how many are euthanized and even how many dangerous dogs attack people- including owners and their children. And these effects may also make the new puppy you buy or adopt with high hopes harder to train and live with.

Our practices of caging dogs need to change- because there's a darker side to the utopia of owning dogs. Many people still remain unaware of it, but it is increasingly starting to touch the average person's life in negative ways. Our communities host huge numbers of dogs currently suffering in puppy mills, substandard "shelters" and the homes of hoarders and dog fighters.

And average families are starting to face real risks. These range from the emotional and financial costs of training dogs with unprecedented behavior problems, to the risk of injury, or even death, from dog attacks in this brave new world where the animals most inclined to love us are often caged to the point where some become dangerous. Those who benefit from the status quo desperate try to hide or to downplay this dark side. But excessive crating changes absolutely everything about our dogs in ways none of us would want.

Scary Facts About Dog Ownership Today:

(1) Average families increasingly require professional help with serious behavior problems in their dogs and puppies:

Fixing these problems goes beyond ordinary "self-help". **For example, families increasingly report "bizarre" or disturbing behavior in young puppies, including true aggression in pups as young as two months.** As canine psychology and home training specialists we often hear, "It's spooky. I've owned this breed all my life and I've never seen a puppy act like this."

Scientists and veterinarians have identified many of the most extreme symptoms as likely to arise from Excessive Crating. This includes true hyperactivity (including spinning and never staying still); compulsive behaviors; self-mutilation; inability to ever be housetrained at any age, coldness and lack of bonding with humans and cases where young puppies aggressively growl or bite. According to scientific findings, all these problems are consistent with puppies that start their lives in puppy mill or backyard breeders' cages without sufficient stimuli and socialization with people. And every additional day these puppies continue to spend the majority of their waking hours crated in a family's home can worsen the problems, creating a vicious cycle.

Today individual families increasingly require animal behaviorists with advanced degrees to help them with their dogs. Surprising numbers of dogs are put on prescription medication for anxiety, hyperactivity and aggression that are similar to human psychotropic meds. And increasing demands for veterinarians to solve behavioral problems are lately changing the face of veterinary medicine.

In a pet industry with revenues of approximately $50 billion annually in our country, much of this money is spent on problem solving. And lately dog owners are spending unprecedented amounts on a proliferation of home dog trainers and training classes- including classes offered by doggie day care facilities, pet stores, veterinarians, groomers, shelters and municipalities.

Dog training is still experiencing double-digit growth according to the fascinating, if ironic, book *One Nation Under Dog*. And, as we describe in Chapters 7 and 8 , the last five years has been the era ruled by "celebrity" dog trainers like "*Dog Whisperer*" Cesar Millan. These public figures, whose names seem to be on everyone's lips, often train Hollywood stars' dogs. And these trainers seem to attract as many obsessed fans as the screen idols they like to work with. Many of the memorable problem dogs featured on their television shows are aggressive to animals and humans. Others have crippling neuroses and fears such as separation anxiety that keeps owners from ever leaving home or shockingly dirty habits like leaving bowel movements on kitchen counters! And many thousands of dog owners watch these shows not only for pleasure, but to look for answers for the same behavior difficulties in their own dogs.

Many owners today, especially in more cosmopolitan cities, spend up to $600 per month to send their dogs to "doggie day care" to burn off energy because they feel that, otherwise, they couldn't live with their dogs. Other owners spend on repeated sessions with certified pet massage therapists, holistic healers, herbalists, aromatherapists and practitioners of Reiki, acupuncture and acupressure for help with dogs' serious behavior problems. And it's not uncommon for owners to consult with pet psychics or pet communicators, sometimes over the Internet.

Meanwhile Bark Busters, an international dog training franchise, boasts that their representatives have trained over half a million dogs. This statistic is particularly scary, since Bark Busters doesn't specialize in basic obedience training, but rather in solving behavior problems. And a first session with Bark Busters costs hundreds of dollars.

Also the use of increasingly complex targeted supplements for dog behavior problems has rapidly increased. Supplements and "natural" behavior treatment aids are not only available in specialty pet and health food stores, but they are now widely available in chain pet stores. **Many other owners treat their dogs daily with expensive and potentially hazardous pills- powerful tranquilizers, anti-anxiety and anti-aggression drugs including psychotropic medicines that are commonly used for humans or their derivatives (like "doggie Prozac",** or Fluoextine, a reformulated version of the widely popular human antidepressant). And many "problem" dogs will take these medications, prescribed by their veterinarians, for life.

If you're thirty-something or older, you may not remember serious everyday problems with dogs on this scale from when you were younger. We believe the vital **difference in how well dogs live with their families is the amount of time, starting from the earliest puppyhood, that dogs spend crated. Many families that raise their dogs the old-fashioned way, without ever thinking of crating, still enjoy dogs that are helpful and loving family members that bring greater joy and meaning to every moment of life.**

It's also almost impossible to rehabilitate a dog with emotional/behavioral problems while still crating to the same extent. **There is simply no historical precedent for trying to train a puppy between 6 months and a year old to be obedient and have great house manners when the dog is never in action. When a young dog spends more than 18 hours a day total in a crate, basically immobile and with no stimuli, he doesn't ever have the opportunities he needs to learn.**

Like Bouncy "the terror at 5:30" in Chapter 6, a dog may leap out of the crate when released by the owners at the end of a workday and start making trouble in the house. **Pups that rarely encounter the world outside of their crates lose the ability to make sense of it.** They are not called upon to practice judgment and so they never learn the skill; nor do they use their intelligence or athleticism in productive activities. The dog may only know two things: the contrast between motion and total lack of motion. By abruptly releasing dogs from up to 12 hours of total immobility at the end of each workday, families inadvertently teach a modern "breed" of dogs to go from zero to sixty in a frenzy of pointless motion- exactly the kind of behavior they don't want.

(2) Millions of Dogs Have Originated from Horrible Puppy Mill Conditions:

If your dog originally came from a pet shop/puppy shop or was ever sold and shipped via the Internet, it's he likely he suffered a stressful early upbringing, devoid of necessary stimulation and socialization and characterized by cruel and constant

confinement. Because of this, your dog will likely carry some lasting physical and/or emotional damage, which will likely impact your quality of life with him.

All across the country, purebred and "designer mix" puppies sold to retail pet stores and over the Internet are raised in shockingly cruel conditions in out of state "puppy mills". And buyers are deliberately misled about their origin. (True cases of puppy mill abuses are discussed later in this chapter and in Chapter 11.)

Each year the Humane Society of the United States (or HSUS) assists in investigating multiple puppy mills and saving thousands of dogs (for example, in the past two years they rescued 5,000 dogs). Increasing media exposure and the work of agencies like HSUS and many private rescue organizations small and large helped prompt recent legislation to put reasonable controls on puppy mills and puppy shops in states including California and Pennsylvania.

The state of Missouri, which alone accounts for about 40% of puppy mill dogs, or approximately 1 million puppies sold per year, voted yes on a Dog Breeding Regulation ballot initiative in November 2010 meant to protect dogs in that state from some of the very worst puppy mill abuses. The law, which prohibits stacked cages and wire flooring, and allows dogs access to outdoor exercise and a minimum of 12 sq. feet to 30 sq. feet floor space depending on the animal's size, along with other provisions, was still facing legal challenges from legislators and private groups months after it passed...

Missouri currently has 1,000 licensed commercial dog breeders, representing a powerful lobby with some powerful supporters who fear the potential $1 billion impact on the state's economy if all affected dog breeders were shut down. And, since laws like this only put controls on the very worst breeder abuses, tougher laws, in many more states, are still needed.

When police and humane society investigators finally raid criminal puppy mill operations they often rescue hundreds of dogs from each location (as detailed in the individual cases described in Chapter 11). And sadly some of the dogs rescued are in such bad condition physically or behaviorally after extended imprisonment in cages and related abuses that they cannot be rehabilitated and are ultimately euthanized.

Each day Americans learn more, and feel more outraged, about the conditions dogs suffer in puppy mills. In order not to support puppy mills, large popular chain pet stores like Petco, Petsmart and Pet Supermarket will not sell puppies, but will only host rescue organizations with dogs for adoption. In 2008 many Americans first learned about the scope of the puppy mill problem through a much talked about television expose by Oprah Winfrey. Dog lovers were also shocked by a highly publicized case against Pets of Bel Air, a popular pet Beverly Hills pet boutique that was frequented by glamorous stars including Paris Hilton and Britney Spears. Yet despite all the increased awareness, and increased legislation, at the moment the puppy mill business continues to flourish.

Every day Americans who follow the headlines or watch popular shows like *Animal Cops* hear about extreme cases of animal abuse and neglect. Cases of dogs being left to dehydrate, starve or freeze to death in crates are common, including cases where owners watch their dog dying in a crate over the course of weeks while the dog is near them indoors in plain sight. (In Chapter 11 we describe a case that outraged an entire Florida Space Coast Community, where a young woman abandoned her 3-year old German Shepherd to die in a crate. The dog's body was left long enough to mummify, so that forensic investigators couldn't even determine how many days or weeks the animal suffered before dying.)

Preparing this book has forced us to research literally hundreds of puppy mill cases across many states, most involving abuse and neglect of hundreds of dogs on each property. Each case is appalling in its own way, but one of the strongest testimonials against puppy mills came out years ago, before most people even knew the term, in the now well-known February, 1999 *Reader's Digest* expose, "Scandal of America's Puppy Mills."

In the article, author Michael Ecenberger, who visited 53 puppy mills across the country in order to see the conditions firsthand, first reports on one in Lancaster County, Pennsylvania (the "Amish" country that has received so much recent media coverage, because of scandal including the expose on the Oprah Winfrey Show and new tougher Pennsylvania legislation). The author visited the farm, where dogs available included *"Poodles, Yorkies, Schippierkes, Maltese, Jack Russels, Shih Tzus, Pekinese, Boxers, Cockers, Labs, [Bichons]"* and he peeked into a barn where he saw, *"... the animals lived in small wire cages stacked four and five high. Some puppies had open sores or hairless spots from lying on the metal wire. Urine and feces from upper cages dropped into the ones below. Food was tossed in among the waste. Some dogs had no water."*

He also describes another puppy mill in rural Florida where police and humane officials seized 358 dogs and horrific images included *"...a stack of filthy cages where the decomposing carcass of a terrier dripped fluids onto a live poodle below."*

Not surprisingly, living in such unnatural conditions has a destructive effect on puppies. Some of the dogs seized from the farm mentioned above were beyond help and had to be euthanized for medical conditions. And it's becoming more widely known amongst the veterinary community that puppy mill dogs often suffer serious long-lasting psychological consequences.

In the *Reader's Digest* article, Ecenberger quotes ASPCA consultant Sue Pressman, who explains that some of the worst victims of the puppy mills are the breeding bitches that "... spend their entire lives in one place, producing one litter after another..."

Ecenberger explains how, *"... in many mills, the bitches are restrained in wire cages or pens and get no exercise. The stress induced in these bitches by such conditions often results in hostility to their offspring. The pups end up treating littermates in the same way. ... Such aggressive behavior does not yield good pets... Lack of human contact is why puppy mill dogs are so often aggressive, distrustful and hard to train."*

He also quotes George Whatford of ASPCA investigations, as saying, *"A lot of...[puppy mill dogs] end up abandoned in shelters because owners can't deal with them."*

In this book, (in Chapters 1 and 5) we describe "kennelosis" or kennel-craze, a well-documented syndrome with many far-ranging physical and behavioral symptoms that affect dogs after excess confinement, especially during formative early weeks of life. (Chapter 4 shows an hour-by-hour example of how a family dog starts to develop these symptoms.)

At the moment there's still legal/legislative debate on the extent that it's acceptable to cage dogs in commercial facilities like large-scale breeders, and laws vary from state to state. **As of the publication of this book, current animal welfare standards, used as a guideline by the USDA, do not even specifically prohibit keeping dogs in a wire cage, never to come out, for their entire lives!** And this is why individual states are pushing so hard to enact additional legislation to control puppy mills in their borders.

The newest law approved in Missouri, if and when it ever goes into effect fully, should prohibit wire flooring. But, in other states, there's still heated legal debate about whether wire flooring in cages where dogs live out their entire lives is acceptable. This is despite abundant evidence of dogs that have had feet wounded, infected and amputated because of standing on wire for months and years.

But we wonder how people can feel sufficiently outraged at wire cages in puppy mills when so many people use wire cages at home, and when trusted "experts" in the dog world keep telling us that crating is great for our dogs. The fact that dog "professionals" have convinced so many families to crate their pet dogs blurs lines and may make it harder to enforce legislation against the puppy mills. And unfortunately, the large percentage of pups coming from pet shops/ puppy mills with behavioral problems beyond average owners' patience or understanding feeds the vicious cycle.

Consumers need to raise the bar and we should demand at least the same standards as when we purchased purebred puppies twenty or more years ago. Every reputable breeder should invest time, energy and money in their dogs' breeding, veterinary care and health screenings. They should also allow buyers access to information and allow buyers to physically tour their facilities and meet the pups' parent(s). **Buyers should also demand that every puppy they purchase will grow up to live with proper house manners in their house, and not just in a cage.** Proper husbandry is, of course, up to the owners. But breeders should ensure that puppies come to new owners properly socialized, at least partially housetrained and already at ease around people and in the home.

(3) Dog Attacks:

As excessive crating has increased in puppy mills, pet-shops, private homes and no-kill shelters, dog attacks in our country have also increased in number and severity. For example, according to the American Veterinary Medical Association or AVMA, in 2006 dogs bit 4.7 million people and 800,000 of these victims were injured severely enough to require medical treatment. While this statistic might not seem very high considering there are currently 77.5 million dogs owned in the country, it actually represents more than 1 incident per 100 dogs where victims were bitten seriously enough to require medical attention.

Even more concerning is the fact that the majority of the victims of serious and fatal attacks are children and the elderly. The AVMA reported that children were more likely to be seriously attacked than adults, with the majority attacked "during everyday activities and while interacting with familiar dogs".

In the past two decades we also seem to hear more about incidents of packs of wild dogs "hunting" and killing people. A recent Animal Planet special estimated that there are approximately 100,000 feral dogs, or dogs that have reverted to their wild state, currently roaming free in the United States today. For example, an Associated Press article by Kate Brumback from 2009 describes one of the 22 fatal attacks that year in which a large pack of feral dogs attacked and killed an elderly Georgia couple- who happened to be dog lovers- outside of their home.

Some of the more highly publicized and more vicious dog attacks have been against owners and their children, and several fatal attacks on children have happened this year. A good number of serious and/or fatal attacks have occurred in homes where families either crate, cage or tether their dogs. One recently highly publicized case in

2009 where a child was seriously injured involved popular pro-football player James Harrison of the Pittsburgh Steelers. Harrison's Pit Bull was released from his pen and viciously attacked the ballplayer's four-year old son, who was immediately hospitalized, and the dog also bit and injured an adult who attempted to rescue the boy.

Closer to our home, in a well-publicized case in Davie, Florida several years ago a Presa Canario attacked and killed his adult female owner. And in February 2010 in Central Florida a tethered dog that had previously been contained in an outdoor kennel killed his owner's 3-year old daughter in the time it took the woman to step back out after using the restroom.

We strongly believe that isolating puppies through crating or caging or tethering, especially during early formative weeks when puppies should be properly socialized to humans, contributes to many dog-on-owner attacks. Constant crating also prevents puppies from practicing proper manners with humans in a thousand individual contexts each day. By constantly putting a cage between puppy and owner, it puts distance into the relationship and takes away from the dog's naturalness with humans and his feeling of being family.

Isolating is well known for bringing out ferocity in dogs and the fact that dogs are deliberately tethered on short chains with limited stimuli and socialization in order to make them aggressive is known to the point that certain cities have outlawed the practice. The fact that excessive kenneling can make dogs extremely aggressive is also well-documented. And now Excessive Home Dog Crating is adding to the problems of excessive kenneling and tethering.

Note: THE MAJORITY OF DOGS WILL NEVER HURT A HUMAN NO MATTER WHAT CONDITIONS THEY ARE FORCED TO LIVE IN! But, in some cases lately, the combination of excessive confinement and other factors leads to an explosive mix. Neurological studies described in Chapters 3 and 5 demonstrate how excessive caging can be a causal factor for reactivity (the inability of a dog to respond correctly to new stimuli) and aggression. **And, unlike other causes of aggression such as health or genetics, whether we cage our dogs is one factor we can easily change. But if our society allows the widespread practice of crating dogs as a way of life to increase, then dog attacks on humans will likely increase also.**

(4) Dogs still dying in dog pounds & shelters

Even though shelters for homeless pets are becoming increasingly popular, trendy and "prettied up" and fundraising has become more intense, shelters still euthanize at

least 2.1 million dogs each year. (This statistic is based on a highly conservative study done by Tufts University. And many respected dog charities estimate the number millions higher.) Many dogs that are put to sleep are perfectly healthy and "adoptable". And a number of dogs are even euthanized in shelters advertised as "no kill".

A frequently quoted statistic is that 85% or more of the dogs in shelters are surrendered because of behavior complaints. And many people will, oddly, point to this statistic as publicity for adopting dogs and supporting the work of shelters rather than wondering what created all these behavior problems in the first place.

Some "doggy" behaviors are natural. And we certainly can't expect dogs to act like stuffed animals. **However, serious and/or continued problems in healthy well-bred dogs are NOT normal. And healthy well-bred adult dogs should overall *enhance* family life while living free in the home, rather than causing problems.** We suspect that many owners today are creating "problem" dogs by excessively crating them, starting during the formative weeks of puppyhood when dogs should be learning and maturing into their future personalities. Or, by crating, owners may try to put a "band-aid" on problems that already existed when they obtained their dogs, rather than making the extra effort to shape and rehabilitate them.

Certain shelters and rescues may report high adoption rates, but not all shelters are equal when it comes to preparing dogs and their adoptive families for a healthy future together. **And a large number of dogs adopted from shelters quickly "boomerang" back into to the shelter system or repeatedly change hands via free adoption classifieds like Craigslist.**

Acceptance in a "no kill" shelter or rescue may bring more problems for a dog with behavior issues. To our knowledge, private shelters and rescues around the country are still not subject to any standard federal government oversight, so each facility can choose to euthanize due to arbitrary personal standards that they establish. Or they may house a dog that acts "wild" in a tiny cage, with no heat or air conditioning, in bleak and stressful conditions similar to those in puppy mills for years, or for life.

Since owners frequently dispose of "problem dogs" between 1 and 2 years of age, a dog can theoretically spend up to 14 years of his life in rescue, locked in a tiny cage with only occasional walks or socialization by volunteers. We have personally seen individual dogs housed in small cages in no-kill shelters and rescues in a number of communities for years at a time. Dogs that start out "hyper" can develop much worse problems after months caged in shelters. And they may begin showing symptoms of a syndrome known as "kennel craze", "kennel syndrome" or "kennelosis" which includes fear, unfriendliness or aggression.

Quite often shelters, including many with large budgets and ample staff, never attempt to screen a dog for "house manners" before telling a family he's totally adoptable, because they expect the new adoptive owners to crate the dog for life and never allow it freedom in their home.

Many adopters today are shocked when they find the adult dogs they brought home from shelters and rescues aren't properly housetrained, pull painfully on leash or react improperly to people and household pets.

We feel shelters should advise potential adopters if a dog isn't ready to live with good manners free in a home, or if his house manners are a mystery. This way, only families that are truly qualified to rehabilitate such dogs would take them home. And, to prevent the problem, shelters should use their funding and donations to teach dogs house manners in real home settings- for example, by placing more dogs in foster care while awaiting adoption, rather than housing them long-term in cages or crates.

Otherwise, shelters and rescues can easily make dogs appear attractive in photos on the Internet and boost adoptions by making the process seem "fun". But if adoptions don't "stick", the same dogs that were never properly rehabilitated at the first shelter end up "boomeranging" back, or passing from home to home and from shelter to shelter. This can take precious "no kill" space from the millions of other potentially adoptable dogs that are quickly put to sleep in public facilities.

Every day, no-kill shelters turn away large numbers of callers who attempt to surrender their pet dogs, and of these shelters have waiting lists in the hundreds. If an owner is truly desperate and their dog is turned away by five, ten or thirty no-kill shelters and rescues, truly desperate owners may feel they have no options. They will then surrender their dog to a county pound where, even if he has perfect house manners, the dog may be put to sleep within the week due to lack of space.

Despite the fact that some very dedicated staff and volunteers save dogs every day in shelters and rescues, we feel that a system that kills millions of dogs a year and allows others to languish for years at a time in small crates is a system that, overall, isn't working, and must be improved.

(5) Health problems and dog deaths covered up, even as the pet industry makes so much money on dog pampering and festivities

Read the book *One Nation Under Dog*. These days many people support an upscale dog-positive culture. But meanwhile, thousands of puppy mills, dog auctions and Internet puppy sellers still openly operate without adequate legislation or powers for police to raid them. And this means a shockingly large percentage of young puppies die in puppy mill cages or during transport. Other young pups die in pet store "back rooms" while they're dosed with antibiotics for illnesses like Bordatella and Parvovirus. These deaths are an expected loss in the burgeoning pet industry. And, as a rule, they are concealed from the public.

In the State of Florida pet store pups are sold as-is. They cannot be returned. Buyers often encounter problems the first day and struggle with serious health and behavioral issues for the rest of their pet store puppy's life. Vet bills sometimes run in the thousands in the first weeks and months.

In puppy mills, female dogs in puppy mills are kept solely to produce litter after litter and many never experience fresh air or life outside of a cage. One they are "used up" and can no longer breed their owners have sometimes been known to shoot them. In fact, the practice has been legal in some states for years although currently laws are changing.) Other "used up" dogs, some with physical problems or injuries, are sold at huge dog auctions (you can see some shocking videos on YouTube). One class of people buying at such auctions in includes wholesale "B" dealers, who then sell dogs they acquire to be used in laboratories. So some dogs pass from hand to hand, never knowing one moment in their lives free from pain and stress and never knowing a moment free from a cage, except perhaps while being held up by their scruffs for display at auction.

We believe that when the public recognizes that isolating a pup in a tiny cage without adequate stimuli for lengthy periods equals abuse, legislators will support these standards. **And it's important to demand better treatment for our animals because, when so many of our "best friends" experience inhumane treatment, it also impacts our quality of life and expectations of compassion and decency.**

So now is the time to confront the problem of Excessive Crating, arguably the largest source of suffering to the largest number of dogs every day across America. To save dogs from suffering can be relatively easy, as long as the impulse of kindness is no longer treated as a taboo. So this means confronting those people who are spreading pro-crating propaganda.

Busting the most popular pro-crate myths:

These days, people may attempt to pressure you to crate your dog or puppy, citing several popular "facts." But the most common of these facts are based on completely flawed logic and they are not facts at all. Here is the truth about the most common pro-crating myths:

1) The truth is a dog never derives any long-term benefit from being crated!

Even when a crate prevents a dangerous behavior problem (like ingesting poison or running away) the cage is just a physical barrier that blocks the action in that minute. Instead dog owners can use more humane environmental barriers (like baby gates) while practicing easy behavior shaping (like the techniques in Chapter 14) so you have to keep facing the same problems that you would with a dog that's been crated.

A crate, at best, can keep your dog away from problems in a given moment. **But leaving a normal dog in a cramped crate with nothing to do is** *never* **good for his body or physical condition. And it's** *never* **good for his overall mood, his happiness, his stability or security or any other aspect of personality- no matter what any dog training expert may say.** Crating a dog never teaches anything positive enough to counterbalance how much the caged dog misses out on opportunities for everyday learning and interacting with stimuli in the real world.

Despite what some experts may say (see Chapter 8)**, since the crate itself is a negative, rather than a neutral stimulus, it has no function as a positive tool for behavioral learning. And the fact that crating stresses dogs and prohibits them from expressing natural behaviors hampers learning.**

On the rare occasion that a physical barrier is needed to teach a behavior, owners can use different barriers that are less stressful. And, in special cases where an extremely agitated dog can benefit from stillness and containment, there are more comfortable environmental tools that give a better sense of security. **Catalogs and pet stores also offer harmless products specifically designed to help dogs with clinical anxieties and phobias. In contrast, crating usually worsens severe anxieties in dogs**. Or it may cause the anxiety to sublimate into another maladaptive syndrome, including eating disorders, self-mutilation, depression ("shutting down"), aggression or physical ill health.

If your dog manifests with clinical anxiety, including separation anxiety, many "dog people" today may tell you to crate him to cure the problem. This is quite dangerous, because crating only makes true separation anxiety worse. Also, in very many cases excessive crating in early life was what caused the separation anxiety in the first place. So crating the dog even more would be like throwing tinder on a fire.

2) The truth is that a dog never "loves his crate".

Both well known "experts" and many folks on online discussion boards like to cite the fact that, even when the doors are finally opened, their dogs rush back to their crates. **But if a dog ever *runs* back to his crate, or seems to seek it out constantly as a place for security, this is actually an extremely disturbing sign that may mean that he's become afraid to seek *people* for his security.**

Whether it happened in your home or at a former owner's, your dog may have become fearful after excessive crating. And he may have learned to fear facing a world that seems intimidating to him because of his lack of exposure to normal stimuli throughout his life. If you bring home a dog that's known nothing but crating for long hours every day and night since puppyhood and you suddenly attempt to free him, when you first release him he may run back to his crate. But if your dog seems intensely motivated to get back inside the cage, this is actually a very bad sign which signals intense anxiety- *not an indicator he loves his crate.* (See the true story of Bridget in the Chapter 15.)

The most common reason many dogs endure confinement without protest is love! Most often, if your dog seems complacent about remaining in a crate, it's because he loves you so much he's willing to take your direction. And he endures caging because he thinks you want him to. Of course dogs sometimes like to relax or avoid stress in small protected spaces, just like people might feel safe in their cozy bedroom or bath. **But a dog no more likes being locked in a crate and abandoned all day than you'd like it if your spouse locked you in your bedroom or bathroom every day for 10 hours while he or she went to work.**

3) The truth is a dog is not a "den animal". And you don't replicate his native environment if you lock him in a cage!

Some people hear this myth about dogs being "den animals" repeated so often they just start replaying it in their heads like a catchy little jingle. The concept, which you can find "explained" at length in online and written literature, is based on the fact that wolves whelp, or give in birth, in underground "dens." (See Chapter 3 for an in-depth description of wolf pups' maturation.) The mother wolf sleeps with and cares for the pups in the den and occasionally leaves them there, concealed from predators, for approximately the first eight weeks of their lives- but not longer.

After this the pups are introduced to the world at large, they wander about quite a bit and the den is replaced by an outdoor rendezvous site. Soon, the pups start accompanying adults on hunts. And, as the wolf pups mature and become adults they primarily devote their lives to vigorous activities like hunting, playing, migrating and freely making choices of how and where to move their bodies. **Wolves are inquisitive, highly active hunting animals that can travel between 30 and 50 miles per day! They seem like the *antithesis* of what we'd think of when we hear "den animal"; wolves are certainly not creatures that spend their lives contained in small spaces underground.**

Animals that seem more aptly described as "den" animals in the sense that people think of the term might include moles, prairie dogs or rats- but *not* wolves. And certainly not pet dogs! Try to envision an adult Irish Wolfhound, German Shepherd, St. Bernard or a beautiful white Standard Poodle in full show coat living their entire lives in a cramped underground earthen den. The concept seems quite creepy. **And if a dog really was a "den animal", why on earth would anybody adopt one, buy it a rhinestone collar, kiss it on the lips and call it our best friend?**

4) The truth is that a crate won't speed up housetraining, and it often makes it more difficult.

Many dog owners who are alert, careful and consistent can kindly and successfully housetrain their healthy normal pups without crates in a matter of days.

In fact, in most cases where a dog is successfully housetrained with a crate, he could have been trained more quickly and effectively without one. (You can read about housetraining without crates in detail in Chapter 13 and in our comprehensive puppy book *Awesome Puppy*.)

In cases where a dog takes excessive time to housetrain with a crate, you probably could have housetrained him faster without it. This sometimes happens because dogs that come from "puppy mills" or pet shops often won't respond to crating at all, since they have already been desensitized to lying in their own filth in the cages they grew up in. These dogs need extensive and compassionate help, and they may take extra long to housetrain because of their previous abuse and neglect. *But, as long as you do it properly, perfect housetraining without using a crate should never take longer than if you'd used one.*

Although a crate may teach a puppy not to relieve himself *when he's in it*, this won't teach him anything about recognizing the house in general as a place to keep clean. When you finally let him dog out of the crate, he'll still have to learn how to respect the entire house as his home and not use it as a toilet. **It's ironic that housetraining is the main reason most people start using crates, because crating is not the best or quickest way to housetrain!**

Many dog "professionals" are less skilled at housetraining dogs than a good percentage of "laymen" who accomplish it quickly, kindly and effectively without crates. And professionals often accept customers' money for using only the crate-training option because it is easy. Mastering how to housetrain a dog that spends almost all of its time in a cage requires little skill, effort or time and little attention to individual dogs.

We believe it doesn't make sense for dog training customers to waste money on crate-training advice or to hire trainers who believe in crating.

There's no need for extraordinary talent or a special "way" with animals to get a dog behind bars not to cause problems- as long as you *keep* him behind bars. If a "professional" therapist locked a person in a linen closet for 12 hours, the person would probably try to hold their bladder and bowels, too, rather than standing or sitting in their waste.

What's your "magic number"? Think in terms of total hours per day that a dog could stay in a crate during a 24-hour period, and determine the number of hours that you personally feel is too much for a dog to stay crated each 24-hour period. Many different factors influence each case, but when you keep this number in mind it will ensure that your decisions always resonate with your conscience and the facts you gather. Clarifying a specific number also prevents you from getting so caught up in the demands of everyday life that you start crating your dog more than you'd like to. And it will make for a common rational ground when you discuss the subject of crating with others.

If someone who wields power over large numbers of dogs and owners declares that crating is great, ask them, "For how many hours a day is crating okay?" And make sure that they answer with a number per 24 hours, not just a number of hours at a stretch. Dog professionals who routinely preach crating as a panacea for behavioral training may be surprised to discover that the owners they've "educated" are now crating their dogs or puppies for as many as 18 to 23 per day total- an amount even these experts would agree is quite harmful!

Who's crating dogs and why some families feel they have no choice:

Aggression towards humans is the most serious symptom that can grow out of Excessive Crating and it's a reason many dogs are surrendered to shelters. Some dogs act aggressive to strangers or guests. Others growl at, snap at or even bite owners or their children. And some of these bites are serious/life-threatening, including cases where dogs leap up and bite people in the face or head.

Some owners change their entire lifestyles because of behaviors they fear, yet have come to expect from their dogs and there's no reliable statistic on how many dog owners currently live with dogs they consider "monsters". But the explosion in the number of dog trainers, television shows, books and websites dealing with canine behavior issues reflects the scope of the problem.

Pet stores are increasingly filled with new products for problem dogs: chew toys designed to be "indestructible", sprays to discourage chewing up possessions, special head halters and no-pull harnesses to deflect dogs' power on walks, electronic devices to remotely shock dogs or scare them off certain areas of the home, a multitude of "calming" pills, drops and sprays and even the $500 "Alcatraz" escape-proof crate, manufactured with chunky bars of twenty gauge steel resembling those in human prisons.

As specialists in helping families with canine problems in their homes, we perceive an almost chilling pattern. Something's definitely not right in the world of dog ownership; and something has definitely changed. Raising a puppy has always been a somewhat irritating or trying time. But, historically, the rewards were usually worth dealing with the few small difficulties. And any problem behaviors faded away naturally as dogs reached adulthood.

In contrast today, dog trainers are frequently called to solve serious problems in adult dogs ranging from extreme hyperactivity to extreme aggression. They also often complain that dogs and pups don't like to be physically handled and never "bond" with people; many never show affection or even make eye contact.

Sometimes it can be hard to distinguish cause and effect. But, in general, dogs that have been excessively crated also seem to show the worst behavior problems. This includes: "cage-aggression" or "cage-craze", a term that used to only be used at shelters, but now also refers to some pet dogs. Caged-crazed dogs may lunge at people like slavering beasts in private homes. They show extreme reactivity to new living things and new situation (for example, going crazy at the vet or groomers). They may attack other animals in the home and bite people. And this can range from nipping children's heels or hands and drawing blood, to deliberately leaping up and biting owners' faces.

Owners often get caught in a vicious cycle. They excessively crate a young dog to try to manage behavior problems. But by depriving him of proper stimuli, interactions with humans and opportunities to learn manners free in a house, they start to create a "monster".

Instead of improving, the dog's behavior problems worsen and new ones begin. As the dog becomes more unmanageable in normal household situations, the family start to crate him even more often until he behaves like a muscular juggernaut that explodes out of the cage whenever they unlatch it and leaps at people uncontrollably (see the case of "Bouncy" in Chapter 6). Family members may start to feel all they can do is to release this unruly creature to the back yard to relieve itself, and then immediately crate him when he comes back inside.

The cycle worsens until the dog is crated 18-23 hours a day for the rest of its life. And most of the owners doing this aren't animal haters, nor do they consider themselves animal abusers. These families may spend hundreds or thousands of dollars on their dog each year and care about him deeply, yet feel they can't safely let him out of his cage for more than minutes at a time. And, instead of offering a better solution, whatever dog professionals they consult may only instruct them to crate him more (as in the disturbing true case study of Bridget in Chapter 16).

It's difficult to quantify exactly how many American families crate their dogs "excessively" since excessive means different things to different people. Two coworkers may chat about dogs, yet never clarify that one crates their puppy 3 hours per day, while the other crates 17 hours!

Meanwhile numerous "old fashioned" owners may not even know what the term "crate-training" refers to. Like us, these owners happily allow their dogs to live in their houses with them freely as family members and cannot conceive of any other way, so they may not even know there is a problem in society.

Wherever you get several people boasting together about how much they love their dogs- whether coworkers, clergymen, government officials, the girls at the gym, the nice ladies who volunteer at your local rescue or your Internet "friends"- **there's no way to know if the dog they boast on spends all his time free with a family or whether he spends all but an hour a day in a cage just big enough for him to turn around in. Even some gorgeous little lapdogs that receive regular massages and pedicures with colored nail polish, and make the scene at "Yappy Hours" each weekend wearing designer dresses are actually caged whenever they're home.**

Whether or not people keep their dogs caged creates a huge variation in way of life for social peers. People who keep their dogs free would likely feel upset to learn that a neighbor or coworker was confining their puppy most of every day and every night, while dog owners who crate tend to say that people who complain about crating are silly or uninformed. Those who crate tend to defend their beliefs by saying that dogs would destroy their homes or hurt themselves if set free. And they'd have the backing of many dog professionals who are saying that crating is the best way to raise dogs.

This is because the practice of crating has become the darling of certain segments of the pet industry, as described later in this book. If you complete a casual Internet search, it's extremely difficult to find information about the dangers or drawbacks of crating. Yet sites abound that advise crate-training as a cure-all for new owners and dog trainers. In fact, **owners frequently tell us they hesitated to crate their pups at first because it seemed cruel.** But then a personal acquaintance or a professional strongly pressured them until they did it.

Unfortunately there are certain owners and pet professionals who cage dogs for truly bad reasons- to criminally profit or to abuse dogs, or because they feel powerful making other creatures powerless. Certain people- including some that work with dogs- actually derive satisfaction from watching puppies whimper behind bars. And in the most extreme cases, like in the case of Ella or many of the puppy mills described in Chapter 11, owners leave their dogs to die in crates.

But even though certain individuals like these deliberately abuse animals, most people *do* care about dogs and do want dogs to be happy. Most people also have a hard time hiding their compassion for dogs, and can barely control their tears when they watch the heart-wrenching television commercials sponsored by humane organizations like the ASPCA that play popular ballads while panning over the sad faces of dogs behind bars in shelters.

Men and women alike bawl just seeing this combination of dogs and cages. But ironically, the cages shown in these commercials are often outdoor/indoor runs, which usually offer dogs vastly more room than the average dog crate recommended for people's living rooms.

In the past few years, society as a whole really started learning the truth about puppy mill breeding, and most of us felt outrage. Widely viewed television specials, like the 2008 Oprah Winfrey expose, graphically introduced many Americans to cruel breeding facilities in every corner of the country that warehouse dogs like pieces of meat- facilities where breeders' fundamental cruelty is to cage dogs for life in tiny spaces.

Seeing pictures of dogs and puppies cramped and stacked in rows of cages like this has made many outraged viewers pledge their help and their money to boycott pet shops and abolish puppy mills. And many Americans also vehemently (and understandably) oppose the cruel caging of animals used for meat, like cows, pigs and chickens.

On a gut level, most of us feel immediately saddened when we see the image of an animal gazing out at us from inside a tiny cage- especially if that animal is a dog. And yet, **these days, dog experts have somehow convinced many of us that, because wolves** whelp in dens and their cubs stay there in early weeks, normal adult dogs should find it natural to spend all their days at home locked in cramped metal cages!

In truth, there's really no comparison between an open den that a wolf pup shares with littermates and a locked cage he sits in alone. And, ironically, wolf pups leave their den enclosure for good when they are weaned at approximately 8 weeks, which is just the age most families *start* to crate their puppies. Clearly the trend of crating dogs has involved media and special interests manipulating people's feelings and beliefs and throughout this book, we discuss who and why.

And in Chapter 3 we discuss include scientific findings about the early weeks and months of dog and wolf pup development and results of scientific studies, including facts about canine brains, senses and social behavior to show the truths and untruths about dens in wolves' lives.

Readers shouldn't feel guilty or shamed. Our goal is to provide alternatives and answers to help modern families live happier, healthier lives with their pets with no need for crates. And, with every word in every chapter, we hope another reader will return to the non-crating way of life and start to experience more fulfilling times with their dogs.

And, if you wish to help free dogs from excessive crating on a larger scale, Chapter 16 suggests easy ways for people to use their different talents and resources to make a difference locally and beyond.

If you've ever wondered what actually happens to excessively crated dogs in homes all around the country, you can read the reconstructed hour-by-hour experiences of Champ, both crated and free (in Chapter 4); and the true case studies of Bridget (in Chapter 15), Smoky (in Chapter 12) and Patton (in Chapter 11).

Many families would like to stop crating, but need suggestions for housetraining. And you'll find detailed instructions for housetraining without crates in Chapter 13, along with training suggestions in Chapter 14 to keep your home protected and your dog or pup safe and secure as he learns house manners. You will also find many suggestions for training, housetraining and activities in our book *Awesome Puppy*.

Please note: although long-term crating is never an ideal solution for training and housing, we always advise families to put alternatives in place in a safe and well-planned fashion. And we acknowledge that temporary crating could be necessary in the particular situations described below:

Appropriate temporary crating: Unique situations where temporary crating may be necessary for safety

Despite our belief that crating family dogs at home has no emotionally therapeutic or behavior training purpose, and that Excessive Home Dog Crating can create pain and long-lasting suffering, we are not fanatical about saying that an owner can't ever place their dog in a crate, anymore than we would tell you that you couldn't take your dog hiking with you, use him as a hunting dog or dress her up in a ballgown! Your dog is part of your family, and a crate, or any type of indoor/outdoor enclosure (or line used for tethering) is only a tool. We hope that you always make decisions about your dog's husbandry carefully and always choose the course of action that is safest and most beneficial for all concerned.

For the record, in our professional opinion, crates should not be used for any type of training, including housetraining, nor should they be used as housing for dogs and we do not crate our own dogs.

We do feel that, in some temporary situations, a crate may be safer than other alternatives available. For this reason, owners may want to gently take a few hours to introduce their pups to crates or carriers just as they would all other novel stimuli, so the dog won't ever panic if he's confined briefly during an emergency or when the owner is not available.

There are a few situations where the authors believe temporary or short-term crating could possibly be appropriate, necessary, or a better choice than the immediate alternatives for the particular dog in question. Obviously these cases include any situation where a crated dog, as soon as released, would likely do immediate bodily harm to itself, humans or other animals. In cases like this, owners/handlers should always have a safe plan in mind for handling and rehabilitating the dog *before* they open the cage.

There are several other situations where we feel *temporary* crating might be appropriate.

1. During travel; to protect your dog;
2. For medically necessary temporary treatment, observation or medical recovery at the veterinarian's office.
3. For short-term veterinary boarding for physically or emotionally delicate dogs, with lots of personal attention and exercise breaks, in cases where this is the safest boarding alternative.
4. In hurricane or other disaster shelters or during evacuations

5. For *short-term* housing in community shelters for homeless pets in order to save dogs' lives or to reunite them with owners.

6. For brief quarantine (usually less than a day) of a dog so that he cannot infect other animals with a dangerous disease or parasite.

7. As a temporary emergency intervention to stop or prevent situations (like dogfights) that could put humans or other animals at physical risk.

8. As a *temporary* holding area for dogs or puppies that might immediately injure or kill themselves on hazards like household chemicals and electric cords, until owners "dog proof" a larger, more comfortable area.

9. For *briefly* training and practicing with your dog to get him used to being calm in a crate in case you ever have to use one during travel or emergencies

10. On the dog show floor- temporarily, to prevent stress, providing the show experience overall does not stress the individual dog

11. Also, a crate can be kept in the home with the door open, so the dog can go in to relax, yet leave freely.

    CAUTION: Danger of death or extreme physical injury to humans who impulsively release caged dogs that are behaving aggressively without first taking safety precautions. The authors advise readers to always evaluate every situation carefully in terms of safety to dogs, other animals and humans before acting.

No matter how much compassion you feel, if you're a layman without adequate training, you should never simply open a cage door with no other plan for safety if the dog behind it is snapping, growling or lunging at you viciously and looks like he is trying to get out of the cage to kill or attack you.

A dog like this can be dangerous. It's true that the dog may have gotten to this point through excessive caging or other cruelty, and this may seem heartbreaking. But before releasing a dog that is demonstrating aggression, you should have a specific and safe plan. Otherwise you or your family could be savagely attacked and the dog would be euthanized, defeating your intent to help. A dog behaving aggressively behind bars might also be physically ill and require care. With proper care and kind, yet effective, training he could possibly be rehabilitated to become a healthy and friendly pet. But this can only happen if you act patiently and logically. If you're a layman without special qualifications and you are faced with a dog viciously attacking his crate trying to get at your family, you should immediately call for qualified backup from people that you know will treat the dog kindly before you open the door.

Even professionals such as shelter employees might need additional backup or expert behavioral advice in cases like this. Rather than attempting to be a hero and immediately opening a cage, dog lovers should realize it's okay to take a few extra minutes or even hours to formulate a plan for releasing a dog that's been cruelly crated or kenneled for years, when it's the only way to protect dogs' or people's lives. Some books noted in Appendix B, Recommended Reading, give tips on reading dogs' body language, vocalization and expression for potential signs of aggression, and you can also find many good books on the subject in your local library and bookstore. Books like this, plus consultation with local experts, can give you insight into whether a dog is dangerous.

Excessive Home Dog Crating takes place across every demographic- every locale and every income bracket. And while some owners crate their dogs out of frustration turned to anger, most people who crate excessively truly care about their pets. This book covers the facts and dispels the myths for everyone who cares about dogs, whether you currently crate your dogs or whether you've never heard of the practice. It also offers easy suggestions to train your dog to live with good manners in your home and to make changes in your community and the world at large.

The next chapter shows why it's so important for pup to grow and develop naturally, rather than in confinement. The chapter breaks down normal puppy and wolf pup development by the week, including details about how young canines develop their senses, skills, social temperament and behaviors during each of the formative early weeks and months. It also introduces research studies that reveal surprising facts about what happens to a young canine if he misses out on any of the critical milestones of early development.

Crating Your Dog Won't Cure Separation Anxiety. But it *can* cause it! Your dog can't express distress about a crate to you in words. But, when you first put him in, he may whine and even "scream" in a frenzied plea to be let out.

This may sound like your dog is being tortured and, in some cases, it's a good indicator of what he actually feels. But pro-crating "experts" don't make allowances that certain dogs (including many puppy mill and abuse survivors) cannot mentally tolerate crating. Instead, some "experts" tell owners that, in order to properly crate-train any dog you should simply let him "scream himself out" until he finally loves the crate. Some even suggest slamming the crate hard with a frying pan to stop the vocalizations.

In many cases, even dogs that protest the most eventually stop their panicked vocalizations and escape attempts. But this is just a sign of despair and resolution· or complete physical exhaustion. Owners have allowed dogs to *die* by leaving them locked in crates (see Chapter 11). And there is simply nothing a caged animal can do but bend to the will of man. So we find it shocking that dog behavior "experts" will point to a time when a dog eventually gives up on begging for help as meaning he *loves* the accommodations. But this is what many experts are currently saying.

Clinical separation anxiety is a serious anxiety disorder in dogs, and crates tend to cause it, even though some "experts" have started telling people the opposite. If a dog screams or pants constantly when crated and never stops, or if you return home to find the crate and the dog slippery with drool and/or loose feces, or you find your dog injured and bleeding from throwing himself against the crate, these are signs that the crate confinement has caused a state of emotional and physical extremity and that the dog should never be crated again.

Once a dog has gone through trauma in a crate, he may develop serious separation distress that prohibits normal quality of life for both dog and owners. And this might never have happened if his owners had listened to their own intuition, rather than the "experts", and immediately released him the second he acted like crating was killing him.

Chapter 3: Stages of Normal Puppy/Wolf Pup Development & Development of Canine Intelligence

<u>Highlights of Dog and Wolf Pup Development</u>

<u>Birth- 2 weeks:</u>

Wolf Pups: Scientists believe that wolf pups' development is essentially the same as dog pups' during ages up to 2 weeks.

Puppies: David Weston and Elizabeth Ruth Ross, in their book, *Dog Problems; the Gentle Modern Cure*, agree with notable American psychologists Professor John Scott and Professor John Fuller after Scott and Fuller studied dog behavior for twenty years and broke development into five periods. Ross and Weston identify the neonatal (or newborn) period, up to 2 weeks as, "a time of life when the pups are highly adapted to living and surviving in a den... [The pups] can neither see nor hear and their ability to move is extremely limited because their brain is underdeveloped. Their capacity to learn is virtually non-existent. The period ends when the pups' eyes open approximately thirteen days after birth.

Note that none of the experts or research quoted in this chapter ever describe dog or wolf pups as needing to live in a den *after* weaning, and certainly not when pups over 6 months are basically functioning as adults. By 8 weeks, the age owners usually start crating their puppies using wolf theory as a justification, wolf pups have already left their dens in the wild.

2 weeks- 4 weeks

Wolf Pups: The development of wolf pups and dog pups at this age is still undistinguishable, according to the research Weston and Ross report.

Puppies: The period from 13 to 20 days is known as the "transitional period" according to Weston and Ross because it "is a time of transition between a very dependent and more adult type of behavior. At this time the development of the senses gives the pups an increasing ability to respond to their environment. The motor nerves, which control movement, conduct stimuli more quickly so pups can move more rapidly and travel further afield. **The first signs of learning appear at around 15 days.**

4 weeks- 5 weeks

Wolf Pups: Development is similar to puppies' and wolf pups still remain in the den, although some may poke their noses out. Wolf pups, and dog pups are still dependent on the mother for nutrition.

Puppies: At four weeks, "Puppies are still dependent on the bitch, but this is a period of extremely rapid sensory development during which they become acutely aware of their surroundings and begin to interact with the environment. Puppies are very vulnerable to psychological trauma at this stage..." according to April Frost in *Beyond Obedience.*

6weeks:

Wolf Pups: Wolf pups are now frequently out of the den, sometimes moving up to a mile away from the den when led by an adult wolf

Puppies: For puppies, the period between 5-7 weeks is important for socializing with littermates, learning normal canine behaviors such as play behaviors, and proper inhibition, such as bite inhibition. Puppies separated from the mother and/or littermates too soon may develop fears and/or behavioral problems relating to either overattachment to humans, or problems with self-control of behaviors. This can happen when pups are separated from their mothers/siblings too soon and shipped cross-country to new homes or to pet shops- a particular risk when you buy over the Internet. Because of dog pups' similarity to wolf pups (and from personal experience) it's also safe to say that 6 weeks is usually the time that pups begin exploring outside of the whelping area. They may also take some interest in eating independently at this time.

7 weeks:

Puppies: A pup at 7 weeks now has a completely developed brain and the learning capacity of an adult, although with a much shorter attention span, according to *Beyond Obedience*. One vitally important fact about a pup at this age is that, "Everything the puppy comes in contact with now leaves a lasting impression, as he enters his time of greatest learning. Because he is assimilating information so rapidly, it is important for safe, non-stressful socialization with people and other animals to begin." The author stresses that, "**[the pup] needs to become aware that there is a whole world beyond the confines of his den area.**"

Many pups bred by substandard breeders do not receive adequate socialization or stimuli of any kind during this period. Instead they stay in a cage, in an environment devoid of stimulating sensory input except for physical discomfort and stress. Or they may experience fear and stress during transport to pet shops or to new homes.

8 weeks- 12 weeks

Wolf Pups: **At 8 weeks, weaning is complete and, at this time the wolf pups now abandon the den and travel to outdoor "rendezvous sites" to hang out with the adults.** According to WolfCountry.net, "once the pups are about eight weeks old (and fully weaned) they leave the den and start using "rendezvous sites". These are meeting places where the wolves gather to sleep, play and just 'hang out'" The pups will spend most of their time at the rendezvous site, often with one of the adult wolves watching them until they are old enough (at about 6 months) to join the pack independently on the hunt.

This is also when wolf pups start learning the skills necessary for hunting and one of the ways to do this is to act out the motions through play. "Wolf pups love to play. They chase each other and roll around the way dog puppies do. Many of their games appear to be a sort of practice for things they will do as adult wolves," according to Wolfcountry.net.

Note that wolf pups are no longer isolated in a dark den at 8 weeks, which would be the earliest that a family buying a new puppy would bring him home. Wolf pups are already out of the den, and actively exploring the outside world, learning skills that they will need later in life.

Puppies: **This is known by canine experts to be the optimal socialization period for puppies.** According to *Beyond Obedience* "This is the time when the puppy should be exposed in a nonthreatening way to everything and everybody he will encounter in adult life- children, men and women, other animals including livestock and especially cats, experiences like riding in cars (to pleasant places, not just to the vet)".

And, owners must be careful in how they socialize the puppy so that the puppy receives only positive, and never stressful stimuli, especially during several "fear stages" or "fear periods". One of these "fear imprint periods" occurs between 8 and 11 weeks. According to *Beyond Obedience,* "Anything traumatic that occurs during this age will leave a lasting impression and will provoke defensive reactions throughout the dog's life." The book advises that, during this time, "Things like elective surgery or shipping should be postponed."

Unfortunately, exactly the opposite happens with so many of the dogs we encounter when we are called to treat emotional/behavioral problems. Many of these pups start their lives raised in puppy mills on one end of the country- an already stressful situation. Then, at exactly eight weeks or slightly less, they are shipped. Those that do not die during transport are then placed in pet store environments where they are again caged and stressed, all before coming to their final home, often right in the middle of a fear period.

Many of these dogs also lose out on the critical socialization period between 8-12 weeks. They are never allowed to see anything outside of their "den" (or crate) area

during the entire socialization period. **These are the dogs that later become fearful and/or reactive to any new stimulus they see throughout their entire adult lives, often completely changing quality of life for their owners.**

Even if the new stimulus encountered is just a neighbor strolling down the street with his dog, an adult dog that was not socialized properly during his socialization period as a puppy may act crazy or frenzied and try to violently lunge at dog and owner. On the other hand, puppies that owners exposed to varied stimuli during these early weeks are likely to remain calm, contained and emotionally balanced whenever they encounter something, or someone, new.

David Weston and Elizabeth Ross agree. In Dog *Problems, the Gentle Modern Cure*, they describe the critical socialization period as occurring between 3 and 12 weeks. "...what the pups learn at this time from contact with other dogs, humans and other animals will have a dramatic effect in later life. It is therefore most important that pups are handled by a wide variety of people and exposed to as many different environments and situations as possible without being stressed. This not only helps them to grow into adults with a sound temperament who can readily cope with change, but it has been shown that extra stimulation actually makes the brain develop more... This is the time when most people acquire a puppy and it is the optimum time for training to start."

Housetraining:

Although pup's bowels and bladders still require additional development, at eight weeks pups are physically mature enough to learn to "hold it" while inside their owners' homes. And they can successfully relieve themselves outside as long as owners don't force them to wait for an unreasonable number of hours that's too long for their physical development. All conditions being optimal, pups can be housetrained as early as 8 weeks with almost perfect success without crating, as long as the owners provide a late-night potty break and don't leave a pup this young for too long at a stretch while bladder and bowels are still developing. And, if a family buys a puppy at 8 weeks and he is perfectly healthy, if the family works with him properly without crating, they should certainly have no problem housetraining him before 12 weeks.

Obedience training:

Dogs are ready to learn and soak up everything amazingly young. And 8 weeks, or whenever you first get your puppy home, is the time to start training him calmness and great house manners using gentle positive methods. (See Chapter 11 for the theories of successful behavior training for your dog or puppy and find detailed instructions for teaching all commands in our book *Awesome Puppy*.) Eight-week old puppies *can* also learn basic obedience. So, very gently, without frightening or hurting the pup, you should start teaching commands like "come", "sit", "down", "stay" and even "heel".

Train by offering rewards and never push or pull harshly on a young puppy. And don't forget that, just like young children have shorter attention spans than adults, young pups naturally have much shorter attention spans than adult dogs. So never overdo or prolong training sessions. But **don't ignore the fact that an 8-week old puppy is already a sentient being that needs constructive things to learn and practice to keep his mind busy and keep him out of trouble.**

6 weeks-10 weeks: Fear Periods and Socialization to canines/humans for puppies:

This stage of development overlaps with other stages, and it is critical according to Ed. Bailey, author of the article, "The Making of Dog-dogs and People Dogs". Dogs in one of his research studies showed widely differing reactions to humans, some reacting with extreme fear. Bailey says, "we have all seen dogs slink away, try to hide behind or under anything available, or sometimes bite, or wildly snap at air, teeth popping, yet simultaneously cower if no escape route is open... We say [these] ... dogs are kennel shy or have kennelosis."

The author explains that, prior to around 6 weeks, nerve myelinization is not yet complete, so pups (or wolf pups) do not experience fear with full intensity. Since other senses including smell, hearing and vision have already kicked in, this is an ideal time for the pup to explore and sense new things without the full intensity of fear getting in their way.

(This is why it's important for pups to encounter humans who handle them gently at their breeders' even before they're weaned at eight weeks. After this optimal window of time for socialization when pups tend to encounter new things with benign curiosity, the next stage in their development kicks in.)

According to Bailey, "Beginning at six to seven weeks, fear gradually develops, to become the full blown emotion by 10 to 12 wks. For the development of the dog-people relationship the onset of fear is most important."

From the time of birth, all the way to the beginning of the fear period, as long as people don't cause the pup discomfort or pain, a pup will naturally associate the presence and touch of people with low anxiety, because the pup is not yet wired not to feel high anxiety. (Puppy mills cause terrible damage here. These breeders still have the pups at the start of their critical socialization period. But they either ignore them entirely or else they cause them pain, by hosing them down with cold water, for example, or by roughly grabbing them by their scruffs. A good breeder, in contrast, will gently handle young puppies before weaning to teach them good associations for a lifetime.)

If all is done right by the breeder, according to Bailey, "By the time fear has developed to an influential level, the pup will have a whole list of acquired associations all relating people to low anxiety, Later, when faced with an anxiety-inducing situation, the pup responds by coming to a person because he has previously found low anxiety associations with people, associations formed during his first two months.

"A pup deprived of human contact during the critical low fear period does not associate people with [comfort] because the opportunity never existed. Having passed the low fear period, a person is forever a large menacing object, fearfully impressive. The people-deprived pup cannot recoup; he will always associate strange people with fear and will be kennel shy."

According to the author, when a pup is acclimated to humans before the first fear period sets in, and also learns to recognize and interpret the gestures and expressions of canine littermates, which will generalize to reading human's gestures and expressions, this can create the ideally "social" dog.

10 weeks-12 weeks

Wolf Pups: According to WolfCountry.net, as early as 12 weeks, wolf pups may accompany the pack on hunts supervised by an adult.

Puppies: Although some puppies have just come out of an impressionable "fear stage" at 12 weeks, this time period is critical for learning. This time also often corresponds with most pups completing vaccinations (other than rabies) so it becomes safer for owners to bring them to public places. Pups can very effectively learn basic obedience at this age (if taught gently and for short periods at a time.) This is also an ideal time for teaching good manners in the home, such as not jumping on people, because pups are quite curious and will note how owners act towards their new behaviors. They will also assimilate any experiences they have- so the richer the pup's experiences now, the richer his "databank" later. Pups still require a lot of sleep at this stage, but **any pup that is left staring at blank wire and blank walls for hours a day during this critical period will never catch up to similar dogs that were given a richer environment**. Owners of pups deprived of stimuli at this age may struggle later on to get the adult dog comfortable with those same basic stimuli.

12 weeks-16 weeks

Wolf Pups: Wolf pups are accompanying older animals along on hunts just to observe. And their play is important for mimicking hunting and also as social gestures with other wolves- adults as well as littermates.

Puppies: **At exactly sixteen weeks, many puppies enter a period when they want to explore the world, which coincides with the longer and more important outings of wolf pups in the wild**. Puppies investigating on their own, and showing greater signs of courage are normal and natural. (This is why it is important to train your puppy to always come when you call prior to the onset of this age when pups usually start to show greater independence.) **A pup crated during this period will lose out on a period of great curiosity and a time when he should be assimilating many details of the world**. Physically, this time also brings rapid growth and an important period for the development of coordination.

16 weeks- 20 weeks

Wolf: Wolf pups at this time are accompanying adults on some hunting trips. Each week they are becoming bolder and practicing more of the skills of hunting. They can now travel far from the den or rendezvous sites.

Puppies: Authors David Weston and Elizabeth Ross define the period from 12 weeks to puberty as "the juvenile period". "This period starts when wolf cubs make their first long excursion from the den and ends at sexual maturity. Wolves mature in size and become physically capable of hunting so they are fairly independent of their parents towards the end of this time... We have noticed that pups learn new responses quickly between eight to sixteen weeks of age. After sixteen weeks they have usually developed a few habits which slow down the formation of new behaviors..."

For many breeds 16 weeks also represents the start of teething,(When baby teeth fall out and are replaced by adult teeth) although it can start later. Many owners may think they have gotten through the stage with no problems, but instead they should check the mouths on their puppies that seem so controlled when it comes to chewing on possessions. The pup just may have not started teething yet! So, if an owner hasn't done it yet, now is their last chance to "dog proof" their house by removing all hazards such as household chemicals and supervising carefully around electrical devices and cords. Meanwhile, you should encourage our pup to enjoy playing with an array of designated chew toys made especially for teething. Teach your pup the value of these toys by presenting them carefully, one at a time, rather than leaving them all strewn around the house at once for him to become bored with. Also teach him which toys are his. as opposed to your children's, and gently teach him "Leave It" and "Drop It" commands, which will be important during teething. (You can find instructions in our book *Awesome Puppy.*)

5 months – 6 months

Wolf pups: At around six months, which may represent the time of puberty for some dogs, most authors agree that we can easily notice a difference between wolf pup and dog pup development. At this time, the wolf pups are close to full size and, most important, they have matured enough physically and mentally that they can hunt on their own- so they have now achieved a time of independence;(although they still depend on the adults in the pack in certain ways.

Puppies: In contrast, human owners like to keep their dogs in a constant state of dependence on us for all their needs, even when they are adults. And the preferred state of an adult dog for most owners resembles an overgrown puppy- not an independent creature. Most pet dogs have taken well to this; and they rely on their owners for all aspects of sustenance throughout their whole lives just as a wolf pup would rely on his parents only during his first weeks and months.

Owners should note that, even though your pup may not appear to be fully grown at six months, and probably isn't in all aspects, this can still be the start of sexual maturity and fertility for some dogs. And a female dog that goes into heat *can* get pregnant, even this young.

Most owners will get their pets spayed or neutered by 6 months and attempt to avoid females' first heat. Another advantage of spaying or neutering this early is that the pup will never experience adult hormones, and thus will benefit more from the effect of docility that spaying or neutering tends to produce. If you do not spay or neuter your pup, watch your pup carefully. It is possible for a female to become pregnant during her first heat, which can occur at six months. And, even though neutering/spaying does tend to help with temperament with both sexes, especially males, owners should realize that it is no panacea and won't always cure specific behavior problems.

__Temperament:__ Another reason to watch a pup carefully at 6 months is if you have other dogs in the household. This is an age when multiple dogs may begin "vying" for position in the pack, sometimes by fighting. Having established a clear order in the home with the owner as the benign yet all-powerful leader when the pup was young can often prevent this kind of spat between dogs. You also want to encourage dogs to live together properly at all moments of the day. Crating one dog can create an artificial barrier and strain and prevent the dogs from exchanging proper canine signals that could lead to peace. Instead, owners should carefully supervise and shape all canine interactions in the home, especially when the puppy is little and again, at around six months when he enters adulthood, and once again when your older dog becomes a senior. Always be highly careful bringing home a new dog, and only attempt after testing if the dog first gets along great with your existing dog(s) in a neutral setting. **To promote the best lifelong balance between dogs, owners should never allow dogs to play in such a way that it becomes violent, "growly" or "snappy" or injures, agitates or frightens any dog.** And they should never let dogs fight violently on the theory that that they will "work it out on their own". **Instead, this early time in your pup's development is a window of opportunity to make it clear that the human sets the tone for interactions- and peace is the only way to go in your home.**

6 months-7months

__Wolf Pups:__ According to WolfCountry.net, the wolf pups now resemble adults and now start actively hunting with the pack. And, even though these young adults may still hang around the outside of the den when food is scarce, seeking scraps that are brought to the younger pups, it would be ridiculous to associate wolf pups at this age with the cramped underground den, which they have long abandoned.

__Puppies:__ Some puppies (especially small breeds) also resemble adults physically at this age, although all pups and some breeds, especially the large breeds, still have a great amount of maturing to do. Puppies at this age are highly energetic and all breeds other than giant breed pups (who have restrictions on jumping and running due to bone and joint development) start to need amounts of exercise equivalent to their young adult requirements. **Pups at this age are curious and at the peak of their energy and**

potential. Handlers will introduce show dogs, sporting dogs and working dogs of all kinds to aspects of their work at this age and earlier. **Pups should already know basic obedience at this age**. And, even in non-working situations, a six-month old pup should have some idea of a useful job to do in his home. Pups at 6 months still are playful, with a much shorter attention span then they would have as adults, yet a six-month old pup (especially those of working breeds) should be mature enough to respect the family's children and/or frail elderly and help out with small things like barking if they hear an intruder.

<u>Housetraining</u>: All pups that started out totally normal and healthy should be housetrained to never have a accidents in any part of your home by this age unless you leave them for abusively long periods of time, or if you made the mistake of trying to housetrain by crate-training. Of course, many pups that come from rescue situations (or puppy mills or irresponsible first owners) won't be housetrained even if they come to you at 6 months, and so you'll have to start training fresh. But if you've owned a pup since 8 weeks and he grows to 6 months still not housetrained, this indicates that either the pup has physical problems, serious behavioral problems and/or the owner has made serious mistakes.

<u>Teething</u>: Your pup is likely at the height of teething at this time, although many breeds (especially small breeds) may have already stopped teething. **Puppy teething and destructive chewing of an owner's home and possessions are two completely different problems and occur for different reasons (no matter what anyone tells an owner). And these problems have a different prognosis and require different treatment**. Teeth falling out, signs of physical distress in the mouth, such as scratching or rubbing the mouth and/or whimpering or groaning are all physical teething symptoms, and a pup that's teething will likely to chew on "off-limits" items even when you're present, because pressure on the teeth tends to alleviate physical distress.

Teething tends to take place between 3 and 10 months and, when the pup finally has a healthy set of adult teeth, "teething" ends. Good solutions for the physical distress of teething include toys specifically made for teething, preparations to ease pain, and frozen items to chew on. This is also a time to "puppy proof" by removing any dangerous or precious items. If the puppy does chew on something inappropriate, interrupt immediately with a sharp sound or noise (but no harsh corrections; don't hurt him or scare him). And then refocus him to accept a "proper" teething toy.

Genuine teething is NOT a behavior problem, but rather a symptom of discomfort in a juvenile animal. And **it's the owner's responsibility to restrict and redirect their young puppy to safe and appropriate chewing items while he's developing his adult teeth, clearly demonstrating which items in the house are okay to chew (his toys) and off limits (everything else). Symptoms of *real* teething will subside as soon as a pup's adult teeth grow in and at the same time the pup will have learned to differentiate his chew toys from all his owners' possessions through the owners' daily efforts.** But if owners do not take the time to correct the puppy when he makes mistakes and teach him which items are hands-off, there's a chance he may continue to chew on possessions for a variety of reasons, even after physical teething ends. Under ideal conditions, housetraining can be completed in a week or two; however teething takes several months to get through and dogs enter the stage at different times.

The only time an adult dog may physically "teethe" is to alleviate extreme dental distress. And if this is the case he will demonstrate similar symptoms of physical irritation to those young puppies show during the teething phase. Chew toys and cold items as described above may help, but a dog with a painful dental condition needs dental treatment from a veterinarian. And If a physically mature pup or an adult dog with adult teeth ever chews on an owner's possessions without signs of dental distress, this problem is *not* "teething" and it will *not* clear up on its own. It will most likely intensify until the environment changes, exercise increases and/or the dog receives gentle behavior modification training by an expert. Physical barriers can protect a dog from ingesting dangerous items. With puppies, this can help owners "wait out" the chewing period. But **physical barriers alone will never train a dog to respect owners' possessions if the problem is caused by lack of exercise, problems relating to and taking direction from humans or true hyperactivity. And, in adult dogs that chew, adding more frustration by crating the dog often intensifies the problem.**

7 months- 8 months

Wolf Pups: According to WolfCountry.net, wolf pups are now hunting with the pack.

Puppies:
Second Fear Period: Behavioral scientists agree that, starting at puberty or just prior, young dogs go through a second "fear period" and so they must be trained gently and kept away from stimuli that might traumatize them if owners notice them acting more wary and reluctant during this period. Unfortunately this is an age when many young

dogs first enter group obedience classes and encounter stressful stimuli, such as intimidation by another dog or an overly harsh trainer. According to Dr. Joel Dehasse, "There follows a vulnerable period of cognitive sensitization at pre-puberty or puberty during which minor trauma can occasionally entrench wariness or fear, (ill) adaptations, and cognitive and emotional distortions that are undesirable in a dog living among humans in a city environment.

"Sensitization... is the process that engenders wariness, fear, phobia and anxiety. The cognitive process that it entails leads to a dog anticipating harmful situations that exist only in the mind... and thus behavior strategies (defense mechanism: flight, aggression, inhibition.)

Note: At this age puppies now resemble adult dogs in many critical areas, although their development is not complete. Show dogs are able to compete in the AKC at this age.

On the negative side, popular larger breeds (notably Labrador Retrievers and dogs of similar size) start to achieve weights of 50 lbs, 60 lbs or much more. If the pups were not properly socialized to have manners in the house when they were younger, they are now big enough to hurt people with bad manners like jumping.

Seven months is the age when we start getting most of our calls to help with behavior problems, especially in larger breeds. Seven months also seems to be an age when large numbers of people, frustrated with their dogs' behavior, start giving them away. And pups at this age are a common sight in shelters and offered for adoption on Craigslist and Petfinder.com.

8 months-9 months

Puppies: Some owners don't realize that certain dogs start teething relatively late and don't physically complete the stage until nine months. Don't assume your pup has stopped physical teething until you check his mouth. But, once all the adult teeth are in, no puppy has any physical reason to try chewing on any item other than designated toys. All pups should have completed the teething phase by 9 or 10 months. There may be some unusual cases out there where it could take longer (or the dog might need dental treatment to remove an impacted tooth) but any dog that chews on possessions after one year is no longer teething! Also no pup at this age has any *physical* reason to not be fully housetrained in all parts of the home unless he is injured or sick. And, even though many breeds still have a lot of growing to do, many pup's size at this age may approximate that of a mature dog.

9 months-10 months

Puppies: Even though some breeds (especially large and giant breeds) have very much growing to do, and even though their personalities will change as they come into full maturity and full temperament, we feel it's a mistake for families to confuse 10-month old dogs with much younger "puppies", especially when it comes to housetraining, chewing on possessions or lack of knowledge of many basic commands, including basic obedience and manners around people.

For example once taught by their owners, all dogs of this age should be able: to identify family members by name; to always return to owners when called; to fetch and surrender items on command; to bark and stop barking on command; to "go to their place" and not bother owners; to "leave" and "drop" items on command; to stay and wait for at least 10 minutes; to walk on leash perfectly (even around other dogs); to travel well; to stand calmly for grooming and veterinary exams; to appropriately greet friendly strangers; to behave well on outings to public places and to show good manners around children.

Of course, your 10-month old pup can't learn all this on their own- but they do have the mental power to learn all of this and more as long as owners take time to train them properly. **Dogs are bred for working and learning new information quickly. And if you don't train your pup useful commands at this age, he can learn just as many negative habits on his own, just to keep his mind stimulated**. People often make the mistake of underestimating their dogs and not introducing challenging mental and physical commands early enough. Even the right games can aid your dog's development, physically, mentally and emotionally (see our book *The Cure for Useless Dog Syndrome* and *Awesome Puppy* for more details and specific instructions for many different games and activities). And the worst thing you can do with a pup of this age is to leave them nothing to do. Instead, you should make a long laundry list of hundreds of things you'd like your dog to learn, and then teach a new one every day from the day you get him home.

Obviously, when a puppy has reached 10 months crated for the majority of their day every day, there is no way to know what he or she did or didn't learn- because the pup missed out on so many opportunities to rehearse good behaviors in the natural environment.

You should still expect a "pup" of 10 months to be more naturally boisterous than he will be in 6 months' time and allow him some leeway if he makes the occasional mistake. But, **provided the animal is healthy, at this age there is no longer any** *developmental* reason that a "pup" isn't capable of living in every part of the home with his family, controlling his bowels and bladder and respecting all human possessions and family members. **Since dogs of this age do resemble adolescents and are a little flighty, however, it's important that you provide plenty of exercise, attention and outlets for healthy play; plus leashed walks and impromptu obedience practices for dog/owner bonding.** Always accustom the dog to new situations slowly and positively. Because different breeds mature at different rates, some young dogs could just be coming out of their second fear period at 10 months. So be careful, and encourage young dogs to get work past their fears with confidence rather than just forcing or pushing them through fears.

1 ½ years- 2years

Young Dogs: This is the age when many families surrender dogs to shelters because they feel they can't handle them. And we receive many calls for help with behavior problems, especially in larger breeds of this age. This is because, by this time, dogs have reached their full size, their highest energy requirements and they're are at the height of their sexual energy and drive if they haven't been spayed or neutered.

Some dog breeds, especially guardian breeds, require a long time to mature in temperament. And some working breeds that might have appeared silly and soft when younger now "suddenly" come into the true temperament they were bred for, which is strong and defensive. This sometimes surprises and confuses owners who may have been unrealistic or who were deliberately misled by breeders or other dog "professionals".

Dogs that were shown clear yet fair leadership when they were younger will not defy owners when they reach 1½ years. But dogs without this kind of guidance may.

It's also important to get the dog used to encountering stimuli like other dogs when they are young, because dogs left to grow to 1½ years with hardly any exposure to outside stimuli may react wildly the first time they see new things. And by this age, just when they're most likely to show sudden defiance, they've also achieved full size and what may feel like supernatural strength. This strong temperament would be only natural in a wild animal at the height of sexual maturity that might have to fight to the death over a mate. But if your dog was not spayed or neutered until now, performing the procedure at this age may not be a total solution because at this age the defiant temperament may have already become a habit- and are just a change in hormones may not be enough to control.

What if zoos crated wolves? Years ago conditions were not that great for animals in zoos. Many of us are still old enough to remember sad spectacles like big cats being held in small cages or toted around in cages for exhibition in circuses. But these days, research has proved that this type of confinement without natural enrichment is damaging to zoo animals, both physically and psychologically. And zoos have gone to great pains to revamp enclosures to be larger and to resemble animals' natural habitat; and to give animals stimulation to occupy their minds. (One example is delivering food in "enrichment devices" so the animals have to think and work for it.)

If you've had the privilege of seeing wolves at zoos, you've most likely seen a pack allowed to roam together in a large fenced wooded area. In fact, wolves often live in the largest and most natural areas at zoos around the country, and they're often on the move. But imagine instead if the zoo kept the wolves like many "experts" are recommending owners keep their pet dogs- locked in small crates, all day long. Seeing the wolves lined up like this in cages would be a heartbreaking sight. And we imagine that it wouldn't be long before public outcry of animal cruelty would either shut down the zoo, or immediately change the conditions. This is, of course, ironic since many dog "experts" are basing the notion that crating is good for dogs on their belief that dogs are "den animals" just like wolves! (See Chapter 6, Part B). Of course caging in a tiny area is bad for any animal, especially a large intelligent predator used to traveling great distances. And, if you ever want a graphic image to remind you of the absurdity of the pro-crating camp's views, just remember the images of the wolf pack in little wire cages!

2 years-3 years

Wolves: At this age the wolf is at full sexual maturity and the alpha pair will have their first litter of pups.

Young Dogs: Full physical emotional and social maturity in every breed, including those giant working breeds that are slowest to mature.

Canine Sensory Development:

Nose: Recently, celebrity dog trainer Cesar Millan has been mentioning on his television shows how important it is to engage a dog's nose to help him to feel more balanced and behave in a more stable fashion. Cesar also explains on his Facebook page that, "while we humans have only about 5 million scent receptors in our nose, the average grown dog has 220 million!"

Learning to discriminate by scent is vital to puppies' development and, in our experience, using the nose properly makes for more stable dogs. An interesting clinical observation we've notice is that the most disturbed dogs we work with seem to also have trouble distinguishing items by scent, even when the task is as simple as finding a small treat partially covered by a blanket, or even a treat that is lying on the floor. When we incorporate exercises in using their noses, along with other senses like hearing and touch, into these dogs' treatment plans we've noticed improvement in their sensory skills in tandem with emotional improvement.

And, according to Diane Jessup in *The Working Pit Bull*, it's never too early to start nose training- owners can start teaching pups as young as eight weeks the basics of how to track.

Canine Brain Development- effects of normal stimulation vs. understimulation on developing dogs' brains:

An influential article by Veterinary Behaviorist Dr. Joel Dehasse ("Sensory, Emotional and Social Development of the Young Dog", The Bulletin for Veterinary Clinical Ethology, Vol. 2, n1-2, pp 6-29, 1994, Brussels) explains the scientific research on puppy brain development, sensory development and behavioral development starting before birth and progressing in a predictable fashion based on the weeks of the puppy's life. The scientific studies summarized in this article demonstrate how **proper stimulation during the puppy's early weeks and months will increase its abilities in all areas, while inadequate stimulation, especially during critical developmental periods, can not only impair physical brain development, but also create fears, neuroses and problems relating to both dogs and humans when the dog encounters these and other environmental stimuli later in life.**

In reference to neurological development, Dr. Dehasse explains that dogs, like humans, are born with immature nervous systems and that supportive parental environment assists them as their neuronal networks differentiate, or are organized specific to the tasks and talents required for their species. This is the theory of selective specialization, which we feel applies to the level of enrichment in pups' physical environment as well.

In a classic experiment that is now well known Weisel and Hubel (1963) demonstrated that young monkeys suffered irreversible visual damage (presumably through disuse) when one eye was kept shut by experimenters for the entire first 6 weeks of their lives even though no specific structural damage was inflicted by the experimenters. Similar experiments (Weisel and Hubel, in Vastrade,1987) with cats showed a critical period for visual development between 3 and 7 weeks and an incapacity to recover vision after three months.

According to Changeux, 1983, "There is a critical period during which the abnormal functioning of a system causes irreversible lesions".

And, in experiments with postnatal rodents, Caston (1993) showed that temporary occlusion of the ears led to subsequent difficulties locating sounds in space, and discriminating auditive patterns. Caston (1993) also found that in rodents, "precocious exposition to other species' odors eases future interspecific socialization (decrease in aggressions, lowering of corticosteroids [stress hormones])".

Dr. Dehasse, points to neuorbiological studies that demonstrate that "prolonged precocious isolation was responsible for long-lasting structural or functional cerebral modifications." For example, a study by Verdoux and Bergeois, (1991) showed that isolation of young monkeys leads to a diminution of the dendritic network in the frontal cortex [center of higher thought and problem solving], along with changes in hormonal centers of the brain which mediate hyperreactivity to stress.

And Cyrulnick (1991) remarks that **"the brain becomes atrophied when [an animal] is raised in sensory isolation,** and it develops more than average in an atmosphere of hyperstimulation in noise, affectivity, odors, tastes, sight, etc...."

We now know that puppies do not complete all their mental and behavioral activity in equal increments, but rather in stages, identified as "sensitive periods". "A sensitive period is a point in the maturing process when events are susceptible to leaving long-term effects, or a period when learning is easier and knowledge gained is stored in the long-term memory." Dehasse points out that **"during the sensitive period, a small number of determining experiences have major effects (or damages) on future behavior".** The authors (Dehasse and DeBuyser, 1983, 1989, 1991) also stressed the role of several discreet sensitive periods between 3 weeks and 3 months in behavioral epigenesist in puppies.

According to Dehasse, scientific experiments indicate that hormones and neurotransmitters responsible for emotion and attachment can even be triggered before birth, based on positive stimulation to the mother through petting. He states that **"a dog's tactile capacities develop before birth, and it is possible that it already becomes used to contact in the uterus, when the mother is petted. Puppies manipulated this way show a greater tolerance to touching than dogs born of a mother who was not petted."**

Research by Dennenberg and Rosenberg (in Fox, 1978) demonstrates how in rats, proper manipulation at a young age or just before birth (by manipulating the pregnant mother) gives greater resistance to stress and disease.

These experiments demonstrate that "when a gestating pet is given a friendly and caring human environment (with affectionate physical contact), the domestication and emotional balance of her offspring is facilitated, as compared with an environment where there is no contact and interaction with people."

Obviously, the results of this research bodes badly for puppies bred in "puppy mills" whose mothers are raised in cages with no human contact or socialization during the gestation period. Since we do not know exactly how much damage might occur while the pups are still in utero, the next opportunity to expose them to proper stimulation would obviously be after they are born and in the new home. **This is why we, the authors of *Dogs Hate Crates*, feel there is such potential for damage to a puppy's development if crated extensively at home during the later sensitive developmental periods if the pup has already suffered from a deprived environment at the breeders during the pregnancy and the early critical weeks.**

Overall, according to DeHasse, "Domestication depends of the presence of humans between 3 and 12 [plus or minus two weeks] in the surroundings in which a puppy develops and this socialization must be continued throughout the animal's life. The lack of human contact between 3 and 12 [plus or minus two weeks] fosters the development of fear/wariness of humans (feral dog)"

For this reason we, the authors of *Dogs Hate Crates*, believe that in many cases, **young pups that come from puppy mill or backyard breeders start with an already shaky foundation of human stimuli and interaction before weaning. But once they come into a home during the remaining 2-6 weeks of opportunity on Dehasse's scale, owners may make it worse by isolating them in a crate.**

According to Dehasse, a pup's early development is also the time he will develop a healthy state of balance, or homeostasis. Dehasse quotes Vincent (1986) to explain. According to Vincent, "Homeostasis is the ability of an organism to maintain equilibrium in a variable environment. Just as we have thermo-regulation..., we can also speak of emotional and relational homeostasis. ...Living in a group and adapting to varied environments calls for a certain degree of emotional equilibrium. "

Dehassse mentions an experiment in which "Fox (1975) experimented with puppies placed in contact with increasingly complex stimuli (enrichment) at 5, 8, 12, and 16 weeks: as they grew the puppies tended to seek out complex environments. Puppies raised in environments poor in stimuli... and placed for the first time in a highly stimulating environment at 12 or 16 weeks are inhibited and search less complex environments."

To our interpretation, this means simply that the more novel stimuli a pup encounters when he is young, the better, and we base many of our most successful treatment plans on this principle. **Sensory deprivation (as in excessive crating in one location with no opportunity to see, smell or interact with everyday stimuli in the outside world) would, by implication create pups (and dogs) that were more hesitant, and less emotionally balanced, courageous and bold. And they would be more likely to display sudden and extreme fear reactions to relatively benign stimuli.**

In contrast, proper interaction with outside stimuli, according to Fox (1975) creates a sensory frame of reference or tolerance level that will help the dog in proper response to any future stimuli he encounters. According to Dehasse, "This referential determines the stimulation level at which the individual must begin to adjust by activating the appropriate emotion (fear, wariness, etc.) and adopting the most appropriate adaptive behavior (investigation, avoidance, flight, aggression, inhibition, etc.)

"The referentials that come into play are level of noise, visual agitation, intensity of olfactory stimulation, number of vibrations, occupation of three-dimensional space, flexibility or rigidity of movements, etc." We must point out that none of those dimensions in experiencing new stimuli would ever take place if the pup was kept in a crate during critical periods! A dog in a crate would not experience such simple sensations as understanding that tile flooring feels different than a rug between the toes; that palm fronds can brush against an outside window, creating harmless but fascinating moving dapples of light that a young dog can chase, but never catch; that a pool of sunlight on a wood floor feels good to lie on; that some surfaces that owners warn a dog not to jump on wobble dangerously if you try; that sound of a vacuum cleaner or even a neighbor knocking on the door is harmless, and that cool water splashes back at you if you try to paw your water dish!

Of course exposure to interesting outside stimuli is also important- rides in the car to go to fun places, a trip to the pet store, the first time a dog sees a large body of water or joggers, bicyclists, and squirrels circling the park- or even the sight of birds flying or trees waving overhead. We've literally treated adult dogs with life-destroying fears or extreme panic or even aggression reactions to some of the situations mentioned and hundreds of similar stimuli (see the true case of Bridget in Chapter 15). And, while the dogs we treated each had different histories (including some with unknown genetics and breeding) one thing they all shared in common was that they had been largely deprived of the chance to encounter novel items and experiences at a young age. **In our experience, those dogs that had been crated excessively during their formative weeks and months of development seemed to react most abnormally when encountering the outside world.**

Dehasse points out that a puppy is initially graced with "malleability [which] enables it to adapt to almost all environments without undue stress." And people have appreciated this quality for many, many centuries. This unique adaptability is what makes dogs such great all-purpose companions, whether a dog is accompanying children on a bike ride, or marching beside soldiers into war; living on a ship or helping his owner through a blizzard. But today, many owners have dogs that literally "freak out" on a simple 5-minute car ride to the pet store, and cannot even be brought inside to sniff at dog toys. Some are even scared or panicked by the toys themselves!

According to Dehasse, "Differences in the quality and amount of stimuli a puppy receives in its environment of development as compared to its adult surroundings determine the degree of risk it may not be able to adapt it's sensorial referential... and thus achieve homeostasis (this includes the development of phobias and anxieties.) Clinical observation has also confirmed that it is easier to transfer from an environment with a high level of stimulation... to an environment with a low level ... than the contrary. A puppy raised in a deprived environment may be tempted to compensate for this lack of sensorial stimulation by self-stimulation; this is how certain stereotyped behavior develops, as well as self-centered behavior (Fox 1975) such as self-induced dermatoses.

"Lastly, stimulus-poor puppies run the risk of developing hyper-attachments to their biological or adoptive parents..." This includes symptoms of separation anxiety such as intolerance to isolation and attention-seeking behavior.

This tendency for dogs raised without adequate novel mental and sensory stimulation as pups to develop acute separation anxiety is also borne out by our own clinical findings in dogs we have treated. We have found that sometimes proper introduction of the kind of stimuli the dog should have encountered as a puppy (with extreme care not to push too hard and induce fear) can help some of these dogs; but first it helps if we know how extreme the sensory deprivation was when the dog was younger.

Owners are often surprised when they realize that **a maturing pup cannot exist and develop a healthy mind and emotions if every day, for 8 to 12 hours straight, the animal has nothing more interesting to stare at than a blank wall and nothing more interesting to do or interact with other than licking, or chewing on, his own paws**. (See the case of "Champ" living in two completely different circumstances in Chapter 3).

The truth is that pups are fascinated by new toys and novel stimuli. And, in general, **the more a pup gets to engage his brain each day, the better**.

Warren Eckstein, the originator of the term "Latchkey dog" and the man labeled by the press in the 1970's as the "first dog psychologist" would agree. Mr. Eckstein, in *How to Get Your Dog to Do What You Want,* a book he co-authored with Fay Eckstein in 1994, emphasizes the vital importance of keeping your dog's mind active, in the face of virtually no one else talking about the subject at that time. "Inactive [canine] minds," the authors state, "can contribute to the development of many undesirable behavior habits and can create unhealthy mental attitudes that take their toll on ... physical well-being."

"[Dogs] need image- and confidence- building as much as we do. And they need a certain amount of self-esteem in order to behave well. They need to develop inner strength if they are to try something new or to learn to trust in you...

"By doing nothing," the authors say, "by ignoring your pet, by not interacting with him on a regular basis, you can do great damage. It is simply not enough just to feed and walk your dog, then treat him like a piece of furniture the rest of the time."

The Intelligence of Dogs:

Learning about dogs' intelligence is fascinating and holds many interesting implications for humanity, yet there haven't been nearly enough controlled scientific studies. This may be partly because humans limit ourselves by trying to quantify canine intelligence only in human terms. And we're also limited by the constraints of the study modalities available. For example, we wonder how we'll ever quantify the "ESP" (extrasensory perception) that all dogs seem to possess naturally; in human terms we see evidence every day that dogs are mind readers. Certainly they are better readers of human character than most of us, and some of our dogs seem able to pinpoint exactly what we're feeling even when we attempt to hide it. If you've watched the movie *The Incredible Journey*, you've also seen animals find their way back to owners who had driven many hundreds of miles away to a new home. The movie is based on a true story and there are many similar documented cases. So there's no doubt dogs possess an internal "GPS" (global positioning system) even though we don't know the exact pathways that make it work. The same is true for dog's ability to know time.

All of these areas open doors for fascinating research and greater understanding and appreciation of dogs. And the future may open many more amazing discoveries about our best friends. Recently, computer technology has provided a bridge to make much more research possible. For example, one study that we hope inspires further research was conducted by Friederike Range from the University of Vienna in Austria.

In this unique study, dogs successfully demonstrated their ability to learn by using computer-automated touch screens. "The dogs were able to classify complex color photos and place them into categories in the same way that humans do... When the dogs were faced with a choice between a picture of a new dog on a familiar landscape and a completely new landscape with no dog, they reliably selected the option with the dog. These results show that the dogs mentally formed a concept 'dog'".

And, if intelligence in dogs and humans share similar benchmarks, then we can find interesting implications in the entry in the *National Association for Child Development Foundation (NACD) Journal*, Vol. 4 No. 3, 1984, by Robert Doman, M.D. entitled, "Sensory Deprivation". Dr. Doman explains, "Stimulation is vital to our brain's efficiency... Proper stimulation leads to the proliferation of more and more connections between brain cells, creating more efficient pathways of brain function.

"Sensory deprivation studies show us that sudden and nearly complete deprivation of stimulation through the five senses can lead to dramatic changes in the brain's efficiency with a partial loss of memory, a lowering of the IQ... [and] personality changes, including withdrawal... A classic example of a withdrawn child is an autistic child."

This article deals with the formation of autism in children. **But we postulate that similar extreme deprivation of stimulation in a developing puppy, as in a pup that is locked in a tiny cage in a dim room, or similar conditions when a pup is crated with no stimuli in a home, can actually create an autistic dog- a dog that displays similar symptoms of avoiding human connection and normal social relations with humans as an autistic child does.**

We also suggest that extreme deprivation of stimuli during a puppy's critical early weeks and months of development can actually reduce the pup's IQ, as well as his ability to function in common situations in family life.

Literature in the field indicates that more and more such dogs that lack the cornerstones of basic functioning are being treated by applied animal behaviorists, who prescribe many of these dogs psychotropic medications, including "doggie Prozac" (an anti-anxiety medication derived from a human antidepressant), tranquilizers, muscle relaxers or medications for Attention Deficit Disorder. And we also see many such emotionally disturbed dogs in our practice. Even though, at this time, there's no official term for "doggie autism", Emma has worked with the condition both in humans and in dogs- and the symptoms appear to be the same.

Stephen Budiansky, in his book *The Truth About Dogs*, refers to the landmark animal behavior studies on imprinting in dogs done in the 1940's and 1950's at Jackson Laboratory in Bal Harbor, including the well known "wild dog" experiment published in 1961.

In this study, "puppies from more than a hundred litters of varied breeds were reared in large outdoor fields with essentially no direct human contact. But for a period of one week each, the puppies were brought into the laboratory for daily sessions of human contact and intervention. The age at which the puppies had their week of human contact was varied from two weeks to nine weeks; a control group had no contact at all until age fourteen weeks".

The study demonstrated the fact that the particular week the pups had their contact with the humans also influenced how well they did with future human handling after 14 weeks. Pups that received their only contact at either 2 or 3 weeks and pups with no contact did the worst when they were introduced to a person sitting quietly on the floor or when they were put on a leash for the first time and exposed to unfamiliar places.

In fact, those in the control group (with no human contact before 14 weeks) were so fearful that they would not come anywhere near a person sitting on the floor. By eliminating these pups' contact with humans during critical developmental stages the pups never imprinted- or formed a concept of humans as suitable "family" for them. **One always thinks of dogs as having a "natural" bond with humans. But by manipulating young puppies' upbringing so they never got contact with humans, as in this experiment, scientists were able to "create" dogs that did not have the bond with humans that usually defines dogs!**

This study was done many years ago, but today millions of pups are being brought up in isolated situations devoid of human contact in puppy mill cages all over the country. And most of these pups are then sold to pet shops where they're again isolated in cages. At 14 weeks many still haven't reached a family home. And when the pups finally make it from the isolation of a puppy mill to a family home, many spend the last critical weeks of their early development again confined to cages without stimuli. **Some spend 18 or more hours a day (often as many as 23) with no physical contact with their humans.** The fact that those last critical weeks are wasted like this, most often on the advice of dog behavior "experts", is particularly ironic when we learn the results of a study like this.

What lack of stimuli does to a dog's mind

In the next chapter, we'll help unveil the mystery of how a developing suburban dog typically spends his time alone, with a detailed reconstruction of what the 8-month old pup would experience each hour of a typical day if locked in a crate vs. the same dog's experiences if left free in the home. This includes behaviors the 8-month old dog exhibits and lasting changes to his mind and body.

We draw on information ranging from scientific studies to our own detailed and documented observations to describe short and long-term mental, physical, developmental and emotional effects of crating vs. household freedom. We also use evidence in behavioral literature, as well as experience in our own canine psychology cases to bring to life the likely ways the young dog relates to his owners and their children in the contrasting scenarios.

Have you ever stayed home with your dog and had the chance to carefully observe him all day? Many owners never get the chance to do this or to fully focus on their observations, while others may not know exactly how to interpret what they observe. Even though owners' "gut instinct" may tell them certain things about their dogs, many still feel the need to defer to the opinions of "experts". This is likely because, despite the fact that we love our dogs so, the innermost workings of their minds still remain a mystery to us in many ways.

We advise owners to go ahead and trust their instincts. And, even if you make an error, it's best to err on the side of overestimating, rather than underestimating, your dog and the complexities and depth of his personality. We rarely have to criticize owners for "anthropomorphizing". **Certainly, dogs are a different species, and they do communicate in a different fashion and live in different ways than humans. However dogs share in common with us the fact that they are social beings and sentient beings.**

In other words, dogs definitely do have consciousness and they do think! Ranging from hundreds of years ago, to recent times there's been scientific debate on whether dogs have consciousness. Applied animal behaviorist Patricia McConnell writes about some of the more radical theories in her book *For the Love of a Dog,* including the fact that, **to this day, some scientists not only believe that dogs don't have consciousness, but that they don't even have feelings!**

If you think this is so radical, she describes in her book how hundreds of years ago Rene Descartes (one of the most highly respected scientists and social/philosophical theorists of his time, whose ideas have shaped much of our perception of our world) "demonstrated" his theory that dogs don't have feelings by nailing them up-alive-onto barn walls- all in the name of progressive scientific thought!

In her book, Ms. McConnell also refers to research studies that support the idea of dogs as thinking creatures- including the fact that dogs have been proven to understand the concepts of larger vs. smaller and the concept of quantity.

Our professional opinion is that, even though dogs may not communicate or think symbolically as humans do, they certainly have consciousness. Proof of this is the fact that dogs can solve problems, they can remember outcomes from the past in order to decide whether to repeat behaviors and they can make independent decisions. And dogs also feel a sense of responsibility and love.

Your dog probably also knows many more words than you think. Dogs with testable vocabularies of 150-200 words or more are not uncommon. Emma's Collie/Shepherd mix knew over 200 words and could also understand when some of these words were combined into unique sentences. She could also demonstrate discernment between past, present and future outcomes based on what was said to her. Living with this dog, you often needed to spell out certain words if you didn't want her to know what was being talked about.

And, just like children do in the same situation, she even learned some of the spellings!) Feats like this, which we hear about frequently from dog lovers, seem even more remarkable when you consider the fact that words are not dogs' strongest language. Many of our pet dogs also communicate with perfect intuition to understand what their owners are feeling, and what they want and need at any given moment.

Some studies have shown that dogs' intelligence is equivalent to that of a human child of 2 ½ years old. (Other studies have placed the number as high as 5 years.) Strangely, we've heard people react to these numbers as proof that dogs are stupid. And this reaction, of course, brings into question *their* intelligence. Because, when you think of what children at these ages are capable of, it's remarkable that a dog could have the same IQ! And knowing about dogs' mental abilities makes it even more frightening to think of the horrendous cruelties some people inflict on dogs (like some the cases in Chapter 9) and the everyday cruelty of Excessive Crating, which leaves dogs basically isolated for life with nothing to do or think about.

If you wish to quantify dogs' intelligence, it's also important to consider the acuity of their senses. If you leave a window open, your dog can smell you literally a mile away, distinguishing your scent from anyone else's. And he could easily find you if you were ever lost if there was any trail to follow. But even more amazing is the fact that you would be the only person he would *want* to find.

That kind of loyalty is pretty amazing in a world where even half of marriages break up within seven years. If you own a large dog, the fact is that he's probably strong enough to easily kill you with his teeth. But instead, he'd almost surely lay his life down to protect you without a second thought. (This recently happened in our area when a local police K-9 dog took multiple bullets, and ultimately died, to save the life of his human partner.)

This willingness for a dog to sacrifice his life for his owner is *not* just instinct or training. Even though your dog doesn't express it verbally, he loves you, and he certainly perceives you as a family member. Your dog loves you and he thinks about you a lot! Even if you went away for five years, he would still know you. So how can any owner doubt that they are on their dog's mind the whole time they are away at work?

In every facet of working dogs, dogs are trained to perform highly complex series of tasks, sometimes completely independently. Our favorites are the ancient flock guardian breeds, such as the Anatolian Shepherds of Turkey, whose work is to protect "their" flocks of sheep by staying alone with them in the countryside for months at a time. And then there are rescue breeds like St. Bernards that can independently search out and assist avalanche victims. **Keeping dogs' mental abilities in mind, is there really any question that your dog won't notice or understand that, for some reason, you lock him in a cage when you leave for work?** And do you think he doesn't fear that you'll do it to him again the next day?

According to Leon Festinger's Theory of Cognitive Dissonance (described in Chapter 7) once a person does something out of line with their own perception of themselves, they will feel so uncomfortable that they will try to seek out some reason that would somehow make their behavior make sense. And then, regardless of traditional logic, they would add that new line of thinking to their beliefs in order not to experience uncomfortable dissonance between their thoughts and actions. (One example of the theory in action that social psychologists frequently point to is Nazi war criminals who found ways to justify their actions.)

And we think that dog owners who sense what they are doing by crating dogs is bad often seek for theories that justify their actions, and then stand strongly behind those theories. One example is owners (as well as dog professionals) who say, "Why shouldn't I crate my dog? All he does is sleep all day." And then, in a bizarre case of twisted logic, "experts" frequently cite observations of *crated* dogs to support their theory that all dogs do is sleep all day. Of course, if a person was only given enough space to either lie down or stand up and turn around, they'd likely do a lot of sleeping, too!

But, it's true that dogs do sleep a lot during the day, and they sleep many more hours in each twenty-four hour period than humans do. This is due to dog's different physiology, energy source, method of obtaining food and their particular Circadian rhythms. Patterns of sleeping also depend on a dog's age and they vary greatly depending upon breed and what type of work the dog is bred to do.

If, as an owner, you carefully watch your dog, you'll notice that his sleep resembles naps. He will sleep for twenty minutes and then stand and move around. Or he may be roused from sleep by a sound that he believes to be a danger to his family and respond to that danger instantaneously by jumping up to check it out. While sleeping, dogs stretch and turn frequently. Or a dog will rise, walk to another room and take a drink. These movements and inquisitive behaviors are just as likely to happen during the night as during the day. And it's not dogs' nature to sleep soundly for eight hours at a time.

Even though dogs sleep a lot during periods of "downtime", under more demanding conditions dogs sleep much less. For example, a Border Collie that actively works on a ranch will not take much time to sleep during daytime hours. This pattern of adjusting the amount of sleep to the day's demands resembles the lives of wolves in the wild. A dog is a sophisticated hunting animal that uses a great deal of mental energy and thinking, planning and communicating with his pack while hunting, as well as expending tremendous physical energy. His actions can determine life and death for his family, so he must be in prime form when he's needed.

And whenever his efforts are not needed, he rests to replenish his energy. Just like your dog at home, a wolf takes little naps when convenient. He may sleep for a while, then get up and stretch, go sniff at something interesting or play with pack members for a while. If it's hot out, he may dig a shallow depression in the cool earth and lie down for another siesta. Resting like this is a good plan when the pack may be on the move again, and on the hunt, at dusk!

We've taken time to observe many dogs from different backgrounds and carefully document what they do in a home environment every hour throughout the day. And **it's never natural for a dog to sleep soundly all day, barely moving, for 8 to 12 hours at a time. It's worse when he sleeps trapped in the same small cage he lay in all day, unable to even stretch properly, for another 8 or more consecutive hours each night**. And it becomes worse still when the dog gets little physical or mental challenge during the few hours he's out of the crate.

While there are many good scientific studies on dogs' senses, and increasing studies on dogs' intelligence, scientific proof that dogs have emotional feelings is basically non-existent. Anecdotal evidence, of course, abounds. And, even though many of the experts whose work we refer to in this book also believe dogs have feelings similar to human emotions, scientists suggesting this risk losing credibility for not sticking to strict scientific method in their inquiries. And this is perhaps a sad throwback to the time when Rene Descartes gave his grisly demonstrations of nailed up dogs, not in the name of cruelty, but rather in the name of science. Unfortunately, for centuries, the prevailing scientific view remained that dogs did not have feelings.

In the next chapter, when we reconstruct the pieces of the hypothetical dog's day, only changing the variable of whether he spends the day crated or free in his family's home, we stick to science and clinical observations as much as possible. The descriptions cover all the young dog's actions, showing how the different stimuli he encounters crated vs. free change his behavior, temperament and development. We reconstructed every action, thought and feeling from scientific evidence and observation. And, even though it's true that no one has definitively proved that dogs *have* feelings, Champ, the 8-month old German Shepherd in the story, took on a life of his own.

So that we could let him live on, in every detail of his day, including what he feels, we made the story of Champ a separate little book, *Dog In a Box*, which will be published soon. Here in Chapter 3, we cover only the highlights of Champ's day- and the specifics on how crating affects behavior and development. Readers who want to know more about Champ, his warm, playful and heroic spirit and his human family can purchase *Dog In a Box* wherever you purchased *Dogs Hate Crates* or our other books, including print, an ebook and Kindle version. For the more concise description of the hypothetical young dog's hour-by-hour experience, crated vs. free (that does not give away the ultimate storyline), simply read Chapter 3.

To our knowledge, a detailed description hour by hour like this has never been published anywhere else. To reconstruct the theoretical dog's day free in the house, we drew on information from breeders, show handlers, agility and Schutzhund training experts, veterinary behaviorists and veterinary textbooks. To reconstruct crated Champ's day hour-by-hour, we used the same sources, plus evidence from studies done in shelters; studies on the effects of housing on laboratory dogs; veterinary commentary; and reports from humane authorities, rescue societies and court reports in cases where dogs suffered criminally abusive crating, as well as our own observations. Even though the thoughts and feelings we attribute to the dog can only be inferred, and not yet proved by scientific method, physical and behavioral effects similar to the ones we describe in this reconstructed case have been clearly and repeatedly documented.

We'd like to end this chapter with a quote from Diane Jessup's fact-based fiction novel, *The Dog Who Spoke with Gods*, which deals with the heroic bond between dog and human that transcended even the abuse of a laboratory setting:

"The dog inhabits a no-man's land between human and animal. Unlike the cat, the pig, the sheep or the horse, he cannot, if given the opportunity, take up where he left off with Nature. In one sense, he is no longer truly an animal. Nor is his canine brain the equal of our primate one, and for this he is forever doomed to be misjudged.

" We struggle to quantify his intelligence in terms of our own particular endowments, which cannot be done. The dog cannot read or write. He speaks with his body and his eyes. He does not use tools. He possesses loyalty, perception and patience in quantities we cannot comprehend. He shares with us our full range emotions; he can sob with terror or sorrow or and grin with good humor. He is more similar than different from ourselves. And the similarities in the ways we think and feel are such that a dog and a human can have perfect understanding, acting together as one while performing complex tasks. A single glance between dog and human companion can communicate subtle and complex emotion and meaning, proving without question that we have more in common than not. Friendships between humans and dogs have proven to be as strong as, or stronger than those found between many humans."

Chapter 4: One Day in the Life of a Crated Vs. an Uncrated Dog- The Story of "Champ"

This chapter is a condensed version of the detailed hour-by-hour day experienced by one dog in two very different situations, described fully in our book, *Dog In a Box*. Champ is an 8-month old German Shepherd dog who lives with a couple and their two boys- 7-year old Aiden and 6-year old Cody in their large house in a gated development on Florida's Intracoastal Waterway. Champ and Aiden are particularly attached to each other. In our upcoming book, *Dog In a Box*, we follow Champ through each hour, contrasting scenarios of what each hour is like for him if he is crated and what happens if he's not crated. You can read the chapter that follows for the most important highlights of how Champ's behavior and personality is impacted each hour, including benchmarks of normal development contrasted with manifestations of symptoms of excessive kenneling listed in Chapter 1. (And, if you wish to read the full story with additional detail and the complete emotional conclusion read *Dog In a Box*, which will be available wherever you purchased this book.)

If you're not sure what existence is like for your dog or for other crated dogs, this chapter and the book *Dog In a Box* will give you many details you may not have considered before. Of course, not all dogs are the same, and neither are their reactions to crating. Each owner can look at their dog's own reactions and behaviors (and reactions and behaviors of other dogs they know that are crated) and use crated vs. free-in-the-house Champ's experiences and behaviors as a jumping off point for inquiry and comparison.

Highlights of Champ's day:

7:00 am-8:00 am:

Mom gives both the crated and uncrated young dogs brief walks to empty bladder and bowels, but she doesn't notice the crated pup is suffering from an impacted anal gland and irritation/infection caused by constantly biting at the area while he's been confined. Dad's been away on a business trip. In the home where Champ's going to be left crated, the goodbye is tearful. Seven-year old Aiden, who has a special bond with Champ protests about crating the young dog, but Mom insists, citing the instructions of their dog trainer.

Several months before Mom and Dad paid a young certified dog trainer almost $1,000 to tell them to crate Champ in order to curb his excessive barking and symptoms of separation anxiety. Now, Champ vocalizes in distress as the boys he feels are his personal responsibility step out the door. So Mom does exactly what the dog trainer instructed. She slams Champ's empty metal water dish onto the top of the crate, leaving his ears ringing. Then, within the 4,200 square foot home with the desirable waterfront address, Mom leaves the energetic and inquisitive 8-month old German Shepherd puppy locked in the cramped crate in a small blank laundry room with nothing for him to look at all day except a recycling bin!

In contrast, in the alternative scenario, Free-in-the-house Champ runs from window to window to see the family off. He'll miss his family waiting for their return, but he feels no anxiety. While he runs around, Champ knocks some papers and windowseat cushions down by accident in Dad's home office, and this gives him a chance to use his own judgment to remember proper house manners. Instead of chewing up a cushion, the young dog exercises his mind, makes a choice and tries to remember where he left his favorite chew toy. Then Champ's fast-twitch muscles kick in as he wheels around energetically and runs to go get it. (This is somewhat similar to how a wolf pup might run in the wild.) Next, playing with the toy in different variations and on different surfaces stimulates Champ's senses and improves his athleticism and balance. It also strengthens his fine coordination and it acts as a healthy rehearsal of normal doggie hunting behavior.

Obviously, a breed like Champ, a German Shepherd Dog, could be doing much more challenging work than playing with toys and waiting for his owners to return, whether he worked as an assistance dog, a herding dog or a police dog. Modern American suburban life while Champ's family goes away to work and school doesn't provide the stimuli/exercise that would be ideal for him. But at least Uncrated Champ gets a chance to practice natural behaviors, move his body and make thoughtful decisions at an age when his body and mind are still developing. In contrast, Crated Champ, frustrated and worried about his owners' leaving, spends the balance of the hour howling forlornly until his voice is hoarse.

8:00 am- 9:00 am:

Crated Champ stops howling and refocuses on his favorite toy that he notices outside the cage. Rather than reaching with his paw (which got stuck on the wire and hurt him yesterday), he vigorously rocks the cage trying to get at the toy. All the exertion makes him thirsty, but his owners deliberately withhold water to keep him from having bladder accidents- and Mom left his empty bowl sitting on top of the cage.

The veterinarian hasn't noticed yet, because of Crated Champ's good genetics, but Crated Champ is not in the same good physical shape as he would be if free in the home. All the daily cramping in the cage without movement or exercise has inhibited some muscle development. And his athletic endurance has dropped to the point where the pup, only 8 months old, tires out quickly when he gets the chance to run and play with Dad on bursts on the weekends.

Constant crating (12 hours on most weekdays, plus 8 hours at night) also means less opportunity for this young dog to exercise his mind. The lack of opportunities to experience small new challenges in the daily environment and to try out different solutions to test whether hypotheses work, has also limited Crated Champ's intelligence (or IQ), so that it's less than his free counterpart. It may be this lack of good sense- or it may be boredom or classic compulsive behavior- that makes Champ start licking at the underside of the water bowl through the bars, even though this hurts his tongue. He continues licking obsessively like this, with his neck bent up, for the rest of the hour.

Meanwhile, uncrated Champ has a "party" all through the family's living room, leaping, dancing and throwing his toy around, rolling, vocalizing and standing on hind legs. Then he notices a large bird strutting around outside. He doesn't overreact, but he does take note and "stalks" it along the wall of glass doors. Then responding to his body's internal needs, he walks to the laundry room and takes a small drink of water.

9:00 am-10:00 am:

Supporters of crating say that dogs spend their whole days sleeping. (Oddly, their evidence of this- literally- is often based on videos that show dogs sleeping all day- in crates!) It is true that dogs sleep a lot during the day; but if left free they do it in small, restorative catnaps, broken up by roaming around. True to his species, Free-in-the house Champ now elects to take his toy bone and curl up in a favorite spot under the dining room table where the boys often lie with him on his dog bed.

For part of the hour, he doesn't quite sleep but meditatively chews on his bone, like a man chewing on a pipe stem in a cozy home library. When he does sleep, he repeatedly stretches and repositions, aiding his vital skill of proprioception- an animal's sense of the positioning of it's own body in space. (This ability will help protect an adult dog from injury. It also keeps him from being clumsy and knocking over delicate household items or carelessly hitting into, or stepping on, family members. Excessively Crated dogs with less of a sense of their own bodies are much more likely to make these errors.)

Crated Champ also sleeps for most of this hour. The difference is he can't help sleeping because he's exhausted from the compulsive behaviors he's tried and the twisting of his neck. Cramped and aching, even while he sleeps, his body twitches with jitteriness.

10:00 am- 11:00 am:

The idea behind desensitization is that when dogs repeatedly encounter a new stimulus in small increments and don't feel threatened by it (especially during early puppyhood when they're most open and accepting) they won't be as likely to overreact to that stimulus later in life. In this case, the garbage truck pulls up and makes noise outside. Free-in-the-house Champ wakes, but then dismisses the sound as something he knows to be non-dangerous, because he's seen the garbage men many times before, in the company of his human family who remained relaxed. His lack of overreaction to the garbage men is healthy.

In contrast, Crated Champ, who can barely hear anything through the walls of the laundry room where he's crated, suddenly hears the unusually loud clanging of the garbage truck. And the sound, which he's unable to put in any context due to his lack of exposure to daily environmental stimuli, sends him into a slavering panic. Crated Champ's reaction characterizes the "reactivity" we see in so many dogs today. He barks and leaps around and his barking sounds aggressive, although he's also terribly frightened. Champ has been a naturally easygoing dog, but when a dog repeatedly feels cornered and agitated by an environmental stimulus he cannot control or get away from, his overreacting can be a precursor to aggression.

Crated Champ also experiences a release of adrenaline, which will stay in his body and increase agitation, for as long as 24 hours following his sudden fight-or-flight reaction. In general, the presence of too much adrenaline will make him overall more stressed, less stable and less likely to properly learn from interactions.

Both dogs again fall asleep. But the difference is that Crated Champ suffers with nightmares based on the terrible noise outside, while free-in-the-house Champ experiences pleasant dreams where he acts out real life scenarios. When another dream is frightening, Free Champ is able to wake from it and simply shake it off. He walks into the other room and, without even thinking about it, seeks out the comfort of a corner of his owners' couch.

No, this is not perfect behavior, but once again the young dog gets an opportunity to make a mental choice. Once his equilibrium is restored after the bad dream, he realizes that he's on the couch where his owners would not want him to be. They never used punishment to train him. But when he was a small pup, they also never crated. They started by keeping the puppy in a safe area of the kitchen behind a baby gate. As they trusted him more, and he passed housetraining and teething stages, they gradually increased his freedom in the house until now, at eight months, he's earned full run of every room.

Champ learned by having his owners give consistent mild verbal corrections whenever he made small mistakes, plus consistent attention every single time he did the right things. This is true positive training. And what Champ has learned about proper house manners generalizes to when the owners are not home because he's learned to associate good behavior with things that are good for him (like treats, petting, praise, or real life rewards like a leisurely walk, or a fun play session with a new toy). Since Uncrated Champ was shaped to do all the right things since earliest puppyhood, he doesn't know himself as the kind of dog that does things his owners don't like. So now he gets down off the couch, leans on it instead and watches the "show" in the river before him- boats, birds and waves. All fascinate him and everything he sees stimulates his mind.

Next he takes a little walk, sniffing around the downstairs and stretching his body. And once again, he has to make a mental (and moral, as some people would see it) decision. Uncrated Champ's bladder tells him a bathroom break would be welcome, and he even scents out one area where he had some "accidents" many months ago. But he makes the decision *not* to relieve himself in the home. Instead, all the good decisions he's been taught to make in the past lead to a good decision today, when he's not supervised. Champ lies down, enjoys a prolonged leisurely stretch (great for his blood circulation and lymph flow) and relaxes. Making proper decisions like this are great for Champ's emotional health and his adaptability as a family dog.

11:00 am -12 Noon

Crated Champ wakes from a terrible nightmare based on the unknown noise of the last hour; he scrabbles in the cage, hurting himself, with nothing he can do to make himself feel better. This sense of frustration, with no way to affect his physical environment to control his fate, even if it's just walking to another room, may have long lasting ill effects on Champ's character. He'll likely have problems dealing with any frustration in future and will likely act less adaptable in figuring out solutions. He may act either too impatient, too hesitant, fearful or depressed. Each dog is different and genetics and structured time Champ spends with his family will also influence how well he deals with frustration and fear in future. But, for some vulnerable dogs, experiences like being alarmed and agitated while trapped in the crate may contribute to serious life long problems.

Right now Crated Champ feels agitated and achy and irritated from his anal gland infection. He also feels disoriented in the small dim space. Desperately, yet irrationally, he tries to escape- clawing, ramming the cage with his face, squealing and whimpering. Then he lies down and starts compulsively rasping at the irritated area on his anus with his dry tongue, only making the irritation worse. Stereotyped behaviors like this- including licking an area until it becomes raw and infected- are common in overcrated dogs, as described in the scientific findings we discuss throughout the book.

In contrast, after sleeping just long enough to feel properly refreshed (but not *too* long) and then completing a natural stretch that gets his blood flowing and makes his mind alert, Free-in-the house Champ gets up to walk around. He roams the entire house, getting some exercise for his body. Then he determines to retrieve a stuffed toy that Aiden has given him and prop it up amongst Aiden's pillows, where he often carries items to leave as "gifts" for his favorite boy. Holding the toy in his mouth and balancing it as he prances up the stairs is great practice for Champ's coordination and following through on a plan like this exercises his mind.

Note that a dog left free run of the house when owners are gone isn't like a caged dog who physically *can't* jump on beds because he's locked up. In contrast, "parents" should be able to feel confident that their dog will make overall good decisions in the broadest sense with no need for them to impose physical control, just like human children gain independence and good judgment as they grow. In this case, Champ generally steers clear of spending time on the beds, a practice he knows Mom and Dad frown on, and spends most of his days downstairs where he feels his owners prefer him to be. He only jumps on Aiden's bed because Aiden often secretly invites him up and they often play the little game of hiding toys and treats for each other there when Aiden's in school. Champ is a naturally healthy and clean dog and does no harm while he lies on the bed.

12 Noon- 1:00 pm

While Free-in-the-house Champ enjoys the closeness to his favorite boy's scent in Aiden's bed, in the cage Crated Champ continues his unhealthy grooming ritual, obsessively licking at the pads of his feet and his groin and "underarms". All these tender areas begin to feel sore. But unlike his free counterpart, Crated Champ isn't making rational decisions. He feels nervous, cramped, frustrated, thirsty and confused. He's in physical distress, and now he's running a slight fever- a combination of the infection, the agitation and the lack of water...

Crated Champ's grooming turns from a ritual of self-care to a rough ritual that he cannot stop. The more the licking hurts, and the more distressed and confused he feels, the more he's compelled to keep doing it. And, with each additional day in the crate and each additional repetition of unhealthy behaviors like the licking that give him some sense of control over his world, Crated Champ's unhealthy habits will become more ingrained and harder to transform. By the end of the hour the areas he's been compulsively licking are now more cracked, irritated and prone to infection. And this distress will only compel Champ to frantically lick himself more, doing still more damage. But right now he's so exhausted that he falls into a sudden stuporous sleep, lying wedged upside-down in the crate.

In contrast, Free-in-the-house Champ takes his time to complete the natural grooming ritual that keeps his coat sleek and healthy. Relaxing up on Aiden's bed, he uses instinct to guide him how to groom each body part. In the wild, instinctive grooming like this would help keep him healthy and resistant to parasites.

1:00 pm-2:00 pm

Free-in-the-house Champ is used to regular comings and goings in the street, including a group of young mothers he regularly watches from different windows as they walk with their children in strollers. Watching people like this intrigues him, and exercises his senses. But, because he was socialized adequately and because he can freely observe that none of the people represent harm, he reacts appropriately.

Today a UPS driver stops in front of the house and talks briefly with the family's next-door neighbor. Then the driver rings the doorbell, waits a second and leaves a package on the front step. Uncrated Champ jogs downstairs to check that all is okay. Even though he's energized, curious and he naturally barks to sound the alarm, he's not overly aggressive or "reactive". Champ recognized their next-door neighbor and watched her exchanging a few peaceful words with the UPS driver when he saw them from upstairs. Watching this, and then smelling the man's relaxed scent through the miniscule crack under the front door as he sets down the package, Champ rightly concludes that the man likely poses no real threat to his family or their home. After the driver leaves, Champ easily relaxes again. He's bred to be defensive and, in future he'll be able to defend his home and family whenever necessary, but he'll never overreact. In general, he'll like friendly humans and he'll always act like a gentleman around people unless they really do pose a threat to his family.

In contrast, Crated Champ, unable to see the driver, hears the doorbell ring and gets the tiniest whiff of a person outside. Confused, he reacts in panic and frenzy. Crated Champ has also been overreacting on weekends whenever he sees people outside, flinging himself at windows, barking unceasingly and even appearing aggressive and this has been making his family increasingly concerned.

Unfortunately, the same dog trainer that insisted the family crate him also instructed them to terrorize him by slamming the water bowl onto the crate whenever he barks. This has only made Crated Champ more nervous and unsure. Crated right now, he's unable to check out the situation on the doorstep himself. And he can't even tell when the UPS driver leaves. So Crated Champ barks uncontrollably for the remainder of the hour; and the more he barks, the more it increases his frenzy. He also jumps around within the crate and finally falls hard so that his jaw hits the floor. Now he enters a state between sleep and waking, flattened, breath hissing, apparently sleeping, yet with eyes open and glazed.

2:00 pm-3:00 pm

Crated Champ has so worn himself out that he sleeps, totally cramped, with no healthy stretching or repositioning. Meanwhile Free-in-the-house Champ takes a precautionary patrol of the house. First he checks the windows to see that there are no further problems outside. (This is a generally healthy behavior in a dog like a German Shepherd that was purchased partly to look after the family's safety.) Champ has no need to attack people, but his instinct tells him he must keep his family safe; and patrolling the home will be his main work while he waits for his family when he is older. But Free-in-the-house Champ is always easygoing and, since there is no danger right now, he easily relaxes as he continues his "rounds" through all the rooms.

Upstairs, he sniffs all the areas where Mom and Dad and the boys got ready in the morning, taking in huge amounts of information from scent. This is a healthy stimulus for a young dog, which allows him to refine use of his sense of smell. While walking the home, he passes the cabinet where his dry food is kept. Though he can smell it, he chooses restraint not to try to break in. He knows he will be fed on time, according to household rules. (As long as owners provide a normal healthy puppy freedom combined with adequate guidance as he matures, they should never have to worry that the animal will act like a grizzly bear in their kitchen!)

Just like Champ's owners taught him, he seeks out a positive alternative to occupy him rather than ripping open the food bag. Instead he plays vigorously with his favorite rubber toy. Although this amount of exercise is not nearly as much as a dog of his breed would receive if he were herding livestock all day, at least free-in-the-house Champ has some opportunities to move his body and develop his mind and senses. In contrast, crated Champ may come out at the end of 12 straight hours with no real movement, physically stiff, yet nervous and wildly overexcited- a bad combination that will make him vulnerable to injury, especially if owners suddenly exercise him too vigorously.

3:00 pm-4:00 pm

Something totally out of the ordinary happens and Dad returns early from his business trip. In both cases the young dogs are able to smell every scent from the road and clearly assess how the business trip made Dad feel. Both also yearn for a favorite moment curling up next to Dad as he loosens his tie and unwinds. But Free Champ has better control of his reactions. Although completely overjoyed, he easily remembers the manners the family taught him as a little puppy and doesn't crowd Dad at the door. But Crated Champ feels more frenzied, overexcited with joy.

When Dad realizes he must immediately leave again, the only difference in the two scenarios is that he feels sorry for Crated Champ having to go all hours without water, so he offers him a full bowl inside the crate. The dog, like many that are crated all day without water (as "experts" recommend!) is so dehydrated that he gags on the water and his belly swells as he drinks madly. And then, too hurried to let him outside to pee, Dad rushes out the door. More overexcitation, leaping and screaming follow- and then an even worse consequence occurs that will disrupt and change everything for the crated dog and his family.

4:00 pm- 6:00 pm

See the book *Dog In a Box* for full details of what happens during these hours, which are normal for Free-in-the-home Champ, but particularly terrible for Crated Champ.

6:00pm-7:00 pm

Several hours later, the family all return again together, but what they find in the different scenarios also makes a profound difference in how they experience family life and life with their dogs. In the case of Uncrated Champ, he takes a nice walk with Aiden. And then all the family members share a unique moment of bonding with him- one of those moments that define the American Dream and why it's so good to return home to family and family dog each evening. In the Crated scenario however, something so terrible happens that it sets the whole family fighting each other. The young crated dog is punished, shamed and terrified. And, worst of all, he feels responsible for making the little boy that he loves cry.

Then follows a bitter irony. Crated Champ shuts down, in an almost psychotic state and he finally loses all desire to even walk outside or attempt to relate to the family. But the owners remember something the trainer told them and, because of this they view his reactions in a completely different light. Crated Champ has been so broken by his wire prisons that now he is terrified to even emerge from it. But the family takes his reluctance to leave the cage as evidence of one of the biggest myths of sudden crating. Crated Champ may never be able to bond again properly with his family without extensive rehabilitation. Yet now, seeing him slink back to the cage after just spending 12 hours in it, all Mom and Dad can do is quote what the dog trainer told them- "he loves his crate"!

In Summary:

In this chapter, we've summarized common observable physical and behavioral results of excessive crating (such as the skin irritation and infection and the aggressive and overreactive barking) using the story of Champ as our example for our hour-by-hour breakdown. There was not room in this chapter to include the entire story, and we know many people would want to read the details of the day of excessive crating vs. freedom in narrative format. So the full story of Champ, with all the details included, will be available as a book, *Dog In a Box*, a novella dedicated to all of those "Champs" out there today still growing up in crates. *Dog In a Box* breaks down the crated vs. uncrated dog's viewpoints and all the dramas of the day, with alternate endings that both sadden and uplift.

The next chapter details the specifics of why daily crating and isolation from stimuli like Crated Champ endured causes a range of problem symptoms in dogs according to veterinarians and other experts.

And the next chapter deals with the society-wide impact of all the "Champs" in all our communities and how our modern world has led us to a crisis in how to spend time productively with our dogs, illustrated by the case of a dog named Bouncy. If your family leads a hectic life, you already know how it impacts dog ownership. Yet you may not know the extent that other families are facing similar challenges. The landscape of America has changed in the past 20 years, changing how we live. And we explore how that changing landscape- in our communities, our greenspaces, our homes and in Cyberspace- has fundamentally changed life with dogs. If you've noticed challenges, you're not alone. But to understand the realities of life with our dogs in this new century, we must first discuss *human* sociological studies and even the history and science of home design.

Chapter 5: Scientific & Veterinary Evidence on the Dangers of Excessive Crating

Ask a scientist. In contrast to some of the currently popular voices in the dog industry who promote crating unequivocally, individuals in the scientific and academic community, including dog behavior experts, researchers and veterinarians, have documented many negative effects of excessive crating, including physical, neurological and sensory changes and associated diseases and ailments.

First we'd like to mention Diane Jessup, an author and internationally recognized expert on dog behavior who also has firsthand experience helping dogs suffering in extreme conditions as a veteran animal control officer. On her website, workingpitbull.com Ms. Jessup points out some very potent facts about crates. For example, she explains that, *"Crates are (only) designed for short term housing while a dog is in transport... [Crates] are not meant to house a dog all day, every day, while you are at work. Housing a dog in a crate- even a large one-does not meet the (very) minimum USDA standards of living space for dogs kept in research laboratories."*

On her website Ms. Jessup also quotes the findings of Hetts (1991) who states, "It is unlikely that such small enclosures can provide for the dogs' psychological needs"; Hubrecht, (1993) who states, "A good housing system should allow the dog to exercise an element of choice, to manipulate or chew safe objects and provide opportunities for human and canine socialization"; and Fox (1986) who states, "It is also recommended that, optimally, dogs be housed in "separate sleeping and exercise areas which provide complexity, choice and allow(s) the dog to defecate and urinate away from its sleeping areas."

For years, Diane Jessup has advocated for Pit Bulls, a breed that have been much abused and misunderstood in recent years. Many of us already know that problems like aggression are usually caused when an owner abuses the Pit Bull and deliberately encourages the bad behaviors (for example, by forcing them to fight). But many people still don't know the best ways of giving this versatile, eager to please high-energy breed productive tasks to do in life. In her classic book *The Working Pit Bull*, Ms. Jessup gives examples of Pit Bulls that win championships in sports as diverse as agility, Schutzhund and tracking and introduces Pit Bulls that work as therapy dogs.

Also, in her powerful novel, *The Dog That Spoke with Gods*, Ms. Jessup shows us the plight of a Pit Bull used in animal research, including feelings from the dog's perspective. Although the book is fiction, some of the terrible scenarios in the research laboratories are based in fact. Dogs in many research laboratories suffer unique stress and pain- often leading to death- as experimental subjects. In between the experimental manipulations, they spend their lives waiting interminably in crates/cages.

The dogs wait day after day, month after month, under fluorescent lighting that never changes to even indicate the difference between day and night. These dogs are intelligent and sensitive and athletic animals that have been bred for centuries to eagerly serve their owners. And, even in a laboratory environment, most eagerly await brief moments of human contact- even though any encounter might represent another experiment that brings pain, fear and even death.

Many people are outraged as they learn more about the treatment of research animals. And even as laws are established for reform and oversight of the practice, these laws come slowly and they are often not effective enough. PETA (People for the Ethical Treatment of Animals) is a well-known and high profile organization that lobbies for humane treatment of animals, including laboratory and farm animals. And it is no surprise that PETA would also speak out about Excessive Home Dog Crating.

PETA speaks out reasonably and conservatively against Excessive Home Dog Crating:

The wide-reaching and outspoken humane organization supported by many Hollywood Stars is known for making news in the media. And, sometimes, extreme activists have associated themselves with various PETA causes, staging public protests that extend far beyond the mission statement of the organization.

But, on the subject of Excessive Home Crating of dogs, PETA's official stance is quite reasonable and conservative and is based on the work of established scientists and dog behavior experts. PETA's official website (PETA.org, under Animal Rights Uncompromised: Crating Dogs) states that:

"Crating began as a convenience for people who participate in 'dog shows' to keep their dogs clean, but they did not take into account their dogs' social, physical and psychological requirements. Dogs are highly social pack animals that abhor isolation and crave and deserve companionship, praise, and exercise. Forcing dogs to spend extended periods of time confined and isolated simply to accommodate their guardians' schedule is unacceptable."

PETA also agrees with our opinion that, "Crate training does not speed up the housetraining process... Puppies do not develop full bladder control until they are about 6 months old. It is counterproductive to crate young puppies in the hope that they will "hold it" because they are physically incapable of doing so and will be forced to urinate in their crate after experiencing great discomfort while trying not to soil their bed."

They also explain ways crate training can backfire, for example, it can sometimes make housetraining more difficult than without a crate. The PETA website explains, "Puppies who repeatedly soil their crates often lose the urge to keep their crate clean, which in turn prolongs and complicates the housebreaking process."

Another way excessive crate training can backfire is by producing, or exacerbating emotional and behavior problems. For example, the PETA website explains, "Pet store and puppy-mill puppies who are born and raised in crate-like structures may experience severe anxiety and develop fearful and/or destructive behaviors if they are confined to a crate. They may even injure themselves trying to bite or scratch their way out of it.

"Studies have shown that long term confinement is detrimental to the physical and psychological well-being of animals. Animals caged for extended periods can develop... antisocial and/or aggressive disorders or they can become withdrawn, hyperactive, or severely depressed."

And PETA is not unreasonable, making sure to put dogs' safety first when it comes to housing arrangements. Like us, they do not rule out limiting the areas a dog has access to if it promotes the dog's well being. For example PETA, "does not oppose keeping a dog in a small area if it is in the dog's best interest (e.g. when cage rest is ordered by a veterinarian or when confinement will keep the dog safe during travel)" as long as the dog is provided reasonable "access to water, fresh air, food, and other basic requirements."

PETA, like us, also recommends humane obedience training based in effective communication to shape dogs into well-behaved companions that owners can feel safe leaving in their homes while they are away. They also recommend having a trusted person, such as a pet sitter, available to take a puppy out for a midday walk if the owner must stay away at work for prolonged periods.

Steven R. Lindsay speaks out about crating in the enormously influential behavioral science text, *Handbook of Applied Dog Behavior and Training*:

Some of the most compelling scientific evidence against crating comes from research scientists. *The Handbook of Applied Dog Behavior and Training* by Steven Lindsay consists of three volumes of in-depth physiological and behavioral facts, research and theory. Combined, the three volumes make up approximately 1,500 pages. And the *Handbook* is so well respected that some dog training schools and accredited colleges that teach animal behavior base much of their curriculum on it. This exquisitely researched, well-rounded and highly theoretical book **also speaks out strongly in every aspect against crating.** For this reason, statements in the book are often quoted by those of in the dog community who are serious about stopping the popularly trendy belief in favor of excessive crating.

One example is KP's Dog Blog website. (You can now access the information through PETA's main website in the "Living" section, http://living.peta.org). KP has been a librarian for PETA , and her writings are just one resource associated with the organization's anti-crating policy.

The ideas expressed on KP's blog (in common with PETA's official policy on crating which is quite conservative) are highly readable and highly reasonable. And KP zeroes in on some of the ideas expressed by Stephen Lindsay in the foundation dog behavior text, *Handbook of Applied Dog Behavior and Training*.

For example she mentions how, "Most puppies and dogs show a high degree of aversive arousal when first exposed to crate confinement. After learning that the crate is inescapable, however, dogs appear to treat the crate in a paradoxical manner analogous to persons affected by the Stockholm Syndrome: that is, they appear to form strong attachments with the crate, which becomes the place they identify as home."

"Stockholm Syndrome" was first identified by psychologist Nils Bejerol in 1973 in Sweden after captives assisted bank robbers in their crime. The syndrome refers to the mental/emotional construct that can cause victims (for example, people who have been kidnapped) who are isolated from other stimuli for extended periods to become emotionally attached to their captors, even after they are released. In addition to the case discussed by Bejerol, we believe another probable example of Stockholm Syndrome is the case of American heiress Patty Hearst who gained notoriety in the 1970's when she was kidnapped by the Symbionese Liberation Army, and later criminally assisted that terrorist group in a bank heist to further their cause.

KP explains in her blog entry how Steven Lindsay points to the theory of Stockholm Syndrome as the explanation why some fans of crating may observe behavior that makes them think their dogs love crates. Many web postings and published observations refer to dogs that "love" their crates so much that sometimes the first thing they want to do when released from the crate, or exposed to any new stimuli, is to immediately run back inside the crate. Dogs like this may get in the habit of insistently running back to their crates, even though when they were first crated they fought to escape the crate and found it highly distressing. But this behavior (bonding with the crate) is *not* an example of a natural happy canine behavior. Rather it's a maladaptive behavior that only developed as a result of the excessive crating, just like the human captives suffering from Stockholm Syndrome eventually helped their captors, not because they really liked them, but because they had already been abused by them.

In the *Handbook* Lindsay also asserts that it is a mistake for advocates of long-term crating to make inappropriate comparisons with wild canids (such as wolves) that use dens during some periods of reproduction and rearing young to claim that dogs are phylogenetically predisposed to living in crates.

In fact, Lindsay says that, **"A crate has far more in common with a trap than it does with a den."** He explains that a house a dog shares with his human family actually has the most in common with a den, since it provides access to communal spaces. In contrast, "The crate serves the express purpose of separating the dog from social attachment objects [family or pack]... Instead of promoting comfort and safety, the inescapable exclusion imposed by crate confinement appears to confer an increased vulnerability for disruptive emotional arousal and insecure place attachments."

Lindsay points out that most dogs at first show a high degree of aversive arousal to the crate. Later on, he explains, many display a paradoxical attachment to the crate, which advocates of long-term crating may erroneously identify as love for the crate. Lindsay explains that this almost desperate need to rush back to the place of confinement when first allowed freedom in the outside world is actually similar to "Stockholm Syndrome" as described above, and that the behavior is unhealthy.

Says Lindsay, "The daily repeated exposure to the sterile environs of the crate may significantly undermine a developing dog's ability to habituate and adjust to the wider domestic social and physical environment." To an undersocialized/underexposed dog, many stimuli that would be welcomed by a dog normally habituated to home and family life can instead become stressors.

Either the dog reacts inappropriately, or it may seek immediate relief for its desperate feeling of stress by hurrying back to the only thing it has ever known- the confinement and control of the crate. Since dogs like this are unused to making their own decisions or reacting calmly when faced with novel stimuli, they may instead turn to a flight (or even fight) response. "For dogs exposed to excessive crate confinement... their search for comfort and safety may gradually turn from the family and home to the crate."

PETA offers free posters and educational materials and agrees that dog don't "love crates":

PETA offers free downloadable posters/flyers on their website, which anyone can print and distribute in their community, school, animal business, etc. PETA also offers a poster that simply and concisely instructs dog owners how to succeed at housetraining without crates.

On another free poster entitled "What's Wrong with Crating?" PETA points out that "Crates do not promote a feeling of security" and that many dogs develop separation anxiety, depression, hyperactivity and even anti-social behavior after long periods of crate training. Nor, they say is, a crate similar to a playpen, crib or den, as many advocates of crating like to argue. They make clear that, **"A crate is a cramped, impoverished environment that prevents dogs from engaging in basic normal activities, such as looking out the window, walking around and stretching out comfortably."**

And, like Steven Lindsay, PETA contradicts the odd, yet sadly popular saying that "dogs love crates." The wording of their poster simply states the obvious and begs owners that are just looking to promote their own convenience to stop denying, and acknowledge that a crate is not good for dogs and that "no animal on the face of the Earth 'loves' being locked inside a cage, including your dog."

Shelter veterinarians speak out on cage-rage

As could be expected, some of the most knowledgeable experts on the negative effect of excessive crating are those who observe and investigate the most extreme scenarios of excessive crating/caging- including abused dogs and dogs confined long-term in animal shelters.

One highly respected researcher and theorist is Dr. Randall Lockwood, currently senior vice president for anti-cruelty initiatives with the ASPCA and former Director of Education for the Humane Society of the United States (HSUS). The HSUS investigates abuse on animals on a national level including some of the largest scale cases of abusive crating of dogs, like puppy mill breeding facilities described in detail in Chapter 11, where many dogs died and others were irreparably damaged after suffering for years. HSUS has assisted in putting many facilities like this out of business. Dr. Lockwood's highly referenced research has also included studying the sociological parallels between the abuse of dogs and extreme human-on-human violence- such as in sociopathic killers.

In *The Guilt Free Dog Owner's Guide* author Diana Delmar quotes Mr. Lockwood, who has also studied wolves in the wild, to debunk the pro-crating notion that dogs are den animals. Lockwood explains that, in the wild, wolves only live in a den for the first 6 to 8 weeks of life. He also believes that crating is a method that has great potential for abuse and is too often used as an "easy way out" by people who don't want to take the time to train and socialize their dogs.

Ms. Delmar also refers to the opinions of experienced humane dog trainers Warren and Fay Eckstein, who, in their book *Understanding Your Pet*, call crating the "wrong environment" for a family pet. She says that, in their opinion "having to open the crate to interact with the dog interferes with the socialization process. Crated dogs can have emotional problems later on and the Ecksteins say that they've seen dogs that have, "really created havoc in the house when they were let out of the crate because they never learned how to behave in the house." (An example in *Dogs Hate Crates* is Bouncy the Labradoodle in Chapter 4.)

Not all veterinarians have the same perspective on crating, even though it is safe to say that all would agree there is a point at which crating becomes excessive. Obviously, it is those veterinarians who treat the more seriously abused and damaged animals coming out of puppy mills, fighting rings and shelters who see the most severe cases of "cage-rage" (also known as "kennel-craze", "kennelosis" or "kennel syndrome"). The symptoms show up in family dogs as well. But unfortunately, when dealing with average families, veterinarians may not always diagnose the syndrome officially because they assume that regular "concerned" owners would not crate their family pets this excessively. And many owners don't even bring up the fact that they crate, or how much they crate, when they bring their dogs in for veterinary exams.

Symptoms associated with excessive confinement, however, are well known enough to be included as an entry in *The Veterinarian's Encyclopedia of Animal Behavior by Bonnie Beaver.* The entry states, "Problems can also result from excessive confinement with minimal exposure to conspecifics, people, different environments or adequate exercise. For the deprived individual, stereotyped behaviors are common. Other problems include improper socialization, digging, kennelosis, barking... and self mutilation."

Policy makers in many animal shelters around the country are placed in a position of great responsibility when they're faced with the subject of crating. Dogs that come into shelters are often rescued from abusive and neglectful situations, including large groups of dogs and puppies that are rescued from puppy mills. Unfortunately, despite their best efforts, shelters and rescues are sometimes unable to reform some of these dogs behaviorally after what the dogs have suffered. And shelter management and shelter veterinarians are often in the best position to observe the depth of emotional and behavioral illness brought on by excessive crate confinement.

These dogs are often in a vicious cycle. Excessive crating made them less adoptable to begin with. Then, being less adoptable, they stay in shelters for longer amounts of time. The next risk is a common syndrome known to shelter management and staff- "kennelosis", or "kennel-craze" in which excess confinement, in combination with insufficient socialization, physical and mental activity and stimuli in the outside world creates serious symptoms, including aggression.

Many veterinarians associated with shelters advise how important it is to remove the dogs from kennels at regular intervals for exposure to socialization with people and novel stimuli in the outside world. And some progressive shelter programs/protocols include daily walks and regular interaction with volunteers. (Ironically, in the best shelters dogs may actually spend more time out of their cages engaged in focused activities with humans than pet dogs do in many modern homes!) Even though this is often the case, and even though the "kennels" provided in shelters are usually substantially larger than the tiny crates barely big enough to turn in that many dogs live in when in their homes, shelter veterinarians tend to speak out most strongly on the serious ill-effects of long term crating.

In one example, multiple veterinarians were interviewed for an article in *Veterinary Forum* (January 2008). The first vet quoted, Dr. Haisley, stated, "The traditional animal shelter sets an animal up for failure." And another veterinarian, Dr. Eddlestone, explained further, "Confinement is a horrible situation for animals. We saw this with [Hurricane] Katrina. Animals that had been from loving homes... when we took them into our shelters we couldn't adopt them because they had become too aggressive. They had no enrichment, no interaction with people and it became personally damaging...

"The veterinary community argues about exactly what depression is in an animal, but anyone who spends time in a shelter knows exactly what depression and misery look like."

And the last vet quoted, Dr. Moyers, explained that shelters can be mentally damaging because the shelter environment "forces the least adoptable behaviors, but it can also be physically damaging... The traditional shelter is one in which you place a traumatized or stressed animal in an environment that encourages him to decline physically, mentally and socially... If [dogs] are held in the kennel all day... they become bored and stressed out. They need interaction with people and other dogs." And Dr. Moyer points out how, "steel cages and cinder blocks... create barrier or cage rage, negatively affecting an animal's psyche..."

Observed symptoms and veterinary behavior prognosis in puppy mill dogs:

Shelter veterinarians and shelter staff tend to be familiar with the effects of "kennel craze" (or "kennel syndrome" or "kennelosis") on a personal basis. Another group of people who encounter the symptoms of kennel craze firsthand are professional investigators (such as those with the HSUS) and volunteers who rescue dogs from the puppy mill conditions, where the animals have been crated, sometimes for years, without exercise or socialization. Unfortunately, even after the canine victims of puppy mills receive desperately needed medical care, they are still often not suitable for placement in private homes because of emotional problems.

Many suffer lifelong fears or other behavioral symptoms. Others are so far gone that they cannot be placed at all, and they are often euthanized. Some require extensive rehabilitation in foster homes. And some finally do go to private homes, where caring new owners must compensate for what happened to the dogs or puppies when they were cruelly caged.

One example was on the Yahoo! Answers website. One of the participants in the discussion group described her experience as follows: "[I got my dog] from a second chance rescue and she was crated for about 12 hours a day for a year before I got her. ...For the first 6 months after I got [her] she didn't know where she should go to potty. She also had no muscles. It was hard for her to walk with me. She had a hard time on steps and couldn't jump. Now after having her for 3 yrs she is so much better."

Another participant includes an in-depth description of the symptoms dogs can suffer when confined too long as follows:

"There is a well-documented condition called "cage madness" that shelter dogs can suffer (especially the "no kill" shelters who keep them caged for months on end.) Symptoms:

Spinning (non-stop); Non-stop barking; Self-mutilation; Aggression; Hyperactivity; Inability to be housebroken; Some dogs "give up" and are lethargic and just stare for hours; "OCD" type rituals (for lack of a better term). They do the same thing over and over; Oral fixations. They MUST carry a toy or have something in their mouths at all times;

If puppies are crated and not given proper exercise, bones and muscles are stunted; Muscles atrophy and bones deform in adult dogs.

"Improper socialization [associated with caged dogs being separated from people and outside stimuli] causes plenty of problems too:

Fear biting; Aggression; Possessiveness/food guarding; Inappropriate urination; Complete intolerance for other animals."

Another website (Puppygal's English Bulldog Medical Information) agrees, describing symptoms consistent with kennel craze and stating clearly that:

"Excessive crate time causes behavior problems... [and] compulsive behaviors such as, but not limited to obsessive tail rubbing, spinning and barking. Most dogs who are deprived of adequate stimulation or change of environments for long periods of time will at the very least become hyper and unruly with uncontrollable jumping and bouncing when released."

In Chapter 9 we describe in detail a real-life example of a likely case of kennel-craze syndrome, with many of the symptoms above, in the true case of "Patton- the Whirling Dog".

Even the Champaign County Humane Society Pet Library Online, which generally recommends careful crating, concedes what harm Excessive Crating can do, touching on the symptoms of kennel-craze. They state, "Ironically" the very device designed to provide safe confinement indoors, the dog crate, is sometimes used, or misused, so that it crates problems rather than ...preventing them. Dogs confined in crates for long periods of time can develop undesirable behaviors, and excessive crating often exacerbates any underlying behavior problems. Overuse of the crate can result in a dog that is hyperexcitable outside the crate.

Conversely, some dogs that are crated too long become depressed. A preexisting problem such as aggression or timidity may intensify in response to the dog's frustration at being crated aggressively." They also advise dog owners that, "if you will be away for more than five or six hours at a time, your dog should be left in a confinement area (a dog-proofed room or portion of a room), rather than a crate."

Canine Behavior Experts recommend methods other than crate-training:

Best-selling authors David Weston & Ruth Ross do not advocate crating. In their book, *Dog Problems; The Gentle Modern Cure* they describe alternatives for housetraining young puppies without crates (for example, using a child's playpen near the owner and in the owner's bedroom for containment.) They provide truly gentle alternatives for training and they also dispel one of the major pro-crating myths. Many individuals who advocate crating today say that dogs, like wolves are by nature "den animals". But Weston and Ross explain, "Adult wolves do not actively seek for shelter... [although] they will circle around a few times on the same spot before lying down." And they also mention something we all know if we grew up in rural areas and were observant during the dog days of summer, "Dogs will dig large holes in the dirt or may excavate under the house in an effort to find a cool shady spot." This is not, of course, the same thing as an adult animal living in a den!

Dr. Michael W. Fox

Dr. Michael W. Fox is a classic pioneer in behavioral science who advocates understanding animals in order to better train them and provides us a basis for understanding how isolating a developing puppy in a crate can damage its future ability to bond properly with its owners.

In his book, *Understanding Your Pet; Pet Care and Humane Concerns* Dr. Fox describes how vital proper socialization and sufficient stimuli are to producing a well-rounded dog that gets along great with humans. "If we raise a puppy with very little human contact, it will not become emotionally bonded to people," he says. "Being less dependent, and not so adequately socialized, it will be much harder to train than one with much human contact during its formative weeks. This is one of the problems in buying a dog that has been in a kennel for four or five months or caged in a pet store for a prolonged period, or obtaining one of obscure origin from a humane shelter; a dog that has had a lot of contact with other dogs and inadequate contact with people is one that will misbehave. Being less emotionally dependent he will be less concerned with pleasing his master. The key to trainability is an emotional link of dependency and affection..."

Knowing information like this, we wonder how any "expert" could advise that a dog that comes to his new human family after spending his first months in such conditions of isolation should be crated even more!

Dr Fox continues, with facts that may explain why some dogs, after long-term excessive crating, seem eager to run back to their cages. "One of the saddest human-induced behavioral disorders found in dogs," he says, "is kennelosis, or institutionalization syndrome, which seems to result from containment and lack of stimulation during the critical formative months of puppy-hood. When a dog is plunged from a cage into a complex human environment, it commonly suffers a crippling nerve overload and withdraws into a dark corner- both psychically and physically."

He points out an interesting example in which, "The army's training program for attack dogs was upset temporarily by kennelosis, when the handlers neglected to provide a sufficiently diverse environment for puppies. Although the dogs' intelligence was well developed and they were entirely acclimated to people, they freaked out when they first reached a forest, where they would spend most of their adult lives working. The mere rustling of leaves was enough to make some of them defecate in fear... We have found that those pups given a regular program of stimulation- noise, lights, cold places to walk- become more responsive and adaptable than non-stimulated peers."

If enriched stimuli shapes dogs positively, can deprivation of stimuli act as punishment?

Positive reinforcement trainers don't believe in using punishment to correct dogs' behavior. But they do frequently use what's called "negative reinforcement"- depriving dogs of things they want in order to shape behavior. For example, positive trainers frequently use "time out" similar to the "time-outs" we give children, to briefly deprive misbehaving dogs of the contact with family they desire so they will learn not to repeat the behavior.

Some of these same trainers also tell customers to crate train their dogs. And they tell them never to use the crate for "punishment" or time-outs for bad behavior so the dog will never associate the crate with anything unpleasant. But to us, this seems illogical since there's not much you can do to make a crated dog *not* feel he's experiencing time out. Being locked away in a crate certainly has all the hallmarks of social isolation that make time-out feel so negative for dogs.

Steven Lindsay's *Handbook of Applied Dog Behavior and Training* the comprehensive 3-volume work, which is often used in college level classes for dog behavior professionals, describes in Volume 1 why time-out works as a negative reinforcer, based off the work of J.P. Scott, the first researcher to describe in detail the motivational aspects of canine social behavior. According to Lindsay, dogs' need to be social and connect with others is strong, and losing that contact causes immediate and noticeable distress in canines.

"These primitive separation-distress reactions," he says, "reflect the dog's psychobiological need for close contact with other dogs and people with whom the dog has formed a strong attachment. Besides withdrawing social contact and control, time out also removes reward opportunities that might otherwise be available to dogs if they had remained in [a] training situation."

Of course training opportunities also include any situation throughout the day where a dog can perform a behavior and receive a positive or negative response to it. With repetition, the dog learns whether it's advantageous for him to repeat the behavior. This is the basis of learning. And as much as it applies to obedience commands or tricks, it also applies to good manners and gentleness around people. Since a dog isolated in time out- or a dog in a crate- cannot perform "good" behaviors and get rewarded or perform bad behaviors and see they don't pay off, learning can't take place.

According to Lindsay, in addition to the social isolation, the fact that dogs can't perform actions to earn reward is part of what makes time-out feel so uncomfortable. "The response-dependent withdrawal or omission of positive reinforcement is a strong form of punishment [negative punishment], especially in contexts providing valuable and frequent reinforcement opportunities."

Lindsay points out research findings to prove this point. For example, he explains that, "Time out as a loss of positive reinforcement is aversive, and animals work hard to escape or avoid time out from positive reinforcement" based on the research of Leitenberg (1965). And he also mentions how, "... under laboratory conditions, time out compares favorably with shock as a punitive contingency. (McMillan 1967)."

So if, in some instances time-out can prove just as punitive for a dog as shock, then how can we possibly say time in a crate doesn't have the same effect? After all, extended crate time is the most extreme example of social isolation, leaving the dog alone and frustrated while the family may go about their activities in another room or part of the house. And crating certainly represents exclusion from any chance for the dog to alter his environment and receive any positive stimuli- especially in the form of interaction!

Paul Loeb

Paul Loeb is a nationally recognized animal behaviorist who, in 1974 introduced the idea of using animals to comfort the sick and elderly at New York's Bellvue Hospital and is also a recognized leader in the training of companion aide dogs. He has been featured along with Jane Goodall and Konrad Lorenz in National Geographic's Behavior Education Series, and has also been featured in articles in *Newsweek*, *The New York Times* and *Wall Street Journal* among others. Loeb was one of the pioneers who offered more humane, effective and holistic alternatives to harsh dog training. In his book *Smarter Than You Think*, along with co-author Suzanne Hlavacek, he explains how owners can create the well-behaved dogs they've always wanted through rational methods of shaping behavior and a bond of true understanding based on learning to speak their dog's language.

While the authors *do* advocate limiting your puppy's freedom while housetraining, they advise against crating and suggest more humane methods of containment. To start, they point out the importance of having water available at all times, something most dogs are deprived of while crated. They also point to one of the central problems with crating, and one of the biggest ironies- the fact that crating doesn't work well or quickly as a housetraining method.

According to the authors, "Housetraining with a crate or a cage could take up to a year or even longer and sometimes forever." And the problems they point out extend far beyond housetraining, to a dog that, overall, does not look to his owner for guidance or bonding.

"Instead of depending on you for his security, your dog becomes dependent on a crate or cage. This can have an insidious effect on his well-being. A dog is a pack animal and so he needs contact with other living creatures. Without this contact he may become withdrawn and not grow to be an integral part of the family... Although we know that many trainers and veterinarians believe in caging or crating a dog, reasoning that dogs are cave animals and need their privacy, we believe that's a lot of nonsense."

And Mr. Loeb agrees with us that crating does not teach house manners or how to respond in positive fashion. After crating, he says, "You will never really trust your dog not to be destructive until he's an adult and then some. Teaching him to come to you becomes a major problem because of his bonding to that crate or cage instead of you."

As we have pointed out, it is ironic that people are now *striving to teach their dogs to bond to their crates*, without realizing that the only way to do this is to break down the natural social and emotional mechanisms of the dog until the dog no longer bonds as well as he could with *people*...

The authors continue, "People get lazy and rationalize how great the cave is for their cave animal, and they can end up leaving their dog in the crate for long periods of time, too long. Your dog is a social creature and doesn't want to be isolated in a box anymore than you would want to be isolated in a box."

The authors also point out a little fact we all know intuitively- the fact that a cage or crate does not fit in "with any interior decorator's schemes". Humans seem to share uniform responses to certain stimuli, and the sight of a cage is one that we tend to react to negatively. Most of us like to keep our homes soothing and welcoming places. And, instinctively, we recoil when we see the bars- associating cages with imprisonment and pain. So just following our natural reaction about how disturbing a cage looks in otherwise attractive homes might be enough to turn many homeowners against having a dog crate as a central part of their lives.

Chapter 6: Useless Dog Syndrome, the Real Estate Bubble, Open Floor Plans; and Bouncy the Labradoodle, the "terror at 5:30"

It's 5:30 pm on a weekday evening- picture an open-floor plan suburban home with a large "great room" where a 10-month old Labradoodle (Labrador and Standard Poodle mix) named Bouncy has been in his crate all day. His owners, a family that might resemble yours, just released Bouncy to go outside as soon as they returned home. Statistics prove that, in today's America, family members, including husband and wife, may spend no more than minutes per day in conversation with each other. But, in this case, imagine that the family is lucky for once, with everybody gathered together in the great room...

Picture their 4-year old, just home from day care, now spreading out armloads of small stuffed animals and tiny interlocking plastic toys on a corner of the wood floor, getting ready to play.

Mom stands in the kitchen heating up her long-anticipated dinner, gourmet leftovers from a catered work conference today, where she never got a minute's downtime to eat despite the mouthwatering spread. Standing at the counter now, still wearing her uncomfortably high pumps, Mom efficiently multi-tasks, briskly paying bills on the kitchen computer while reheating the aromatic salmon with wine sauce that will be her first solid food in the last twenty four hours. Meanwhile she cradles her cell phone between her ear and her shoulder, once again trying to reschedule a lunch date with her best girlfriend who's going through a tough divorce.

The family's overachieving eleven-year-old Calvin, though sweet and highly intelligent, is also noticeably introverted- quiet and shy in a way that wouldn't have won him many friends back when his parents went to school. And sometimes they wish he'd have more fun. At the same time, they're enormously proud of his excellence in science and the fact that he attends a prized charter school, saving them thousands in private school tuition and increasing his chances for acceptance into MIT's engineering program- their goal for him since he was four.

Tonight, like his parents, eleven year-old Calvin looks a little pale and generally bushed after a long weekday. But he's also really eager and excited about getting online and completing a major group science project with several of his friends. This is the last day for finishing touches on the final project and Calvin feels confident. He just has to compile his friends' data along with his and then send the entire project off to a computer across town, where his science teacher is also eagerly awaiting the results on a project that he considers groundbreaking, even if it though it was completed by middle-school boys.

Despite the months of skill and diligence Calvin put into this very special project, the truth is that the eleven year-old feels a bit silly tonight and craves to finally kick back and act immature for a moment. Right now, he's enjoying glancing at the silly guests on the *Dr. Phil Show*, which his father switched to on their new television. Calvin also plans to finally goof around a little with his young friends with the fascinating new webcam that his parents just bought for him.

In order to send out the research for the project, and to video chat with his friends, Calvin has to first get online. Even before that, he must get seated comfortably. And he's also starving hungry at the moment. Not willing to miss out on anything, he balances his laptop computer (even at eleven, Calvin's a devout Macintosh man) and a bowl of Cheerios with strawberries that he took for himself for dinner- and he scoots back onto the middle of the sectional sofa in the great room.

His father sits near him, but at a distance on the vast new couch, instant messaging online on his smartphone trying to secure plane reservations for a business trip tomorrow. Meanwhile Dad abruptly flicks channels back and forth. He stays for a few minutes on CNBC and all he sees is more bad economic news. But, to him, frequently checking the financial news is a lot like running your tongue obsessively over a bad tooth and he can't seem to stop himself. Each time more bad news about stocks falling and banks failing makes his migraine throb more, he switches channels to soothe himself with the mental balm of the *Dr. Phil Show*, which the whole family seem to be glancing at and enjoying at the moment.

Right now Dad still wears his beige linen pants from work; he also plans to wear them again tomorrow with their matching suit jacket when he gives a talk as the featured speaker at the conference. He seems unworried about damaging his best clothes and indeed he's managed the balancing act of leaning back in his favorite corner of the sectional and dipping tortilla chips into bright red salsa- his first meal of the day, while responding to frustrating instant messages regarding his frequent flyer miles.

Before Dad sat down, Mom asked him to let the Labradoodle Bouncy out to the back yard so the pup could relieve his bladder. And, since everyone views Bouncy as a valued member of the family, Dad has left the patio doors open so the young dog can come back whenever he's ready.

For a moment, everyone seems somewhat lost in their own activities, but still enjoying their time together. And this is what the newly popular American floorplan prominently featuring a "Great Room" was specifically designed for- to appeal to modern families by bringing an extremely busy family together even as they work on separate activities. And indeed, the Great Room of the family home seems to be serving its purpose tonight.

But now everything changes as bright mischievous eyes in a bouncing mound of curly gray fur appear at a run outside the patio door.

If he could speak, Bouncy the Labradoodle would tell you the truth in his heart- that he loves Calvin best of all the family members- eleven year-old Calvin whom the pup was bought for, yet who's also the person who seems least interested in him. But Calvin's reticence doesn't seem to trouble young Bouncy. Bouncy who still loves Calvin fully in his free-spirited way- Bouncy who just dug through the earth in the backyard and rolled in something dead that he buried there several days ago!

Bouncy now enters the room at a run, claws flailing on the slippery floor, but not enough to lose any momentum as he charges. Calvin becomes Bouncy's first "victim".

The sixty-pound puppy launches himself full force onto Calvin's lap- and onto Calvin's laptop. The computer hits Calvin's front teeth hard, slightly chipping one.

But this is not the reason Calvin starts to scream. The young boy's wails seem to come from his very soul for the computer that has just been ruined, the semester-long science project that he never backed up ruined along with it, the upended bowl of cereal not only staining the white couch, but also drenching and destroying the electronic screen and keyboard. Bouncy understands none of this.

As his beloved child wails, the horrified dog goes into a panic and tramples Calvin's lap even worse, his feet gauging through Calvin's satin basketball shorts to leave deep bloody claw marks. Finally, panicked Bouncy tries to get off of Calvin. But he does it by running across the sectional and leaping directly onto Dad. The sofa was a ten thousand dollar designer sectional that the family had to buy more as an investment than as a convenience. A professional home stager assured the parents that a modern low slung light-colored sectional was the only thing that could help them sell the house if any prospects ever showed up to take a tour. But now it looks as though the arctic white sofa has taken a bloodbath of red salsa and it's ruined also, along with their last meager hope for selling the home.

Four-year old Justin now begins to scream and cry.

Mom's eyes seem to pop halfway out of her head as she observes what's going on, and she yells at Dad to please do something- because she can't just hang up on her friend without at least explaining the emergency. And somehow Bouncy seems to think it's all a game. He springs from Dad's lap directly onto Justin's toys and he grabs one, Justin's favorite, and tries to swallow it.

"Get him!" Mom screams, no longer able to keep out of the situation.

Dad tries to scruff Bouncy, but he can't, especially since he's walking with a waddle, attempting to keep clumps of salsa from running down his pants onto the expensive white and black ponyskin rug. Now Bouncy drops the toy, deciding instead to start licking up salsa from couch and floor.

The last time Bouncy did this exact same thing (which had ruined their last sectional only a few months ago) eating salsa also gave the puppy terrible diarrhea. So now Mom steps in, glares darkly at Dad and tries to grab the dog while juggling her phone call, cradling screaming Justin and flinging scattered toys toward the corner in a compulsive urge to clean up, as though this may somehow avert more damage, stress and pain.

Meanwhile Dad rushes to bend over Calvin trying to see if there's any way at all they can salvage Calvin's two-thousand dollar computer and/or the expensive orthodontic work they just completed on his teeth. For the moment, nobody in the family sees Bouncy, although they still smell the earthy, dead reptile odor, which he's now trailed all over the once-fancy sectional along with muddy footprints.

They don't find Bouncy until they hear a terrible rattle in the kitchen and discover he's somehow jumped onto the granite countertop and the hot stove in order to eat Mom's reheated salmon! What they heard was the pan falling after he got the fish. Mom rushes in ahead of all the other family members and, as usual, she's the one stuck with Bouncy's discipline.

The medium-sized gray dog now huddles trembling on the far corner of the counter, his coat singeing under recessed cabinet lights. He coughs while wolfing down the salmon in wine sauce and he trembles in fear as Mom approaches. She reaches for him, admonishing, and he shakes harder, like a comical bundle of bones in loose fur and skin. And then unbelievably, in fear and shame, Bouncy launches himself. He lands on his side with a thud of air leaving him, sounding literally like a sack of potatoes hitting the tiled floor. For a second Mom fears he's dead or seriously injured.

But Bouncy is only stunned, and just for a minute. He struggles upright and returns to Mom leaking a little urine and he sloppily licks at her feet. Again, Mom smells something- not only the odor of dead things and earth. And her nose leads her to look back at the corner of the counter to find something she would never have imagined. Bouncy has actually gone to the bathroom, depositing urine and loose feces all over their kitchen counter!

When would *you* let Bouncy free if you were this family?

If this family called us to their home, we wouldn't be surprised at the problems they were experiencing with Bouncy, and we'd likely offer to help right away. If the family didn't currently use a crate, we'd never mention one as part of problem solving. And, if they were using one, we'd inform them that we hoped after a few weeks working with us they'd see all the behaviors improve to a point where Bouncy would be safe and they'd no longer need to crate him. Ultimately a dog learns house manners by living in a house (as long as it's dog-proofed for safety) and not by simply being locked away. Once they know what to do, owners can easily shape common "puppy mischief" into positive behaviors that they want. (See Chapter 11 for more positive alternatives).

A lot of other trainers would charge this troubled family a fee ranging in the hundreds or possibly much more and then offer a Faustian compromise- an immediate solution that could prevent everything that happened on the terrible afternoon described above. The downside would be that using the "solution" wouldn't actually solve the problem- it would just put the dog behind bars.

Would you take that deal in the example of Bouncy above and can you see why this family would? In their world Mom wakes well before six to get Justin ready for day care. She lets Bouncy out in the back yard to relieve himself, but when he's ready to come back in she crates him again so he doesn't get underfoot. Dad and Calvin only have a little window of time to grab some more sleep. Then Dad must dress properly for his high-profile job. Meanwhile he needs to be able to concentrate when he checks overseas financial reports and then he wants a moment to bond with Calvin as they eat their morning cereal. And Bouncy is always jumping, tormenting Calvin. Who can blame Mom for crating him after he's peed to leave her men a tiny bit of sleep and peace? Who can blame Dad for leaving Bouncy crated for a few minutes so he can have some juice, straighten his tie and catch up with his son?

Dad and Calvin customarily let Bouncy out once more to relieve bladder and bowels, but then they must rush him back into his crate so they can leave on time. The first person to return home in the afternoon is usually Calvin, and the dog won't stop jumping on him, hurting him and interfering when he tries to work on his laptop. Mom and Dad can only instruct Calvin, "Just let Bouncy out of the crate to the back yard when you get home. And don't mess with him."

So Bouncy stays out there, uncrated for two and a half hours on those days when Calvin gets home early. But more often, Calvin stays for afterschool activities. On these days, no one in the family returns home until five-thirty. On these days Mom or Dad let him out, and he only likes to go outside long enough to relieve himself. Then, feeling lonely, he barks loudly outside the back door as he watches the family moving around in the house and he won't stop until someone allows him in. But when Bouncy does come in, he acts so crazy that the parents usually put him back in his crate, at least until they put Justin to bed at seven thirty.

On days like this Bouncy only spends a half hour outside. Now he's allowed free inside until approximately nine. The family believes he'd certainly damage the upstairs, where he's never been allowed if he were free, so they always put him into the crate at 9:00 pm for the remainder of the night. So, on days like this, Bouncy only spends about two to two and a half hours total free. He receives basically no exercise and no structured play or activities. And this will continue almost every weekday of his life.

Weekends can mean a lot more free time for Bouncy. But, on the other hand, weekends can sometimes be busier for the family than weekdays. The dog is too wild for the family to take him to public places and too wild for them to consider him safe around guests out of the crate. And the family always seems to be busy, sometimes even more than they'd like. Trips, social obligations, school events, shopping and important errands often keep them out all day and into the night on Saturday and Sunday. They also try to efficiently complete household chores on the weekend and they can't constantly stop to "fight" with Bouncy or clean up his bathroom accidents. So, sometimes the family admits they actually crate the young dog more on the weekend than on weekdays.

The description of the chaos when the dog got free on the couch graphically portrayed the family losing thousands of dollars in just moments with Bouncy. So, is it really surprising that they might leave him crated for 18 to 22 hours a day for the rest of his life to avoid ten minutes of destruction like this? And, if you and your family owned the dog and no one told you that there are actually fairly easy alternatives to get family and dog functioning together successfully- when would YOU want to let Bouncy free?

The Real Estate Bubble- Suburban Dream or Collective Shame?

Was the last decade a true portrayal of Paradise on earth, with everyone's goal a brand new home in the priciest subdivisions in the most coveted zip codes? Most of us know people who won the lottery of real estate investment and flipping homes in those days, or benefited from the booming economy that went with it. And many of us believed that we too could possibly live like these friends and neighbors- with at least twenty-five hundred square feet of space or four thousand, five thousand or more.

Many people also came to expect fantasy amenities including infinity pools with hot tubs, water features and swim-up bars, chef's kitchens with granite and stainless and wine coolers (both indoors and out), custom his and hers closets, three-car garages and dedicated home theaters. And there was only one possible downside to these mini-mansions that sprouted on every corner. Many of these grand new homes were surrounded by other large houses just like them, all with "zero lot lines" and restrictions against fencing that left no place suitable for keeping or exercising large high-energy dogs. But this didn't stop families lucky enough to purchase such homes from buying or adopting large-high energy dogs, because this was also a part of the image of the American Dream.

Imagine a generation where the luckiest families received constant offers of interest-only financing for such "McMansions" with little or no down payment nor financial documentation required. And in the "hottest" areas, like the part of South Florida we lived in, home buyers could sometimes make hundreds of thousands in easy profit simply by "flipping" a home several months after they bought it! Even though this oddly supersized "American Dream" now sounds like a cynical joke at the expense of the naïve, the "Real Estate Bubble" of the past decades was actually a significant historical event that altered perceptions of reality and changed the actions and lifestyle choices of several generations.

And, even though families of two, three or four frequently lived in modern homes the size of museums, because of the popular floorplans of these new homes, their dogs actually got less chance to move around comfortably than they used to in smaller, traditionally-designed homes.

Of course, sociologists, psychologists, land developers, planners and even decorating experts have always known that the moods, morals and concerns of a society at a given moment shape and influence how people in that society construct their environments around themselves.

Taking this concept further is the theory that our environment, both in our community and public areas, and particularly in our homes, can actually change who we are. **Not only is our daily environment a stage for our feelings, but the environment can actually shape or create those feelings.** This fascinating premise is proposed in the book *House Thinking*, which walks us through the concepts behind the impressive entryways and warren of individual rooms with unique functions common in Victorian homes all the way to the ubiquitous "great rooms" and "open floor plans" so common in new construction today.

House Thinking explains how the popular home designs of each period were related to the particular needs of the people of the time. (For example, a craving for privacy and private spaces made concrete in the divided floor plans of the Victorian era coincided with large numbers of people newly thrust into city environments during the Industrial Revolution, all looking for a room they could call their own.)

Today, some of us still live in those Victorian homes with many small rooms. But the majority of us are more familiar with the "McMansion" idea of function and luxury that became so popular during the real estate "Bubble" era. Between the mid nineteen and approximately 2007/2008, especially in the Sunbelt states, hundreds of thousands of homes undistinguished in appearance aside from their embarrassingly huge size sprang up at dizzying speed in subdivisions where lax government planners allowed land developers to rapidly destroy every shred of nature, replacing grass with Astroturf and marshes with manmade ponds. Even while removing almost every shred of nature, the developers gave these developments ironically woodsy names like Forest Estates and

Deer Lake and ran away with profits equivalent to Arab sheiks' to invest in the next venture.

Many homeowners with either good timing or good luck also benefited enormously from this "real estate bubble" that was perhaps the biggest single shaping factor in America for the past fifteen years. And then that real estate bubble burst, leaving the country in a tailspin of foreclosures, bank failures, tremendous reductions in wealth, rising unemployment and economic uncertainty that has created ripple effects throughout the world.

These days, most of us wouldn't try to buy a home beyond our ability to pay for it expecting eternally rising values. But, in the days of the "Bubble", families' ability to succeed at this risky game became a primary determinant of our quality of life, self-esteem and even our definition of who we were. And this success without much effort also brought on a unique sense of entitlement for some.

Unfortunately if a young career person chose to remain in one of the less "hot" real estate cities, they'd likely lose out- forever. Meanwhile, a peer of theirs who chose to dabble in real estate at the right time and place couldn't lose. Especially in our area of South Florida, it wasn't unheard of to buy a pre-construction condo for $700,000 and, within three months, with no improvements, "flip it" for over one million. Success like this, without any real work and in such a short amount of time, seemed to make ordinary people feel like spoiled heiresses or hedonistic rock stars. And it made their friends feel terrible if they didn't also "live large". So many took on second and third jobs and enormous credit card debt just to mimic the lifestyle.

Suddenly, the notion of a "starter home" no longer seemed practical. Many of us internalized a feeling of entitlement plus a burning jealously of friends who had luck where we didn't. Many felt willing to do anything to have the new "necessities". Twenty-somethings came to expect gourmet coffee rather than instant, Egyptian cotton sheets, manicures, pedicures, spa treatments and housecleaning services. And developments of massive new homes designed to resemble mini palaces of Versailles huddled together in the middle of alligator-infested swampland, miles from the nearest grocery store, but convenient to major highways.

Guests in these homes could first crane their necks up at the crystal chandelier in a three-story marble tiled entryway. And then they'd step into the "Great Room", the massive space we've come to identify with the modern notion of home. As most of us know, the Great Room of today is characterized by openness- incorporating kitchen along with family room and dining areas, so that all members of the family and their guests can engage in their own individual activities while still being together.

Some upscale housing developments were literally called Versailles. Dinner may have been pizza- every night- eaten straight off six thousand dollar granite countertops after an exhausting 90 minute commute. But, with that Dominos pizza, guests could sample expensive microbrew beer or aged wine from the custom cooler or wine room. Luxury finishes and furniture continued throughout every inch of the home.

Housewives in their early twenties quickly were schooled by their neighbors to become intimately familiar with terms like exotic hardwood, honed marble, stainless steel, jetted garden tubs, custom closets and chef's kitchens. But the most ubiquitous term of all- the one that most defined the Bubble generation has been "Open Floor Plan".

In reality, ranch houses with open floor plans first surfaced in the 1950's as a way for developers to use cheaper materials in tract houses. But the open floor plans that America fell in love with during the 1990's and the turn of this century were different. And it was no coincidence that the popularity of this style coincided with other changes in lifestyle. Women were working more than ever before, for longer hours and in higher powered and more stressful jobs. As a result of these two-career families, preschool children spent more time in daycare, while more school-aged children became "latchkey kids" who'd return home alone after school while both parents still worked. Along with more people working, commuting time in most large cities increased, with many of us becoming "supercommunters" (over ninety miles each way) just to afford the lifestyle and the quality of home that we wanted.

Toward the later years of the "Bubble" even while so many enjoyed an endless party of unimaginable financial success, others struggled to hold on. If your family happened to live in the wrong city (like Miami or San Francisco) you were likely to be completely "priced out", even if both parents worked at respectable jobs like teachers or police officers. This meant that in order to afford a home at all, you would have to move a great distance from where you worked.

Some breadwinners retreated further to suburbs or exurbs where new developments kept springing up with new mini-McMansions to meet the needs and desires of what was left of a middle class. Others just extended themselves further- taking on more competitive or more stressful careers or counting on infinite gains in home equity to finance enormous mortgages that they could never pay under normal circumstances. (Monthly mortgages in excess of twenty thousand dollars were not uncommon amongst our in-home dog training clients in these years.)

The odd thing is that families were getting more house than their wildest dreams, but less time to enjoy these homes. While parents' work schedules expanded, so did their kids' activity schedules.

This was the decade that it became common for high-achieving children in grade school to complain that they were overbooked and stressed by all their formal sports, clubs and other activities. And some of these children started requiring professional help for anxiety and sleep deprivation brought on by the lifestyle.

The only thing that seemed to exist in great abundance during the height of the Bubble years was material abundance. And some of the standards that were introduced in those years still continue today. It became common to have high-end computers and televisions resembling those in movie theaters in every room, including outdoors and in the bath. A good number of children as young as four years old came to expect personal computers in their rooms.

Now they could also use their cell phones as computers, as well as television (and these capabilities expand exponentially each day). Teenagers who started out by spending enormous amounts of time chatting with friends on their cell phones now retreated even further into technology and emotional isolation from their families- earphones hooked to personal iPods while continuously visiting social networking sites on the computer or texting on their phones. Yet while expectations grew for material abundance and technological power in the average home, the expectation for free time shrunk.

First two-career parents, then teenagers and then even elementary school age children were affected, to the extent that the first thing that many mothers, and even some children, say they'd want to do if they were given some unexpected free time would be to catch up on sleep!

The book *Distracted, the Erosion of Attention and the Coming Dark Age* eloquently describes the changes in our society, including results of psychological research studies that confirm frightening facts that many of us are already acquainted with. For example, one study mentions family members communicating with each other via text messages (rather than approaching each other and talking) while in different parts of the same house- or even different parts of the same room!

Meals taken together as a family are rare. In fact over half the meals eaten are eaten out and, of those meals eaten out, 25% are ordered from the car! People no longer prioritize eating as important for purposes other than fueling the body- hence the fact that convenience foods increased by 50% in the year prior to the book's publication, with many people taking their nourishment solely in the form of protein drinks and shakes.

When not accounting for multi-tasking, it would seem many women *do not eat*. In one survey cited in *Distracted* women reported no formal time for eating when they logged their days. Instead of sitting down to meals, family members "graze" alone while they complete other tasks, eating items like the frozen crustless peanut butter and jelly sandwiches described in the book.

In fact, a significant percentage of people report they'd rather not eat at all if they could get their nutrition in pill form! In other words, the ritual of eating together as a family that has cemented human "tribes" together for thousands, even hundreds of thousands of years, often interwoven with religious and cultural elements, seems to have become a bygone thing in the past decade.

Some parents may feel twinges of regret at letting the old rituals go. Others encourage their grade-school children to heat up their own microwave meals while rushing out the door to one obligation or another because they're so desperately pressed for time or because it's what their kids seem to want.

And it's true that since life has so speeded up, including so many distractions and temptations in technology, most kids would feel too antsy to sit down to a traditional meal. And they'd likely see no point in it. Of course there's actually no inherent value in shared family meals like *The Waltons'* other than the opportunity for bonding. Since, unlike previous generations, our kids' generation didn't grow up with the custom of taking family meals together, why *should* our kids feel that shared family dinners every day are important? This appears to be the first generation truly growing up without families touching base when they eat together.

With such an important ritual as eating with family gone, what's happening to the traditional rituals of how we should bond with our dogs? Unlike the hundreds of thousands of years humans have upheld traditions like family dining, "traditional" American notions about the ideal ways to bond with our dogs only go back approximately a hundred years. And the "golden era" that most of us remember for suburban families and their dogs in America actually was as recent as the 1950's.

As described in the book *Distracted*, family members of all ages can now elect for independence, and a loosening of ties from real things in their immediate surroundings in preference for the much more vital-seeming worlds on every front that we now live in whenever we're in Cyberspace. We already know that community has taken on a very different meaning in the world of impersonal chain stores, superhighways and brand new gated communities filled with homogeneous builder homes. Inside harried commuters who have never met, or sometimes never even seen, their next-door neighbors feel isolated if they're not "plugged in".

In light of worlds of "friends" in Cyberspace and our increasing ability to live all aspects of our life there, including shopping, dating and career changes, not only do many of us prefer the Cyberworld to the real one, but we may start challenging the notion of which is actually more meaningful and which is actually more real- the riches of our Cyber life, or the blandness and alienation of our generic "communities". The book *Distracted* hints at the concept that this independence of constant "wiredness" for adults and children- the ability to immediately connect with anything we might need by simply plugging in, may go so far as to make the concept of the nuclear family something that the members may consider optional.

All of this occurs in a world where research studies that film families during their days have shone that spouses and children almost never take time to greet a father returning home and average parents and children now spend only 16% of their free time at home in rooms together. This does not take into account whether the parents and kids are actually interacting, or are "plugged in" in some way, like listening to music on earphones or texting while they are together.

Children commonly retreat into playing increasingly complex video games. We all know of children who now never move to go outside on their own, but will choose to spend literally all of their waking hours in front of a video screen if no other demands intrude. And many adults show similarly intense interest in video games. It's a chance to unwind and unstress, they say.

To meet the needs of today's new families, as explained in the book *Distracted*, the food industry has quickly pioneered a whole new category of convenience foods. Television commercials often advertise these foods showing younger and younger children preparing them alone. Most families no longer eat dinner or any meal together, especially on weekdays, and parents often allow grade school or younger children to prepare their own meals in a microwave. And this is the same fare everyone in the family eats, except perhaps on weekends or for holidays or parties.

How The Great Room and Open Floor Plan concept represent a solution- or a last chance

The Great Room and Open Floor Plan concept have come about as a way to resolve the essential ways today's notions of success isolate us from our families, while we still "have it all" in a material sense. And many families cling to the tenuous link to family togetherness this floor plan provides. In a luxury home of three thousand square feet, a young family can still create some physical togetherness by breaking down the walls that would ordinarily separate them during the solitary or tech-driven activities that occupy them every minute they are home. So, even though Mom is emailing work, Dad is checking stock quotes and the kids are texting while the sixty-inch plasma television competes for attention, all are still in one room.

This is an era, according to Maggie Jackson, in *Distracted*, when "*Nearly half of Americans say they eat most meals away from home or on-the-go.*"

Sitting down with the nuclear family to eat at the end of the day is rare. Even greeting a returning family member is often dispensed with entirely. *Distracted* also describes the results of the exhaustive videotaped study by Elinor Ochs, head of UCLA's Center on the Everyday Lives of Families, in which every aspect of the thirty-two diverse modern families' lives was taped, cataloged and interpreted.. In the study, "*wives stopped what they were doing and welcomed home a returning spouse only a little more than a third of the time. Mostly, they were too irritable or too busy to do so. 'In half of those occasions, kids were absolutely distracted and didn't stop an activity to recognize a returning father,' said Ochs. 'They did not look up to stop for even a millisecond.*"

According to author of *Distracted*, when she, "*talked to dozens of parents about their return at day's end, they … grew wistful and sometimes bitter, recounting the many nights they'd returned home to silence from a house full of busy kin.*

"*Perhaps because we virtually check in with each other all day, the idea of moving across a physical threshold naturally becomes devoid of meaning. In a placeless world, who needs to acknowledge the return to a location? Moreover, a boundaryless world means that coming home doesn't signal the end of the workday anymore than... being under one roof marks the beginning of unadulterated family time. The physical and virtual worlds are always with us, singing a siren song of connection, distraction and options. We rarely are completely present in one moment or for one another. Presence is something naked, permeable and endlessly spliced. Add to this portrait of American home life the rise of networked individualism, and you begin to see why family members are not at the door, greeting each other. To cope and keep up with our pulsing personal orbits, we live in worlds of our own making, grazing from separate menus, plugged into our own bedroom-based media centers, adhering to customized schedules...*

"*[Only] 17% of the families in the UCLA study consistently ate dinner together. On weekdays, the* parents *and at least one child came together in a room just 16% of the time.*"

With statistics like this, one can see why suburban families treasure an open floorplan that at least allows the parents and children to remain in physical proximity with each other, even if pursuing separate digital activities. Most families today also highly treasure entertaining time, the only occasion they get to actually use that chef's kitchen and to spend warm moments with equally harried and overscheduled relatives and friends.

Emma is a big fan of the show "*House Hunters*" on the Home and Garden Network. And the single most frequent comment of new home buyers seems to be, "I like how open it is" or, "I need the kitchen to be open so that I don't feel isolated when I entertain".

Successful builders and developers targeted buyers' requests as they filled the Southern half of this country with new houses as quickly as they could play a game of Monopoly. Buyers said they loved kitchens with luxury finishes like stainless and granite that could stand open to the living areas of the house not just as showpieces, but as facilitators of forced physical connection between family and friends. Unlike in older homes where family members could retreat to their own small rooms and shut doors behind them, the newer homes now keep family members in the "Great Room" for most of their tasks and leisure/media time.

But some of the aspects of the Great Room that make it so great for today's families also make it a bad layout for managing a young boisterous dog in a healthy fashion. And, according to the AKC, over half the AKC registered dogs today are those considered high-energy- breeds that were specifically created to perform extremely taxing physical tasks like hunting, retrieving or herding livestock.

According to the definition in the book *High Energy Dogs* by Tracy Libby a high energy dog can get by with no less than two hours of intense physical activity per day, but would be happier with even more. These dogs, including dogs like Labrador Retrievers, the most popular breed in America, have to move! And while a large Great Room may give a large, extremely high-energy puppy of five months and up space to move, it will also ensure that if he runs around, he will always be underfoot and interfering in some important family activity.

Modern homes without the room divisions of older homes often don't give these dogs anywhere they can move around where they are not interfering with some activity or endangering some expensive item, and they spaces are not constructed ideally for managing a dog while still letting him move around and be in proximity to the family. Many of these spaces have no doors to close, no doorways, and no obvious places to temporarily affix baby gates or room dividers.

Because these Great Room areas are now used so intensively, most families want highly comfortable furniture made for total relaxing and indulgence. And because these areas are always seen by guests the furnishings have to look impressive, too. It's become the norm to include super-high-end decorator-quality sectional sofas, in finishes like light-colored suede, in the new open Great Rooms. (This is in contrast to the rattier sofas of yesteryear's hidden-away family rooms, dens, game rooms or rumpus rooms). In these open Great Rooms, whenever guests are not present, family members sit on these sofas or sectionals to watch television, work on laptops or play video games.

And they spend just as much time, or more, congregating at the high-end countertop, squatting briefly on stools as they gobble Pop Tarts or takeout pizza, pack up homework or hold brief family powwows about vacation plans or the kids' grades. Life, fast-paced as it's become, increasingly takes place in the kitchen and the open layout has helped families manage.

Soon after its introduction and increasing popularity, the Open Floor Plan became not only a response to a quickened pace of life, but an expectation in itself. For many of us, the sight of what appeared to be chopped-up little rooms in older homes came to turn our stomachs. We had come to expect an uninterrupted vista of the swimming pool seen through the chef's kitchen and the cavernous Great Room- and very many families absolutely refused to expect less.

Often Great Room areas including open kitchen, dining and family room areas were as large as one thousand or two thousand square feet. But this interior space came at a price. Because, no matter how much interior square footage or how high priced, these new Open Floor Plan homes often were designed with tiny yards and no option for fencing that might be against subdivision regulations.

During the last years of the real-estate bubble, average families bought some of these new homes for a quarter of a million to a half a million dollars or more without blinking, and without complaining about the lack of extensive fenced outdoor space. Family members, whenever they were home, were all plugged into individual electrical devices indoors, each making their own noise, and rarely finding time to go outside other than for occasionally entertaining on the patio. Many families never saw or met their neighbors. And, given the choice, they preferred to wrest every additional square foot out of the indoor spaces- namely the Great Room. It became common for homes of three thousand square feet to devote two thousand of that to a single living area.

The problems of Great Rooms and dogs:

Here is the problem of the "Open Floor Plan" as it relates to owning a dog: If all the space in the Great Room area is carpeted or contains valuable furniture, flooring, electronics or decorations- as is the case in many homes- a dog, especially one that's not housetrained, might do enormous damage if not contained.

In contrast, in "old-fashioned" older homes with distinct small rooms, including a separate kitchen with a door and a normal size doorway, this isn't such a problem. In a traditionally designed older home with distinct rooms, a puppy during housetraining can stay in one small room like a dining area behind a baby gate, and still have plenty of room to stretch and still see his family. In the past, a common solution for containing a pup when owners were away was to keep him in the kitchen- a generally happy area with lots of traffic. And kitchens have been historically easy to "dog proof".

Safety Note: Even though kitchens can be the basis for safe containment, this does not mean that a kitchen, or ANY area you leave your dog free in is automatically safe until you take action to make it safe. Never neglect dog-proofing any area your puppy or new, unfamiliar dog is free in by removing all accessible chemicals, poisons, garbage and hazards, including small sharp objects, electrical hazards and dangerous foods or plants. Consult the Internet and and/or your vet for a full list of hazards and poisons if you are not sure, and always assume dogs can jump and climb high! Until it learns what is off limits a teething puppy can easily kill itself if left free in an area with hazards! This is especially true when the dog is alone, but deadly incidents sometimes also happen while owners are present. This does not mean that you must crate your dog or puppy, but that you should always protect him. It is generally safe to leave emotionally balanced adult dogs with good house manners free in an ordinary home environment, just like you might leave your young teenagers.

But you should always be aware of extraordinary hazards like chemicals and manage them accordingly, even when your dog matures. It's best to always err on the side of safety. And, as you leave a dog sufficient room to wander the home and feel comfortable, you can always shut doors on certain rooms or areas for safety.

One reason kitchens used to lend themselves as generally good places for puppy containment was because the floors were easy to clean up. And, just like in older homes, kitchens in newer homes may have stain-resistant floors like tile, which would imply that a puppy that was not fully housetrained could stay there without doing damage while the owners went away. But the truth is that the floor plans of newer Open Floor Plan-style homes sometimes leave the authors baffled. It becomes frustrating to think of alternatives for humanely containing young dogs during housetraining in these homes, or containing adult dogs in treatment for severe behavior problems temporarily so they won't injure themselves because of the architectural designs that sometime leave no logical way to affix a gate.

Often the wide-open design of the kitchen rules out that obvious setting for containment- because no normal baby gate could block off some of these spaces! Manufactures do sell much wider versions of baby gates, in custom wood finishes that look somewhat appropriate with higher-end décor common in so many homes these days. But even the widest cannot help in many new kitchens that offer literally no division from the rest of the house.

We've seen owners' housing their dogs in baffling conditions that we couldn't even understand at first. For example we found a small thirteen year-old terrier housed long-term in a closet in a multimillion-dollar waterfront home whenever the owners went away. Meanwhile three younger dogs stayed in crates lined up in the only enclosed room in a vastly open floor plan filled with breathtaking antiquities and luxury finishes.

Here in Florida, we've been introduced to dogs and puppies housed in crates in laundry rooms, garages, sun porches and back patios with no air conditioning while the owners worked. Meanwhile central air conditioning was left on all day, chilling thousands of square feet in other parts of the lovely empty homes. (Unfortunately, leaving crated dogs without climate control, especially in very hot or very cold regions, can be extremely dangerous. Yet it's quite a common practice when owners are afraid to mess up luxury flooring and finishes inside their homes.)

Other times, we've encountered dogs or puppies kept in the common areas, yet crated so subtly that, if you didn't know the owners had a dog, you wouldn't see it.

As we repeat frequently throughout this book, the offenders in many of these cases are not deliberate dog abusers. Instead they are respectable families who are quite likable under other circumstances. Dog owners who leave their dogs in tiny crates inside giant houses are only living in the society of their time, and doing what they've been told to do by so-called qualified "experts" in the professional dog world. But it is still hard for us to relate to the lifestyle, where activities of family life go on with no input from the dog behind bars except for glowing eyes staring at his owners as they watch television or work on the computer. The children are frequently the only ones that remember to say hi to the dog. But sometimes they are too engrossed in technology to seem to want to.

Other times, the children seem shy, or even afraid of the dog or puppy. And, as trainers, we unfortunately witness the vicious cycle that occurs when an animal (like Bouncy the Labradoodle) that has been caged for ten hours is suddenly let loose in a large open area with luxury finishes the second the family gets home! Through no real fault of their own, but just a natural response to a multi-faceted problem made infinitely worse by excessive crating, problem dogs often run out of their crates like the tornados they are often compared to.

And, if left alone even briefly when they run wild in a Great Room like Bouncy did, a dog or pup is not just a danger to a three-hundred dollar sofa like many in older generations grew up with. In some homes today, a dog could literally do tens of thousands of dollars worth of damage in minutes- especially "neurotic" and highly distressed dogs that immediately attack items like high-end designer sofas, window treatments and wall molding or who break through glass windows or destroy entire car interiors. Of course, behaviors at this extreme are not natural or normal, especially in adult dogs five years past teething. But putting the problem dog back in a cage and refusing to look at the problems in the environment is no solution either.

These dogs need to be gently and yet intensely and expertly trained, until they become civilized and mannerly members of the family that can always be trusted to contribute positively to all family activities.

This is especially true when the individuals closest to the floor are the children, and they are the ones getting painfully jumped on or nipped or scratched (sometimes drawing blood and leaving permanent scarring) whenever the family dog is released. Again, this is usually a vicious cycle- and no professional should leave a family in a situation where this is happening with no long term treatment plan for safely removing the dog from the cage. With a little attention and direction (as we will explain in later chapters) most of these dogs' and puppies' behavior can be properly channeled, so that the dogs are a pleasure and no longer damage people or possessions.

But, admittedly, changing an already established lifestyle that feels like it moves like a freight train for all its members from 6:00am to midnight can seem daunting. Even thirty years ago, regular suburban family life was very different, especially as it impacted dogs. Families spent much more time together and individually doing "real" things- whether conversation, working on projects, games or crafts, sitting down to dinner or playing with the dog on the living room floor or in the back yard.

Children seemed to like to stay children longer, and they naturally gravitated toward dogs as part of that lifestyle. In other words, within reason, kids had the endless patience and energy to be interested in exactly the kind of game that growing puppies needed. And influencing the dog, whether through play, obedience practice or activities like grooming, provided fascination for the kids. Families that were lucky in those days likely still had one parent staying home from the workforce. And/or members of their extended family lived in the home or visited frequently to interact with the dog in the most natural fashion.

Of course dogs, which are wired to do best in a social, or family, context thrive with this kind of attention. And they need it consistently every day, and spread throughout the day, for the most benefit. The absolutely best lifestyle for most dogs would also include some clear purpose or work that the dog would do throughout the day directed by his owner. But clear purpose and structure and consistent attention is exactly the opposite of what most suburban nuclear families give their dogs. Parents and children alike suffer from health-destroying lack of sleep during weekdays that are just too jam-packed with work and other obligations for us to ever get off the treadmill, or stop stressing about what we have to do next.

Multitasking is mandatory, even when we are having fun. The book *Distracted* cites Barbara Schnieder and N. Broege, in "Why Working Families Avoid Flexibility: The Costs of Overworking, to say that *"working parents spend a quarter of their time multitasking"*. Another example is the findings of Eulynn Shiu and Amanda Lenhart. The study they conducted demonstrated, that, *"more than half of instant message users say they always Web surf, talk on the phone, or play computer games while iM'ing"*.

When it comes to dogs, this lifestyle might mean that, at eleven thirty at night, a working mother might be replying to an email from the office while talking to a friend on her cell phone, while attempting to catch up on a favorite television show, only to get up distractedly to let the dog out into the yard for his last bathroom break of the night.

More frequently in the cases we see, the overburdened mom might not catch the two-year old dog's desire to go to the bathroom in time and, after her other activities, she would also be mopping up a big puddle of urine and feces on the marble entryway floor. In frustration with another twenty minutes of her schedule now wasted on cleaning the dog's fifth "accident" that day, she would not be inclined to spend any more free time that evening trying to interact with the dog.

Perhaps she might "reward" herself with a bath, followed by a few more quick work emails, school emails regarding the children and a few regarding purchases and maintenance for the house just to stabilize things until morning and then, finally, a little Internet surfing and social networking to finally touch base with friends and family. A bedtime of two or three o'clock would not be unusual, with the alarm clock set for before six, and an expectation of hopping off the freeway and a big latte from Starbucks to make the next day even possible.

Life for the children, whether teenage or grade school, might not be that different, only their drug of choice to keep themselves awake would be cola and/or energy drinks. Time seems to get lost in the midst. After a day that's not only physically, but primarily mentally, demanding the human soul craves for a relaxing outlet. Ironically, even though high tech is what makes demands on so many of us all day long, high tech is also where we turn for comfort, whether in the guilty pleasure of a reality TV show, a video game, downloading some new tunes to our iPod so we can tune out the world or a completely silly interchange with "friends" that we don't even know on the newest social networking site.

In all of this, it is easy to simply forget a dog, especially on weekdays. **Unfortunately, a "forgotten" dog will tend to pester the family and it's hard for owners to envision that all would run smoother if they simply initiated interaction with him**. Most dogs today have no real jobs to do. They are certainly not out herding sheep, hunting deer, pulling carts or rescuing hikers. Most don't even actively guard their properties.

But **just petting a dog is not nearly enough to stimulate his mind and body**. The family may realize that they do not spend enough time with their dog, but the way most families attempt to compensate creates its own problems. On a weekday, family members may start leaving the house at six in the morning. Even if someone stops in at 3:00pm to quickly allow the dog to relieve his bladder, the whole clan may not come together from work, school and afterschool activities until seven-thirty at night.

This is when they may decide to play vigorously with the dog. The home that looks like a palace now gets lived in like a roadhouse, with a brief time of screaming, running and chaos that overexcites both children and dog, and frazzles the parents even worse.

Weekends are similar. On certain weekends, the family may finally get some free time and attempt activities with their dog. This may be the only time the dog or family members exercise. It may also be the only time the dog gets out of the house. Once again, the family may attempt to squeeze in so much vigorous physical activity outdoors, and exposure to so many novel things that the dog once again goes wild and reactive and dog and family members alike become overheated, overtired and mentally "fried".

Or sometimes, it is once again the parent left with everything. As the kids retreat to the dim bowels of the house and the glow of their computer screen to finally relax or they use their Saturday for more prescheduled activities like birthday parties, dance classes or part-time jobs, it is usually Mom who decides to exercise the dog.

This could involve a sudden midday three mile run around the community for a dog that has barely moved in the past three weeks, or a trip to a sun-scorched art fair where hundreds of people reach out to pet him, even after he has not met another stranger outside of the home in the past three months. It is not like the "old days" when kids just naturally played outdoors, and constantly involved their dog in a casual fashion. And the kind of extreme ups and downs we impose on our dogs today simply are not healthy for the dogs' behavior.

Whether or not the children love the jangly, yet physically isolating environment they live in is not their choice. Children tend to be adaptable, and the same kids who thirty years ago might have spent a lot of time simply hanging around outside and playing together in imaginative games with brothers and sisters and dogs have now learned to play hand-held games on their cell phones or connect with their teenage peers next door with the touch of a button, rather than lacing on sneakers and walking over.

But we must remember that these children did not choose this Brave New World. And usually they are not the ones who chose to bring home a dog. Parents may suddenly be faced with a ridiculously luxurious, oversized, overpriced and impractical "dream home" that is killing the Norman Rockwell, *Leave It to Beaver* or even *Brady Bunch* environment that these thirty and forty-somethings imagined when they pushed so hard to bring home the dog.

It was very hard to believe we'd lose something like our connection to dogs when so many of us traded up from the old American dream of the white picket fence in the friendly small town in exchange for the new dream of the mini-Versailles where we never meet our neighbors. Now that the real estate bubble has burst many families again crave a simple life. Yet they can find no way economically to unload the enormous house and no hope in sight in the near future, so they must work even more hours just to support a bloated mortgage.

The question becomes whether owning a dog and owning and open floor plan home can be reconciled. More importantly, we should also ask how our lifestyles might change to bring more real fulfillment, including the kind of bond we were meant to enjoy a dog in the first place. Of course, the first step is to stop considering a dog crate as a solution. The next is to ask where the conveniences, technologies and habitual patterns of action that have been defining our lives have actually begun to strangle our highest potential to keep us from what we really want. If you love dogs and crave quality time with them, you know intuitively what we mean. And that knowledge is all the start that is needed.

Remember that dogs, no matter how smart they may be, live only in the real, and not the virtual, world. The quality of their lives is the quality of all the actual minutes they spend and it never has anything to do with any symbol or video image. In further chapters, we can help by providing simple solutions that allow dogs and families the best kinds of interaction even in our tech-driven Red Bull world. (Or, read our family-friendly activity books: *The Cure for Useless Dog Syndrome* and *Awesome Puppy* or some of the other helpful books included in the Appendix.) Never despair of solutions, for dogs are essentially positive creatures, and they are almost always open to grow and change.

The purpose of this chapter, however, is to hypothesize how **the rise in busy lifestyles and open floor plans left so many of us in despair- prey to false prophets who vigorously preached the gospel of almost constant crating for dogs entire lives. These people, unfortunately most of them "dog professionals" advocated a type of care that they could have known would injure dogs. But they promoted crating for purposes including monetary profit and keeping their own businesses alive and thriving when faced with families asking them for help with problems with deeper roots that they had no real notion how to solve.**

Crating was never a true solution. But for many (though absolutely not all) dog trainers and writers it proved a good way to shut down the complaints of desperate suburban families, while still collecting profits and proclaiming themselves experts. Without facing the real soul-wrenching disasters happening in their homes every evening, families could keep their dogs, keep their lifestyle and keep buying dog products and services as long as they caged their dogs. This was all the multi-billion dollar dog industry needed to know, because many in the industry had their own McMansion or mini-McMansion payments to make!

We wonder how many of these dog professionals that compromised their creativity to the doctrine of crating have already lost their ability to connect with dogs in the deepest fashion. This is sad for us to think about, but dog owners have always been our priority. And we believe dog *owners*, not dog professionals, will be the first ones to shift the trends and change the world for the better, so that it will become as politically correct to turn away from caging dogs as it's become to protect our treasured dogs from tainted dog food.

For suburban families who lost quality time with their little "Bouncies" because they gave in to crating doctrine, we believe the prognosis is still good, even in our tech-driven society. Dogs are adaptable and, above all, they do wish to love and serve us as long as they understand what we want them to do. As soon as owners are ready to dispense with crating as a catchall solution, they can start to live in real solutions. And, once that happens, a new dog industry with new creative ideas can pioneer new ways for families and dogs to really share quality time even in this demanding modern era!

Chapter 7: Dogs Gone Wild

Do you ever feel as frustrated with your dog as Bouncy's family in the last chapter? Do you ever feel afraid of your dog? Does he make your life more miserable than fun, so you sometimes wish you didn't have to come home after work because of him? The truth is that average families are increasingly feeling they need extreme help for their dogs' behavior.

Marley & Me ("the world's worst dog") vs. St. Shaun (the normal Labrador)

Millions of Americans made *Marley & Me,* John Grogran's autobiographical memoirs of his family's traumas with their out-of-control Labrador Retriever, a hugely influential bestseller. If you read the book, you'll remember the author believed he owned "world's worst dog". And, apparently, much of the country could empathize. In 2006, shortly after its release, *Marley & Me* spent multiple weeks on the *New York Times* and *USA Today* bestseller lists, including two weeks as *USA Today's* #1 bestseller. Since then, the book has sold at least 6 million copies and inspired successful spinoffs.

It also inspired the blockbuster movie, *Marley & Me*, which starred Jennifer Anniston and Owen Wilson and earned $14.75 million dollars on its first day at the box office and over $50 million its first four-day weekend. The phenomenal success of *Marley & Me* indicates just how deeply many Americans relate to the concept of family life being rocked by "out of control" dogs.

America's #1 favorite problem breed. It's interesting that the infamous Marley, who made life crazy for author John Grogan's family in *Marley & Me* happened to be a Labrador Retriever, while Labs also happen to be America's favorite breed according to AKC registrations. Labs also represent a disproportionate number of our calls, with owners begging the authors for help with their adjustment problems. One problem is that high demand for any breed often leads to puppy mill breeders, irresponsible breeding practices, flawed genetics and poor early husbandry. But also families often forget that Labrador Retrievers are a sporting breed, characterized by extremely high energy level, and they require a great deal of physical exercise. This need for physical activity frequently collides with the unrealistic expectations of owners who expect Labradors to be "perfect" couch potato family dogs that can live without exercise or stimuli. And, in our experience, Labs are a breed that does terribly when they are crated- yet they're the breed we see crated most often!

While *Marley & Me* is heartwarming and elegantly written, it's quite different from traditional iconic dog books like *Old Yeller*. The Grogan family had to endure a lot of stress and evasive maneuvers in order to "enjoy" love and warmth with hyperactive Marley. And this seems like something today's dog owners can identify with more easily than they can identify with the fictional canines of yesterday that were presented purely as family heroes. *Marley & Me* constantly weighs the young Labrador Marley's friendliness, loyalty and heart-of-gold against his life-disrupting misbehaviors and his family's frustration. For example, in addition to being responsible for various destruction in the house, Marley suffered severe thunderstorm fear. Once, his owners returned home to find that, "An entire wall was gauged open, obliterated clear down to the studs"- the result of his panic.

Full grown Marley liked to pick up and eat random items and John Grogan compares the dog's mouth to a "salvage yard" which often contained, "paper towels, wadded Kleenex, grocery receipts, wine corks, paper clips, chess pieces, bottle caps" One day he pried open Marley's jaws to find "my paycheck plastered to the roof of his mouth." And, in one of the more memorable scenes in the book and movie, Marley consumes a gold chain that was a gift for Grogan's wife. Then the author must wait days to retrieve it after it passes through the dog's digestive system.

Grogan describes Marley as having, "his default setting... stuck on eternal incorrigibility", walking on a leash like a "runaway locomotive", rearing up on hind legs and bolting forward to try to greet dogs and people- even dragging a cafe table while trying to follow another dog.

At one point the author seeks help in the writings of one of the earlier influential canine behaviorists, Barbara Woodhouse, and he's horrified by her opinion that some dogs with highly serious anxiety disorders can't be cured and need to be euthanized. We certainly agree with the Grogans that poor anxiety prone, yet goofy and friendly, Marley never needed to be euthanized! In fact, we feel if the family had known how to subtly change their responses to Marley's everyday behaviors, along with some relatively painless changes in environment and activities, they could have better shaped his actions for a more normal and easy to live with dog.

In our opinion, knowledgeable and customized treatment could have helped even Marley's more serious anxiety symptoms including extreme thunderstorm fear, drooling during car rides and separation anxiety that likely caused the worst of his destructive tendencies. And all those millions of dog owners who relate to the story of Marley because they have similar problem dogs in their homes should understand that there *is* hope.

Unfortunately many dog people today advise owners to simply cage a high-energy problem dog like Marley most of every day and night with no plan for behavioral treatment. But this can be cruel and terrible. And we believe the Grogans were absolutely right in caring for Marley enough not to continue crating after they once attempted it briefly.

The truth is that owners *can* find effective treatment for all the Marleys of the world, although not every dog trainer or expert out there can provide it. And the owners of 77 million dogs should understand that having to live with a dog with Marley's behavior problems untreated does *not* set the bar for the experience of dog ownership. Our dogs *can* be well-behaved, even though we sometimes have to put in an initial effort to show them what we want and need from them.

Those of us now in our thirties, forties and older were among the lucky ones because most of us grew up with dogs that blended easily with family life. And, for future quality of life, it's important that everyone remember this, rather than forgetting and believing that dogs, by nature, behave so badly that they must be locked up at all times. **Most of our generation grew up with dogs that acted like helpful and loving family members** and brought joy and meaning to every moment of life. Many owners still enjoy these great dogs every day. And it's fascinating to discover that *so did the author of Marley & Me!*

Because John Grogan, famous owner of infamous Marley, actually got his introduction to Labrador Retrievers in his childhood and teens with a wonderful dog nicknamed "Saint Shaun".

As described by Mr. Grogan, Shaun, *"was one of those dogs that give dogs a good name. He effortlessly mastered every command I taught him and was naturally well-behaved. I could drop a crust on the floor and he would not touch it until I gave the okay. He came when I called him and stayed when I told him to. Never once did he lead me into hazard."*

It's clear John Grogan's parents never crated Shaun, and it's clear they didn't have to. This was a dog that heeled perfectly beside the author without a leash. And the Grogan family *"could leave him alone in the house for hours, confident he wouldn't have an accident or disturb a thing."*

This dog Shaun was not a actually a saint- he was simply a normal Labrador Retriever with normal strong points of his breed, given attention and a clear purpose in life and treated fairly by his owners. In return, Shaun gave John Grogan, "the childhood every kid deserves."

It's a shame how many families today forget that naturally cooperative behavior like Shaun's should be considered a healthy baseline for doggie behavior- with no force necessary to train it! **Families should be able to trust their adult dogs to behave properly in their homes, with no need for cages**. Instead, more families seem caught in a society-wide Catch-22. They lock dogs up in crates to control problems, then the problems worsen and expectations continue to fall.

How extreme are the training aids average families use today?

Much of our country's explosive fascination with prime-time television celebrity dog trainers started in 2004 with *"Dog Whisperer"* Cesar Millan, whose shows on National Geographic Channel feature Cesar training completely intractable dogs whose symptoms include extremely aggressive behavior to other dogs and people. And it seems many families relate to the show because they personally live in an embattled state with their pet dogs that would have been unthinkable years ago.

Unfortunately, rather than seeking the root cause of the problems, many owners simply try to subdue or break the disturbing behavior. Dog owners shell out more money than ever to control their dogs' energy, paying for training that ranges from group puppy classes to private in-home behavior specialists. Some leave their dogs in "doggie daycare" every day for a respite from their bad behavior, while others seek the services of dog masseuses, dog astrologists, dog acupuncture practitioners and dog psychics or communicators. And many owners purchase expensive natural supplements, herbs and essential oils to change their dogs' behaviors, along with books to explain how to use these holistic methods. Other owners buy mechanical aids like special no-pull harnesses and head halters; and others get veterinarians to prescribe powerful medication ("doggie Prozac") for their dogs for years at a time.

These days, everyday owners frequently use extreme methods of canine control like muzzles and devices that deliver electric shocks (including e-collars). Veterinarians and groomers increasingly muzzle dogs. And some groomers even sedate dogs (sometimes without the owners' knowledge) before they work on them. All of these extreme coping strategies are signs of the erosion of comfortable relations between dogs and man.

The growth, and change, in the dog training industry and why some trainers today don't have better solutions than crating:

It's no coincidence that in recent years, as an increasing portion of our population suffers with dogs that won't meld with their lifestyles, the industry of professional dog training has exploded. For example, just one organization, the Association of Pet Dog Trainers (APDT) now boasts approximately 6,000 members since its founding only seventeen years ago.

Dog training has also moved into the mainstream. As recently as fifteen or twenty years ago, most people didn't purchase formal training or behavior interventions for their pet dogs. Twenty or thirty years ago and before, "dog training" tended to be a discreet discipline, usually involving specific skills for military, police, guide or show dogs, and not a service purchased by average suburban owners for their pet dogs. But now families find cultural acceptance when they reveal to the world that they have problems with their pet dogs that require professional treatment.

This coincides with the enormous popularity of celebrity television trainers. Several years ago, Cesar Millan, of *Dog Whisperer* on National Geographic Channel, intrigued our whole nation with the concept of an all-powerful and charismatic dog trainer able to come into our homes and take away our dogs' dysfunction and disrespect. Next Victoria Stillwell of *It's Me or the Dog* on Animal Planet appealed to dog owners who wanted a gentler, more positive approach to save their families from falling apart.

Lately the concept of dog training has become so mainstream that, in thousands of chain pet stores across the country, like Petsmart and Petco, shoppers almost collide with large sign-up displays for in-store obedience classes when they first walk in. Dog owners learn training jargon like "being the pack leader" from television shows and many free sites on the Internet, where they also spend many hours searching for solutions to their dog problems and commiserating with faraway peers in similar distress.

Years ago there used to be a certain mystique around the "art" of dog training, and individuals only attempted professional dog training as a career if they felt sure they had a special talent to influence animals (similar to the talent for training wild animals, for example). It was also customary for new dog trainers to have to endure a long and often demoralizing apprenticeship under a highly experienced "master trainer". Thirty years ago and before then, professional dog training also tended to be a male-dominated industry (with a few notable exceptions). But today, the bias towards males has changed.

Entry into the industry has changed in other ways. These days, dog training is presented more as a technical discipline than an instinctive "art". And the career is made to seem more appealing to individuals who might have feared attempting it in the past because of an implication of guaranteed success for anyone that invests time and money in particular educational programs. Some schooling for dog trainers is quite expensive (running into the tens of thousands) while other options include $300 certifications over the Internet and many 2-week certification classes. And we believe that so many well-publicized options have encouraged thousands of new people to enter the dog training business with unrealistically high hopes, not realizing that, to be fully effective, they would have had to start with an extraordinary inborn- and quite rare-power to influence dogs.

In the past ten to fifteen years, as "reform" of the dog training industry has started to replace compulsion/dominance methods with standardized positive behavioral reinforcement strategies, new dog trainers sometimes assume they can walk into strangers' homes and solve totally mystifying canine behavior problems just because they've completed requirements of a particular class and/or learned specific behavior modification techniques. But it's not that easy.

We doubt these individuals would try their hands at training out-of-control *bears* using the same techniques, no matter what technical training they'd just completed. Most people would only try rehabilitating troubled bears if they knew in their heart with 100% certainty that they possessed a unique, almost magical talent to influence bears and that it was safe to bet their lives on it. And getting paid to train strangers' dogs is not that different.

The authors certainly believe that schooling (along with personal research and study, and experience in a variety of situations) is vitally important. But, unless a dog trainer is born as an almost freakishly special "dog whisperer", we feel believe that no amount of technical training will be enough to guarantee that they can master extreme challenges in customers' homes. Unfortunately many dog trainers may not want to admit to themselves when they are in trouble. And, **if a trainer has serious difficulty with customers' dogs, they may look to anything for a quick fix. Years ago, this often meant harsh physically corrections that made dogs surrender in fear. But these days, the "fallback" solution is usually crating- simply locking the dogs up in cages as a supposed treatment for behavior problems.** (Unfortunately, this even extends to some of the better-known behavioral theorists, as in the case of Jean Donaldson's book, *Culture Clash*, in the next chapter.)

Why has "Gentle" or "Positive" Dog Training Become So Popular, Replacing Violent Training of the Past?

Prior to the late 1980's, when people thought about "dog training" they tended to picture a strong militaristic man controlling large dogs like "police dogs" through compulsion methods. This style of training included physical positioning and rough jerks on the collar, so dogs learned to fear consequences from the trainer if they disobeyed.

Humane dog trainer Donald Hanson explains how the "dominance theory" teachings started back in the early 1920's (with Thorlief Schelderup-Ebbe) and were commonly used with military and police dogs. Then in 1978 the Monks of New Skete, who bred, boarded and trained German Shepherds, popularized paternalistic training techniques for family dogs in their book, *How to Be Your Dog's Best Friend*, published in 1978. And their techniques influenced people's concepts of proper dog training for decades in what turned out to be quite a negative direction.

As Donald Hanson explains, the Monks and the great majority of other trainers of the era advocated training techniques that sometimes included hitting dogs under the chin, scruffing, shaking and "alpha-rolling" (turning a dog over onto its back and holding it immobile until it surrenders and stops all movement). Even though compulsion methods like these may have been behind the creation of some stellar obedience (including that of many guide dogs, military dogs and police dogs) most people gradually realized that using pain was unnecessary. And some of these physical corrections seemed frightening or cruel. Also, in the hands of individuals who became excessively forceful, these methods often backfired, creating worse behavior problems.

A dog will surely respond to training sessions- if that's the only time he's let out of a cage... One of the most disturbing training methods, popularized years ago, and used with some working dogs (including German Shepherds) was to deliberately house the dog in a kennel or a crate for all the hours of their day except for when a trainer actively worked with them. These training sessions- the dogs' only freedom- might only last one or two hours a day, and the theory was that the dog would come to crave the stimulation of working and being with people so badly that he'd learn and obey perfectly whenever he was out of his cage. **Unfortunately, some trainers still swear by this method for dogs from all walks of life, and they advise customers to deliberately keep their dogs locked up, only interacting with them during obedience practice sessions.** Other trainers will check your dog into their training facility and charge thousands of dollars to take the dog out only for those brief hours they work with him.

Of course some individuals used kinder dog training methods even when compulsion-style methods were popular. These individuals who went against the tide in favor of a more humanistic approach included some of the visionary trainers, veterinarians and naturalists whose works, published in the 1970's and 1980's, we frequently refer to in this book.

And, even while compulsion/punishment-based training was popular for dogs, years ago some wild animal trainers, such as dolphin trainers, were already using positive, reward-based methods and clicker training, which was clearly the best way to elicit willing cooperation from large animals that people couldn't physically overpower.

Yet it wasn't until the mid 1980's and later that the general public first started listening to and respecting the voices in favor of "gentle" or "positive" training for dogs. Pioneers who advocated positive methods included veterinary behaviorist Dr. Ian Dunbar (who later founded the 6,000 member Association of Pet Dog Trainers or APDT); Paul Owens, the original "Dog Whisperer", who wrote the book of that name and Karen Pryor, whose book *"Don't Shoot the Dog* was published in 1984.

Another highly influential dog expert who promoted positive-reinforcement training methods was Jean Donaldson, who wrote *The Culture Clash* in 1996. At this point, the tide of public opinion about dog training truly started to turn and positive reward-based methods (including clicker training) became more widely known and accepted.

Overall, starting in the 1980's and continuing into the present, popular methods of training dogs have increasingly shifted from punishment, correction or intimidation to "softer" methods based on behavior modification.

A notable exception is Cesar Millan, who often uses physical techniques including collar corrections and alpha rolling aggressive dogs on his enormously popular *Dog Whisperer* television show. The general public seems to be split in opinions on his methods, but Millan has been publicly criticized by numerous respected veterinarians, trainers and experts in the dog field, including Dr. Ian Dunbar, representing the APDT. And, even though many financially successful and locally popular dog trainers are still training based on handlers physically intimidating and overpowering dogs, famous trainers like Cesar Millan and the Monks of New Skete (perhaps responding to overwhelming criticism) are now publicly starting to "soften" their methods.

For example, Cesar now frequently trains with treats on his show. In addition to heeding the criticism of the dog trainers' associations, he's likely also been influenced by the increasing popularity of his biggest television competitor, Victoria Stillwell. Stillwell, featured on *It's Me or the Dog* on Animal Planet, is a charming, yet uniquely outspoken, British lady who uses positive methods creatively to gently cure serious canine behavior issues. And Victoria also has a knack for convincing American families to take more responsibility for their dogs' behavior.

Rough old-school methods that used to be considered the norm, like kneeing, scruffing and shaking dogs can seem truly awful when people apply their conscience. So it's obvious why dog owners, finally offered an option, would prefer to hire trainers who use methods labeled as gentle or "positive", and why more and more dog trainers would advertise themselves this way. And this prevailing change in the public attitude may also be one of the reasons just one group- the Association of Pet Dog Trainers (or APDT), founded in the 1990's on a shared belief in education and positive ethical training methods for pet dogs, grew rapidly to approximately 6,000 members in less than twenty years, with similar growth throughout the industry.

Why many trainers feel they must cage dogs to make "positive training" effective

Even though "positive training" seems so attractive today, there *are* problems inherent in the method. Dr. Bruce Fogle explains in *K.I.S.S Guide to Living with a Dog* that "Positive reinforcement is a term taken from [human] behavioral psychology, it is a reward given immediately following a behavior, which is intended to increase the likelihood that the behavior will occur again". So, we can train a dog to perform a new, desired behavior by introducing a reward (for example a treat) that always follows that behavior. According to positive methods, the best way to extinguish negative behaviors is by ignoring, making sure that the dog never again receives reinforcement (reward) of any sort for performing the undesired behavior.

At first glance positive training might not seem powerful enough to extinguish problems, but, in most cases it works better than correction. For example, turning away from a dog each and every time he jumps on people, coupled with consistently offering him praise, petting or treats whenever he sits politely to greet people usually stops jumping more effectively than the old method of kneeing the dog in the chest.

To treat more serious problems such as dog-on-dog aggression with positive methods, owners must show 100% compliance over a longer period of time, yet the benefit of avoiding force with fearful or aggressive dogs is obvious. **The biggest challenge comes when dog trainers attempt to use positive methods to treat problems like chewing possessions or soiling the home, because these behaviors can be what's called self-rewarding.** Since chewing or relieving bladder or bowels on impulse can feel good to a dog, these behaviors act as their own reward. So just ignoring these behaviors won't extinguish them.

And **if a modern dog trainer believes physically punishing self-rewarding behaviors is not an alternative, they're faced with a challenge. They can fail to solve many of their cases, risking their popularity. They can get highly creative and try unique or obscure treatment modalities whose purpose might not be immediately apparent to customers and might be met with resistance. Or they can fall back on crating/caging dogs, which only appears to solve problems for the moment, but usually satisfies customers in the short term.**

Of course, how well a dog trainer can solve the presenting canine behavior problems in each of their new cases is a measure of their skill, and it can prove a welcome challenge for a trainer who enjoys solving difficult puzzles under pressure as a matter of professional pride. But realistically, many dog trainers overbook their schedules, leaving no time to give special attention or to try novel modalities. And others start with only a few weeks of technical education, so they cannot fall back on extensive knowledge of animal psychology and behavior.

Ideally, for intense chewing or housetraining issues, a hard-working and creative trainer might recommend any combination of: new products and preparations, video surveillance, alarms, room dividers, interactive toys, change in schedule or customized activities to challenge dogs' minds, veterinary help, dietary improvements and/or healthy physical activity/exercise. And they would coach owners how to present kind and consistent leadership through actions, tone of voice and body language. But success with innovative methods like these depends on many factors including scheduling, timing, consistency, patience and a unique ability to educate and motivate both dogs and people. And many practicing dog trainers can't, or won't, make this level of effort.

For example, the authors never use rough or compulsion methods. Yet our treatment goes far beyond stimulus-response and operant methods of reinforcement. For each and every dog we start with completely customized methods based on in-depth home observation, diagnosis, temperament testing, history and research. And we formulate a treatment plan that covers every aspect of dog/family interaction to make owners and dog enjoy ideal moments together for the dog's lifetime.

Our methods usually include some basic and advanced obedience. But, depending on the case, we may also include: intuitive communication with dogs; communication through body language, tone of voice and expression; helping dogs overcome fears and encounter new stimuli; outings; teaching adults and children calming methods of touching/interacting with dogs; teaching families games to play with their dogs to shape behaviors and increase intelligence; and teaching owners how to read small but significant changes in dogs' body language. We sometimes advise changes in diet, holistic treatments and/or cooperation with a veterinarian's treatment plan. And we even teach dog owners therapeutic canine massage. The in-depth nature of our practice and expertise allows us to improve situations where basic positive reinforcement training methods alone might not work, without having to use force or compulsion- and without giving up and crating dogs.

We're proud to help dogs not only become better behaved, but to show a new luster and pride- manifesting to their own highest potential, sometimes wagging and "grinning," for the very first time in their lives. Our customers usually graduate from in-depth sessions with us feeling empowered, with a new appreciation of their dogs. And, after a few sessions, it's not uncommon for them to learn more theory and technique than a good number of starting dog trainers.

Of course, customers sometimes want a quick fix. But we always warn owners of the delicacy of working with dog behaviors, likening our practice to human psychology. Unfortunately other trainers often cave to unrealistic owner demands just to get business- and some even accept payment over the Internet before they've met the particular dog.

Yet professional ethics dictate that dog trainers cannot- and should not- guarantee specific results when working with living animals and that it is only safe for "master" dog trainers should attempt to cure serious aggression.

Many dog trainers will guarantee to stop a dog from chewing on items or soiling on carpets without realizing that the dog comes from an abusive background that makes his problems deeply embedded and hard to treat. Owners have sometimes called us in tears, reporting problems with new dogs that are so fearful they slink along in a crouch, run from people and refuse to look at them or act aggressive. Some dogs act violently and insanely towards any new person or dog that they see. Others are so hyperactive they can't remain still even for a second and they run around in such an uncontrolled fashion that they painfully trample their owners' kids unless they get the right kind of help. Many adult dogs these days even have daily bowel and bladder movements on their owners' beds!

We're often asked to cure dogs with lists of behavior problems miles long, along with challenging physical problems, multiple allergies and genetic disabilities. Some families have already spent thousands on veterinary bills and on other dog trainers before they call us. And some seem to be so angry, or in such despair, that we fear for their well-being along with their dogs'. But we enjoy empowering and educating owners and walking them through the process of how we plan to help their dogs through canine psychology. And even though we often do hours of research to formulate the best treatment plans for individual dogs, we often charge no more than many trainers who offer little more help than instructions how to crate-training

For highly complex problems (like true separation anxiety or problems arising because of past abuse or lack of socialization) a careful mix of different modalities works best. And, once we help owners shape each dog into the balanced and happy dog of his highest potential, **housetraining and chewing problems usually become non-issues. This is because it's not in the nature of physically and emotionally healthy dogs to soil their owners' homes or damage possessions!**

But these days it seems like many people forget this. **When a dog trainer uses strictly positive, reward-based methods, yet fail to include complex and creative techniques customized to the particular dog, they may find that they *can't* effectively cure the specific problems the owner called them for! And we suspect this is why many trainers turn to crate training.**

A dog trainer may arrive at a home, or enrolled a dog in their group class, and the owner will tell them, "All I want you to do is to stop Coco from pooping on the rug". If the trainer wishes to absolutely guarantee the dog won't defecate on the rug tomorrow, they can make the owner immediately lock her up in a crate. This always works because the dog cannot physically be in two places and she can't defecate on the rug as long as she remains locked in the cage. She also can't chew on the owner's couch cushions, jump on visitors or get underfoot *when she's in the cage*.

But using imprisonment to stop teething or to stop bowel or bladder mistakes only prolongs and intensifies the problems. Once the dog's crated, she's also deprived of exercise and physical movement, making her even more stressed and unstable and more likely to continue the problem behaviors or start something worse.

But today many dog trainers and dog professionals will prescribe crate time as a cure-all for every problem, probably fearing their customers won't pay them if their dogs make any mistake. **Ironically, owners will pay trainers large sums of money to teach them to lock their dogs up to physically prevent problems. But this is something they could have done on their own with no trainer input at all, and no expense, other than the cage.**

Solving canine behavior problems in today's world with such a large proportion of dogs coming to owners already damaged by puppy mills and other abuses is a difficult and intricate task. And to be well-paid for this challenging task in today's world (as most dog trainers are) should require a smart, careful, cautious, kind, well-studied, yet imaginative individual with a knack for getting tough answers right. The trainer also shouldn't schedule too many home sessions in a day or overfill their group classes. And they should devote generous time and attention to each dog without rushing straight to band-aid solutions.

It's time to take dog training to a higher level. In a crowded field with so many thousands of choices of dog trainers, dog owners should start voting with their wallets. They should demand that dog trainers work hard to teach their dogs and pups good manners that fit with every aspect of their lifestyles, so their dogs can be trusted free in the home. And they should stop wasting good money hiring trainers who don't even attempt to think of better alternatives than locking their adored family members up in cages.

A Scary Lesson in Moneymaking: One apparently well-liked dog trainer sells a video training program that seems like a throwback to worst of the old-school correction methods. One his video, the trainer demonstrates using such hard leash corrections that he warns owners to muzzle their previously non-aggressive dogs, because often dogs that have never bitten before respond by striking out in aggression. It sickened us as we watched young children on the video forced to wear padded gloves in order to administer violent corrections to their dogs! And then we found out something even more shocking. This trainer was offering a six-week certification program to teach new dog trainers his methods- and he was charging each student $50,000!

Chapter 8: How Crating Caught On Like Wildfire & Helped the Dog Training Industry Grow Explosively

Part A. Power of multiplication and the dog training industry

We're not surprised that an established crate manufacturer would state on their website, "Most dog owners, expert authorities and veterinarians recommend dog cages (also known as crates) as the best way to raise a puppy" because this statement may be true. Many dog owners use a cage as a substitute for training and communication; then crating makes their dog's behavior even worse, leading to even more crating.

Or a dog may suffer in a crate for his entire lifetime while his owners fail to enjoy their time with him the way they could have. Dogs don't do well spending years in such frustration, while isolation erodes the normal bond between dog and owner. And often dogs that are excessively crated become ill, prematurely run away or are given away or put to sleep.

Sometimes animal "professionals" use crates to keep a larger number of dogs in their homes than they can care for properly. Abuses like this happen in some non-profit rescues that take in more dogs than they can possibly find homes for, and in the homes of animal hoarders who keep excessive numbers of dogs as pets. (One woman featured on the Animal Planet series *Animal Hoarders* kept 87 small dogs in her trailer home.) Crates enable people like this to keep extremely large numbers of dogs indoors, with no barking in outdoor kennels to alert police or zoning officials.

NOTE THAT: **MOST RESCUES ARE RUN BY CARING, REASONABLE PEOPLE WHO DO THE BEST FOR DOGS, and they need all the help they can get from dog lovers around the country!**

But the fact that crating dogs for most of their waking hours is no longer viewed as abusive can make the public fail to notice problems when "dog people" do wrong. Puppy mills that breed between 2-4 million new pups a year are the most obvious example. But we've also seen excessive crowding and inhumane caging at well-liked boarding kennels where cramped cages referred to as "suites". And dog owners must also be cautious about abuses by dog trainers who take dogs away to train them at their kennels but only free them to work with a person for an hour a day. (And one dog trainer earned hundreds of thousands per year by stacking pups in crates sky-high in his home while customers paid for pricey "housetraining" programs; when pups "failed" he'd convince some customers to surrender them to him and then resell them.)

Almost as many searches for Dog Crates as for Britney Spears! According to Google Adwords statistics, during just one recent month, June 2010, there were 368,000 Google Internet searches for the keyword "dog crates"!

Chain letters, Pyramid Scams and crate training advice

Pro-crating propaganda has been spreading exponentially- especially over the Internet- based on the same principles as chain letters or pyramid scams. Once a certain number of "experts" each tell five people to crate their dogs, and then each of those five people tells five more, and this continues indefinitely, by logic pro-crating dogma will soon infect the minds of every American. And when people are surrounded by this much hype, it can deprive them of *personal* choice based on their own instincts, core beliefs and values. Today erroneous "facts" are also speeded up many times over through digital media, so what used to take weeks to communicate now takes seconds on the Internet. And anonymous opinions can easily be presented, and accepted as expert knowledge.

What happens when 6,000 dog trainers must decide whether or not to crate?

In 1993 veterinarian Ian Dunbar founded the Association of Pet Dog Trainers (APDT) to promote continuing education, ethical professional conduct and gentle dog training methods as opposed to old-style punishment, or compulsion, methods. And in less than 17 years, just this organization alone has grown to almost 6,000 members. Yet we're concerned that this incredibly influential organization, which was originally founded to stop training abuses to dogs, isn't doing all it can to prevent Excessive Crating, which is perhaps the biggest abuse of dogs today. For example, even though the APDT has issued official position statements on several other ethical and political dog issues, they have not issued any position statements on Excessive Crating.

We also were quite surprised when we watched Dr. Dunbar, a pioneer of positive training and also a knowledgeable, humane behaviorist with a genteel style that we personally admire; recommend crate-training puppies in one of his early videos, which is still a popular gold standard in the industry.

Even though we are personally opposed to the method, we understand that when Dr. Dunbar recommends crate training, he certainly means it for a limited purpose and with appropriate cautions. And other well-meaning dog trainers who recommend the crate certainly aren't advising it for 18-23 hours a day. But the problem is that when their message gets passed down through enough people, this is exactly what happens in real life!

There is no official government licensing or oversight for dog trainers. Dog training certifications are entirely subjective based on the individual schools or coaches who provide them. And organizations like APDT can do nothing more to sanction a trainer whose conduct towards dogs is abusive than to terminate their membership if the organization receives complaints. In the meantime **certified dog trainers in their hometowns who advertise themselves as "gentle" often use choke, prong and even electric shock collars when they can't get the results they want. It seems like now that old-school punishment training methods are no longer considered acceptable in the world of positive dog training, many frustrated individual trainers are turning to other methods that can be equally harsh. And, when it comes to crate training, individual dog trainers are passing on damaging advice to hundreds or even thousands of their customers each year.**

Caging dogs is the one method- short of euthanasia- that immediately, if temporarily, stops every canine problem. **But Excessive Crating is just as inhumane as any violent training method. So we hope that well-respected dog training organizations like the APDT recognize the problem.** We also feel that APDT should release an official policy statement to all its member trainers and to the media on the dangers of Excessive Caging and Crating, including the specific number of hours per day that caging becomes abusive and negatively impacts canine behavior. A formal statement like this, by such an influential organization, would also work against puppy mills and pet shops that are housing and caging dogs in inhumane conditions.

"Dog Whisperers Are Born, Not Created"

Not every dog behavior problem in a customer's home is easy to solve. These days there are so many schools and training opportunities for dog trainers to learn the business that many people interested in dogs can forget that it's not actually easy to solve dog behavior problems in customer's homes. We believe, to succeed, an individual must possess something more- a unique personal talent and an almost psychic connection with dogs.

People like this truly have "magic" and this is why laymen should pay them- to train dogs using gentle, yet uniquely effective methods. **Saying that crating a dog is necessary to train him *anything* is just as much a cop-out as when some old-school dog trainers said you had to knee a dog in the chest or hang him by his collar.** All these excuses mean is that *the individual dog trainer is having trouble getting results.*

Unless a trainer is blessed with a natural influence to lead animals and speak their language, then attempting to suddenly get significant results when a dog's owners have given up can be an uphill battle. And a home dog trainer also needs to have extraordinary patience and empathy with people of all cultures and walks of life under highly demanding circumstances.

The work of a specialist in home dog training is humbling. Even at its best there is no glamour, other than the satisfaction of making a difference to dogs and their families. And, years ago, if you wanted to be a successful dog trainer, having an extraordinary inborn talent was pretty much a mandate. At that time, except in certain specialties (like selling protection trained dogs), the job of dog trainer didn't promise great income. And before the era of celebrity dog trainers, it certainly didn't offer any glamour. Dog training wasn't perceived as a particularly noble or enviable career to pursue. And it wasn't a career that offered great opportunities for marketing, promotion and networking through huge national organizations and Internet directories the way it does today.

The popularity of dog training as a career changed hugely when Cesar Millan came along with his primetime *Dog Whisperer* show. It seemed like everybody in America quickly got to know Cesar with his white teeth, his charisma, his lightning-fast interventions with aggressive dogs and his catchy philosophical sayings. On television Cesar happily controls large and small spoiled housedogs that fight and snap as viciously as psychotic wild creatures until they finally dissolve into intoxicated submission. Meanwhile he never breaks a sweat and keeps talking the whole time, mesmerizing his viewers, along with his uber-stressed celebrity clients.

Cesar came along at a time when the growth of positive dog training was already changing the face of the industry and making it user-friendly. And, while Cesar certainly trains with physical methods and not standard positive ones, he still struck a nerve with the public.

We think part of it was timing. *Dog Whisperer* premiered at one of those "moments" in society, a time of general jadedness and belief in immediate gratification that was an outgrowth of so much expendable income at the end of the real estate bubble. Just like people wanted the biggest homes, and the best finishes for every surface in those homes; just like they demanded plastic surgery to fix their bodies in record numbers, they also demanded certain things from their dogs. As pointed out in *One Nation Under Dog*, there was no amount of money that certain segments of society wouldn't lavish on their dogs, as long as it promoted "the dream" and didn't cause them stress. People wanted dogs they could show off and lavish lots of presents and professional services on, even though they could not spare enough time in their hectic schedules to really bond with these pets.

Many people wanted an easy solution, and they thought they should be able to buy it. After all, dog trainers like Cesar that they watched on television graphically proved on their shows that even the most out-of-balance dogs could be fixed. So this was a time when many people rushed to hire their own home dog trainers, just to prove they could afford their own personal "Cesar". Yet many of these dog owners still weren't ready to take on the 24-hour responsibilities of shaping their dogs' behavior.

At this time other individuals watched Cesar's show and began to crave the power his almost magical control over dogs seemed to confer. Dog trainers fed into this belief system by rushing into the profession in record numbers and promising dog owners that they could shape any canine into the owner's ideal with their services. Unlike other careers, dog training allowed almost immediate access to the "fun stuff" with no official requirement for college, no legally mandated testing or licensing- and not even a high-school degree. In a span of approximately five years, a huge number of people rushed into the field of (home) dog training, many of them with the mentality of would-be rock stars. And many of these new trainers were determined to train dogs like Cesar did at any cost because failure would destroy their self image.

The problem with a show like *The Dog Whisperer* is that many fans took it wrong. People who call us for employment often demonstrate an almost fanatical drive to experience the "highs" of dog training with little thought about the reality. And since these people tend to feel training *has* to go perfectly, according to what they see condensed into a half-hour on television, they can be highly susceptible to frustration. **This frustration can then make trainers turn to the only one-minute solution for stopping canine problems- the crate.**

Years ago Emma worked in an occupation that's actually surprisingly similar to home dog training- visiting homes to investigate child abuse for the Department of Social Services. That job offered gratification similar to dog training whenever you assisted children and families. And that job felt equally frightening when you faced the magnitude of your responsibility standing in kitchens where the drone of television sitcoms was the backdrop for the terrible sounds of children and their parents crying on the worst day of their lives.

The only difference is that people didn't excitedly line up wanting to do *that* job the way they often crave to train dogs! Yet the level of responsibility and expertise called for as a caseworker is really no different than walking into a home to train a dog. As a home dog trainer, you will strongly influence the quality of a family's life with their dog for what may be the next 10 to 15 years. It's your responsibility to first dry up the family's tears (and the tears of the dog that don't show) and then turn all the problems around to get the family back to the blessing dog ownership should be.

Some experts publish theoretical explanations for crating as a behavioral cure for aggressive or fearful dogs. But we urge all our readers to carefully question such explanations. Taken objectively, these theories shouldn't present much appeal or seem very logical. But we're afraid, when it comes to difficult or mysterious dog problems, crating dogs can look like a welcome life preserver to dog trainers who really don't know what to do next.

Starry-eyed positive-style dog trainers (some with no more than 2 weeks' education) may walk into some homes expecting to have fun with dogs. But instead they often find themselves bombarded with demands to immediately fix situations that are beyond them. For example, even housetraining can be harrowing when multiple adult dogs have been using an owner's bed as their only bathroom for years, or when a puppy is having accidents because he is ill. Other times dogs have bizarre behavior problems- like some dogs that get so compulsively "amorous" on people's legs or other surfaces that they cause lasting injury to themselves or humans.

Some trainers will accept payment for every case over the Internet before ever seeing the dog, so there's no way for them to know if they can help the animal's problems. And sometimes an experienced trainer may visit the home to make the initial sale, but then send out a low paid novice to do the actual training. But home training can cost in the hundreds. So we feel that ethical professionals should only accept cases if they can map out specific treatment plans. And they should never guarantee unrealistic results that they could only accomplish by caging.

Why dog trainers might want to run from some dogs, so instead, they crate them

Owners of dogs with problems should feel for empathy for dog trainers. If a home dog training specialist is doing their job right, it's never easy. Like us, they might walk into a home, and immediately have to talk two hysterical, extremely dog-aggressive hundred-pound Golden Retrievers down from their favorite perches on the headrests of two adjacent sofas without inciting more violence between them. Or they might have to make progress in an hour with a little Dachshund that was so terrified and feral that his owners hadn't been able to touch him since they bought him a year before at a pet store.

Sometimes a trainer may instinctively feel like running away to keep their own sanity- or to save their own skin... But they may be the only hope that a family, and their dog, have left. **And we feel that just closing the door of a cage as a behavioral training method is essentially no different than taking the owners' check, pulling the front door of the house shut and running away from the troubled dog.**

Sometimes owners may unrealistically demand that their dog stop a problem behavior immediately and one hundred percent. And a trainer who's new or lacks that magic combination of talent, skill and conviction may fear the dog and/or the owner, or they may fear that they will fail. And this is the moment that many dog trainers turn to a crate or cage as a "foolproof" solution.

A true case of ours demonstrates how the crating solution only prolongs and intensifies problems. In this case the family crated their severely overboisterous 7-month old Labrador too much and she ran around wildly and jumped on everyone whenever she was free. They had started with another trainer whose website listed impressive certifications, awards and positive training experience. But, according to the family, this trainer spent the entire first session with the Lab locked away in the crate in another room as she took a history. (Good trainers always take a detailed history, but this usually be done while interacting with and observing the dog.) The family told us that, during the second session, the trainer let the pup out briefly, but then she quickly returned it to the crate the moment it jumped on her vigorously enough to scratch her arms.

But the problem we found was that this lack of results was leading to much more dangerous risks than just the jumping. We immediately noticed that the young Lab's constant rough play was terrorizing, hurting and annoying the family's other 7-month old pup, a nervy Chihuahua. The little Chihuahua had been pushed to her breaking point and was starting to growl and snap. And this was endangering their 5-year old daughter, who liked to cuddle and kiss her. And the other dog trainer (with all the great credentials online) hadn't even noticed or addressed the Chihuahua's aggressive behavior towards a child in her treatment plan.

It was clear to us that too much crate time had bottled up the high-energy young Lab's problems so that, each time she exploded out of her crate, she immediately took her frustration out on the smaller dog. The harassed Chihuahua in turn, started to take out *her* stress by snapping and growling at the child. We worked with the Chihuahua to get past her serious fears and anxiety so she could react consistently and respectfully towards people. And we taught the family how to read her body language to head off problems in the future. Meanwhile we showed them how to exercise and work obedience with the young Lab and how to shape better house manners, especially around the child and her tiny dog. It was a pleasure to help this nice family. But we only got the chance to work with them because the other trainer hadn't been able to complete her sessions. And this made us concerned that if they had continued training with her, despite her qualifications, she might have continued relying on crating as a solution, while missing dangers to both dogs and the young child.

Just like a stuffed dog, a dog in a crate CANNOT do any of the bad things that owners complain about WHILE HE IS IN THE CRATE. So many dog trainers offer the crate as a solution to behavior problems and the owners accept it. Not only don't these owners complain that they paid a trainer for this "solution", but they actually thank them because their rug is not getting soiled, their couch is not getting chewed, etc. But, in the long run, caging our dogs and never allowing them to make mistakes and get kindly redirected is likely to create a race of dogs that may never grow into house manners. And all the behavior problems return-even worse the second the excessively crated dogs are set free.

And we fear that, as more dog trainers give up searching for creative solutions that work for dogs and families and instead resort to the 100% environmental solution of crating, much of the real "art" of dog training will be lost and innovative new ideas will never get attention.

The "elephant in the middle of the living room":

In twelve-step recovery jargon ignoring the "elephant in the middle of the living room" is a metaphor for dysfunctional families going to great lengths to cover up their single biggest problem. In the world of dog training, the "elephant" is the crate. And the underlying dysfunction is owners trying to maintain lifestyles that are incompatible with helping their dogs' serious behavior problems while many practicing dog trainers lack effective strategies to heal their dilemma.

The ancient Greek philosophers set a precedent for learning through discussion. So we'd think the trend in recent years for dog trainers to form networks to exchange information through organizations like APDT or online discussion groups, would give struggling trainers a place to brainstorm creative alternatives other than just locking problem dogs up in crates. But unfortunately, in large groups of trainers, nobody seems to be addressing the "elephant in the middle of the living room".

Instead, many well-meaning dog trainers, writers and other professionals continue to share positive feedback about other interesting dog topics like holistic pet care or dog-friendly venues or events. But whenever professionals, including writers, skirt around the biggest potential hot button in the industry- the "great crate debate" it does a disservice to dogs.

In today's climate, speaking out openly against crate training can initially make a professional feel like a pariah among other dog people, yet not speaking out Excessive Crating- both in puppy mills and private homes- is ethically and morally irresponsible.

More dog owners than not actually prefer having their dogs trained without crates if they are given a choice. Eventually, as dog owners speak up for their needs, business will go to people who excel at training dogs kindly and effectively without caging them.

If you own a dog or a new puppy, **there's never a reason to hire a dog trainer who will only suggest crating as the sole solution for housetraining or behavior problems.**

If you ask, many trainers will openly tell you they plan to teach you to crate train, with no alternatives. And a number of trainers who insist on crating also lecture or even yell at owners. Some families (as in the story of Champ in Chapter 4) may think they have to endure verbal abuse because an "expert" knows best. But being yelled at or snapped at reveals a dark side to what should be a nice industry. And an angry outburst can reveal ignorance or anger that might come out towards your dog during training.

Methods that hurt dogs, and why some dog trainers shouldn't be training:

Unfortunately, just like with other professions, the services of some practicing dog trainers can do more harm than good to dogs and their families. In our opinion, this includes trainers who recommend Excessive Crating, along with those who use highly physical old-school dominance methods and those who act blatantly sadistic to dogs.

Some trainers still make a good living using violent training methods. Recent extreme examples include two female trainers prosecuted in separate states. One tortured a dog with several shock collars, including one on his gonads; the other accidentally killed a puppy when she "alpha rolled" it to assert dominance. Other trainers who use methods rough enough to make some dog owners wince still teach classes and force owners to replicate these same rough methods, often creating fears and more serious behavior problems in the animals. And other dog trainers who are comfortable working with basic obedience in group or generic settings may not be expert enough to extinguish severe canine behavioral problems in private homes- and yet they may advertise this service.

Unlike applied animal behaviorists with advanced academic degrees, many practicing dog trainers don't research and scientifically diagnose the causes of behavior problems nor formulate individualized treatment plans to share with owners. Rather they may prefer to just "wing it" each time they're with a dog, or just train the basic obedience commands.

But they may find it difficult or impossible to teach these commands to deeply troubled dogs. For example, dogs with dominance issues often have barriers to lying down on command, and hyperactive dogs may have problems remaining in a "stay". Usually, a trainer with talent, patience and an open mind can subtly adjust their methods to eventually help most dogs. But some serious behavior problems have medical causes and a common mistake is for rushed or impatient dog trainers to neglect to take a medical history or ask for veterinarians' opinions. Another common mistake is when trainers who've worked only a few months advertising guarantee that they can cure even the most serious cases of aggression, even though professional ethics dictate that only highly experienced "master trainers" should work with such cases.

Even though, as this book goes to press, there's still no required or standardized licensure or certification for dog trainers in any state, a large number of schools and programs offer to train, and "certify", dog trainers for a price. More of these programs surface each day and, just like so many other aspects of the dog training industry, they vary greatly. **Most of the educational institutions and programs for dog trainers are not accredited colleges and thus they're not subject to any oversight, nor are they eligible for government financial aid**. And certificates from these programs can't transfer to other occupations or degree programs in the way degrees from accredited colleges can.

Some of the schools and programs offer irresistibly cheap certification- as little as $300 online- while other programs, including many that aren't accredited colleges charge $10,000, $20,000 or even more for several months' education. Many new dog trainers pay additional for club memberships and Internet resources, directories and marketing tools before they ever start seeing dogs in customer's homes. (Others choose to become part of a huge international dog training franchise like Bark Busters, where individual investors, with no requirement for previous dog training experience or education, can purchase a local franchise for approximately $50,000.)

Learning the theories of animal behavior is vital in training dogs right, but it seems like the educational options offered right now for dog trainers are a mixed bag. In the industry formal education of any kind at a university level is the exception. And, even though there are so many new dog trainers; and so many of them invest in schooling to some extent, most don't seem prepared well enough to stop the nationwide epidemic of dog behavior problems discussed in the last chapter or prepared well enough to stop the "kill" shelters from filling up when these dogs are surrendered. We wonder if some of these new dog trainers, who've been led to believe that their job would be easy and fun, fail at solving customers' problems and then turn to crating as an emergency stopgap measure, rather than facing the fact that they may have invested the money, effort and personal commitment to prepare for the job in vain.

Obviously, the solution is clear. Customers desperately want help from dog trainers. Now dog trainers must become more careful and more expert so they can deliver well-behaved dogs to customers rather than taking customers money and then just telling them to lock their dogs up.

The Power of Semantics: Just using different words can "spin" the concept of crating, making an idea that otherwise appears distasteful seem appealing. And expert dog journalist Bardi McLennan expresses the same view in her book *Dogs and Kids* (although she actually *applauds* the way that twisting words has accelerated the increase in crating). "Over the last ten years there has been a great improvement in the pet owner's conception of the dog crate," she says. "It really only took two things. [And] one was semantics. The now universal use of the word *crate* instead of *cage*."

According to Ms. McClellan, the second reason for the enormous spike in America's acceptance of the crate between the 1980's and 1990's had to do with people's acceptance of the much publicized "fact" that dogs are den animals and feel secure in crates. McClellan explains that, *with the modern practice of likening crates to bedrooms, dog owners can also happily associate crates with baby paraphernalia, like playpens and cribs*. Thinking this way, dog lovers don't have to feel they're abusing their dogs. After all, "we do not "cage" members of our family!" as McClellan puts it. But what an enormous difference words can make if we can cage our dogs, and yet believe that we are babying them... In fact, the latest trendy product we've seen in pet catalogs is consistent with this view of dogs as babies. Now, loving dog owners who hate the sight of a frightening-looking cage in the middle of their living room can have their choice of colors and lock their canine babies up in lovely pastel pink and blue coated wire cages!

Part B: Extreme quotes and policy from some of America's Favorite Dog People

Don't believe everything you hear- because some of the worst purveyors of crating misinformation are "experts", who range from dog trainers in your neighborhood to the best-known, most influential people in the industry. For some reason, these people seem to believe that if they band together and keep repeating their message strongly enough, they can force American dog owners to buy what they're selling. But we believe dog owners aren't that naive.

In the remainder of this chapter, we shine a spotlight on some ideas and actions that show particular hypocrisy and flawed logic, while at the same time influencing the opinions of large numbers of people. Even though some of these "expert" quotes are so extreme they might make readers laugh, thousands of people, including other dog professionals, took these statements seriously at one point, and many dogs and pups are living in crates right now because of it. This includes the last case we discuss- recent actions by the nation's best known- and most controversial- dog trainer that may influence millions.

1. Without even knowing it, some businesses and public facilities may hand out free dog training and husbandry information that recommends crating dogs with no alternatives or cautions. Several years ago we picked up a free puppy training video at an enormously popular Southern supermarket chain that was piled on a table for shoppers to take home with them. The video featured young dog trainers from a private company wearing continual smiles as they demonstrated standard positive training techniques. But then we were shocked to see them introduce crate training for puppies- never mentioning that were alternatives or that there could be dangers.

We wonder whether the liability the supermarket risked by putting out a video like this was worth the potential gain- a few brief spots for them on the video promoting their house brand of dog food. We also wonder if the supermarket management that okayed free distribution of the innocent-seeming video ever watched it and noticed the pups being locked in crates, or whether they even knew that dog cages can be dangerously abused by casual owners who aren't given adequate warnings. And we wonder if this otherwise pleasant supermarket contemplated whether many of their formerly loyal shoppers- like us- might consider caging pups in small cages cruel and disgusting and might start looking for other places to shop.

This supermarket is just one example of many businesses and public entities that are now giving out crating information mixed in with other materials. And managers or administrators may not even be aware of all the information people are receiving through their business, organization or website.

Lately we've noticed very many innocuous-seeming pamphlets that tell owners to crate dogs (without adequate cautions or alternatives) offered free at venues like humane shelters. And crating recommendations constantly show up embedded in online links to many organizations, shelters, rescues and animal networks- this even includes some large groups and organizations that decry puppy mills or rescue puppy mill dogs. We feel the management of businesses, government entities and non-profits must be more careful and "clean up" potentially damaging information before they offer it to the public.

2. The Internet can easily go "viral". And when erroneous information promoting Excessive Home Dog Crating is multiplied exponentially and at light-speed online, it's as damaging as an infectious disease. Compelling scientific evidence proves that excessive crating seriously damages dogs. Yet the laws of Internet optimization make it almost impossible for the average dog owner to find negative information about crating because it's obscured by thousands of optimized results that recommend dog crating.

Much of the highly optimized pro-crating information and advice is connected to advertisements or publicity for dog products, professional services or non-profit organizations soliciting donations. Even more search results supporting crating are simply opinionated posts by individuals.

Pro-crating information tends to be bottomless because of profit and personal motives involved (as we detail in Chapter 10). And much pro-crating information that's been posted and publicized also tends to be simplistic and repetitive and the authors don't seem ashamed to contradict themselves. The tone is often patronizing, sarcastic or angry when directed against people who speak out against crating.

An example of confusing information delivered with an authoritarian tone comes from the DPCA Breeder's Education Website. Although the writer tells us that 4 hours is the limit to how long a dog can stay in the crate before it needs to potty and stretch, they also reassure that many dogs live "happy lives" crated all day and night with the exception of one potty break at lunchtime and then a few energetic hours with visits and play when their people get home in the evening.

Interestingly, two paragraphs before, the same writer conceded that there's a point where crating becomes too much, which they describe as follows:

"Many dogs are on schedules that are more demanding, even to the point of 10 hours crated while their owners are at work five days a week. This level of crating is very challenging over the long term and some, if not many, will end up with anxiety as a result and become difficult to crate, destructive when they are out, hyperactive and generally neurotic as they have few options in dealing with this level of stress."

But the "experts" who posted this entry don't offer solutions, despite their own conclusion that excessive crating *produces* the neurotic behaviors. Instead, they next tell owners:

"To suggest that these [unstable] dogs would be better left loose in the house is equally irresponsible as [these dogs] are so stressed as to now lack (assuming they ever had them) the skills to deal with good behavior when loose." In other words, these people first tell owners it can be okay to leave a dog crated all those daytime hours but, if that amount of crating makes the dog truly uncontrollable, they offer no solution at all.

Researching *Dogs Hate Crates* we found literally thousands of similar articles and postings in favor of crating, some so disturbing they left Emma tearful and both of us sleepless. This is a case where the Internet seems to have worked almost entirely in favor of those who promote crating. But now it's time (as we discuss in Chapter 16) for dog lovers to harness the unique power of the Internet to let everyone know there are kinder *and more effective* alternatives than Home Dog Crating.

3. Many popular books on canine behavior and training/housetraining on bookstore and library shelves, especially those published after 1995, don't offer very helpful solutions. We were especially disappointed to find some of the most disturbing and unreasonable statements about dog crating in a book, *The Latchkey Dog*, that we'd had very high expectations for because of its title (and reviews).

The term latchkey dog, actually coined in the 1970's by Warren Eckstein- a pioneer of canine psychology we quote throughout this book- refers to a bored modern dog without any active functional tasks to perform that simply "waits" all day for his people to come home from work. This concept resonated with us because we wrote our book *The Cure for Useless Dog Syndrome* to help stressed families find purpose for their dogs in our ultra-busy, ultra technical world. *The Cure* includes hundreds of positive ideas and easy activities to promote dog/owner bonding despite challenges like condo-living and physical limitations.

We started out eager to read *The Latchkey Dog*, expecting useful information that we could recommend to families in trouble. Instead we read nothing but repeated case studies where the author describes treating dogs with serious emotional and aggression problems with-of all things- crating! The book falls back on the idea that extremely stressed dogs that feel abandoned without their pack seek to hide.

And then the author builds on this one idea to prescribe the use of crating as a panacea for every problem. She fails to mention that attempting this without comprehensive screening and assessment may put families at risk from kennel aggression syndrome in susceptible dogs and/or prevent diagnosis of medical conditions.

The author, Ms. Andersen's most disturbing quote seems to come from a scary science fiction future. *"Is time spent in a cage simply time spent in a cage,"* she asks, *"or is it a temporary reprieve from the stress of daily life? ... If you look at it as a modern dog would, you'd probably view a crate as the one sacred shrine you have left- one that pays homage to your ancestry and represents the only constant future in your life."*

All Publicly Known Dog Experts Should Tell the World Their "Magic Numbers": Sometimes semantics can be confusing. So we hope all experts, policy makers and celebrities in the dog world will clearly advise the public of their recommendations for crating in a specific format- by stating the *total number of hours in a crate per 24-hour day* that they feel would have *no ill effect on the average dog*, and also the *total* number of hours (if any), per 24-hour period, that they feel would most *benefit the average dog*. Many suburban owners who don't intend to abuse their dogs are now crating for 18-23 hours a day total, often on the advice of experts who advised them to crate their dogs without giving a specific time limit. So, we hope all dog behavior experts and celebrity trainers, especially those whose views we discuss in this book, will make public statements of their updated "magic number" to clearly communicate with their readers, fans and followers so that their advice can be followed precisely. We've also noticed that **a few of the most influential and learned applied animal behaviorists and veterinary behaviorists with advanced degrees whose work we most admire seem to conspicuously skirt around the issue of crating, not mentioning the subject *at all* in their in-depth**

books about dog training and behavior. Although these experts also never recommend using the crate or mention crating in any details of their own personal dogs' stimulating lifestyles, we believe this is not clear enough. If these particular scientific experts formally publicized their exact "magic numbers" on when they believe crating is beneficial and when it is damaging, it would influence the perception of the new dog professionals who study under them and this would start to help dogs immediately.

4. Pro-crating doctrine that contradicts itself or does not make sense even extends to more well-known and more influential authors in the field of modern dog training. For example, Jean Donaldson, who wrote *The Culture Clash* and *Dogs are from Jupiter* is a pioneer of advocating reinforcement-based dog training techniques (operant and classical) vs. old-school punishment-oriented training of decades past. Ms Donaldson believes that dogs are neither devious nor angelic, and it's not in their nature to perform tasks based on an innate desire to please their owners, but simply based on the availability of rewards for the desired behavior. Ideas like these have been revolutionary for the field of modern dog training, since they mean that there would be no point in punishing a dog for behavior humans don't want.

In her writings, which have strongly influenced the dog training industry, Ms. Donaldson seems completely forgiving of dogs, particularly those that bite, and strongly against using cruel training tactics in any situation- even where dogs have attacked humans. And yet she is a strong supporter of crating. In *Culture Clash* she makes one of the stranger statements we've encountered, saying that crating gives the dog a "solid history of reward." Even in behavioral/experimental terms, as she likely meant this, she must have forgotten that time in the crate is *not* neutral, but a highly negative reinforcer in itself, as described in classic research studies in Chapter 3.

And, while writing about the benefits of crating in *Culture Clash*, this positive-reinforcement behaviorist contradicts herself by mentioning that it would be "against conscience" to leave a pup in a crate for "more than a few hours". But unfortunately, like so many authors who write in favor of crating, Ms. Donaldson does not, anywhere in this book, make clear if by "more than a few hours" in a crate she means more than a few hours *consecutively* or in total during a day.

The problem is that when owners make a point just to avoid crating consecutively, as long as they allow a pup out of the crate for ten minutes at a time just to empty his bladder and bowels, they could still be crating him for 23 hours total in a 24-hour period. And a good number of owners don't realize that 23 hours of confinement in a 24-hour period is not okay even if the dog or puppy gets frequent ten-minute potty breaks.

Since so many popular writers, trainers, behaviorists, dog sellers and dog adoption personnel warn against not crating for too many hours *while never indicating whether they mean number of hours consecutively, or total hours daily,* we wonder if this omission of detail is deliberate, rather than accidental. Perhaps some "experts" hope that deliberate vagueness about the number of caged hours they recommend can protect them from bad press or liability claims for dogs that die or suffer injury due to excessive crating.

Along similar lines, in *Culture Clash,* **as in many other books by the most popular experts, we could personally find no mention of at what age (if ever) Ms. Donaldson recommends an owner should stop crating a dog.** So a truly confused owner could crate their dog for life simply because they were given no further instruction by "experts" about when, if ever, to stop.

Interestingly, Ms. Donaldson advises that owners move the crate from room to room with them and into their bedroom at night so the dog can have their company. These statements which acknowledge dogs' fundamental need to be involved with their family are much more consistent with her stance against cruel dog training. But we'd prefer to see a behaviorist who is this influential in the industry take much more care with her statements about crating- because her statements influence the beliefs of so many other dog trainers and, in turn, the actions of families and their dogs' quality of life. If Ms. Donaldson's opinions on crating have changed in any way since her highly influential book was published, then we hope she will clearly advise the public.

5. An enthusiastic celebrity dog trainer who mentions "love" more than we have seen in any other book, sets up bizarre contradictions between her ideas about bonding with dogs and her ideas about crating.

Even though it seemed like it would be a highly positive book, we were deeply disappointed by the time we finished reading popular celebrity dog trainer Tamar Geller's book, *The Loved Dog.* Ms. Geller, who lists among her credits training Oprah Winfrey's dogs and acting as an advisor to the Humane Society, explains she considers it her personal mission to help dogs, including millions dumped into shelters and euthanized each year. She states that she supports "play training based on love" and explains that, after studying wolves, she determined that her future was to train dogs *"using the wolves' natural methods."*

Geller labels herself as *"a non-violent life coach for dogs"*... *"Part of a natural and harmonious world..."* And she explains that, *"...peace begins with interactions among*

...families... including our pets" and that, *"each element of your dog's daily routine should involve relevance training."*

We definitely agree that a dog learns most from a wide variety of everyday interactions, especially when the desired behaviors have value in real life. And we were next impressed when she stated, *"Dogs need to feel connected to their owners and to their [owner's] lives... Similar to a toddler, a dog needs what psychologists call 'secure attachment', an invisible cord of love that connects one being to another."*

But apparently, this unique "cord of love" she describes can extend even into a cage! For suddenly, the book that so frequently mentions love for dogs now changes its tune, as Tamar Geller starts explaining why she feels it's necessary to crate.

"Because dogs are den animals," she states in the latter part of the book, *"they love small places, so they will not dislike the crate. The only thing they may not like is that they cannot come and go as they please..."*

These are not statements to be thrown around lightly. As described in depth in Chapter 3, dogs are not "den animals" and neither are wolves!

Wolves are by nature athletic hunting animals that travel vast distances as a group searching for and stalking prey. Their only natural connection to "dens" is that females whelp in underground dens, and the offspring remain only about eight weeks until they are weaned.

It's true that when it's time to rest, adult canines will sometimes seek out semi-enclosed areas (for example they may dig up the ground a bit to expose cooler earth before they lie down on a hot day or they may curl up under tree boughs that shield them from view). Adult canines, by nature, sleep in short catnaps interspersed with frequent periods of waking and moving around anywhere they want to; they do not, by nature sleep for eight, ten, twelve or fourteen hours at a time without stirring. So clearly a canine locked up in a tiny space and prevented from coming or going "as they please" for this many hours would feel marked physical and emotional distress, although Ms. Geller refers to the problem so lightly.

She continues, *"After his initial reaction to the crate, which may include whining, crying or barking, the dog will relax and take a little nap. Make the experience pleasant by talking to your dog in a soothing tone of voice, and help him realize that the crate is his own private bedroom- not a jail cell."*

We certainly hope nobody ever tries locking up their *"Loved Husband"* or *"Loved Wife"* in a small cage (or a closet, pantry or powder room) all day to prevent bad behavior, although it's true that, after an initial bout of whining or crying (and desperately searching for a cell phone to call a locksmith and a divorce attorney), your spouse might also give up and feel exhausted enough to "relax and take a little nap."

After dealing with the subject of crating, Ms. Geller's book next returns to its former loving tone, condemning those people who *"still abuse, choke and beat up their animals and call it training."* And she begs, *"Please join me in becoming a dog advocate... Spread the word that abuse is unnecessary and unacceptable... We must do whatever we can to end abusive dog training and to speak up for all creatures that cannot speak up for themselves, whether they are homeless or living next door. Please interfere. Tell your family and acquaintances they can choose a different way."*

These statements seem sincere and heartfelt, and we're glad if the book convinces some people to go out and speak up for abused animals. But the authors of this book must also "speak up" and "interfere" about squeezing a dog into a cage just big enough for him to turn in for the majority of his life. And we feel allowing our dogs reasonable freedom from confinement should be an essential part of Ms Geller's plea to *"respect* [dogs]*, appreciate them and celebrate them in each and every moment of your lives together"*.

6. The celebrity dog trainer American has been wildly infatuated with for half a decade goes against the philosophy that made him famous.

Dog Whisperer Cesar Millan, with his influential primetime show on National Geographic Channel, his best-selling books and now many other products (including videos, a magazine and a dog food with his name) is arguably the most famous dog trainer the world has ever known. And, in the past few years, his unique philosophy has changed America's beliefs about our ways of living with our dogs.

In six seasons on television, Cesar Milan has popularized the idea of training dogs based on their "psychology" and their innate nature as dogs. He's made his fame by going into the homes of dysfunctional owners, notably celebrities, and demonstrating how families tend to create canine behavior problems by failing to relate to dogs as animals. Instead, Cesar shows owners how to combine his catchphrase of, "exercise, discipline and affection, in that order" to effectively communicate with dogs in a manner that dogs are born to understand.

Cesar advocates for dogs to live as much like wolves as possible, explaining in *"A Member of the Family,"* his book about puppy rearing that, in nature, dogs must work for their food. *"From the time [young dogs in nature] are old enough to hunt with the pack,"* he states, *"they... migrate together, sometimes walking for many miles, until they find the nourishment they seek."*

In all of his writings, and his television shows, Cesar advocates that owners duplicate canine's natural activities as much as possible at home. One example is his no-excuses prescription for walking your dog, which he suggests that you do in the morning before you feed. *"Remember,"* Cesar says, *"your dog must have two walks of a minimum thirty minute duration each day, no matter how big your backyard is, or whether or not your kids play Frisbee with your dog every day!"* One requirement of dog rearing that Cesar will not compromise on, ever, is adequate exercise, especially when it comes to the vast exercise needs of high energy breeds.

There's been growing controversy and outrage about Cesar Millan. While literally millions of people have been impressed by him, and used his suggestions to learn how to present confident energy and lots of exercise when with their dogs, others have called his instinctive and often highly physical methods harsh and even abusive. Some owners have hurt, terrified or brought out aggression in their dogs trying to duplicate Cesar's methods physical correction methods incorrectly at home. And highly influential groups of veterinarians and dog trainers, including many trainers representing the APDT, have recently spoken out about Cesar's methods because he often demonstrates potentially painful corrections including harsh collar corrections and "alpha rolling".

Personally, we treat the subject of training "Cesar's Way" with the same caution that we regard any trainer's methods. We learn from what we believe is good, and we'd never imitate anything we saw any trainer, including Cesar, do if we believed it might hurt dogs or families, nor would we advise it to readers. Over the years, we have related to some of Cesar Millan's methods, while completely avoiding many others that we feel might harm dogs. While we train primarily with positive-reinforcement methods, we also train based on intuitive connection and influence with dogs, as Cesar often does. And, like Cesar, we do believe that dogs respond well to consistent leadership from well-balanced owners (as in pack theory). However, we never use dominance, attempt to overpower dogs or tell owners to try this. Instead, we teach owners to use personal energy, body language and consistent responses during daily interactions to change dogs' state of mind.

We also avoid strong collar corrections and flooding (repeatedly pushing a dog past its fears and/or triggers to the point of exhaustion or surrender) especially with the highly fearful and potentially snappy dogs we specialize in treating. We do most training off leash and, whenever we do use a leash, we use it "softly", with just turns and stops and no choke or prong collar corrections. And, with no harsh corrections, our in-depth multi-pronged approach makes less stressful, but traditionally slow, desensitization and reward training work more quickly.

Watching Cesar's show, we've sometimes had the impression that he unnecessarily stressed particular dogs by physically confronting aggression that was based in fear. But, even when he uses muscular methods, Cesar's precision and unique intuitive connection with dogs seems to produce less harm than when viewers or other trainers try to imitate him. Viewing Cesar's show we see many positive outcomes. And, from what we've seen on television and read in his books, our impression is that Cesar, at heart, seems to honestly live for dogs.

The authors believe that Cesar Millan's unimaginable popularity has contributed both positive and negative to human/canine relations. Much of his unique positive contribution to modern life with dogs comes from some of his well thought out philosophies that encompass other disciplines, and that are explained in detail in his books. And much of his Cesar's pivotal philosophy centers on dogs feeling they have jobs to do in life, rather than just sitting idle. We feel this is vitally important.

Because of the importance of philosophies like this, we didn't rush to join all the "Cesar bashers" even when we disagreed with some harsh leash corrections and alpha-rolling that we witnessed on particular TV episodes. More recently, Cesar has backed off some of his signature physical methods in many cases, probably due to the major criticism from positive trainers. And it was nice for us to see him use more positive methods. But then in a few cases he started using a training device that could do even more emotional/physical harm to dogs- electronic shock collars! The shock collars disturbed us quite a bit (we never use them and we've had to rehabilitate dogs that suffered lasting emotional trauma after their improper use). But we still didn't give up on Cesar and we still had to credit him for all the good he's done for dogs (notably his recent work helping rescue and puppy mill dogs.)

And then we saw something else that we completely couldn't understand... On a visit to a Petco store we almost tripped over a plastic, airline-type dog crate on wheels with Cesar Millan's name on it!

Cesar has talked so fervently for years about dogs needing to run great distances in natural settings to express their inner canine that we thought perhaps he'd endorsed the plastic crate only for travel. (It did look convenient for dragging through an airport.)

But then we saw a special *Dog Whisperer* show about Cesar raising and training four different breed puppies. Everything seemed fine until we saw a shot of the puppies lined up next to each other in four individual crates in a room that looked like the garage of Cesar's home! We did not believe what we were seeing and now we are unsure about Cesar's policy on crating. But for him to recommend crating would *have* to be hypocrisy.

One of the best things Cesar Millan did for dog owners in America was to (re)popularize the notion that dogs need vast amounts of physical exercise and stimuli to be happy and emotionally balanced, especially in this time when tech-driven owners have so little time to spend with them.

In his books, Cesar explains how Mexican farm dogs that he observed while growing up lacked pampering but enjoyed the benefits of moving around freely outdoors and living purposefully. **He explains that dogs lack something natural to do all day in most modern American homes. And he stresses over and over again that the more natural life can be for dogs, the better**.

For years, along with all of America, we've watched Cesar's "pack" run free together in the yard of his dog psychology center. **We've also watched Cesar jogging for miles through the hills of Southern California with a huge pack of loose dogs running behind him in elemental freedom- and the sight is beautiful!** Both authors have experienced similar lifestyles with dogs as children and we know how transcendent it feels for dogs (and their owners) to run or roam together and be one with nature.

We believe one of reasons Cesar's methods always worked almost magically for him is that he stayed 100% convicted in his beliefs and instincts regarding dogs. But now we cannot imagine why Cesar Millan, an inspired dog trainer who constantly expresses how much he believes in freedom and the laws of nature, would start caging dogs. To be fair, we don't know the whole story. So we wish Cesar will tell it to us and to America, by formally releasing his views on crating and his own definition of the "magic number" or number of hours total per day in a crate he feels is the maximum a dog can endure without damage.

We know Cesar has already stood against puppy mills, by rescuing and treating some of the dogs that were victims. And because excessive fear and undersocialization of a puppy mill dog was one of the symptoms that he dealt with on one of his specials, we know he has personally encountered the syndrome known as "kennelosis", as we describe in Chapter 3, Chapter 5 and throughout the book. So **we believe the scientific evidence, combined with Cesar's own instincts and experiences, will be enough for him to want to speak out against Excessive Dog Crating, whether it happens in puppy mill breeding facilities or in private homes**. And we hope he will lend his support to our mission. **If Cesar Millan publicly announces that there *is* such a thing as Excessive Home Dog Crating and that it *does* damage dogs, this one thing alone can change our world for the better**.

Does Victoria Stillwell still hate crates? In the past few years, many TV viewers who prefer gentler training methods have chosen to watch charming celebrity dog trainer Victoria Stillwell, featured on Animal Planet's *It's Me Or the Dog*, rather than *Dog Whisperer* Cesar Millan. The authors have always been fans of Victoria's, both for her creative and intelligent positive training interventions involving the whole family dynamic, and her stance on television against Excessive Home Dog Crating, while she trained dogs in the UK. The fact Victoria stood against Excessive Crating was no surprise, since she is known for being humane and believing that dogs need adequate mental and physical stimuli in order to stay happy and out of trouble. And Victoria is also from England, where crating dogs tends to be viewed unfavorably.

What did surprise us was seeing a recent *It's Me Or the Dog* puppy special where Victoria's American clients admitted to crating an older puppy for "70% of her life". While Victoria *did* obtain a much larger crate and many more walks for the dog, it was her omission that frightened us, because she didn't tell the owners onscreen that they should be crating less or transitioning the dog to live free in the home! She was even shown luring the puppy (whose symptoms, including snapping at the owners, were consistent with kennel syndrome) back into the larger crate with treats. And later in the show Victoria *introduced* a crate (shown with the door ajar) to another home with a puppy.

We are sure that Victoria Stillwell is a champion for humanity towards dogs and that she would never support excessive crating. In fact, we've have heard her speak out about excessive crating on past *It's Me or the Dog* episodes. But the danger is that just one episode like the one above can do vast damage. If viewers observe the crate used without adequate warnings, many are likely to purchase one and use it negligently or excessively without understanding proper limits. So we wish that Victoria Stillwell will understand how much influence she commands in this world and that her influence is growing every day to perhaps soon equal or outdistance Cesar's Millan's. With this influence comes a responsibility. So we hope Victoria will carefully consider and craft an official public statement of her policy on dog crating, along with her own formal "magic number" for the amount of hours per 24-hr period the average dog can tolerate in a crate with no ill effects, as well as the number of hours in a crate, if any, per 24-hr period that she feels would be most beneficial for the average dog. And, just like in the case of Cesar Millan, we sincerely hope Victoria Stillwell will read this book and speak out to help those dogs in puppy mills and those excessively crated right now in private homes, for it can literally make a world of difference!

We urge dog owners to always make your own best choices, trusting your own best instinct, and only using what famous people, or dog experts, tell you as general information- not gospel. Our advice to our readers when watching or reading about Cesar Millan or Victoria Stillwell training dogs is to simply learn from any good information these trainers provide, while always remaining cautious and skeptical. This is a good rule of thumb when dealing with any discipline as important as shaping your dog's behavior. Tap into varied information. Screen it by your own gut instinct, and never replicate any training technique that doesn't fully resonate with your conscience.

And, before you spend any money on stopping a dog behavior problem, ask yourself whether the people who are selling you a particular device or service, such as dog training, would actually profit more if the problem *didn't* get completely cured than if it did. Problem dogs represent great profit for a multi-billion dollar industry, as we explain in detail in the next chapter.

Chapter 9: The Cost of Bad Dogs

The dog industry currently profits from "bad" dogs; and it creates more bad dogs by Excessive Crating:

Throughout the book, we detail the amounts of money people are willing to spend just to train and/or physically keep their dogs controlled. Dogs these days seem to cause their owners more serious problems than they used to. And this is partly due to the cycle of excessively crating young puppies.

Ironically the downward spiral for most "bad" dogs usually begins if their breeders caged them excessively during their early formative puppy weeks (as explained in Chapter 3) and didn't given them adequate stimuli, socialization or introduction to the world. (This can be true for many puppy mill dogs and many dogs adopted from shelters and rescues.) Often behavior problems start with excessive crating, cruel tethering and/or inadequate socialization, with no opportunity for pups to learn self-control in a home environment. Or problems start when pups are abused or neglected in early life.

Of course, these dogs all deserve a chance. And most canine behavior problems (other than some extreme aggression) *can* be treated if new owners devote sufficient time, money and proper interventions to get the dog past a potentially rocky introduction to normal family life and house manners.

Rescuing animals (even the most ragged strays on the brink of death that we have personally taken off the streets) can be deeply fulfilling. But new owners have the right to walk into the process with their eyes open when they bring home a dog with serious pre-existing problems. Unfortunately, for their own benefit, people in the dog world frequently convince families to buy or adopt dogs by misrepresenting the facts.

It's deceitful for a breeder to charge a family hundreds or thousands of dollars for what they describe via email as a perfect purebred pup, and then deliver a pup that's abused, undersocialized and physically ill. And it's also negligent if any expert who influences dog selection fails to inform a family that they're choosing the wrong dog for their lifestyle, or tells them obedience (or crate) training will make the wrong breed- or the wrong dog a perfect fit.

Even though all dogs need a general introduction to house manners, obedience and communicating with their owners, you will have a much tougher time training a dog that was not the right match. But some breeders, trainers and shelter personnel may tell you that all dogs- regardless of breed or background- are equal in how happy they'll make your particular family feel. This ideology is considered "politically correct" by many people today. But it often encourages families to rush into dog ownership, rather than waiting and acting picky about selecting the exact "dream dog" that meets all their criteria. And rushing to adopt a dog that is not exactly what you want can cause serious future adjustment problems for the dog and the owners. It may lead to a dog being crated all day because his new family finds him too high-energy for them to manage. And it may eventually lead to that dog being euthanized rather than going to a family that would have been a better fit.

Mismatches between dogs and owners are painful for both humans and dogs. Yet segments of the dog industry profit hugely from these cases, either by offering training to change the dog, medications to sedate him or a wire crate to physically corral him. While these modalities, with the exception of the crate, sometimes have therapeutic uses, **we don't feel extreme measures should routinely be imposed on healthy, young, normal high-energy breeds in an effort to completely change their essential nature**. It would be healthier for professionals, including breeders, to match these dogs with households that can comfortably provide the exercise and stimuli they need.

1. The profit of selling crates

One reason the pet industry doesn't mind problem dogs is that, for every problem dog, at least one dog crate, with prices ranging around $100, can be sold. Crates now sell in all the large chain pet stores and giant retailers like Wal-Mart. Cages are even featured prominently for sale in upscale pet boutiques, right next to designer dog fashions, rhinestone collars and holistic food and treats that are more expensive than the food many human families can afford to eat.

Crates sell in all the biggest pet product catalogs and all over the Internet, so with one click you can easily buy one at four in the morning. These days employees in puppy shops are instructed to send home a crate with every puppy as a necessary housetraining tool and most new owners agree and purchase one the same day they purchase their puppy.

If dogs love crates so much, why do we need special "escape-proof" crates? Some dogs develop a serious anxiety disorder when locked in crates (especially if they've suffered former abuse crated while growing up). A dog in panic has amazing physical power, and some owners have to replace crates when their dogs dent or break them in a frenzied effort to try to escape. Our best advice is to get dogs like these highly qualified help for their anxieties and discontinue the crate in favor of safe, yet more spacious, housing. But the pet industry offers an alternative solution. For dogs that are repeat escapees, for approximately $500, families can purchase a heavy escape-proof crate nicknamed the "Alcatraz" crate. The squared off bars of this real item sold in catalogs are twenty gauge steel, reinforced by half inch steel tubes constructed strong enough that they look like they could repel a bomb blast or a real prison break.

So perhaps some of the experts who tell the world "dogs love crates" will have to think up a reason why any dog would need a product like THIS!)

Lots of dog owners (like us) have never crated our dogs and never purchased a crate. But many people in the dog industry now insist that EVERY dog, even those with no problems with housetraining or house manners, should stay crated every workday, all night every night and whenever people are away, from puppyhood until the end of their lives. So, if there are 77.5 million dogs in America according to the Humane Society of the United States, we could multiply this number by $100 (the estimated of cost of an average crate) to calculate theoretically how much money crate sales alone could generate if every dog owner bought one. An estimate like this makes it clear why anyone involved, however peripherally, with selling dog crates would want to convert as many people as possible to the practice of Home Dog Crating.

But behavior control for problem dogs only starts with selling crates... And the dog industry's motives for wanting the average family to have problems with their dog go much further...

2. Profit from selling products to cure dog behavior problems

The pet industry sells many products for people to enjoy with their good dogs. But they likely sell as many products to frazzled customers who feel compelled to spend any amount just to solve dogs' behavior problems. (For example, in one home we met three neurotic- and nippy- small dogs with about $300 worth of toys at retail in *each* of their toy baskets. And most of these toys were mangled and half destroyed, soon to be replaced by new ones.   Highly frustrated dogs with no exercise (such as those who are crated constantly) and neurotic dogs with serious problems (like the three above) often chew violently, and they quickly destroy any toy they are given. But the industry has offered a solution for owners who don't want to seek treatment for their dogs or give them a healthier, less frustrating, lifestyle. For all the "bad" dogs and desperate owners, manufacturers keep coming up with increasingly indestructible (and correspondingly expensive) toys. And the more the dog is crated, the more he tends to need the outlet of these toys. (In fact, esteemed Dr. Ian Dunbar of the APDT even goes so far as to suggest in his writings that you should try to "bond" a pup to toys by leaving him nothing else when he is crated!)

Some frazzled families spend as much as a hundred dollars a week just on rawhides and bones (some two feet long!) to momentarily engage their rude or "crazy" dogs and deflect bad behavior.

It's natural for dogs to love to chew, but *frenzied* chewing like this is a sign of a serious problem and/or a dog that needs more exercise, purpose and stimuli in his life. And when disturbed dogs rip up bed after bed, this is just more profit for the pet industry.

The same is true when dogs (usually the same dogs that are crated all the time) are so out of control on walks that they flip around like a fish on a line and immediately chew up expensive leather leashes.

Once a dog has been excessively crated and deprived of regular walks it can feel like a nightmare when owners do attempt to walk him. This often creates a vicious cycle of more crating, less walks and even worse pulling and lunging. To help the problem many owners buy products that range from the more gentle (like the Gentle Walker head harness, which costs approximately $30) to the more uncomfortable (including choke and prong or "pinch" collars). Purchase of all these products is more profit for the pet industry.

On the surface, all these problems might seem to make a case *for* crating dogs. But the truth is that crating only delays and then intensifies problems the moment that the understimulated and underexercised dog is set free to be with his owners. In Chapter 6, this is what Bouncy's family endured when they let their frustrated pup out of his cage at the end of a long day. **Bouncy was not a bad dog, and he loved people. But only by learning to live in the real world- and not in a crate- can a dog become the productive member of your pack that he's meant to be, follow the house rules and not revert to instinctual ways.**

If you kept a zoo animal in a tiny cage in your living room 18 hours each day, you could expect to have serious problems when you finally let that animal out. And this is what's happening to many dogs today. A practical connection between dogs and owners fails to happen and, instead owners simply focus on controlling problem behaviors in an immediate sense. Unfortunately, many dog trainers prefer this to deeper change, knowing that there will always be assignments for them as long as owners only control, but never fully cure, their dogs' problems.

In Chapter 13, we describe correct housetraining technique and why "crate-training" actually makes housetraining less efficient. Crated dogs do a strange thing that house dogs rarely did when we grew up- they sometimes continue to urinate and defecate all over their owners' homes when they're adolescents and even adults! This is not normal. Housetraining should only be an issue in young puppies. But pet stores these days sell an unprecedented number of cleaning solutions, diapers and other housetraining aids. Many days many people buy these supplies in bulk for years- another financial benefit for the pet industry.

And the latest fad owners have been trying for all forms of behavior problems are highly painful electronic shock collars, sometimes euphemistically referred to as "e-collars" or "e-touch training". These electric shock collars have been known to cause serious physical damage and lasting emotional trauma to dogs, and their use sometimes backfires, turning dogs' minor behavior problems into aggression. We have seen dogs emotionally damaged for life after their owners bought these products and shocked them too young and too hard. Yet recently many trainers (including Cesar Millan on some relatively recent episodes of *Dog Whisperer*) have been using and recommending shock collars. And, even though e-collars cost approximately $300, they are available in chain pet stores and many families have been buying and using them casually.

Another similar product- anti-bark collars that deliver electric shock (another item we warn against) are also highly expensive (ranging from $50 to well over $100), yet they're highly popular as well. And dog trainers are often advising families to use these devices.

It's scary that average suburban owners are now starting to see these extreme corrective products as "normal" everyday necessities to control their pet dogs. Muzzles have also become a common piece of normal household equipment. We've literally seen dogs decked out for walks in their neighborhoods with two leashes plus a Gentle Leader head harness (which looks like a horse's bridle) worn over a muzzle, so that the animals must have looked to passerby like Hannibal (the Cannibal) Lechter! Ideally, dog trainers would be able to shape dogs' behavior so that they wouldn't need all these devices for control. But, perhaps to keep people from feeling bad, the pet industry has recently come up with a product called the "Happy Muzzle" that's decorated in pretty pink polka-dotted gingham fabric.

Muzzles are sometimes necessary for safety. However, when the majority of people start believing that the definition of a normal dog is a creature that *must* wear a muzzle just not to attack people, and that this is all they can expect from a pet, we think this will prove tragic for dogs and for the human community. And raising dogs as caged animals that have little real contact with people may be hastening this scenario.

4,000 Authors, 12,000 Items and Still No Improvement

One day we searched Amazon.com and turned up 4,147 different books and as many as 12,057 items, including books, related to dog training. With so much training information so readily available, it would seem that dogs in our society must be very well behaved- or else they must be very badly behaved. We suspect the second. As long as dogs won't behave the way owners want them to, owners will keep seeking more information for any way to solve the problem, and this means more profit for the pet (and related) industries. As soon as special interests convince new dog owners to crate-train their new puppy, the pet industry profits from the sale of the crate. And then the industry profits more if the crate training leads to a cascade of more serious behavior problems. The problems can last a lifetime, and the dog's owners will keep on desperately purchasing books, products and services to fix the situation.

3. Profit the huge industry of dog training makes on bad dogs:

Many families don't know how to remedy deep-seated adjustment problems that are actually caused by excessive caging, so instead, they turn to solutions they can buy in a store. Then, if the dog behavior problems don't respond to all the pet store devices, many families finally decide to purchase professional dog training. And, even when behavior problems are bad, most families usually first start out with a group puppy or basic obedience class.

These classes, offered through vast numbers of trainers and commercial and community venues are relatively inexpensive. For example $99 classes, with multiple one-hour sessions, are offered on Saturdays at Petco and Petsmart stores around the country, and these classes are usually full. But classes like these, which teach only basic commands in a group setting, really aren't geared to the intense canine problems many owners need to solve. So, following the basic class, a number of owners will then purchase additional individual private sessions with the store's trainer, which cost an additional $99 for each hour.

Dog owners often keep returning to "cheap" community obedience classes until their bill amounts to hundreds of dollars. And, since the settings are crowded and don't address problems unique to the home, the behavior issues may still continue. Even worse, group trainers sometimes make serious mistakes when dealing with more vulnerable dogs and this may aggravate, or cause, damaging fears or aggression. Then, for these dogs to be rehabilitated, requires more expert private behavior help, adding hundreds more to the training bill.

Many dogs act so out of control simply because they are given no outlet for the high intensity physical exercise and sufficient mental stimulation they need every day. The problem is compounded enormously by Excessive Crating. But unfortunately, the attitude of many in the dog training industry is that the more training each dog needs, the better. As long as so many dogs keep behaving inappropriately, trainers will never lose business. (Interesting, this even applies when a dog's behavior problems originated with crating, *which the trainer themselves suggested*).

Obedience training for problem dogs represents a large amount of income for a large amount of people. Group dog training ranges from formal classes conducted by trainers with varying levels of expertise and experience, to informal sessions led by individuals with no qualifications who advertise informally by word of mouth and through free services like Craiglist. Across the country, all these dog training services combined account for a huge amount of profit.

In every community, legitimate dog obedience classes of every sort, including "puppy kindergarten" are run by experienced trainers, veterinarians' offices, community centers, large community rescue shelters, doggie day care facilities, groomers, pet stores, obedience clubs and breed clubs, etc. And these classes seem to tempt to families because, at less than $100 for several one-hour sessions, they seem relatively affordable.

Especially in today's sluggish economy, offering a seemingly inexpensive group class like this can be a sure way for dog trainers to earn money. While it is often hard to fill up a class, it can be much easier if a trainer is willing to admit dogs with more severe problems, notably aggression even though it can harm other dogs and it goes against professional ethics.

And because classes usually just focus on basic commands and often don't work for problems that occur in the home, owners of problem dogs may eventually have to hire more expert trainers and pay much more to the training industry than they originally expected. And dog owners who pay for "puppy classes" or "puppy kindergarten" just looking for housetraining solutions may be surprised to find that they paid $100 just to be told to crate their pups.

Many thousands of people charge to train dogs in various capacities and their ranks grow exponentially every day. And, even though there are some large organizations of thousands of dog trainers, there is still no uniform licensing, testing or certification requirement for dog trainers or for obedience instructors to practice. There are also no requirements for businesses or schools that train people to be new dog trainers.

At any time, a hundred or more "dog trainers" may operate in any small city. But it's difficult to keep an accurate count. While many dog trainers are dedicated to serving their community and acquire a good deal of education, experience and expertise, many others fly completely under the official radar.

There are more "dog trainers" in each community than most people might think. Some of them work part time under the umbrella of large organizations like pet stores, where they may also perform duties as cashiers/store associates. Many young people also work as employees or subcontractors under the businesses name of more mature well-known trainers, so while it appears that customers will meet the one certified trainer, they are more likely to receive services from one of his 5-10 employees.

We travel a lot and find it interesting how many "trainers" show up through non-traditional sources in every town! For example, for a few bucks, many people's neighbors happily offer to train their problem dogs...

How a trainer got their start and how they find business really has no bearing on how good they are with dogs. And often trainers with the greatest rapport with dogs have started on the grassroots level with no formal education. But, unfortunately, some unskilled and untalented people rush to train dogs because they can make quick cash with minimum education or accountability.

"Trainers" will sometimes ask abnormallyy low rates (such as $20) for a home training session. But then the family may find their dog needing twenty or more sessions, where the "trainer" does no more than walk the dog in circles and violently jerk a choke collar- which can make behavior problems worse. Unskilled trainers often hurt or frighten dogs, leading to worse problems and the need for much more expensive rehabilitation. And they often instruct owners to crate dogs if they have trouble making behavior changes through their own lack of skill. Unfortunately Excessive Crating then adds to behavior problems like hyperactivity- so the family may eventually spend more than they ever imagined.

Qualified trainers with more experience and education commonly charge in the area of $100 per hour. And applied animal behaviorists with doctoral degrees may charge a stratospheric fee just to meet the troubled dog. This is often the best way to help dogs. But it's sadly ironic that such extreme cost in interventions and training for one dog can start with needless caging in a puppy mill breeder or a former home!

Depending on the prices in different areas of the country, training a dog with significant problems can cost $300-$800 for satisfactory results from a trainer visiting the home. And, if owners choose to leave their dog full time at a kennel for his training for weeks or months, they can pay multiple thousands. And wealthier owners with bad dogs sometimes keep paying for training for the rest of the "bad" dog's life.

Ironically, Excessive Crating may account for 95% of the behavioral intervention and treatment many families have to pay trainers for. And crating never cures behavior problems. Rather it just "boxes" the problems up, for them to emerge again and again or to morph into different symptoms.

But all these **dog behavior problems only add to the bottom line for the dog industry.** Just for an estimate, you can take the number of dogs and puppies in the country (approximately 77.5 million) and estimate how many could be considered "bad", "wild", "hyperactive" or "uncontrollable". Then plug in $50, $100, $500, even $1,000 or your own best guess on how much each of their families spends on training. Include the cost of training books, magazines, DVD's, Internet consultations and then do the math and you will see clearly why the dog training industry loves bad dogs so much.

4. Profit made by doggie daycare to burn off bad dogs' energy:

Some dog owners who feel they can't manage their dogs never try training, or they may try training and give up on it. Instead, just so that they can live with an out of control dog, they may decide to just lock him in a crate whenever they are home and then let a "doggie day care", or "doggie day camp" facility deal with him whenever he's allowed to move around freely.

Theoretically, day care can have great benefits. Running around outdoors with other dogs, *all things being equal*, can be a good way for dogs to exercise their bodies and minds and, *under perfect conditions,* it can keep a dog's mind and body healthy. Being in a facility that allows the dog room to move around is certainly better for the animal than being left crated for hours. And, in many cases, it can be better than the dog having to stay home alone with nothing to do while his owners work long hours.

The huge increase in popularity of doggie daycare has paralleled the increasing demands of peoples' careers that keep them away from home for longer and longer hours. And, as people have even less time for their dogs and their career, and online/technical, lives demand more and more, we predict this industry will continue to grow dramatically. The doggie daycare business also targets childless two-career couples or singles (often metropolitan) who have lots of disposable income but little time, and are willing to pay anything for their dogs, which they consider their "children". Rates for basic day care can run as high as $35 for approximately 8 hours at facilities in larger cities, with the idea that the owner will bring their dog every workday for the rest of his life.

Some people bring their dogs to day care simply intending for them to have fun and not be lonely. But many other owners now bring dogs to day care for more desperate reasons. They feel their (usually large) dogs are out of control and that they can't exercise them enough to get them to calm down and act civil in the home. So these owners will bring their dogs to day care to warehouse them and tire them out as much as possible, by letting them chase the other dogs around all day. They then hope that when the dog comes home in the evening, all he will do is sleep and this is what usually happens.

When day care is functioning at its best, and when structured activities are actively supervised by adequate staff people, it can be a great place for dogs *that are already completely emotionally balanced and friendly* to have fun, play and socialize. **But day care was never intended as a therapeutic treatment for dogs with serious emotional or behavioral problems. It's also not healthy to lock a dog inside a cramped crate every hour that he's in the family's home and then only release him to run around at the day care facility and it can be dangerous for the other dogs present.** Even so, since regular day care attendance can bring in $600 a month for each dog, it is easy to see why certain day care owners and managers often take risks and admit dogs that are completely out of control because they are constantly crated at home.

5. Profit from self-help & holistic treatments for behavior problems (from massage to psychics)

Today many pet owners are intrigued by the concept of holistic pet care and they're willing to pay high prices for holistic interventions for their dogs' behavioral, as well as physical, problems. **Overall, holistic pet care represents a hugely growing segment of the pet industry, and profit from holistic solutions to behavior problems is growing just as fast.** Proper use of holistic products and techniques can be complex, so owners often hire professionals in each of the disciplines for continued service or advice. They may also purchase highly involved books and educational materials, the sale of which is also a growing industry.

One example of a holistic technique that's become relatively mainstream is massage. Canine massage is a unique professional discipline with schools and programs that train practitioners. It can be used therapeutically for injuries and medical conditions and also for stress reduction and to target specific behavior problems Some owners swear by canine massage and hire professional dog masseuses who charge approximately $70-$100 or more per hour.

And the authors strongly believe in the therapeutic benefits of massage (especially specific techniques like Tellington Touch) for dogs with emotional problems. (And we sometimes incorporate massage in treatment). But professional dog massage sessions can be expensive. Sometimes, specific massage techniques help an emotional issue in just one session. But, more often, treatments must continue, sometimes for the life of their dog. And **we find it sadly ironic when owners have to use massage to treat physical and emotional problems caused by dogs being kept immobile day after day! This happens surprisingly frequently. And what dog *wouldn't* need massage after being held for 12 hours consecutively in a tiny cage?**

Another growing trend in treating behavioral, as well as physical, imbalances is canine acupressure (which requires no special license) and canine acupuncture (which must be performed by a veterinarian). Dog owners must sometimes travel a distance to find a practitioner. And, while these modalities sometimes cure a dog on the first session, other dogs need to repeat sessions indefinitely, and sessions are expensive. Canine acupuncture and acupressure have a reputation for good results in some very difficult situations and, these days, many caring dog owners are willing to pay the bills. But it is also ironic when a dog needs these treatments just as a result of daily crating.

Another surprisingly popular and costly investment lately for people whose dogs have uncontrollable behavior problems are the services of "pet communicators" or pet psychics who will either meet the dog or just charge for services over the Internet.

Holistic treatments vary in their effectiveness, but most- if not all- are helpful to some degree. But the biggest problem we find with using holistic professionals, protocols or products to treat the symptoms of anxious, angry or overactive dog is the same problem we find with the use of many other costly treatment modalities. **Many families try all forms of heroic and expensive interventions for their dogs' well-being while they are meanwhile crating the animals 18 hours or more a day. And, while treatment modalities like massage can be very helpful, the very first treatment many dogs need to ease their emotional distress is to be released from the tiny boxes they've been locked in for a chance to stretch.**

We also think that, if any dog that was locked in a crate truly established communication with a pet psychic, the first thing the poor animal would do would be to express his distress and beg to be set free! This actually happened to a family who adopted a horribly abused pup, as described in the heartwarming true story *Oogy*. In the book, the loving family that rescued Oogy was having trouble getting him accustomed to the crate that dog experts suggested, and they hired a pet communicator. The communicator immediately informed them that poor Oogy was so unhappy in his crate because the people who had violently abused him had also crated him! His new loving family immediately released him from unnecessary confinement to share a joyful life with them in every way.

6. Profit from supplements and prescription medication for behavior problems:

A more drastic step many of today's owners resort to is to medicate their dogs to control behavioral issues. One option are the many generic calming supplements offered in pet stores and online, which cost from $10 to $75 or more per bottle. Dogs usually remain on these supplements long term. Just as frequently, owners will try several types of supplements in a row, because the first ones they try aren't effective. And many dog owners now have a whole cabinet of unfinished bottles of "calming aids". Dog trainers and other dog professionals (including breeders) who are not trained holistic practitioners have also gotten into this market for profit; they will sometimes enter into a sales agreement with a company that distributes a certain supplement or vitamin that, among its other benefits, is supposed to improve canine behavior, and then they strongly pressure all their customers to buy it from them on a regular basis, so they receive a portion of each sale.

Unfortunately, we did the math on this practice and it is easy for dog trainers, breeders (and even veterinarians) to earn more in a year from ongoing sales of these supplements than from all their other business. (Even so, we personally rejected the invitation whenever we were approached with an offer to sell these supplements.)

Supplements quite often won't help with problem dogs in the highest levels of distress. So owners will often get psychotropic medication from their veterinarian. Unfortunately, prescription medications are powerful, with dangerous side effects (which can include terrible behavioral changes). And many dogs take the prescription medication for life. We've all heard of "doggie Prozac". And it's now quite common for veterinarians to prescribe dogs powerful anti-depressants, anti-anxiety medications, tranquilizers and sedatives, including doggie Prozac (fluoextine), Elavil (amitriptylin), Vistaril and Acepromazine.

Dogs that might otherwise spin in their crates and burst out wildly and perhaps even aggressive, now take their medication and slump or stagger out, acting just a little odd or a little "loopy". Medication for dogs is a complex issue. In particular cases, we recommend that dogs receive in-depth blood tests and laboratory analysis and we work closely with veterinarians' recommendations. Some serious canine emotional problems are caused by physical/chemical illness, so these dogs may require medication at some point in their treatment for their safety and well being. But in this chapter, we're concerned with the cost of a lifetime of psychotropic medications and veterinary check-ups for a large number of dogs. And the bill for prescription medication expenses for "bad dogs" adds a lot to industry profits.

Owners who don't want to give their dogs prescription meds for behavior problems may instead purchase targeted natural holistic supplements such as Bach Remedies. Supplements like these are different from the more generic nutritional supplements mentioned above and the authors believe the right holistic products, used with appropriate caution, are highly beneficial for certain dogs. And, other than cost, the best supplements have no downside.

Often these days, dog owners hire holistic practitioners to give advice or apply treatments and costly sessions/consultations may continue for weeks, months or the life of the dog. To treat behavior issues, some practitioners may recommend: special diet, herbs, pills, hormones, flower essences or aromatherapy. Even sound frequency and different color lights are sometimes employed to treat anxious or problem dogs.

We've studied all these natural modalities for the treatment of canine anxiety, snappiness, fears, phobias and dissociation, and we often incorporate holistic modalities along with multifaceted behavioral programs and achieve good results. **Holistic methods** can help dogs with an abusive background of overcrating (such as dogs rescued from puppy mills or fight rings) and a combination of holistic treatment along with exercise and traditional obedience can be the right prescription to cure your previously troubled dog and make life with him a pleasure.

But we don't feel holistic methods should be used as a Band-aid to treat dogs that are still spending most of their hours in tiny cages. It's a shame to try to use supplements or holistic healing techniques just to treat an animal that's being driven crazy by being locked in a cage! Yet this is exactly what many highly respected and otherwise knowledgeable animal behaviorists and trainers do, and advise their clients to do at home.

When dogs *must* be caged (such as temporarily in a county shelter) these holistic modalities can make them more comfortable, easy to care for and more open to behavioral intervention. **But no one should attempt to use holistic treatments as a way to keep a dog mellow, while they are denying the animal the movement and life stimulation he needs by caging him in their home or training facility for months and years.**

Ironically, however, **when dog owners or dog professionals constantly administer products or medicines to sedate a dog that is frustrated by long-term imprisonment in a crate, this can make lots of money for the pet industry.** When you price some of the natural treatments and products for behavior problems in specialty stores and over the Internet, it's easy to see why many people in the pet industry aren't really complaining about modern owners' trouble with dogs. **As long as these frustrated- and frustrating-dogs primarily stay in cages, all the people who "treat" them can continue to treat them, while keeping owners in just the right equilibrium between management and desperation.**

7. Other businesses that profit from problem dogs (writers, non-profits, etc.):

Our obsessive fascination as a nation with extremely badly behaved dogs explains why we're so in love with celebrity dog trainers Cesar Milan and Victoria Stillwell. Advertising on their primetime shows represents significant money. So do book sales and product endorsements. Cesar is now affiliated with the national giant Petco and he's branched out to endorse a line of dog food with his name, as well having his own magazine (another vehicle for advertisers).

Many owners' later stages of disillusionment with problem dogs are characterized by a lot of desperate reading and information gathering about dog behavior problems. And people in this state of mind tend not to care about how much they spend if they feel there's a chance they can find a "solution". So the profit the industry makes from bad dogs includes all the money spent on books and literature about training and behavior problems. You can find websites where you can buy a canine behavior consultation for a fee or you can choose from a vast number of dog training DVD's and home dog training programs in various formats. Popular dog magazines are increasingly filled with articles about problem dogs. And costly magazines devoted to specifically to training (including Cesar's) are increasingly available in chain pet stores, bookstores and even supermarkets.

Any casual Internet surfer can get online 24 hours a day to find endless directories and lists of dog books, magazines and catalogs, many dealing with training issues. These sites may appear to be free, but advertisers count on selling dog owners with the pop-up advertisements and optimized lists along the side of the screen, and the money generated by all this advertising represents even more expenditures on bad dogs- a problem endlessly perpetuated by Excessive Crating. Even the staggering numbers of online communities, chat rooms, free articles, postings and informational sites often channel dog owners desperate for assistance and advice back to hiring dog trainers from a certain company, or buying a particular product or service- *or even a crate*.

While it is theoretically good to have so many resources available for shaping dog behavior- if they truly help- we question whether some expert "solutions" aren't really just to maintain the status quo. **Because this huge segment of the dog industry grows in profit as owners lose more fundamental control and connection with their dogs, which they often do when dogs are overly crated.**

The industry of solving canine problems also features an ever-expanding field of supporting players, including website designers, dog book publishers, writers, editors and businesses that market all these people. Also an increasing number of non-profit organizations are able to hire more staff and administrators and receive more donations as more dogs are surrendered because of behavior problems.

There are huge national organizations that collect membership dues for dog trainers; these organizations are affiliated with other groups that make money certifying dog trainers, and many different schools and programs collect different amounts of money training dog trainers and or selling them educational materials and books- ranging from how to train dogs to how to run a successful dog training business. There are national conventions for thousands of dog trainers and the hotels that profit when they host these conventions. Then there are organizations for professional dog writers that sponsor networking and awards. And there are companies that specialize in selling business plans, websites, marketing plans and standard documents for all these people that deal with all these bad dogs… There are other companies that manufacture, promote and sell all these products, supplements and literature for bad dogs and retailers and trade shows that provide platforms to sell all these products and services.

And all of this could be wonderful. Yet in a climate of so much spent on dogs, why is the dominating behavioral strategy these days to simply lock problem dogs in cages in our homes? And why are owners spending so much more money these days trying to fix dogs' behavior problems just to maintain lifestyles that feel disappointing compared to what most of us enjoyed with our dogs years ago?

In conclusion, much of the money Americans currently spend on dogs' behavior problems may actually be unnecessary. And, if consumers realized this, much of that spending would dry up. Something has to placate frustrated dog owners while keeping them spending. And the trend of crating dogs functions as a perfect solution, because it gives families the impression of immediate relief, while actually making underlying problems worse.

If crating wasn't seen as an acceptable method of keeping dogs, we believe that consumers, en masse, would demand to buy better dogs from better breeders who socialized them better, and families would only purchase the kindest, highest-quality dog training. Reputable dog breeders actually charge less for a well taken care of and well socialized pup than most pet stores and Internet dealers that sell pups bred in puppy mills. If buyers felt strongly enough about dogs not being kept in cages that they screened where they bought more carefully, the 10,000 puppy mills currently operating in the country would start to go out of business and dogs and families would all benefit.

And, if dogs lived peaceably in their homes like most dogs did 20 or 30 years ago, average suburban families would never find themselves thinking their dog required multiple thousands in remedial training or cartloads of expensive supplies just to control him!

To fully understand the financial motive behind the crating conspiracy, we have to wonder if many people refused to crate because they considered it abusive, but didn't want to give up their busy lifestyles, whether they would simply choose not to own dogs. Or they might learn new ways of living with their dogs free in their homes for an optimal lifestyle. Either scenario would mean more enlightened dog owners and a complete end to impulse buying, this would mean that puppy mills would likely go out of business and much of the demand for products and services for controlling bad behavior in dogs might disappear along with it. Along with it, much profit from this sector of the pet industry in its current state might vanish as well.

Once a paradigm shift like this occurs, we believe dogs and their families will be more content and less stressed. The dog industry would have to change to support positive interventions other than crating to help owners bond with dogs free in their homes. And many dog industry players that currently depend on the old model of struggling to control "problem" dogs might lose millions- or possibly billions- of dollars as business was taken by other service providers who worked harder and cared more about dogs' and families' well being.

And, as we describe in the next chapter, some of the biggest profits that come from excessive crating aren't just made by those who work with problem dogs, but also by other players in the dog industry and beyond. Unfortunately, all is not as it seems in this popular $50 Billion and growing industry.

Chapter 10: The Dog Crating Conspiracy; How a $50 Billion Industry & Beyond Profits from Caging "Good" Dogs:

The dictionary defines "conspiracy" as "a secret plan to carry out an illegal act, especially with political motivation; [a] plot". And, looking at the extreme and widespread propaganda that has recently brought the concept of crating dogs in our houses into the mainstream, we must wonder if the popularity of the practice is not coincidental, but a deliberate effort, orchestrated to benefit particular individuals or groups- in other words, a conspiracy.

Throughout history, extreme ideologies or styles of living have suddenly swept nations, often based on economic motives. Examples include the real estate "bubble" of the past decades when special interests profited from irresponsible land development; the increased demand in the cotton industry because of the invention of the cotton gin that made slavery more viable in the American South pre-Civil War; and, in Hitler's

Germany, the severe economic depression that made the working public (many of them unemployed) more susceptible to his message of nationalism and hate.

An immediate assumption would be to try to blame the entire conspiracy of Excessive Dog Crating in America today on crate manufacturers. But even though sales of crates (which have expanded to more retailers of every size, and online) *do* earn huge amounts of money, these sales only make up a relatively small portion of the multiple billions that the practice of Excessive Crating brings the dog industry and beyond. And, unlike the crate manufacturers who have been in business for decades, most of the people and entities that benefit from the practice are not readily apparent- even though they are influencing the attitudes of our entire nation.

When we first started researching this book, we assumed search words like "cruel crating", "abusive crating", "deadly crating" or "dogs dying in crates" would easily lead us to negative information about crates online. Instead, these searches immediately brought up thousands of *positive* entries for crating. And only a small proportion of these optimized listings came from companies selling crates. Many "informative" articles were linked to other dog sites. These were sometimes otherwise popular and/or "politically correct" organizations or groups, including shelters, rescues, veterinarians, public figures involved with dogs, respected publications and national directories of products and services, or charities.

Other writings were simply postings by individuals, which often showed up as highly optimized parts of huge online communities and discussion groups. Often postings by individuals seemed vitriolic, attacking their peers who tried to speak out against crating. And it was *nearly impossible*, even for professionals searching diligently, to find more than a few optimized results about the negative effects of crating. Usually any negative facts introduced about crating or caging dogs were cited only briefly, and then quickly dismissed. We found similar problems on bookstore shelves, where crating is mentioned positively in almost every popular puppy or dog behavior book. And many newer books, especially those written about puppies and housetraining, never even mention that alternatives to crate training exist.

Writing *Dogs Hate Crates* came after years of treating families' dogs in extreme suffering due to excessive crating and personally meeting hundreds of people in dog-related careers who either crate dogs excessively themselves and/or try to push the concept of crate training on dog owners, even when owners resist. We have also read hundreds of books on dog behavior- both popular and college-level- where dog behavior experts promote damaging crating advice based on flawed logic. And we've read thousands of web articles and postings in favor of crating that show up whenever we type the words "dog crate" on Internet searches.

As we did research, several interesting facts emerged. One fact was that, not so long ago- maybe 15 or 20 years back- when crating family pets for life was *not* so popular, there was some very good literature written by naturalists and dog behaviorists providing better alternatives. Even today, some of the most humane and respected behavior experts either speak out against crating, or don't recommend it and don't use it for their own dogs. In the scientific community some of the most respected experts, researchers and veterinarians publish about the negative effects of excessive confinement on puppy mill dogs, shelter dogs and pet dogs, and they have been doing so for many years.

This information is much more compelling than the largely emotional or circumstantial pro-crating opinions in much popular literature and online postings. But, even though the learned opinions and studies that show a downside to crating/confinement are well known by academics, researchers and degreed professionals in the animal behavior community, this information is rarely discussed online or in popular literature and it seems particularly hard for novice dog owners to find. And it's not only *dog owners* who don't get all the facts about crating. But a good number of *dog professionals* get much of their information from popular literature, quick online searches and word of mouth and so they're never exposed to scientific research and behavioral research on the ways excessive confinement damages dogs.

The authors found it interesting that, whenever we mentioned that we were researching a book about cruel crating in homes and puppy mills, most "dog people" who made a living working with dogs acted negative or uninterested, while the emotional reaction from dog *owners* was just the opposite.

Most dog owners we talked to said they would never crate and that they were horrified by the number of hours they had seen friends, relatives and neighbors crating dogs. Many others reported being bullied by professionals who intimidated them and tried to force them to crate their dogs. And some had given in, thinking that they were wrong, even as they watched their dogs suffer and felt bad themselves every day they crated.

Many dog lovers have told us they were happy someone was finally speaking out and that we were the only dog professionals they'd ever met who gave them training advice that didn't include crating. **Dogs were in distress in crates, families were in distress because of it- and yet someone or something was still making them do it!**

It became clear that if there is a conspiracy behind the thousands of recent articles, books, websites and postings by individuals passionately and aggressively arguing for dog crating, then it had to be something larger and more widespread than anything a relatively small group of retail crate manufacturing companies could possibly control or even conceive of ... It had to be something huge.

$ Money motives behind the crate training conspiracy:

The facts indicate that the increasing popularity of crating pet dogs for life has grown out of money motives on a huge scale. And these forces infiltrate every corner of the gigantic and rapidly growing pet industry, and beyond, to involve huge business forces and segments of the larger economy. The conspiracy also involves social and emotional motives, which we discuss later in this chapter.

The Excessive Dog Crating trend now contributes to surprising numbers of jobs and livelihoods and even includes employees of some non-profits we've traditionally assumed were saviors of dogs. Once people start crating dogs to aid their financial interests, they also tend to feel uncomfortable admitting to themselves that they may be abusing animals. So, to defend their actions, they may begin to alter their fundamental actions and beliefs and seek connections with people who promote similar ideas. And these groups of people are now pushing their ideas through the media and altering the mindset of the general public.

The Theory of Cognitive Dissonance explains why some people push so hard for crating even without a monetary motive:

People need to believe good things about ourselves.

In 1957, social psychology researcher Leon Festinger published *A Theory of Cognitive Dissonance.* This groundbreaking work introduced the concept of people changing their thought processes and beliefs in order to be consistent with actions they had already performed to avoid a state of cognitive dissonance, which can feel profoundly uncomfortable.

In Festinger's original research study, subjects were more likely to adjust facts they told another subject about the pleasure of a task they found personally odious *dis*proportional to whether they felt they had a highly compelling reason to have agreed to the task in the first place. So those that had a *high* financial motive to perform the unenjoyable task initially were *less* likely to lie to another subject about how pleasant they thought the task was than those who *didn't* have as compelling a motive to perform the task in the first place. Festinger's subjects without a high financial motive didn't want to believe they were stupid or naïve to perform the bad task, so they had to convince themselves that they had a good reason for what they had done. And the only way they could do this was to convince themselves that they had actually *enjoyed*, rather than suffered through, the task and that the task **really wasn't that bad.**

Researchers have also hypothesized that people's tendency to adjust our cognitions to make them more consonant might help explain the phenomena of otherwise "nice" humans supporting cruel actions by their government. A frequently cited example of the theory in action was when Nazi war criminals justified their torture of innocent people during wartime in such a way that they could believe they were still good people.

Someone who experiences two or more dissonant cognitions (or conflicting thoughts) will always feel compelled to do away with the dissonance. **So the theory of cognitive dissonance can explain why so many individuals who believed for years that caging dogs was cruel suddenly changed course and began to speak out so strongly *for* crating *after* their friends, the media and/or convenience persuaded them to try it on their dogs.**

Once they tried crating (and especially if they noticed their dogs in apparent distress when caged) these thousands- or hundreds- of thousands- of good people wanted to believe they were still acting like good people. So they had to change their initial belief that home crating equaled abuse or negligence.

And simultaneously a number of "professionals" who stood to profit financially used this change in prevailing attitudes to advance their own criminal or unethical money-making endeavors. They could breed dogs in puppy mills, not train them adequately and get away with housing dogs in cages just by "spinning" the concept with catch phrases like "dogs are den animals" or "dogs love crates".

Criminal profit for Excessive Dog Crating- puppy mill breeders, fight rings, etc.

The group of people who profit criminally from over-crating dogs includes all the owners, middle-men and pet shops that knowingly sell puppies raised in puppy mills in conditions that violate the law, and those who later sell the "used up" breeding dogs to auctions and even laboratories. Across the country, thousands of individual puppy mill owners keep millions of dogs in total suffering in cages in deplorable and illegal conditions that any reasonable person would recognize as cruel. And, as an industry, puppy mills sell millions of pups each year (which each eventually sell at retail for hundreds or even thousands of dollars). These breeders often leave dogs caged and suffering for life, never having any surface to stand on other than wire, and they are known to deprive dogs of food, water and veterinary care and to leave puppies' corpses in their cages amidst their living siblings (such as in cases described in Chapter 11).

And, unfortunately those individuals arrested and successfully prosecuted represent just a tiny sampling of the criminal abuse of dogs and puppies that is only increasing. The Humane Society of the United States (HSUS) estimates that, as of 2010, there were approximately 10,000 "puppy mill" breeding facilities operating across the United States. These breeding operations are all large-scale, usually holding hundreds of dogs. And according to an estimate by HSUS, between 2-4 million dogs are sold out of puppy mills each year!

Breeding dogs is a tough business for reputable breeders who breed only small numbers of dogs to higher standards. But puppy mill breeders save money by not giving their animals adequate care and many puppy millers enjoy all the outward trappings of wealth and success, including big homes and the best "toys" like large boats and luxury cars.

Unfortunately, the Internet has increased the anonymity of these criminals, allowing them to conduct business in secrecy, freely selling abused and ailing puppies to unsuspecting families across the country with no real fear of consequences. Sadly, pups that originate in puppy mills are sold in even the most upscale boutiques (like the infamous shop in Bel Air described in Chapter 11 that was frequented by celebrities like Paris Hilton). And some of the most coveted "teacup" sized dogs that can sell for as much as $4,000 are actually runts that sometimes come to owners so ill they die within days.

Obviously most dog lovers would like to stop the criminal actions of puppy mill breeders and pet shop owners who profit off puppies' suffering. But dog lovers are less likely to realize that, in all our communities, there are also many thousands (or even more) individuals whose collective actions needlessly make pet dogs suffer. These include owners of dog businesses who use Excessive Crating to squeeze the most profit out of their limited floor space or staffing, individual owners who observe their dogs suffering, yet still cage them 23 hours total per day because they find them an inconvenience; and policy makers and experts who choose to side with those who crate purely to preserve their livelihoods, even while they're aware of dogs' distress. And numbers of these people are networking and deliberately spreading misinformation so people won't question their practices.

The misinformation is not always deliberate. Networking and sharing can serve a similar function when individuals are simply seeking to ease their own conscience by sharing the wrong ideas. In this chapter, we discuss various motives behind the Crating Conspiracy, ranging from the purely financial to the purely emotional. Together these motivations have interacted to produce such a potentially damaging social trend.

MOTIVES FOR THE TREND OF EXCESSIVE HOME CRATING IN OUR SOCIETY:

1. Emotional Motives, both in dog owners and pet industry professionals
2. Criminal Motives (such as breeding dogs in illegal puppy mill conditions to maximize profit)
3. Financial Motives for selling products and services to dog owners who feel they can only keep dogs if they can crate. (This includes profit from "bad" dogs with behavior problems made worse by crating; and profit from "good" dogs that busy owners can enjoy and show off without devoting enough time to exercise them or train them house manners.)

Financial Motives for the Excessive Home Dog Crating Conspiracy

The huge financial scope of the benefits of Excessive Home Dog Crating unfortunately parallels the huge financial growth of the American dog industry. Recently, the pet industry overall (much of which is expenditures on dogs) accounts for $47.7 billion in sales estimated in 2010 by the American Pet Products Association (APPA). Other sources put this number higher, at as much as $52 billion. All sources agree that the pet segment of the economy is one that has bucked the general economic recession.

For example, APPA figures show that spending on our pets grew 5.4% from 2008 to 2009, with an additional increase in 2010 and another increase projected for 2011. Most awesome is the speed that the industry has grown. In 1994, spending in the pet industry was only at $17 billion, according to the APPA. So, according to their figures, spending in this industry more than doubled in 16 years.

And APPA figures for pet industry spending in 2010 only cover: Food ($18.76 billion), Supplies/OTC medicine ($10.94 billion), Vet Care ($13.01 billion), Live Animal Purchases ($2.13 billion) and Pet Services: grooming and boarding ($3.51 billion). These figures do *not* include many areas of related spending, such as much of the money collected by shelters, rescues and charities; many training and pet sitting services, which are not reported; and many other categories such as money earned writing about dogs or producing television programs about dog training. If all these figures were included in pet industry statistics, we believe the amount of pet industry spending would be ***substantially*** higher!

A significantly large segment of our population now regularly buys "luxury" products and services for their dogs. This includes super-premium pet foods, raw foods and treats; designer dog clothing, jewelry and accessories; "spa-style" doggie daycare and 5-star resort packages with staggeringly expensive perks for canine companions. These luxury items start as low as $20 and range all the way up into the tens of thousands. Another portion of this pet spending goes to ever more sophisticated veterinary treatments and to controlling behavior issues in an increasing number of problem dogs (as described in Chapter 7).

And in past few years, even as our general economy has slumped further into recession, with families in every income bracket cutting spending on everything from luxuries to necessities like where they grocery shop and what they eat, the healthily growing pet industry has flourished. And the great prospects for money-making in this flourishing industry have not been lost on anyone searching for a profitable business endeavor in otherwise hard times.

We believe that the billions in spending on dogs in our country can be divided into 2 categories- spending on what owners consider "bad" or problem dogs; and spending on what owners consider "good" dogs or pampered dogs that they can enjoy and show off. **And Excessive Dog Crating creates more revenue for the industry by allowing more owners to keep dogs, even if they do not really have the time to really integrate the dogs into their lifestyles. Excessive Dog Crating leads to "bad" or problem dogs by creating a vicious cycle where bad behavior is contained but never really changed. And it preserves the unrealistic perception that any family can easily and effortlessly enjoy a "good" or pampered dog of any breed just by keeping it constantly locked up and "out of trouble" no matter where they live or how much time they have.**

If locking dogs up in cramped cages for 10, 12 or 14 consecutive hours whenever the dogs weren't convenient started to be viewed as inhumane, many families might not elect to keep dogs at all because of their overbooked schedules. This could be a good thing, because it might cut down on the millions of new puppies that are bred every year in puppy mills to be purchased on impulse in pet stores and online.

If people took more time to think it over, they would expect a higher standard for their lives with their dogs and they would take more time to decide on dogs, either buying from reputable breeders or adopting from the best-run shelters and private rescues. And, in this more careful climate, criminally abusive puppy mill facilities would be revealed for what they were and would have to shut down.

But a decreasing number of dogs in the nation could mean bad financial news for some of the people who are currently cashing in to the largest degree from the famously "recession proof" pet industry- including related jobs and businesses that dog lovers may never have even thought of.

If the notion of locking dogs in crates long-term for housing and training was rejected, standards of what life with a dog should be would improve. And a new generation of pet services and products would evolve to fill the needs of busy dog owners in today's challenging world. The dog industry could still flourish, with products and services tweaked to be more useful for owners and more humane for dogs. But as that change and evolution took place, it's likely that many current providers of products and services for dogs would be affected in two different ways...

2 Currently Growing Categories of Dog Spending include:

A. **How the pet industry currently profits from "bad" dogs** (This includes sales of crates, products to control problem dogs, training, holistic & self-help solutions, medication, some veterinary services and the earnings of writers, non-profits and others involved in canine problems). **This trend is examined in detail in the last chapter, and...**

B. **How the industry currently profits from "good" dogs** (This includes luxury and fun products & services, dog events, some functions of shelters and non-profits, veterinarians, groomers, boarders, pet sitters, day care facilities, dog breeders, writers, television shows, dog-themed gift products, dog retail items & the dog food industry. **How all of these businesses profit from dogs is explained in this chapter...**

B. How the pet industry profits from "good" dogs:

Reliance on crates helps the current pet industry by allowing many people to think they can own "good" dogs while putting in no time and effort and keeping their exact lifestyles. In today's incredibly busy world, many of these people simply wouldn't keep dogs if they thought they'd have to put in more effort or change their lifestyles to keep their dogs happy and behaving right.

Not only do pet owners spend a lot on "bad dogs", they spend even more on good dogs and on dogs they can pretend are good, without having to acknowledge if the dogs disappoint them. By locking dogs in crates it can be easy to avoid any troubling issues. The owner isn't forced to provide lots of exercise or engagement for the dog. They only have to take him out when it's convenient, when they want to show him off or when they want to go on a spending spree for him. And this kind of unquestioned spending is exactly what benefits the $50 billion pet industry.

1. Luxury and fun products & services for "fun" dogs

What a wonderful world for fans of dogs. There's never been a wider array of dog products available for purchase on a moment's impulse. It starts with dog-themed products that are really meant for people. These include T-shirts, bumper stickers, cards, statues, collectibles, jewelry for humans in the shape of our favorite breeds or even crystals made from our departed dogs' ashes, dog- themed gifts for the dog lovers in our circle of friends, high-quality pet portraits commissioned by artists, pet photos at every price range and a plethora of warm and fuzzy gift books that tell stories about dogs and our feelings for them.

Dog Television and Media:

More income related to people feeling good about dogs comes from the money made by many recent popular dog-themed movies, some blockbusters, and the money made by all the people involved in producing and promoting all the popular television shows that deal with dogs. There is also all the money made by smaller radio, cable and Internet shows relating to dogs and the money made by guests on these shows, and a portion of all the advertising business that exists because of these shows.

And, although most of the vast number of online communities, discussion groups and dog blogs are free, as people spend time on these sites, they also see pop-up advertising or indirect references for them to buy products and services. Every dog site that sends people to other dog sites, dog directories or dog catalogs draws consumers deeper, and this represents more money for the industry including the salaries of the people who design the sites.

Dog Writing:

People love reading about dog topics. In the previous section we mentioned how much of that writing relates to dog problems. But there's just as much or more written about how much we love our dogs! When you walk through a bookstore or browse online these days, you can find endless humor books, coffee-table photo books of dogs and puppies, dog nutrition and holistic care books and many books devoted to discussion about when our dogs pass away. Every day, more books come out, and they channel through the bookstores and chain pet stores and online book retailers, employing many people in different capacities.

Many people earn a living creating and selling dog magazines, publications and catalogs in print. Many also profit by designing, editing and hosting vast online directories for all these publications as well as centralized sites for every kind of dog issue, breed, organization or charity. And **people will only spend money to read much of the information about dogs as long as they continue owning dogs, and continue believing that dog ownership is "fun" and relatively easy.**

Dog Vacations:

Another moneymaking recent trend is the popularity of super high-end luxury hotels, spas, ranches and various resort getaways that offer packages catering to highly upscale pet owners that are dedicated to their pooches. If you haven't heard about this trend in the dog industry, it's fascinating. Some resort packages include extras like flavored bottled dog water and dog massages, in rooms that sometimes go for over $1,000 a night (plus non-refundable pet deposits that are higher than most of us have ever paid for a room!) And offering all these dog-friendly amenities works to fill vacancies- because, no matter the price, there will always be hard-core dog lovers begging for more.

Dog Parties and Social Events:

These days a certain set of sophisticated dog owners that tend to populate gentrified, yet earth-friendly posh little towns ("latte towns") are happy to pay stratospheric prices to participate in social events with their dogs, partly because it gives them a theme to bond with like-minded owners. The book *One Nation Under Dog* presents a good overview of the trend of dog social events and networks amongst this boutiquey set. In a growing number of cities, groups meet every single weekend for dog friendly "yappy hours" and other events. There are even high-paid party planners for dog parties. When these social events are held at upscale restaurants, all the dogs' "parents" buy pricey food and drinks. And when events are held at posh doggie boutiques, they happily purchase high-end food and accessories.

Obviously, the only way people can attend such events is if they own dogs. And **use of crates or cages enables some owners to ignore their dogs all week while they're busy and then take them out on the weekends for "fun" and lots of luxury spending. Various dog professionals make this worse when they tell owners crating dogs is a good thing. But, when we look at the unprecedented amount of money dog owners spend on dog-related luxury and leisure, it's easy to see that all these people who make a living off dogs fear a great loss of income if they told owners crating wasn't a humane alternative** and then, because they couldn't crate, many busy metropolitan owners decided not to own dogs.

AKC Purebred Dog Shows:

Purebred dogs are big business as well. Traditional events for dog hobbyists include American Kennel Club (or AKC) events ranging from locally judged lure-coursing, agility and many other specialty competitions, to giant all-breed shows all over the country, including giant national championship shows like Westminster, the Eukanuba Championship and large shows sponsored by the UKC.

Events like these are huge, with vast amounts of money changing hands for the venues, maintenance, advertising, hotel rooms, charges for vendors, spectators and competitors and salaries for journalists, photographers and media. (For example, it costs *$10,000* to buy a full-page ad in one of the magazines handed out at the dog shows that showcase champions from individual kennels!)

The AKC organization has existed for over one hundred years. In addition to sponsoring shows, they collect fees for every purebred dog registered with them. And all their profits are predicated on the fact that dogs are wonderful, and it's worthwhile to exhibit them to their highest standards. Along with the AKC, there is the income earned by the breeders that compete at the shows, as well as income earned by all the professional handlers, support staff involved in planning and running the shows; writers, journalists, advertising and publicity specialists and media people who cover the shows.

And recently, an even bigger, more accessible and more popular phenomenon has been taking over the country in addition to competition dog shows. These days, giant dog-related festivals and events are frequently held in small and large cities, attended by thousands who bring their dogs to socialize and be noticed.

2. The profit from huge community dog events and festivals:

There's an old bit of movie industry wisdom that says when a dog walks across the screen everybody looks. And the increased popularity of huge dog events (usually sponsored by dog charities) in centralized public parks and squares is an example of individuals taking advantage of this quirk of human nature. Because the non-profit dog organizations or private community shelters that sponsor these events often get valuable centralized venues donated to them while they collect booth rental fees from commercial vendors and donations from the public.

Thousands of festival-goers are happy to bring their dogs out in public to show them off while they can also spontaneously reach out and pet whatever strangers' dogs they want to! At these huge festivals, even though some canine attendees that usually spend their days crated away from the world may act stressed by sudden exposure to crowds of dogs and people, the human attendees leave invigorated. And these events tend to "break the ice" between strangers and reaffirm our belief in dogs as a traditional icon of community.

3. The profit made by non-profits. How animal shelters profit, even when they don't perform the services the public assumes:

Each dog event generates money for all the people involved with it- from vendors to parks personnel, to journalists, to printers and web designers and everyone involved in promotional material and publicity. But the largest sum of money that changes hands is likely often overlooked- the public donations that support the shelters and non-profit groups that sponsor these big events.

The larger, better known private shelters in many communities are usually not government-run and funded, nor are they run completely by volunteers (like many smaller rescues) where all donations go to animal care and placement. Instead, with the donations they collect, these large private shelters and non-profits pay salaries to many staff people- including managers, administrators and media/publicity specialists who can earn professional salaries up to six figures.

Even though rescues, shelters and dog charities like these officially qualify as non-profit, growth always benefits them because they can pay more generous salaries and guarantee people jobs. And, while some mega-shelters may utilize hundreds of unpaid volunteers, the individuals they pay the high salaries are usually administrators with the least hands-on work with the animals and the most contact with public relations and *fund raising*!

Since some shelters in large cities are huge, and quite efficient in their ever-expanding roles, theoretically they need this caliber of administrators. But no matter how efficient they are at collecting donations, paying staff and promoting community-relations, **we believe that animal shelters around the nation are not functioning at the level of efficiency they could.** (For example, one small no-kill shelter had a waiting list months long and often took many months to place dogs, even though they sponsored many high-profile community events and employed several administrative-level staff and enough unskilled staff to crowd their front office. And they were not the only popular private no-kill shelter in that county where, on any given day, potential adopters would find more paid staff out front (or out back on break) than dogs in their surprisingly small kennel. Meanwhile the county-run shelter or "pound" in the area took all the animals these shelters turned away, adopted out thousands, killed thousands more and faced obstacles like outbreaks of deadly disease.)

In our version of an ideal world, all public and private shelters would pool their resources in such a way as to save the most dogs- bottom line- regardless of who owned the facilities or where in the country they were located. **Just "lack of space" should never be an excuse to kill dogs or turn dogs away to a different facility where they will be killed.** If more shelters are needed, more should be built. Or, an even better solution would be not to build traditional shelters which can stress dogs and make them sick, but rather to reimburse more appropriate foster homes for homeless dogs. This should be the direction of the future. And we feel any government grants or private donations should be divided amongst shelters and rescues based on how humanely they treat animals, how many animals they save and how efficiently they do their jobs. **We don't feel any more dogs or cats should be dying.**

People who donate money often are not clear on whether dogs at a particular animal shelter are being put to death, and how those decisions are made. Some larger progressive shelters now hire highly educated behaviorists and pay them high salaries to follow strict protocol for temperament testing dogs and deciding which to put to sleep if they fail. But, at other shelters, the staff people that decide which animals to kill have only limited qualifications and no advanced education and make decisions arbitrarily based only on personal beliefs. And dog lovers who donate to some well-publicized shelters (including some labeled "no-kill) may not realize how many dogs are actually being put down, and for what reasons, unless they truly investigate.

Why shelters make money for staff, but don't do an adequate job of saving homeless animals:

The authors believe that the killing of homeless pets that could reasonably live healthy lives should stop absolutely, even if it means the government must intervene. **Unfortunately, for all the good work that charities do and all the money and volunteer hours that concerned citizens donate, the present system of dealing with unwanted dogs and cats is still not enough to save all the animals that need it. If the system was adequate, animals wouldn't be dying.** In our opinion the most important change should be to tremendously increase enforcement of laws relating to animal cruelty and negligence. At the same time, the government should make spaying and neutering easy and affordable for *everyone*, while at the same time enforcing zero tolerance on those who don't comply.

Our current jail-like animal shelters come from a less enlightened time, and kennels designed like crowded prisons (no matter how nice public areas are remodeled to look) help no one. (As described in Chapter 5) dogs that have to reside in these conditions can suffer so much stress that they can't adjust well in adoptive homes and often quickly boomerang back into the system.

We believe public shelters, county shelters or "dog pounds" should receive adequate funding to do their job right so that budget is no longer an excuse to euthanize animals. At the same time, they should completely change to be cleaner, safer, more humane and more efficient. And large privately run community shelters should also become more efficient to provide the kindest housing, comprehensive training and careful dog/owner matching. If these non-profit shelters and rescues expect to receive government tax breaks and large amounts of donations, they should make their staff just as accountable for success as other private industry businesses would. And the dogs they rescue should receive first class help, not just long-term housing in cages or crates.

Prison-like shelter environments that seem custom made to destroy dogs' temperaments, and killing thousands, or even millions, of healthy animals for "lack of space" should become a thing of the past in a civilized society, even if the government must take additional responsibility for the system or provide additional oversight. And when private shelters fail to take up the slack in a community, charitable donors should question why, carefully examining shelters' efficiency rather than just assuming the whole problem is too many homeless pets.

At their best, animal shelters can certainly be a blessing and many caring volunteers donate an enormous amount of personal effort to shelters to save animals that others have left to die. The authors have both volunteered at shelters and were both brought up in families that supported animal shelters and adopted pets there. (For example, starting at age six, Emma used to stand out in front of supermarkets on many weekends collecting change for her local SPCA.)

But just because an organization is labeled non-profit doesn't mean they are necessarily doing the best for animals. **We advise anyone who wishes to donate money or volunteer time for homeless animals to be extremely careful and first investigate any charity. Compare how much the organization earns in donations with how many animals they place, and how quickly. Most important- never just depend on Internet contact. Before donating to any shelter, visit in person to observe how all the animals are housed.**

Unfortunately shelters, intrinsically, are no more noble or effective than the people who run them. One trend lately is to build or remodel mega-shelters with all kinds of amenities, like flat screen televisions in the lobbies and obedience classes on site. Another trend is towards more private breed rescues, where dogs stay in people's homes and are only seen by the public online or at pet store adoption events.

But one thing all these non-profits have in common is that they DO take in money, often from public donations, from government grants or tax breaks, from the value of volunteer hours and/or from adoption fees (where some breed rescues now charge as much as $400 per dog). **And, when you combine how much money all the dog non-profits combined collect, and actually do the math from the perspective of efficiently running a business, it seems almost impossible that so many homeless pets are still destroyed each year, and conditions remain as bad as they are in so many shelters and rescues.**

(One example we've noticed is that, in most of the large number of shelters we've visited, the comfortable climate control- heat and air conditioning- in the human areas doesn't extend to the indoor kennels for the dogs! It would seem offhand that lack of funding is the problem. But, the truth is, in these areas where Southern heat indices often run as high as 115 degrees and Southern cold snaps leave every dog in the usually small kennels shivering, a window unit air conditioner can cost just a few hundred dollars and a space heater less than that.)

Another concern is that many dogs offered for adoption at shelters have not learned acceptable manners as family pets, so families often feel they've adopted "uncontrollable" dogs. This doesn't just apply to county dog pounds that *must* have high turnover not to have to kill dogs, but also to many no-kill shelters that keep dogs in their care for months or years, but still send them home to adoptive families not housetrained and not knowing any house manners.

But the shelter may not perceive a problem because many successful no-kill shelters and rescues now crate dogs as long as they host them (which could be months or years) and then tell adopters to simply keep them crated for the rest of their lives, never allowing them free run of a home when the owners can't supervise.

Private shelters and rescues exist and bring in donations from animal lovers on the premise that dogs they send out to homes are adoptable. But if families decided that, in order to be considered "adoptable", dogs should have house manners (and not just be controllable if locked up), then many shelters and rescues that now bring in large amounts of money might go out of business because they only prepare dogs to live in cages.

Is it ethical to send a dog home with a family if the only way they feel they can keep him is to crate him?

Shelters have become a big money generating industry, premised on the fact that any average suburban family with no special training or financial resources can visit on any given weekend and leave with a dog that will fill their next fifteen years with more joy than stress. But if these families knew that their future with the adopted dog might be different, many might not adopt, not wanting to put in the effort to rehabilitate certain shelter or rescue dogs.

We've read blogs where people state that it's preferable for a dog to live out his life in a crate in a no-kill shelter than to be euthanized. But we suspect many people have now expanded this philosophy to the use of crates in their homes, only adopting dogs because they expect to keep them crated most of the time.

Some owners insist on crating just for convenience, leaving a dog or puppy locked up for a 12-hour work shift, plus 2 hours' commute time, and not caring that the dog is suffering pain trying to hold its bladder this long. Other owners keep a well-behaved dog crated every day for life just because they don't want him to shed. People with priorities like this might otherwise never bring home a dog. But if dog professionals convince them that it's scientifically and morally correct to crate dogs for the vast majority of every day, then these people *may* buy or adopt, feeling they won't lose out on convenience. And of course irresponsible dog breeders (including puppy millers and the worst backyard breeders) are happy when owners crate dogs, since it lowers the overall expectations of what dogs should be capable of and encourages more people to buy pups on impulse, never investigating their background.

Diana Delmar, in *The Guilt-Free Dog Owner's Guide* is one expert that agrees. As she asks in the book, "What is the real motivation behind the advocates of long-term crating? Could it be a conscious or unconscious desire to ensure that the dogs they breed or train are good models? After all, a dog who lives in a crate most of his life rarely has a chance to soil or chew. Just about any kind of breeding is going to make the dog look good and any kind of training 'successful'" Ms. Delmar emphasizes that, "Perhaps most disturbing about the crating controversy is the force with which some crating advocates insist upon the method." And she urges owners, "Don't be intimidated by the adamant breeder or trainer who tells you that you are ignorant about dogs!"

A certain number of disreputable shelters and rescues have used the plight of abandoned dogs and cats as a front to collect salaries for uncaring and unskilled staff and management whose lack of efficiency caring for animals and getting them placed would easily get them fired in the competitive sector. Some of these facilities keep dogs hidden away from the public eye in tiny cages with no electric light, heat or air conditioning for years until eventually a number of the dogs go mad. But as long as adopters (and charitable donors) are told to expect no more than wild animals that need to be managed in cages rather than placid, mannerly family dogs, they're less likely to identify other abuses in the way homeless dogs are cared for.

Even caring staff and administrators in reputable shelters now face challenging ethical. If busy modern owners like Bouncy's in Chapter 6 suddenly released dogs after years of excessive crating, many might exhibit problems and might soon be surrendered to shelters. Dogs demand a large amount of time and attention, in a world where many couples working can spare no more than a few minutes quality time with each other each day. **Without crating, millions of people might decide dog ownership isn't the "dream" they thought it was, so they might decide to put off dog ownership, to select dogs more carefully or not to own dogs at all.**

The first effect of a more careful attitude towards dog ownership would be less business for large-scale puppy mill breeders who now make billions and sell up to 4 million pups a year. Today many of the people who buy these pups buy on impulse, with insufficient information. But with a change in attitude about dog ownership, only the people who truly had the resources to take care of dogs would own them. And this would mean less dogs abandoned or surrendered and thus a better chance of adoption for those dogs currently languishing in shelters.

Of course the approximately 10,000 puppy mill breeders around the country and all the irresponsible "backyard breeders" would lose out if families stopped buying dogs on impulse. And even some shelter employees- especially management and fund-raising specialists making $60,000, $80,000 or over $100,000 per year- might be unhappy if their overcrowded facilities with old-school prison-style kennels closed because of less homeless dogs.

Profit loss industry-wide if fewer families chose to own dogs

If Home Dog Crating were no longer considered a humane option, the dog industry would eventually have to change and develop innovative solutions to help families happily coexist with their dogs. But, until a whole new breed of dog services developed to help modern owners in ways they really need, many families might either give their dogs up or choose not to buy dogs. If less families owned dogs, there would also be less income for breeders that depend on impulse buying, for dog pounds and shelters and for all the business that depend on dogs.

If less families owned dogs, there would also be less income for:

Veterinarians and office staff:

One of the biggest sources of revenue industry-wide is veterinary medicine, especially the growing field of veterinary specialists who perform increasingly complex surgeries and treatments on par with human treatments, often costing in thousands. And with so many dogs originating in puppy mills, serious disorders are showing up in younger dogs, and even puppies. Obviously, if less people owned dogs there would be less business for veterinarians and their staff.

Dog groomers:

Professional grooming can be a necessity for many of the popular small breeds. For owners to spend up to $100 each month for dogs' entire lives isn't uncommon, and many owners now springing for highly expensive spa-style extras. Just one dog could easily generate $10,000- $15,000 over its lifetime for a groomer. So it can benefit groomers to keep customers no matter how their customers house their dogs.

Dog Care- Day Care, Boarding Kennels and Pet Sitters:

This segment of the economy includes popular doggie day care facilities with modern features that appeal to metropolitan career-people, who may bring their dogs for "day care" for up to $600/month for the rest of the dogs' lives. In today's increasingly mobile world, upscale day care facilities thrive. And every level of boarding kennel, including the rough-hewn old fashioned ones, get plenty of business from owners who must frequently hurry out of town on business or family commitments.

Pet sitting is another rapidly growing industry where there's an abundance of business. For example, in one hot area of New York City where customers have little extra time but lots of expendable income, one popular pet sitter boasts that she personally makes over 100,000 a year. And many highly successful pet sitters start hiring employees and subcontractors to cover the business they can't handle alone. Just one organization of professional pet sitters, Pet Sitters International, reached 6,000 members several years ago. With families increasingly busy, with less time for pets, there's also an increasing demand for dog walkers. Counting the professionals and the "hobbyists" who pet sit part-time and never officially register as businesses, the amount of money people earn from pet sitting is huge. And, even though pet sitters' income is influenced by many factors, their business certainly depends on the number of dogs that people own.

(Personally we believe **hiring a professional dog walker is a great way for busy families to give their dogs exercise and attention when they're away at work extra long hours**. But lately we've been shocked to discover that many pet sitters these days get paid just to allow dogs out of crates and into back yards for very short bathroom breaks. This is, of course, better than continual crating. But we think pet sitters and dog walkers should be paid to give *alternatives* to crates, not just for servicing dogs that live in them.)

Fun retail products for dogs:

In recent years exciting and appealing new products for dogs debut with increasing fanfare at vast international trade shows where hundreds of vendors pay top dollar for booths and thousands of retail buyers attend. Some new products are useful for dogs. Others, like rhinestone studded designer dog dresses or designer carrying cases that sell for multiple thousands of dollars are obviously made only for owners.

And in gentrified shopping districts in cities of every size a whole new style of doggie boutique now sells upscale dog merchandise along with pricey natural food and treats. And, amongst a certain set of owners, "superpremium" and high-end organic pet food is considered the only healthful way to feed a dog.

In these increasingly popular pet boutiques a fresh-baked bone-shaped cookie costs $2 or more, and shoppers customarily buy them by the bagful. Leashes can easily cost $50- $60. These indulgences, on a large scale, add up to lots of profit for the pet industry. And some extreme dog fans even pay tens of thousands of dollar on dog items that are truly outrageous. This includes room-sized, custom-designed dog houses with heat, air conditioning, flat-screen televisions, custom fine furniture and human-scale walk-in closets to accommodate full wardrobes of doggie clothing. Some of these "dog houses" can cost as much as human starter homes!

Dog clothing, ranging from high-end ball gowns to costumes that customers dress their dogs in for festivals and yappy hours is another interesting source of profit, because once humans get hooked on buying dog clothes, there's no limit. Some dogs have- literally- closets full of clothing and special outfits for every occasion. Even a pattern book in the Wal-Mart sewing section devotes a large section just to dog clothing and decorations.

Another area of "dog" indulgences that really seems more about humans is the explosively growing modern business of upscale dog parties for every occasion, including dog weddings, which can cost in the tens of thousands just like human weddings.

We're not so surprised about all this obsession with dogs. **But, to us, what *does* seem inconceivable is that a person who would spend thousands on their toy dog's fashions would leave that same dog home locked in a cage- 8, 10, 12 or 14 hours at a stretch and 18-22 hours total per day.**

Of course a large proportion of the owners who obsessively spoil their dogs never crate.

But many actually do! And many of the professionals that owners of "high maintenance" dogs interface with actually instruct them to cage their pampered little dogs as a lifestyle, without ever acknowledging the hypocrisy. This includes some: breeders; groomers who charge to put bows in dogs' hair and nail polish on their toes; trainers who market their services showing off cutesy albums full of photos of "graduates" wearing caps and gowns; some obedience and breed club members and even some pet sitters. It also includes a number of upscale dog boutique owners, who sell crates and boast about crating their own dogs, even while selling you $35 ceramic dog bowls and $13 bags of treats made with yam, bison or blueberries or supplements to prevent joint pain. Even shelter and rescue directors that host all the gala parties and events where dogs attend dressed in high fashion will often tell anyone who will listen that dogs- even if they are wearing tiaras- should spend most of their lives caged. We can't say how many of these dog people give this advice strictly to increase their income. But the financial motives are obvious.

Some affluent dog owners who just want to have fun may not be prepared for the full responsibilities of ownership and training of a dog or a puppy. But if dog professionals can convince them to buy the dog anyway and just put it in a crate most of the time for the next 15 or so years, the industry can then count on them as regular consumers of all the items ranging from $2 cookies to $2,000 ball gowns! The more dogs people own, the better it is for the luxury segment of the dog industry.

And the better it is for an even bigger segment of the pet industry...

The industry that could potentially lose the most if people were more careful about owning dogs is the dog food industry:

We believe that the biggest and most important source of income in the dog industry can also be the easiest to overlook simply because it is so huge. And this is the dog food industry, representing every price and type of dog food. Manufacturers range from gigantic corporations to Internet-based mom and pop operations and retailers range from community shops specializing in natural food, to nationwide pet store chains, to the country's hugest supermarket and discount department store chains. Sales of dog food also support diverse jobs ranging from farming, to manufacturing, to transportation, to retail to advertising.

The reason the pet industry might want families to own more dogs even if all the owners did was keep them in cages becomes clear when you do the math, multiplying the number of dogs in the country (approximately 77.5 million,) times the average cost of their food over an average lifetime. And, every day, dogs have to eat. Even a dog that eats only $30/month in food would still allow the industry to net $3,600 on him over the course of 10 years. And many owners who buy super-premium food or raw food diets for larger dogs can easily spend four times this much.

Realistically, the cost of dog food has changed, as more and more owners trade up to premium or super-premium foods to be "politically correct" or to feel safe. The field of dog nutrition has exploded due to a number of factors including our obsession with babying our dogs along with the tainted pet food scare several years ago where many dogs died and the fact that many dogs today suffer serious food allergies. **Today, paying over $50 for a 30 lb. bag of all-natural super-premium kibble or $13.99 for a small bag of all-natural treats is common. A can of good dog food can cost $4-$6** (One local gentleman buys these in *cases* for his Bullmastiff!) **And dogs that eat special frozen or fresh food cost their owners much more**. Many new high-end food and fresh dog food manufacturers now do all their business through online ordering and home delivery. And many also sell special nutritional supplements and vitamins that owners purchase for the life of their dogs.

Loving owners with the resources will happily buy all of these products if they believe they're doing the best for their pets. And a growing industry of books, magazines and online communities keeps concerned dog owners constantly plugged in to the latest advances in canine nutrition and holistic care.

But NO ONE who profits from selling dog food- whether their brand sells at upscale pet boutiques, mega-retailers or dollar stores- would want people to stop buying dogs. It's essential to dog food manufacturers and dog food retailers that families keep buying dogs, no matter how they house them or how many times the dogs change hands. Along with all the other income in the dog industry, the huge expenditures on dog food make it clear why so many people, and such powerful forces in our society, would be okay with dogs living in crates.

If people really desire to baby their dogs, they cannot crate them. And many in the dog industry may fear the loss of profit if less people owned dogs because of this. When people own dogs and want to boast that we love them, we buy them lost of pricey items including gourmet food, fancy toys, beds, leashes and everything material.

The authors also love to personally lavish the best food, toys and treats on our dogs that we consider our "babies". **But we feel it becomes deeply and cruelly hypocritical the second an owner purchases all of these extreme items of love and devotion for an animal that spends most of its life waiting in a cage!** If all the people who cater to their dogs with material things realized how they were failing their beloved pet dogs by crating, and if they fully understood the plight of all the other dogs in our country suffering in cages, they might no longer have the stomach for buying the "fun" and luxury dog products, and they might not want to have much involvement with the dog industry in its current state, threatening the income of many people, including many whose connection to the industry is not obvious.

Animal Wellness? We Love Our Dogs So Much That...

Whole Foods Supermarket is synonymous with a healthy, eco-friendly and politically correct lifestyle. And the progressive magazine called "*Animal Wellness*" that we found at a local store (priced at $5.95 for 106 slick, slim and eye-popping pages) promoted a wide array of holistic dog products and politically correct dog activities and causes. Featured topics and advertisements ranged from all-natural super-premium brands of pet food that typical Wal-Mart or K-Mart shoppers have never heard of, to multiple ads for doggie "wheelchairs" and sport-style carts designed to increase mobility, independence and quality of life for doggie amputees and dogs suffering from bone or joint disease. *Animal Wellness'* ten year anniversary issue saluted female pioneers in animal wellness, including a woman who operates an animal hospice where she treats canine "hopeless cases" with modalities like hydrotherapy, acupuncture, massage and flower essences, a person who obviously feels that dogs deserve the best quality of life possible even in the most extreme circumstances. In the issue retailers advertised products for owners who clearly consider pets treasured members of the family, including memorial items such as the "Furry Angel Memorial Candle", the book "*Animals and the Afterlife*" and several alternatives to convert departed pets' ashes into unique crystal style jewelry.

Readers of this progressive magazine obviously love their pets! So at first we saw this as just the kind of magazine we thought would embrace our dog books with positive reviews and we contemplating sending them copies. But our minds changed quickly when we came upon an article in the very center of the issue about general practices for *safe crating*! This article, entitled "*Crate Craft*" talked about crating as if it was the most natural thing in the world (as long as you could avoid a disaster like the author described when a dog in her family lost circulation in her leg that got wound in a blanket when she was left crated). The *"Crate Craft"* article features a photo of a cute dog, of indeterminate age, in her crate, where, for photo's sake, the door just happens to be shown left open (even though the article describes crating where you "make sure the door is securely shut and locked").

Ironically, we flipped through the very same issue and we found another piece entitled, "Down with Puppy Mills", which urged people to boycott pet stores and do their part to actively abolish puppy mills. And the photo subject in the article about the abused dogs happened to look exactly like the dog photographed for "Crate Craft". And the dog was posed in the exact same sized crate! The only notable difference was that the "Down with Puppy Mills" photo was moodily shadowed and the dog look troubled, while the same (?) dog depicting the happily crated dog in "Crate Craft" was posed with a cute dog bed patterned with paw prints! We think these two photos clearly typify the madness and inconsistency of modern beliefs about crating! And it's bizarre and troubling for us to find a magazine that seems so progressive overall in beliefs about the freedom of motion and the naturalness and love dogs deserve to include such a potentially dangerous and damaging practice as crating as just another part of canine "wellness".

Since we only picked up this copy for research, we have not read the most current issues of the magazine, so we certainly hope the magazine has since changed its editorial stance on the practice of Home Dog Crating. We do feel that, overall, *Animal Wellness* is a progressive magazine that can inspire many readers to do good things for animals. So, we would certainly be willing to write a piece for the magazine about Excessive Home Dog Crating and more humane alternatives as well as sending the editor a copy of our activity book *The Cure for Useless Dog Syndrome* with hundreds of positive activities to promote great house manners, emotional balance and bond with owners with no need for crates.

Once excessive crating is acknowledged as a heartless practice, income might dry up for the worst players in the dog industry, especially puppy mill breeders:

In a different world, where constant crating was not an option, we believe there would be many less impulse buyers of puppies. And families' needs for healthy pups with their good socialization and good house manners already started would be met by the many reputable smaller breeders who already raise dogs to the highest standards at reasonable prices. Based on public outcry, legislation and enforcement against puppy mills would also toughen.

And the puppy mill breeders that overcharge and specialize in churning out millions of damaged dogs at an unreasonably fast rate simply could no longer compete with the good breeders.

With puppy mills going out of business- considering they now produce 2-4 million pups per year according to the Humane Society of the United States- a huge income amount of income would be lost. The same applies to pet stores that are commonly believed to sell puppy mill pups. (For example, the Petland chain, which had a much publicized class-action lawsuit brought against them several years ago, as described in Chapter 11, was alone responsible for selling approximately 30,000 pups per year at that time.) This portion of the industry could only recover once more reputable breeders replaced the puppy mills and started breeding pups to the standards that newly enlightened households would demand. But right now existing breeders that are profiting by keeping large numbers of dogs caged have every reason to support the status quo.

The shake-up would also apply to anyone working in the dog industry- be they a groomer, a seller of trendy pet products, a boarding kennel owner or even a veterinarian if their appeal to consumers was based solely on speed, impatience and immediate gratification or the fact that there were not enough services to meet demand during the recent pet industry "bubble".

Some people in the dog industry have always put in tremendous hard work and inspiration to provide the best for animals. And, in a more enlightened world of dog ownership, even if less people owned dogs, these hard workers would get plenty of business. And, even in a country with less dogs, caring dog owners would willingly pay more for a higher quality of service so the "good guys" would not lose out.

For a long time, and even in today's more cautious economy, the dog business has run on a gold-rush mentality. And, although there are lots of exceptions, many people have made quick money in the business in recent years simply because it was booming, even while acting rude or "flip" with owners and rough and neglectful with dogs.

We believe if the philosophical climate changed and people realized that dogs deserved a better quality of life than life in a crate, they might also question if all the other services they were paying for were acceptably humane. In an atmosphere with less dogs and more discerning owners, individuals in the dog industry would have to take full responsibility for their effects on dogs just to stay in business. Eventually, those that were most skilled, worked hardest and acted nicest would prevail. And it's easy to see why many people who make lots of money in the dog industry today would fear that, if dog owners stopped crating, they might suddenly become much more demanding customers.

The Emotional Motive So Many People Maintain the Crating Conspiracy:
In some ways, our love affair with dogs is a way that many of us keep believing that life is, by nature, good and that we can have wonderful things happen to us. Many of us need to believe that our dogs love us. In fact, for a significant number of us, our dogs are actually our most meaningful relationship. There have been many surveys that prove this. And Chapter 12 includes quotes from many experts on all the real ways dogs enhance our lives. The authors personally have been blessed to share our lives with many kind and noble dogs and we know that dogs can immensely exceed our expectations with their abilities, intelligence and goodness.

But **we think something needs to change when we hear people speaking obsessively of their mutual love with their dogs, while they leave those same dogs in tiny cages for up to 22 hours a day!** It's simply human nature for most of us to want to believe that we are kind and ethical people, even in a society at large where morals and values are constantly trampled. The theory of cognitive dissonance demonstrates in a research setting that people have extreme difficulty believing contradictory ideas about ourselves, and we like to believe that, at heart, our character is good. And the unconditional love of our pet dogs helps to prove this for some of us. So how could we live with ourselves if we suddenly had to face the fact that we had treated our dogs cruelly for years simply for convenience, because of fears or because people who we believed were experts had duped us?

Because such a large enough number of dog owners are motivated to protect their self-concept at whatever the cost, this has created a conspiracy even without anyone expressly plotting. **As long as "everyone who matters" cages dogs and agrees that you can crate your pet and still be a good "dog mommy" or "dog daddy", then average Americans can still go on comfortably functioning no matter what we've already done to Fido. Many people share this lie about the positives of crating with our peers in order to support each other in our frailty. The professionals who profit economically in all the ways discussed in this book promote the conspiracy to support their own views of themselves and to protect their livelihoods. And more and more dog owners join in to allow themselves to feel good, rather than guilty, once they've already taken the step and started crating their dogs rather than leaving them free in the home.**

Nice average people want dog ownership to be good! We want the joy of cuddling our dogs when we get home from work, or the pride of showing them off on Saturday while strolling around the park, or watching them play in our yards and feeling a week's worth of stress melting away. **We certainly don't want to think of ourselves as lacking because we can't seem to housetrain our dogs without caging them, even though our parents and grandparents could. We certainly don't want to acknowledge that we are ever afraid of our dogs, ever hate our dogs or ever feel disgusted by our dogs or that we ever feel completely overwhelmed by the burden of dog ownership added to all the other stressors in our lives.**

Some of the theories of the development of domestic dogs say that dogs came from wolves, some of whom turned into scavengers that circled our campfires and our dumps. But modern dog owners don't want to think of our pets as strange feral animals to be feared. We'd rather think of them all as cuddly big puppies. And it can be easier to ignore the existence of many dogs, including the millions in puppy mills, thousands tethered and/or tormented for the purpose of fighting and even next-door neighbors' dogs that could be locked inside tiny cages for almost all the moments of their lives. **It's a sad irony that thousands of years of selective breeding and careful husbandry shaped initially wild dogs into tame animals that lived beautifully in our homes, but now crate-training suggested by "experts" is starting to damage those house manners that took so many thousands of years to build.**

In our drive to worship the CONCEPT of dogs, we have to wonder however whether some dog lovers, including those who make policy and influence public opinion, have also been evading the facts. This is because, **the moment a person in power in the world of dogs understands the truth about cruel crating, they will inevitably feel compelled to speak out. Otherwise, by their silence, they'd support the vocal pro-crating majority fueling the spread of the problem. Yet so many dog lovers feel reluctant to make waves.**

For example a new rescue volunteer might hesitate to challenge ten other hardworking volunteers when she learns that they all believe in crating, and that they crate all the rescue dogs in their care, because she doesn't want to downplay all the rescue's other efforts to save homeless dogs. Or a director of a metropolitan shelter that takes in millions in donations might feel she couldn't start refusing to send dogs home with people who intend to crate, knowing how many less dogs would be adopted. Or the staff at a busy might find it difficult to break the news to eager families that crating isn't a good option, and certain dogs wouldn't suit their lifestyles because of a mismatch in energy levels or free time.

But ultimately, no matter how difficult the moral dilemmas, the authors believe **lying to ourselves isn't a real choice. Policy makers and opinion shapers must face the truth and start speaking out so we can bring dog ownership back to that idyll we all**

crave so much, both for ourselves and for our dogs. If we don't, and we continue to lie about what our dogs need, eventually this bubble will burst because dogs simply are *not* den animals, nor crate animals. The way we coexist with our animals has deteriorated so badly at this point, with such widescale acceptance of such an obviously cruel and unhealthy practice as Excessive Home Dog Crating, that the time has come for a change, and it's just a matter of how we chose to get to it! And we believe once people *do* face the truth, they will devote more time, attention, effort and efficiency to finally build a *real* utopia for dogs and their owners that go far beyond diamond collars, cutesy websites and dog-industry celebrities.

Chapter 11: Extreme Case Studies, Puppy Mills & Abuses of Dogs

America's Puppy Mills- a horrible beginning for millions of pups

Definition of puppy mills for those that don't know:

Not too long ago, the majority of Americans had never heard the term "puppy mill", and most didn't know about the grisly and heartless conditions where most of the cute little puppies for sale in puppy shops had been raised. But today, even though many people still buy from pet shops not knowing about puppy mills- huge wholesale dog breeding operations where dogs are abused and neglected- and even though laws against puppy mills still aren't strict enough, the truth about how pet shop and Internet puppies are raised is becoming more mainstream.

This is due to the efforts of investigating anti-cruelty organizations like the Humane Society of the United States (HSUS) and numerous other national and local rescue organizations. When information about puppy mills reached the public in an Oprah Winfrey television special in 2008, it also reached critical mass. This show, along with a scandal at an upscale pet boutique in Bel Air that was frequented by celebrities like Paris Hilton has made average Americans more suspicious when they buy a dog. The latest scandal has been the well-publicized civil suit brought against the well-known chain Petland, for knowingly selling sick pups that had come from puppy mills while misrepresenting their health and backgrounds.

The term "puppy mill" is a label for the at least 10,000 substandard large scale dog breeding facilities nationwide, where hundreds of dogs and pups at each kennel are used like inanimate objects. These facilities are overcrowded, cruel, filthy and disease ridden and they often operate with multiple violations of the law. The heinous cruelties of the breeders- which include leaving dogs in stifling filth, with agonizing untreated injuries- sometimes living beside the rotting corpses of their dead littermates- leave the average person sickened and appalled. Dogs in puppy mills receive no positive human contact. They are usually cramped together in stacked wire cages and never released, except when the puppies are transported hundreds of miles across the country to be sold.

At the puppy farms the breeding bitches are forced to give birth to one litter after another no matter their health. They usually spend their entire lives in cramped cages, often standing on wire that causes constant discomfort, because the kennel operators don't want to take the time to clean solid floors. In these housing conditions, excrement from the higher cages is left to descend onto the dogs below and dogs often suffer from illness and infection due to the ammonia and the lack of cleanliness. Dogs are often cold or overheated and deprived of proper food and water. Pups are sometimes left to die in cages beside their littermates and then left to rot with nobody bothering to remove the corpses. And dogs coming from these facilities are known to suffer from all manner of serious medical and psychological illnesses.

Pups often leave puppy mills with illness ranging from highly infectious kennel cough, which can lead to other more serious illness if not treated, to a serious and highly contagious illnesses like Parvovirus, which is frequently fatal. These pups quickly spread illnesses to other pups in pet stores and pet store owners sometimes try to save their investment by dosing all the puppies in a store with antibiotics, a practice that can be dangerous. Other pet stores try to sell the pups soon enough that disease symptoms don't manifest until the buyer gets them home. In their first weeks with the puppy, these new owners often spend hundreds or thousands on veterinary bills, and face emotional anguish trying to treat the pups' illnesses. And many pups die anyway.

Individuals who run puppy mills profit from doing bulk business, investing almost nothing in the care of the dogs, and then selling the pups cheap to middlemen, who put them through a brutal trip- often drugged- on their way to retailers. Ironically, the same puppies- usually small breeds- that spent the first months of their lives in the most squalid conditions are often displayed in cute little baby cribs in stylish boutiques like the now closed Pets of Bel Air, and sold for thousands of dollars.

Because of this opportunity for tremendous profit when the pups sell at retail, the individuals who run the puppy mills and all the middlemen they deal with do everything in their power to keep their abusive practices secret. This has been made much easier by the Internet, the latest venue of choice for criminally negligent breeders to anonymously sell sick or abused puppies to families around the country. And **Internet sales of pups entirely unregulated.**

Recently, some progressive legislation has passed in several states aimed to control puppy mill breeders. And efforts by private organizations to raise awareness and to investigate and stop puppy mill breeders are increasing.

But the law still makes it hard to collect evidence and prove the wrongdoing of the individuals who run the puppy mills. And even advances like tougher standards on obvious abuses such as wire floors in cages have been limited and extremely watered down. Even the wording in some of the new legislation to control puppy mills and pet shops (such as California's) remains quite vague and depends upon personal notions of cruelty, including under what conditions caging a pet dog becomes cruelty.

The legislation that passed in November 2010 in Missouri does mandate periods of exercise and define specific dimensions for cages. Floor space would not have to exceed 30 sq. ft., even for a large breed. But this legislation is infinitely better than the current regulations for volume breeders in Missouri that do not dictate *any* limits on space in cages, nor prohibit dealers from keeping a dog confined to a cage for every minute of its entire life. Unfortunately, even though the Missouri Dog Breeding Initiative passed, as of the publication of this book, it was still facing major legal challenges that threatened most of its provision.

Many other states still continue with no new regulations to limit puppy mill breeding, other than the broadest animal cruelty laws and USDA regulations which are meant to control farms and agricultural animals. And, currently, breeders who sell puppies directly to customers over the Internet (an increasingly popular practice) are not subject to *any* required licensure or standardized regulation at all.

And as recently 2008, regulations in Pennsylvania hadn't yet been changed. And breeders were still shooting unwanted dogs, rather than humanely euthanizing them. In one case, in Berks County, Pennsylvania, two brothers who owned kennels on adjoining farms avoided facing legal violations for improper care of their dogs by simply shooting 80 of them before a visit by investigators.

Many charitable organizations promote adoption as an alternative to purchasing dogs and advise potential new owners that puppy stores are a terrible place to acquire dogs. **Yet, according to the Humane Society of the United States, puppy mills still sell 2-4 million pups per year.**

And pet stores are still selling many sick pups. (One example is a customer of ours who bought a pup from a local shop that was ill with potentially fatal Parvovirus. After $2,000 in treatment, this pup survived, but her owner had reason to suspect that she wasn't the only sick pup at the store.)

It's common practice for pet stores to quarantine newly arrived puppies in back rooms for a few days while they pump them full of antibiotics. So many pups die in these "back rooms" that **one South Florida store was storing dead puppies in a freezer,** in the same refrigerator where employees were told to keep their lunches. Rumor had it that another South Florida store customarily buried dead puppies in the yard behind their building where they held their group dog training classes. And employees of these stores like these are instructed by management to answer customer questions according to a preset script- always stating that the dogs come from reputable breeders, not puppy mills, and that they are in great health.

Unfortunately, as customer awareness about the dangers of puppy mills has grown, the tactics of those who sell the puppies have simply become more deceitful. Customers may come to a store after hearing the horror stories and naively ask a salesperson, "Do your pups come from puppy mills?" And the salesperson will emphatically tell them "no". Instead, employees are told to tell customers the dogs come from "a great breeder" in Nebraska or Iowa, or even Pennsylvania, where Lancaster County Amish country is a known epicenter of puppy mill breeders, or Missouri, the so- called "puppy mill capitol".

A documentary that exposed the upscale Pets of Bel Air pet store for selling puppy mill pups showed how employees had been coached to always say that dogs' health was good, and that they were obtained from wonderful breeders. If a customer noted that a puppy seemed sick, one of the pretty young salespeople demonstrated how (rather than admitting the pup might be seriously ill) she would say he was suffering from, "sniffles" because it "sounds cuter".

Every time that police and humane officials raid a puppy mill, multiple dogs, sometimes multiple hundreds are seized. And unfortunately, raids like this seem to make headlines somewhere in the country almost every day.

Lancaster County Pennsylvania, the charming and bucolic Amish Country holds a dark side that many Americans have become aware of in recent years. Pennsylvania has also passed legislation to put some controls on puppy mill breeders, because of public outcry after some of the terrible discoveries in puppy mill raids in the state during the past several years. When, Main Line Animal Rescue, a private charitable organization, launched war on the puppy mills in Lancaster County Pennsylvania's Amish Country by erecting a billboard on a local turnpike to warn tourists, and then followed this with another billboard conspicuously in sight of Oprah Winfrey's Chicago television studios, they scored big. Oprah did a television special and now many Americans know that Lancaster County is not just the home of charming farms and religious men in old-fashioned garb driving horses and buggies, but also the home of many puppy mills.

In one case a breeder had 18 dogs seized. The dog warden testified in court that she had witnessed "dogs housed in kennels with decaying dead rats in them and dogs with food receptacles contaminated by feces, spiders and moldy food." Some of the dogs seized included dogs with fight wounds, a Jack Russell with a broken leg and dogs with ear, foot and gum infections. One puppy's hind feet had been chewed off. A veterinarian also testified that, "some of the dogs were so matted that they essentially could not defecate... Those dogs had to be treated with antibiotics to make sure bacteria didn't back up into their systems."

In another case, the *Animal Cops* television show followed the Pennsylvania SPCA during the raid and filmed conditions. PSPCA representative Elaine Scapalia reported that, of the 100 dogs on the farm, "All were in crowded cages, their nails were turned under, and two had embedded collars. Others had eye inflammation and untreated abscesses".

The raid on the farm happened because two weeks earlier an ad in a Lancaster newspaper for free breeder dogs had caught the attention of Bill Smith, founder of Main Line Animal Rescue in Chester Springs. Volunteers went to the farm and took nine dogs, all in deplorable condition. Teeth on one dog were so bad that he couldn't close his mouth. "Two [dogs] were missing their eyes," Smith said. "They had big gaping holes with flies in them. One of the dogs had his eye hanging out. Two were missing ears." (These types of injuries are consistent with either fighting, or caused by crowded and rusted and broken wire on crates.)

One particularly interesting fact about this case is how all this unspeakable cruelty hid behind a seemingly pleasant façade. According to the newspaper report, "the so-called puppy mill [Amish farmer John] Blank operated at his 73-acre farm along Route 10 was not visible from the highway. Instead, a sign advertising brown eggs and cut flowers greeted motorists." The property was reported as "immaculate, with carefully tended fields of corn and tobacco, and a large garden in front of the farmhouse".

One amazing thing about puppy mills is the number of dogs that are the victims. It seems like every time a vast number of dogs are seized from a single property, a newer raid occurs with even more dogs. This is, of course, facilitated by cages and the fact that many puppy mill operators focus on small dogs, trying to squeeze the most animals possible into a limited space.

One of the more shocking cases, where an entire menagerie of almost 1,000 animals ranging from dogs to swans, monkeys and miniature horses were living in horrific conditions was revealed during a raid by SPCA agents in Lehigh County Pennsylvania. ("SPCA raids 'horrific' LeHigh County kennel", Amy Worden, Philadelphia Enquirer, October 2, 2008). **700 of the animals on the property were dogs**. The article relates how agents reported, "Small dogs were crowded shoulder to shoulder in double-deck kennels, and larger breeds, including Great Danes and St. Bernards, were housed four to six in an outdoor pen. Inside one house were dozens of dogs, cats, parrots, chickens and hamsters, some roaming wild and others stacked in cages stuffed in every room." They also reported that most had no food or water and were covered in their own feces. Dead guinea pig carcasses had littered the ground between outbuildings and agents found 65 animal corpses in a freezer and the stench of ammonia and feces drifted onto a busy highway alongside the property.

Reading about cases like this a person is left to wonder about whether it is really right for humans to have the kind of authority and ownership that can allow this kind of abuse at its most extreme degree. In other words, are these 700 dogs really no more than objects to be maintained for breeding and personal gain? At what point does unimaginable selfishness and heartlessness on the part of the owner turn to prosecutable cruelty? Should dogs, that in so many homes are our family members and our friends and soul mates, be used like animals that are raised specifically for human food? And this, of course, opens up the philosophical question of whether it is moral/ethical to use farm animals in this manner either... Unfortunately it is beyond the scope of this book to address these philosophical questions.

But there is another question that baffles and shocks us in ways even more. The article reports that a sign on the road by the puppy mill, which was ironically called

"Almost Heaven Kennel", "advertised pet grooming, boarding and breeding." So **we wonder who were the clients of this hellhole, who voluntarily brought their pet dogs to be worked on in such a place?** Perhaps the reason the thought horrifies us so is that we are sure, basing it on our own observations, that this man *did* have clients.

A few years ago we personally saw a dangerously cramped boarding/day care facility owned by a smiling couple who referred to small cages as "suites" and looked forward to installing webcams *in the small, crate-sized cages* so that owners could go online and check on their dogs lying there for hours. Despite several negative incidents in the few months the facility was open that involved dog-aggression and contagious intestinal parasites, local people were saying good things about the place and hurrying to make reservations.

As we describe in other chapters, we've also seen a few no-kill shelters whose "back rooms" where the animals live would leave some people with lifelong nightmares. Yet these organizations feature appealing/heartwarming brochures and websites, bring in plenty of donations from an elite crowd and are welcome at some chain pet store adoption events in their local cities.

These places all have in two things in common. The first is that they're not committing any prosecutable violations or crimes in the way they house dogs because of the wording of current laws. And the second is that, like "Almost Heaven", they continue to be beloved in their communities, with loyal followings. In fact, the no-kill shelter where we've seen dogs housed in the least comfortable and most squalid (although not technically illegal) conditions for the longest periods also advertises *grooming and boarding*, and apparently they make money off this business...

In the case of the Almost Heaven Kennel in Pennsylvania, according to Dan Sheehan, writing for the *Morning Call*, "A woman who said she was a dog grooming client at Almost Heaven defended [the owner] Eckhart and his business. 'This man tries to be good and people are trying to take his livelihood away from him,' said Millie Altomore of Allentown. She says she's been in the kennel and it is clean. 'He does a beautiful job grooming the dogs,' she said."

Unbelievably, even this was not the largest or most heinous of puppy mill raids. In West Virginia in 2008 The Humane Society of the United States acted as the lead animal welfare organization to raid the Whispering Oaks Kennel, where nearly 1,000 dogs were surrendered. Breeding dogs were housed in small rabbit hutches, many with no access to water in the 95 degree heat. Like most puppy mill dogs, these dogs had never left their dank cages, nor felt the touch of a loving human hand.

Researchers, like Dr. Randall Lockwood, currently of the United States SPCA and formerly of the HSUS, have established links between cruelty to animals and cruelty to other humans, notably in cases of sociopathic killers. So it's no surprise that one of the puppy mill cases we came across was more horrifying than just the abuses to the dogs. In "Truth About Pet Trade: Extremely Sad Case in Mississippi" *The Daily Journal*, May 22, 2008 reported an "unspeakable case of child and animal neglect." The suspects, a couple, used to breed dogs including English Bulldogs, Shih Tzus, Yorkies and Pugs that they sold at various flea markets in Mississippi. A doctor tipped police off that their adopted two-year old daughter may have suffered abuse. When police visited the home they discovered 25 cats, several ducks and 180 breeding dogs on the property and eight other children- all in bad shape. They found the toddler in dire condition, and the child subsequently died.

So where does one draw the line? **We can't help but wonder if America's current acceptance of caging dogs in homes has blunted us to some of the horrors of puppy mills.** Of course, when we hear about the kind of extreme injuries, disease and filth described in the cases above most normal people are horrified. And yet, "regular" people walked into the kennel called Almost Heaven, saw the dogs stacked in cages and still, apparently, left their own dogs there for grooming and boarding- encouraging the owner at least enough to keep his sign up and not worry that anyone would report the conditions he kept 700 dogs in.

An associated phenomenon that is similar to a puppy mill breeder is what's been labeled a "backyard breeder".

In some cases backyard breeders are actually nice families that raise litters of puppies from their own pet dogs and then sell them, always treating them humanely. So, sometimes we advise people to take a chance on dogs bred in this manner, as long as they are *extremely* cautious, visit the home, meet the pups' parents and receive the same health guarantees that any reputable breeder would offer. And some of the best examples of breeding and early husbandry we have seen have been in private homes.

Equally common however, are many disreputable backyard breeders that treat their dogs and pups abusively, depriving them of proper attention, housing and veterinary care. **Some individuals that are "backyard breeders" may also tether or kennel dogs cruelly outdoors, depriving the dogs of proper shelter and proper socialization with humans. This includes some individuals who breed and sell dogs (notably Pit Bulls) for the purpose of fighting them.**

Effects of tethering, including isolation from proper socialization with humans, are known to create aggression in dogs. And some experts on fighting dogs, including Diane Jessup (who has also seen cases from the experience of working as an animal control officer who investigated dog fighting rings) agree that overcrating can produce effects similar to tethering. Improper tethering of dogs is commonly accepted by most experts to be cruel. Most experts also agree that excessive tethering can produce aggression. And, for these reasons, many municipalities have banned, or put controls on the practice.

The common denominator, in cases of puppy mills and backyard breeders who tether is forcing dogs to live in conditions that are not natural to them. These levels of containment and lack of proper exercise and stimuli stress the dogs and eventually interfere with the natural canine behaviors that most of us cherish.

In other cases the people committing the abuse are not even aware that they are abusing dogs, even though they may also keep excessive numbers of animals on their properties, also with cruel containment, insufficient care and little time to relate positively with humans.

Animal Hoarders and the Case of Barbara Woodley:

Another area where law enforcement is seeing increasingly shocking abuse of dogs is in cases of animal hoarding. The conventional definition of "animal hoarder" most people used to be aware of was the stereotype of the "eccentric lady with cats" stereotype. But these days authorities are walking into homes and finding literally hundreds of animals at a time, all indoors, living in squalid conditions- all kept by one individual. Of course, it's difficult to fully understand the motives of hoarders who attempt to keep this many animals as personal pets.

But today there's a new type of hoarder emerging as well- hoarders who actually started out as animal "rescues". The Internet makes it easy to impulsively obtain large numbers of animals that owners surrender; easy to apply for status as a charitable organization and easy to network with others without anybody ever physically seeing where animals are kept. This has encouraged a new breed of hoarder. Unfortunately today some private charitable animal rescues don't adopt animals out properly like other rescues and don't really try to. Instead, they just keep acquiring more, even if they cannot provide proper housing, sanitation or vet care. Unfortunately **whether an organization is a legitimate rescue that has just become overcrowded, but is still functioning properly, or a smokescreen for a hoarder who has so many animals in a small area that the animals suffer has become a strange "gray area". The distinction**

must be interpreted based on the condition of the animals after they are examined by veterinarians and humane organizations. And this is difficult to do, because most animal hoarders will take great pains to prevent these people from seeing their properties.

Unlike with puppy mills, hoarders who keep excessive numbers of dogs in crowded or unsanitary conditions don't usually do it for a monetary motive. Many go bankrupt spending their own money out-of-pocket to feed the multiple animals, and they may truly believe that they care about animals more than anyone else could. Animal hoarders may suffer from a compulsive mental illness that makes them unable to understand that collecting dogs and forcing them to live under overcrowded or unsanitary conditions is cruelty.

In *O; The Oprah Magazine*, Barry Yeoman describes one such case in 2005 in rural Sanford, North Carolina where the homeowner, Barbara Key Woodley's, motives were unclear (although she did have a past history of breeding and selling dogs). At any given time, Woodley was keeping as many as three hundred dogs on her four acre property, with breeds including: Boston Terriers, Boxers, Miniature Pinschers, Pomeranians, Pugs and Jack Russell terriers. And police and rescuers were literally sickened by the stench of dogs' housing quarters that were connected to the same area where Woodley and her husband lived and prepared their meals.

"Many [dogs] were confined to open-top wooden boxes or wire crates with no access to fresh air... Some of the crates were stacked and had wire bottoms, and the dogs' legs trembled as they tried to maintain their footholds. These animals were never released outside, so those in the top cages were forced to eliminate onto those below."

When one of the first law enforcement officers entered to investigate, she found that, "[the dogs] were either petrified of you or aggressive, or they would fight each other just to get some human contact."

Getting all of the dogs safely removed from the property involved a three-year legal and civil battle. There were very many sick dogs and court-ordered veterinarians had to repeatedly visit the property just to treat the serious cases. Veterinarian Laureen Bartfield reported that, dental disease was so rampant that, *"their jawbones were actually rotting."* Twenty percent had significant eye problems, including one pug that had literally been blinded by ammonia fumes. A Miniature Pinscher with a paralyzing neurological condition was left lying in a filthy wire cage, and the vet discovered beetles feeding on six Boston Terrier puppies in a lidded shipping crate.

In court, the defense attempted to make the case that the Woodleys hadn't abused the dogs under strict definition of the law- for example kicking or shooting them. But eight respected veterinarians testified that, "Cruelty can be passive" and the judges agreed. The Woodleys were found guilty of criminal charges, with suspended sentences. And, finally, after a successful civil suit, a California rescue group was allowed to remove, rehabilitate and eventually place approximately three hundred dogs.

After their unimaginable ordeal, almost all this hoarders' dogs had health problems, many serious. Many also displayed behaviors typical of dogs that are excessively crated. Some acted aggressively and snapped at or bit humans at first. Some acted hyperactive and "mischievous" in strange and unexpected ways. Others displayed lackluster behavior, and showed difficulty relating with humans at first, while others were so extremely fearful that it took months of coaxing to get them to like contact with the humans in their new adoptive families.

The good news in this case is that eventually all the dogs adapted to life with their new families, although some continued to show diminished capacities in some areas. These behaviorally damaged dogs were all able to recover to have somewhat normal lives because they found patient adoptive parents who were willing to make needed modifications- the kind of owners who were willing to applaud progress in some of the dogs that had never previously even stepped outside.

Unfortunately, people have recently heard about so many cases like this one that many of us are no longer surprised to read the headlines. Neither was it surprising to learn that, even while keeping hundreds of dogs caged in squalor, Ms. Woodley appeared to "live a double life", coming out into the community in her white Lincoln luxury car, "all gussied up". What would seem surprising, except for the fact that it happened in the cases of other extreme dog abusers as well, is even after what had happened on the property was exposed, Woodley still received a lot of support from her local community.

And cases like this are not uncommon. According to Randall Lockwood, Ph.D, now senior vice president for anticruelty field services at the American Society for Prevention of Cruelty (ASPCA), animal hoarding is not a benign- or minor- problem. In fact, according to the agency **"an estimated 250,000 animals are victims of hoarding in the United States in any given year."**

Dogs suffering from these hoarding situations are an overlap with dogs we describe as suffering from excessive crating.

And the actions of hoarders are often made possible partly because they have crates. Just like in puppy mills, using crates stacked on each other almost to the ceiling enables the person to physically maintain their substandard facility without ever worrying that there is not enough floor space for large numbers of dogs. Indoor cages- as opposed to larger and more humane indoor/outdoor runs- also have the advantage that they keep dogs locked inside all their lives with no outside barking to alert the authorities to an excessive number of dogs.

Oddly also, people have become so used to the sight of dogs in crates, that the sight of an extreme number of dogs stacked in cages in a friend or acquaintance's home no longer shocks some people. A new popular show *Animal Hoarders* on Animal Planet features cases of hoarders who seem somewhat sympathetic as their families try to get them help. One of these women, with some knowledge on the part of family members who finally intervened, had been keeping *87* dogs inside her home. Just like in puppy mill conditions, it's easy for hoarders to keep this many dogs hidden if the dogs are small. And crates are central to physically maintaining numbers of dogs like this in small spaces. One woman was using cages to keep 340 cats inside her home!

On the show, one constantly hears visitors and therapists exclaim how keeping so many animals in such squalid filthy conditions is cruel. But we've only heard one of the hoarders' visitors specifically mention the cruelty of *caging* the animals. Maybe this is because, even if the normal American family doesn't keep 87 dogs at once, we *have* become used to the sight of dogs in cages- because this is what it's like in our own homes.

Chapter 5 describes syndromes and symptoms that can result from excessive crating and includes quotes from veterinarians who worked in shelters and who rehabilitated puppy mill dogs. And these veterinarians are on the front line in treating the common canine behavioral symptoms- some of them bizarre- that result from excessive crating, especially if the dog is overcrated and deprived of healthy stimuli during the formative weeks of puppy development. **Dogs are often pulled out of shelters or puppy mills suffering from the most extreme symptoms of kennel craze or kennelosis. But what happens when the dog is someone's pet? And how are we to know whether the symptoms developed from flawed breeding, initial upbringing in a puppy mill, followed by time spent in a pet store- or whether the worst of the symptoms resulted from the dog being crated in the owners' home?** This was the question we were forced to ponder in a true case we were called in to work with, which progressed as follows:

The True Case of Patton, "the whirling dog" - a case of kennel craze

Schipperkes, little fuzzy black dogs of approximately 18 lbs. were bred in Belgium to be "little captains" who worked on canal barges as watchdogs and ratters. And they're relatively rare in this country at the moment. But anyone who knows the breed also knows their high-energy. When you picture a Schipperke, you can easily picture him on a boat looking all around, taking in every sight, sound and smell with his nose wriggling and his pointy little mouth open, revealing bright white teeth in a friendly exuberant panting smile.

These dogs just characterize natural zinginess combined with a happy ability to engage with everything they see. Lately, Schipperkes are known as great companion dogs- highly loyal, highly curious and active and able to always make their owners smile. And, while they're not known as the most docile dogs, their charisma is part of what makes them so appealing.

So, when a lady called us about a problem Schipperke, our initial reaction was interest in training the breed. But we also took her complaints quite seriously- because her little dog Patton had aggressively bitten her husband's hands on many occasions, in addition to showing other emotional problems.

We entered the home to find the middle-aged husband and wife sitting on their couch with little Patton on the other side of the room, closed inside a tiny crate right by the front door and barking up a storm. The wife told us she'd trained Patton in a group obedience class at a pet store and that she was the only one who could "lay down the law" with him, even though she admitted he often bit her whenever she tried to cuddle him on the couch. And her husband, who was home with Patton all day and had the most contact with him, confessed he was completely terrified of Patton's frequent attacks on him.

He was responsible for all of Patton's bathroom excursions to the unfenced backyard, and he'd take Patton out several times a day. But almost every time he took Patton out, the dog would start acting crazed and madly run at distractions- falling pinecones, a distant neighbor's dog, even birds flying in the sky. Patton would also try to eat unsafe items in the yard. The second the gentleman tried to control him, bring him back inside or remove items from his mouth- whack! Patton would bite his hand.

Sometimes Patton struck so hard and strong that he could not be removed. The hundred and fifty pound man would shake his hand, violently trying to save himself while the growling and gnawing 15 lb. dog held on- fiercely embedded! There was no mistaking the accumulation of old scars on the owner's hands, plus some fresh bleeding wounds he explained came from the most recent encounter.

Patton was locked in a very small crate in the living room, across from the sofa, near the television and directly facing the front door. When we entered, he immediately launched into a frenzy of desperate and fierce barking. Simultaneously, the fuzzy little dog began to spin in circles, literally rocking the tiny cage. Neither the barking nor spinning let up even after we were seated and talking with the owners.

Over the barking, the wife owner did almost all the talking, explaining how she had acquired Patton at approximately six months from a now-closed local branch of chain pet store that has recently been charged with selling pups from puppy mills. She told us Patton was always hyperactive from the time she had brought him home and that, any time they attempted to free him, he would constantly run in circles in the house without ever stopping, and would violently chew on baseboards and other household items. The only solution that worked, she said, was to crate young Patton to prevent him from chewing. So the dog was never allowed loose in the house except for rare times when she tried to cuddle him on the couch.

When we first interviewed Patton's owner on the telephone, we had explained that we did not believe in crating. She had agreed that she was crating Patton too much and said she wished she didn't have to.

But when we evaluated the case in the home, we started to see a clear picture of Patton the Schipperke's daily life. The truth is that, other than those brief moments when he was running circles to evade the humans- or striking at them like a serpent- Patton was caged. His only time outside was when the man of the house walked him on leash in the unfenced yard to allow him to evacuate his bowels and bladder. And these moments of fresh air and movement were quite short. Out in the yard, the gentleman feared what Patton might ingest and he feared having more confrontations and bites when he tried to take items away from him.

So after bathroom breaks he would rush the dog back to his crate as quickly as he could. Neither of the owners ever walked Patton outside in the neighborhood- absolutely never, even though he was a year old. This was partly due to his behaviors, but mainly due to the judgment of the wife who didn't feel comfortable doing it. Obviously, Patton was never taken to pleasant places away from the home-no car rides, pet stores or public park outings for him. He was not allowed toys, even supervised, because his owners said he immediately chewed them up (and this overly rough chewing is not uncommon in dogs with severe stress and anxiety). He was not allowed to explore anywhere in the house at all, ever, because his owners said his chewing was uncontrollable.

Ray was initially able to calm Patton's fevered barking and snapping by simply crouching outside his crate, back turned. But, when he attempted the scary task of removing Patton from the crate, Patton moaned, squirmed and attempted to nip. But he never got a toothhold and he finally calmed in Ray's arms, although his demeanor remained tightly wound.

Most dogs, even those that are so called "red zone", don't act aggressive to us because of our personal energy, our calm, psychology-based techniques and the way that we mimic canine gestures that deflate tense situations. Unfortunately, some dogs- especially those deprived of healthy early socialization in puppy mills- are so damaged they can't properly read calming signals. In Patton we were dealing with a dog like this, and we understood each bit of progress had to be achieved with great care. Ray made peace with Patton. He was able to hold him and then set him free on the floor. (According to his owners, this was an unusual position for Patton to be in on a regular day, because he was never, ever allowed to wander in the house...)

With the little dog free at her feet, Emma, armed with treats, started his first lesson for the day- the "watch me" command. We first had to get past barking, spinning and frantic movement. But much of Patton's destiny rested on whether he could focus enough to obey that one little command.

The little flash of black fur and white fang looked like he was unceasingly dancing the can-can. But Emma tried her best to portray calm confident energy while praying that the treats would work. Dogs in the very deepest extremes of agitation usually aren't able to take food, but it was encouraging that Patton could. Electrified little teeth grazed her fingers as he snapped up his food rewards. But he was able to stop his spinning long enough to obey the "watch me" command and look at Emma. Next Emma walked him around the room off leash, leading him with treats so he'd heel beside her. And next she practiced the "come" command.

Once we knew what Patton might be capable of, we asked his owner to practice some obedience. But when she demonstrated the technique and style she had learned in the group class it included an extremely harsh tone of voice and a violent stamping of her foot. It seemed like this intimidating style might cause the little firecracker to at any minute and we wondered why a class obedience instructor would encourage such harsh techniques with a pup with such serious problems. But the good news was that his owner could easily learn to soften her style of giving commands and Patton seemed stable enough to learn to respond. We advised that owners start off-leash obedience practice using a calmer and more consistent style in order to improve the dog's focus and his bond with them.

Next Ray took Patton outside and walked him briefly on the residential street with encouraging results. Even though his owner never took him on walks in the neighborhood, he behaved well enough that carefully supervised leashed walks on the street would be another good way to bond and a way to work off huge amounts of frustration. Walks would also introduce Patton to the world at large that he'd been deprived of for very many months.

One of Patton's biggest problems was his frenzied barking whenever there was any movement at the front door, so we did a little practice desensitizing him, starting first by just opening the door. He did well, but, since his case was extreme, we explained to the owners that they'd need to practice in small frequent intervals, gradually increasing the challenge and that progress would only come after many repetitions. With the cooperation of his owners, we planned to move on to desensitizing Patton when a visitor knocked, and then when a visitor walked in the door.

All of this was with our intention to start freeing this dog from the crate, letting him move around the house, see a little more of the world and get vastly more exercise, which was a necessity for his breed. Yes, Patton was extremely disturbed, certainly one of the most disturbed dogs we've treated. And, sadly, because of his symptoms of "kennel craze" he might have even been to the point of some puppy mill dogs where rescuers finally decide to euthanize. But, in our single session, we saw significant glimmers of hope with several of the modalities we used.

Our next line of defense, in addition to the multiple homework assignments we gave the owners, would have been to start natural calming supplements and specific therapeutic, anxiety-reducing massage. We had also discussed further veterinary exam and possible blood testing.

So, when the owners' veterinarian offered to personally treat and train Patton, we thought this could be a good idea. The veterinarian did work with him, but she didn't feel she obtained satisfactory results, even when she used strong medication. And, rather than pursuing further training, Patton's owners, who cared deeply about his well-being, felt the best thing they could do was to re-home him.

Patton's owner did care about their little dog, but perhaps finding him a new home was the most realistic and positive solution. Patton had some serious, deep-seated issues. And every one of his symptoms represented the most serious symptoms of kennelosis or kennel-craze, a disorder caused by excessive crating. Every piece of the puzzle indicates that Patton came to owners already damaged by puppy mill breeding, including unstable genetics, inadequate socialization and stimulation in his early weeks, followed by trauma in transit and in the pet store and the cumulative effects of constant crating during the first six months of his life.

But Patton's story hadn't ended there. No matter what the six-month old puppy's problems were when he came to them, no matter what he attempted to chew on around their home, we feel the only way these owners could have ever integrated this particular dog to the world and introduced him to people is if they ever *let* him move around in the world and actually interact with people.

Little Patton was a dog over a year old that spent all day, every day in a tiny cage, looking out at the movements of his owners and listening for the screen door to creak so he could bark at it until he was hoarse. To substitute for movement around the home, playing and natural curiosity seeing new things, Patton spun circles. In those brief moments he was let out of the crate, he had no tolerance or patience to wait to have his immediate needs met and no tolerance for touch or petting. The only touch he experienced consistently was the touch of wire brushing his whiskers and puffy black fur, so this is what he had become used to.

When his owners ever did attempt to touch him, Patton felt unaccustomed to this type of interaction. He'd probably had no experience interacting with people back at the breeder or pet shop, and little experience interacting with people during all the hours he was caged at home. So whenever people moved towards him, he felt scared and cornered and reflexively snapped and bit. And, when the humans screamed, shouted and fought back he became even more panicked and bit harder.

Patton "the whirling dog" never got to do any productive work task, nor did he ever get to play and all of his days were exactly the same. And, unless his owners would have been ready to stop worrying about him chewing on items in the home enough to try letting the naturally curious dog move around, play with stimulating interactive toys, exercise as much as he needed and live in the real world, there would have been no chance of recovery. **Patton was a dog whose total time out of the crate on many days was likely measured not in hours- but in minutes.**

We sincerely hope Patton found a home where his new owners were able to keep everybody safe while integrating the highly compromised young dog successfully into a world he had little experience with, and we hope this dog eventually got more time out of a crate.

We also hope that too many other unsuspecting families- especially families with children- don't find themselves living with dogs with Patton's background and Patton's problems. But if they do, then they need to ask themselves whether they feel the raging creature in their living room filling up the whole of its cage with its fur and the scary clang of teeth on metal is really a feral aberration, rather than a normal pet. If so, they need to rethink keeping the animal in a family home at all, where it may potentially injure- and definitely frighten- young children.

If keeping a dog with problems is literally too much, and if owners perceive danger to family members, especially children, then there's no shame in finding the dog a new home- as long as the new owners are qualified to work with the problems.

Or a family may choose not to give up a pet like Patton no matter how bad his behavior issues are and they may decide that the scary creature is indeed really just a dog, a potentially loving member of the family that has suffered a physical/behavioral disorder set in motion by excessive crating at a breeder, shelter or pet shop. But if a family makes a commitment to rehabilitating a dog, we feel they can't just prolong problems by caging the disturbed or distressed animal rather than attempting to treat the problems so that everyone is comfortable, safe and fulfilled.

Some families probably just leave these dogs caged because they want to put off facing the problems, but we know that others are being told by professionals to cage these dogs as a cure for their aggression. However, **constant caging, without rehabilitation, only makes aggression worse.** In cases where dogs are disturbed, owners should first learn the theories of canine fear and aggression in depth (see the Patricia McConnell, Nicole Wilde and Bruce Fogle books recommended in the Appendix). Once they have a broader view of what they are dealing with, they should next consult an applied animal behaviorist, or a veterinary behaviorist with an advanced degree. The professional they choose must be qualified to keep everyone safe. And whatever it takes, they should make sure that whoever trains the dog believes in gentle methods, with a foundation of canine psychology- and does not believe in crating.

Unfortunately, until the problem of puppy mills and related cases of excessive crating has stopped, there will probably be an increasing call for individuals with this unique skill set to help extremely disturbed dogs like frenzied little Patton.

The pet store/puppy mill scandal:

If you purchase a puppy at a pet store or if you order a pup online and have it shipped to you, the pup is likely came from a puppy mill where dogs are kept in substandard conditions.

One retail store that was accused of selling pups raised in puppy mills was Petland- a well-known pet store chain that sells puppies in shopping malls and strip malls around the country.

In a recent class-action lawsuit, customers who had to pay for treatment of new puppies with dire illness sued Petland stores for deliberately selling sick puppies and misrepresenting where the pups came from. The lawsuit was well publicized and even more consumers became aware of the suspicions that Petland sold puppy mill pups after an Animal Planet television expose about Petland and the case.

For many, the accusation that Petland sold puppy mill pups didn't come as a surprise. Petland, like many other puppy stores, houses pups in small crate-sized like enclosures, kept behind glass.

While we absolutely cannot claim any knowledge about where any Petland store obtained its pups, or any knowledge that the store caused damage to pups in any way, we have had a number of customers consult us about behavior problems in pups they bought at individual Petland stores that are now closed. This includes poor little Patton, "the whirling dog" in the story above, and other pups with emotional, and physical, problems.

Overall, pups we've treated for some of the most serious problems have come from either pet shops or Internet dealers. Some of the problems we've seen in pet shop and Internet pups of all ages included: marked inability to focus on, or connect with, humans; inappropriate behavior around strangers/guests or new stimuli; elimination problems continuing well past normal housetraining age; separation anxiety; extreme, non-directed hyperactivity; and extreme OCD (Obsessive-Compulsive) behavior (for example one pup would drink water compulsively to the point that it could kill him and incidents costing his owner thousands to treat him). These extremes are *not* "normal" puppy behavior problems.

Usually also when we see aggression towards owners and "autistic" inability to bond with owners in very young pups, it is in puppies that have come from pet stores or pups that were sold directly over the Internet- in other words, pups that have endured excessive crating and separation from important stimuli and socialization early in life. It's also not surprising that pups that came from pet shops and Internet dealers were also the ones that came to their new families physically ill, many costing hundreds or thousands in vet bills shortly after they were purchased.

How Much Is Too Much? For the record, the authors don't believe crating is *ever* beneficial to a dog for behavioral reasons or that a small crate is ever a good form of long-term canine housing. We *do* feel *temporary* crating- only briefly- may sometimes physically protect dogs- for example, preventing harm during travel, surgical recovery or disaster evacuation. But we believe alternate arrangements should be made as soon as possible.

Otherwise, we believe *any* amount of dog crating is negative to some degree- and there are almost always superior alternatives. But *how much* crating hurts dogs depends on multiple variables.

And usually damage is directly proportional to how many hours the dog spends crated per 24-hour period, and for how many days, weeks, months or years the daily crating continues.

Some owners rarely leave their homes except for an occasional trip to the post office, the doctor or a lunch date and they only crate their dogs very briefly. And, even though a crate is not the most comfortable accommodation, we rarely see any serious, or even noticeable ill effects, when dogs are crated only a few hours a week total.

At the next level, most dogs that are crated for only 2-3 hours a day every day, but given reasonable exercise, mental stimulation, attention and kindness for the rest of the time also seem to escape the most serious physical, emotional and behavioral effects of excessive crating.

But, in our observation, dogs enduring 5 or more hours total per day in a crate are noticeably more deeply damaged and disturbed than uncrated dogs, especially if crating continues long term. Over 8 hours total crated is another benchmark, where dogs suffer greater damage and emotional effects. And dogs enduring 12 hours or more total per day will with almost always suffer the most serious consequences, along with noticeable behavioral problems ranging from hyperactivity to abnormal emotional withdrawal. It's at this level (12 hrs crated per day total or more) that almost any dog will become one of the "lost souls", suffering extreme distress and extreme damage to emotions, behavior, character and spirit. And the damage tends to be worse for every additional hour the dog is crated, up to 23 and more. Dogs enduring these levels of crating *can* usually be rehabilitated, but it takes a special effort, and they will likely have greater problems integrating into the home once they're freed.

For this reason, **we always recommend reducing number of hours in the crate for owners who aren't ready to give up the crate altogether. Just by reducing the total hours, owners can significantly improve their dog's quality of life.**

When crating opens the doors to even much more horrible abuses:

Laboratory Dogs:

All over the country, dogs are still being used in lab experiments. It is estimated by the USDA that, in 2002, 1.4 million animals (not counting rats, mice and birds) were used in research and almost half a million of these were used in experiments that caused pain or distress, with over 100,000 of these animals given nothing to ease their pain or suffering. In addition to what they may suffer during experiments, dogs kept for this purpose are also deprived of all that makes life meaningful and joyous for their species- human companionship, exercise and mental stimulation. Instead, these dogs spend their whole lives in cages until they are finally euthanized, facing continual boredom, stress, discomfort, fear and unique types of pain during experiments that can sometimes end in death. Their only hope of leaving the lab is not to go to a loving family, but simply to have their pain stop when they die during an experiment, or when they are put to sleep.

If you ask most people, they'd tell you they're opposed to, and outraged by, the cruel treatment of dogs in laboratories. And it's surprising the public wouldn't generalize the plight of how laboratory dogs are housed to similar housing conditions for pet dogs and realize how wrong Excessive Home Dog Crating is.

Perhaps this is another case of the Theory of Cognitive Dissonance (as explained in Chapter 10) in action. The average person hears about the unimaginable imprisonment, terror and injury inflicted on dogs in laboratories in the name of science, and we feel distressed. Yet we're unsure what is right or wrong or how we can possibly help. In the end maybe it soothes us to think that caging dogs the way they do in laboratories is not actually that bad. Because how could we be the kind of people, and how could this be the kind of society where we would allow torture to happen? Thus, the Theory of Cognitive Dissonance allows us to salvage our image of our own goodness by thinking that perhaps caging dogs is not actually so bad... And so not only don't we help lab animals enough today- but now we're starting to cage all our *pet* animals as well!

Chinese Eating Dogs

In one attempt to Google dog crating problems online we turned up something so horrific that felt we must include it in the book. What appeared when we typed in combinations of "dogs" and "cages" was a photo of small primitive crate-stuffed with approximately four highly distressed looking medium sized dogs. This crate was so small that you could barely distinguish where the intertwined body parts of one dog began and the next ended. This photo, on the Squidoo website, was shown with many others. The photos came from China, where the dogs were being caged prior to being brutally killed- and *eaten*- as menu items in restaurants.

Some readers may have already heard that it's still common for some Chinese to eat dog meat, and to serve it as a delicacy in restaurants, even though many Chinese people have recently begun to protest the practice. And even though in the past year an "Anti Animal Cruelty bill was submitted to the Legislature and State Council, China still has no animal cruelty laws in effect, and it's estimated that as many as 14 million dogs and cats per year are slaughtered for food.

To make the practice of eating dogs in restaurants even more horrific is the fact that the dogs are deliberately tortured prior to their slaughter. This is because of an ancient belief that fear, and the release of adrenaline, make the dog flesh more "vital", thus more of a delicacy. For this reason, the dogs, kept outside restaurants in cages for passerby to view them, are openly slaughtered, right out on the street, often by clubbing them to death while the dogs scream. At the time of the 2008 Olympics in Beijing, the government closed some of the restaurants in the vicinity of the ceremonies not to offend foreigners with the sight of the dogs caged and awaiting their fate of a brutal death, prior to being cooked and served as menu items.

Part of the torture these dogs endure, acknowledged by those that kill them to produce stress and heightened adrenaline levels, is the way they are stuffed into cramped cages and transported for days without food or water. Ironically, **the first step in the horrid journey of these dogs that are killed and used in a way that would give the average Westerner nightmares is not actually so much different than the everyday life so many "loving" suburban owners are right now offering their treasured and otherwise spoiled pet dogs right in their own living rooms...**

This is not to compare an American family locking a pet dog or pup in a crate on the advice of some dog professional with the inhumane way Chinese dealers in dog meat dispatch so many innocent dogs. Yet we must wonder why cage confinement- which is the first hallmark of this atrocity- is the same lifestyle many of us now offer dogs we say mean the world to us. If the Chinese who brutalize these meat dogs are aware that excessive crating causes their stress suffering to begin, then why aren't we?

Americans are often pioneers in terms of freedom and humanity- for humans and animals and we often find ourselves shocked at some practices towards animals in less developed countries. The eating of dogs in China is one example. Another is a unique cruelty to dogs in parts of Africa where dogs not only don't have a good life, but many also suffer the fate of being boxed up, literally, for the first years of their lives. Some African owners believe that by isolating a dog from all human contact and all stimuli in a hot wooden box (similar to a fruit crate) with limited visibility and ventilation, they can create extreme aggression and make a fiercer guard dog.

Most Americans would feel horrified seeing dogs coming out of darkened boxes barely big enough to contain them. Yet, in essence, these conditions are not that different are these conditions than the 23 hours total per day that some nice, normal American owners now crate their dogs. It's easy to react with outrage when we see a skinny, flea-bitten cur emerging from a dark and dank shipping crate. But, just because most Americans usually feed our dogs well, clean their wire crates regularly and spotlessly and schedule them for frequent trips to the groomers, the essence of what makes the boxes so stressful to African dogs- lack of mental and physical stimuli- and lack of opportunities for appropriate socialization- are the main factors that make crates in our homes so stressful.

There are the most extreme cases of home crating that result in death and, for every case that makes the headlines, many more likely go unprosecuted and unreported. **The most shocking thing about dogs left to dehydrate, starve or freeze to death abandoned in crates like this is the fact that some cases occur in full view of the owners!** In one case on the television program *Animal Cops*, a dog died inside its crate in the owner's kitchen with a bag of dog food in sight. This owner had been able to calmly eat their own meals for weeks at a time while watching their dog wasting away and dying a slow death!

Reading this, one would be tempted to simply label such individuals as monsters, like other violent criminals. But we wonder if society's overall acceptance of caging pet dogs as a convenience has made it easier for certain individuals to indulge their own selfishness- even to the point of murder. One such case made the headlines in Brevard County Florida in 2008, when an otherwise normal-seeming young woman named Christine Abrams was charged with animal cruelty and unlawful confinement for abandoning her white German Shepherd, Ella, to die in a crate.

The Case of Christine Abrams & Ella:

Eventually, Ms. Abrams was convicted of abandoning Ella to die, but on reduced charges that required no jail time. The reason for this was that, even though the state called in multiple veterinarians to examine Ella's body for cause of death, none were able to form a definite conclusion- because the body had become mummified! Ella had died with one leg stretched out of the crate, as if beseeching for help, while flies swarming around her remains led police to finally enter the home. Although the exact time and date of the dog's death will never be known, Ella likely suffered the torture of dehydration and starvation for weeks before expiring.

Ms. Abrams had moved from the home and knowingly left the dog there for months! According to news reports, Abrams indicated that she couldn't take Ella with her to her new home because her roommate did not like dogs. During the time frame when the dog was dying in the abandoned house, web postings by Ms. Abrams on social networking sites indicate that she was happily partying with friends.

Hundreds of animal lovers throughout the community were outraged, organizing demonstrations, signing petitions and writing letters to the judge, begging to charge Abrams with the more serious crimes rather than the reduced charges. And the local Humane Society dedicated a new walking path to the dog. There was no doubt that the community was horrified by what Christine Abrams had done, something no dog lover could relate to.

And yet we wonder if the ubiquitous presence of the crate as an accepted tool for controlling dog behavior makes it easier for someone like Christine Abrams to do what she did. After all, neighbors had seen the girl in her early twenties act attentive to her dog, and no one ever thought she was an abusive to her dog. And yet she was easily able to kill her...

Of course, the wire crate itself did not kill Ella- it was the unimaginably selfish and self-centered actions of her owner that did. When Ella was no longer convenient to Abrams' lifestyle, she simply boxed her up and left her, rather than trying other alternatives like giving the dog away. But, again we must wonder whether the availability of a dog-control item like the crate at any supermarket or discount store made it easier on Christine Abrams' conscience. If nothing else, easy availability of the crate made it easier for the young woman to leave the dog caged rather than free in the house and it also made it easier for her not to have to think about what she was doing in the end.

The second of the original charges against Ms. Abrams, "unlawful confinement of an animal", is defined by the Florida statutes as she "did impound or confine an animal, to wit: DOG in any place, and failed to supply said animal during such confinement with a sufficient quantity of good and wholesome food and water, or did keep said animal in any enclosure without wholesome exercise and change of air, or did abandon to die..."

At the same time so many people were outraged at the crimes against Ella, we found the following post on one of the vast number of online dog discussion groups- just another ordinary comment from an ordinary average dog owner on the Terrific Pets website:

"[My dog] was in her crate today while I was at work (4 hrs) and she managed to hurt her face very badly. It is swollen, bloody, and her left nostril is swollen shut. I have a vet appt. this afternoon for her, and until then I'm going to be icing her face. I don't know what to do, though... When I put her in, she shakes and drools incessantly. I feel terrible for her. She's never in more than 4hrs. [with the exception of overnight, which the writer mentions, but doesn't count in her time calculations] but she is just so upset. Any suggestions?"

Another writer, also presumably a normal average person, no different from those in any of our neighborhoods, proudly and for all the world to see, offers this advice to the "concerned" owner:

"So sorry. Hope she gets to feeling better soon. Another good idea is to always take off their collar when they are in the crate. I have always been afraid of them choking themselves to death. Sorry she hurt her little face, but [it] might help her settle down some. Hope so!"

Chapter 12: How Dogs Help Us & Why Our Kids May Never Know the Love of a Lassie or Old Yeller

"Compassion, in which ethics takes root, does not assume its true proportions until it embraces not only man but every living being." -Albert Schweitzer

When you read the true case of Patton "the whirling dog" in the last Chapter, the case of Smoky "the dog in a dumpster" in this chapter and the case of Bridget in Chapter 15 you may wonder, for good reason, whether dogs with serious behavioral afflictions can ever bond with families. But life hasn't always been this way. As a rule, dogs' behavior used to fit better with our families and today, if you excessively crate your dog, you're likely depriving your family of optimal dog/owner bonding. You too may remember the "good old days" when dogs acted more like Lassie or Old Yeller than like Marley of *Marley & Me* as described in Chapter 7.

Even John Grogan, creator of the wildly successful *Marley & Me*, and owner of Marley, the "world's worst dog", had his childhood and lifetime perceptions shaped by Shaun, a naturally well behaved Labrador. Shaun, the dog of John Grogan's youth, walked beside him off leash, behaved perfectly on car trips and bike rides and was his caring and watchful companion for all the milestones of growing up. Shaun had a purpose in life- to take care of his family and make their lives more fulfilled. And he performed this purpose well. As Mr. Grogan describes, "never once did he lead me into hazard." Like the true standard for the Labrador breed, "Shaun was spirited but controlled, affectionate but calm." And he gave John Grogan "the childhood every kid deserved."

The truth is- great dogs like Shaun were the dogs that many of us grew up with. They set the bar for our expectations. And many of us today still experience that kind of fulfilling, and mutually helpful lives with our dogs. This truly warm and magical bond that sometimes transcends words is the reason Americans have cherished our companion dogs so strongly. And it's why owning a dog has become part of the American Dream. We all know that the traditional stereotype of suburban success includes not just the two children and the home with the white picket fence- but also the joyful and loving family dog...

Dogs don't just enhance our experience of the good life; they are also proven to enhance our health, both physically and mentally. Every day, studies prove more about how interacting with pets can help us heal, and even prolong our lives.

In addition to the comfort and the healing and homey feeling dogs bring individuals and families, they also help us collectively in deeper ways. The authors and many experts believe **finding oneness with nature is a critical new frontier for our highest manifestation as humans**. It will be cruelly ironic for us to discover more about how necessary it is to bond with our dogs in the deepest ways, while every day more families lose the essence of that bond by following the wrong advice and setting their family dogs apart from them behind the bars of a wire crate.

How Life With Your Dog Should Be:

An example of the benefits of bonding with your dog is described in this very meaningful quote from Dr. Marty Becker, (popular veterinary contributor to ABC's *Good Morning America* and Author of *Chicken Soup for the Pet Lover's Soul*) in his book *The Healing Power of Pets*:

"Pets are like us and yet other than us," he says. "In our symbiosis, we've found that pets are often more humane than humans reflecting the kindest, best impulses of humanity..."

This is perhaps why we have pets, perhaps to remind us of the essential goodness of our universe, even in trying times, and also to reassure us of the potential for goodness within ourselves.

Dr. Becker also powerfully explains the belief that the authors share so strongly, that **pets serve as our ambassadors to connect with the mysteries of nature**, so that we can be fulfilled in an essential manner.

"Through our pets," he says, "we have a trusted; routine way to relate to nature, to break out of the shackles of mankind and its creations. This relationship, this special affective connection, the Bond, gives us an unparalleled sense of unity with nature; it tells us that we aren't above it, but part of it. Our dogs and cats represent an intimate and enduring look at another mammalian mind and spirit and serve as a thread connecting us back to the expanse of nature. Embedded in this Bond to life is simple, surefire, healing power.

"Pets are totems of the values we hold dear and a conduit to our basic historic connections between humans and nature. They help us cultivate the awareness that we are not alone in the world, but united to all living things. They take us outside of ourselves and reacquaint us with the world we live in."

Dr. Becker also points out why pets are so healing. "Our need for each other," he says, "which is part spiritual, part visceral, helps keep us happy and healthy."

Just like Marley the "world's worst dog" in John Grogan's mega-bestseller *Marley & Me*, contrasted with Shaun, the well-behaved Labrador of his childhood, customers often tell us that their current problem dog is completely different from naturally well-behaved dogs in their past.

John Grogan describes his childhood Labrador Shaun as, "...one of those dogs that give dogs a good name. He effortlessly mastered every command I taught him and was naturally well behaved. I could drop a crust on the floor and he would not touch it until I gave the okay. He came when I called him and stayed when I told him to.... We could leave him alone in the house for hours, confident he wouldn't have an accident or disturb a thing."

This directly contradicts the notion that many people who crate their dogs for life have been made to believe- that adult dogs cannot be left free in a home without destroying it. But most of us in our 30's, 40's and up remember that family dogs used to be safe left alone in our homes with no need to cage them.

If You Want to Guarantee That Your Dog Will Never Save Your Family's Lives, Just Crate Him. There are many aspects of our dogs that we understand and appreciate. But some other essential qualities of dogs are so fantastic that they seem almost magical. And one of thing that stands out as most remarkable about dogs is that they save owner's lives. Many of the larger working breeds are bred to protect and/or watch over their owners. And most dogs will sacrifice their own lives to save their owners from potential attackers- home invaders, robbers, rapists and armed individuals intent on killing. And it's not just large dogs that bravely protect their human families. Small dogs will also courageously attempt to save their owners' lives.

Dogs also save owners' lives from accidents, such as fires. Due to their superior senses, they are able to detect problems long before their human owners. And dogs possess a "sixth sense" that we don't and can intuitively sense danger and give the alert to save their humans. Based on instinct, dogs tend to use good judgment to protect your children in particular from harm. And historically, people have kept dogs for their instinct to protect.

But one way to absolutely guarantee that your dog will NEVER save your life, or the lives of your children, is to lock him up in a crate! Imagine your poor dog imprisoned in a cage, barking his lungs out as he helplessly watches a home intruder attacking and killing his beloved human family- a horror the dog could have prevented if he had been free.

And these days many families leave large adult guard dogs like German Shepherd Dogs, Rottweilers, Mastiffs and Pit Bulls imprisoned in small cages within the home, even at night!

One of the great things about a big strong protective dog is how safe he makes his humans feel when they sleep, so we can't imagine how a family could feel safe with their quick and powerful dog rendered helpless in a cage. A dog doesn't mind roaming the home all night like a watchman, keeping it safe for his family. His superior senses of hearing, smell and intuition make him good at it, and he enjoys protecting the humans he loves.

We can't imagine a more compelling reason for not crating than leaving a loyal dog free to protect a family's lives. But arguments in favor of crating have become strange and irrational. One dog trainer defended his policy of keeping a houseful of Mastiffs crated all their adult lives by claiming that, if anyone broke in, his most ferocious dog would just bust out of his crate to defend the elementary school age children in the home. Unfortunately this is impossible or all the dogs (like Ella in the previous chapter) that die abandoned after days or weeks locked in crates would be able to free themselves. The truth is, a dog can't escape a locked crate to save his own life- and he also can't get out of a locked crate to save yours!

As those of us who grew up loving dogs know, our dogs do more than just protect us and nourish our well-being emotionally and physically. Many of us already sense that our bond with dogs is spiritual.

In Chapter 6 we already presented many facts about how our current "wired" and ultra busy world allows us less time to connect with our families and pets in a traditionally nourishing and replenishing fashion. And we have said in all our writings that one of the reasons that our bond with dogs is so important in the post millennium world is that it represents the last connection to nature for many of us. In *Beyond Obedience*, April Frost describes that natural bond between man and dog as an essential of spiritual nourishment. She eloquently points out that:

"A lack of spiritual nourishment pervades our fast-paced culture. Because so much time is given to outer work, people have developed the habit of looking without really seeing and hearing without really listening. Many are afraid or have lost their ability to trust or express their feelings. Perhaps this shutting down comes about because of an attempt to ward off the negative influences of media, noise, unhealthy food, bad air, landscapes devoid of nature, fear of the future, and fear of being controlled and judged by unhappy, unfulfilled people."

Yet we often feel frustrated and sense that we need something more. Many of us feel compelled towards animals and when we're near our pets we often feel immediately uplifted- a feeling people unmistakably and commonly recognize.

As Ms. Frost puts it, "We are incredibly blessed to have animals, with their ability to fully accept us without judgment and as wonderful examples to help us.

"... while evidence of spiritual malaise is everywhere, there is [hope]. Many people are actively seeking, reaching out to nature in record numbers for soul-sustenance to gardens, to travel in remote, untouched landscapes, and especially to those animals who are accessible because of domestication. Dogs are more popular than ever before, and they are being asked to play a big part in creating a deeper feeling of connection with the inner life."

How Dogs Help Our Health:

Years back people were less aware than they are today about the documented health benefits of owning dogs. But today findings about dogs helping individuals recover from serious illness appear more frequently in the popular media. The concept of therapy dogs that visit physically or emotionally compromised individuals in hospitals, nursing homes and facilities for children with various disabilities has caught the public's attention and imagination. Through research as well as anecdotal evidence, we're discovering that just touching and interacting with a pet is sometimes enough to increase quality of life and improve the prognosis for seemingly hopeless patients. Autistic children or stroke victims who may not possess the capacity of speech to communicate can also benefit because animals seem able to communicate with them on a deeper, shared intuitive basis. Therapy dogs have become so popular that just one of the nationwide organizations boasts 21, 000 dog/handler teams.

Not only do these therapy dogs improve the patients' mood and well-being, but studies document that just stroking a dog can reduce blood pressure and increase immune function.

A recent cover story in *New York Magazine* (Feb 2010) described many reasons single people treat their dogs like kids. It also pointed to studies that proved just having a dog look at a person can spur the release of oxytocin, a natural feel-good chemical that is associated with stress reduction, an overall feeling of well-being- and the feeling of being in love!

Canine psychology expert Alexandra Horowitz, in her book *Inside a Dog*, describes the unique juncture where our dogs help our health and our outward manifestation as better versions of ourselves. She also indicates what can go wrong if this bonding process goes awry.

Ms. Horowitz first explains the physical benefits of this bond, which have already been well documented:

"Our bond with our dogs is strengthened by contact," she says, "by synchrony... So too are we strengthened by the bond. Simply petting a dog can reduce an overactive sympathetic nervous system within minutes; a racing heart, high blood pressure, the sweats. Levels of endorphins (hormones that make us feel good) and oxytocin and prolactin (those hormones involved in social attachment) go up when we're with dogs. Cortisol (stress hormone) levels go down. There is good reason to believe that living with a dog provides the social support which correlates with reduced risk for various diseases, from cardiovascular disease to diabetes to pneumonia, and better rates of recovery from those diseases we do get..."

And the prescription many of us are seeking may also be the one that our hearts compel us toward. ""Bonding with a dog can do the work that long-term use of prescription drugs or cognitive behavioral therapy can do," according to Horowitz.

As we humans live in a wired world increasingly lacking in deep, meaningful and natural interactions between each other (described in detail in Chapter 6) Ms. Horowitz explains how we increasingly find a place to once again recognize ourselves in "the feel of the relationship between person and dog." Although we all tend to sense intuitively how to engage in that unique relationship with the most unique of animal species, we may find it difficult to put that magical-seeming, multifaceted bond into words. *Inside a Dog* explains, "that feel is made up of daily affirmations and gestures, coordinated activities [and] shared silence."

Dog/human relationships, the author says are, "happily double-seeing." Dogs know much about us, for example: "our smell, our health, our emotions- due not just to their sensory acuity but also to their simple familiarity with us. They come to know how we normally act, smell, and look over the course of our days, and then they are able to notice, many times in ways we cannot, when there is a deviation. The bond effect works because dogs are, at their best, acting as extremely good social interactants. They are responsible, and, crucially, they pay attention to us."

Attention, on the truest deepest level is a commodity that many in today's society will do anything to find, even if it's just that "fame for 15 minutes" that Andy Warhol spoke about back in the 1960's and 1970's when our world had just started to speed up. Today, the consequences of a society feeding so much on shallow, and always unfulfilled, striving for attention can be dire- and dangerous. Yet that recognition of being recognized- attention in its most life-affirming sense- is always there in the healthy connection between dogs and humans- and perhaps this is why we enjoy dogs so much.

As Ms. Horowitz puts it, "this bond changes us". And it can be an affirmation and encouragement of our highest potential and a refreshing reminder that we do indeed have an individual place in the larger world. "Most fundamentally, this [dog/owner] bond changes us, it nearly instantly makes us someone who can commune with animals- with this animal, this dog. A large component of our attachment to dogs is our enjoyment of being *seen* by them. They have impressions of us; they see us in their eyes, they smell us. They know about us and are poignantly and indelibly attached to us."

But there are instances when the special bond described goes awry, and humans can no longer automatically achieve that bond they remembered having with dogs. Ms. Horowitz describes this problem by pinpointing feelings we experience if we ever feel we're not connecting with our dogs. People tend to experience a "mild betrayal... a feeling of disconnect when a dog one reaches for ducks her head away, preventing contact... betrayal is felt when the simple communication *come!* isn't followed by a dog coming. And it would be heartbreaking to approach your dog and to fail to prompt a tail to wag… or a stomach to be bared for scratching."

Ms. Horowitz also says that, in many cases, the dog receives nearly the same positive effect from the dog human bond, especially through touch. "Human company," she says, "can lower a dog's cortisol level; petting can calm a racing heart."

So what about all those cases, society-wide, where it all goes awry? What about all the dogs that are separated from humans in their first weeks of life in the confinement of puppy mills, only to be locked away from humans again behind the bars of cages in their new homes, until the day when it seems they no longer care anymore? This is just the kind of tragedy, for both dogs and humans that happened in the disturbing true case of "Smoky".

A Spiritual Illness? The True Case of "Smoky"- "the dog in a dumpster"

Smoky, the black Akita mix, seemed to have started his life under a dark star, but then it seemed his luck might have changed. Young Smoky's first owner believed Smoky was garbage, literally. The man was caught attempting to dispose of the puppy and his ten-week old sister in a dumpster, wrapped in up in a suffocating black plastic garbage bag.

Luckily a Samaritan intervened just in time, saving the pups from a horrible death. She took the female puppy home to raise and sent Smoky to her sister, Donna, out of state. Donna immediately fell in love with Smoky and felt strongly that fate had stepped in for her to "save" this puppy that had been treated so cruelly through no fault of his own.

Donna was also a cat lover who kept two highly independent cats in her very small one-bedroom apartment. By the time Donna was able to retrieve the pup from her sister's, Smoky was already several months old (past his sensitive socialization period), already fairly large, and he and he cats did not get along, so she and her boyfriend began separating them.

We weren't called in on the case until Smoky was approximately two years old. The presenting problem was that Smoky was persistently nipping at the owner and her boyfriend in attention-seeking fashion, with such intensity that the nips often drew blood. Donna complained that Smoky would not allow her to watch television in the evening because he continually nipped at her ankles.

When we met Smoky, we first saw a threatening spectacle of fluffed-out jet black fur and bared white teeth up on a table, raging at us through the front window. Then when we stepped inside the medium-large dog climbed onto the back of a couch and continued to rage at us.

Despite the feral spectacle of Smoky's barking and growling that initially put us off, it took us only minutes to realize that the dog was more frightened than we were- and that his extreme threat display was likely just an extreme reaction to the unknown. While we deal with each case of potential aggression differently (and readers should treat such cases with extreme caution), in this case, we called the dog off the couch and asked him to come to us by offering treats. Soon the wary dog was complying with us when we asked him to sit- a good indication that he might respond to other training and that he was not totally "gone".

Smoky had dark fur and, when his teeth weren't showing, he tended to blend into the room, which was kept extremely dark in daytime. The quarters were close to a claustrophobic degree and this tended to make us edgy, since we were confronting a borderline dangerous dog. As specialists in canine psychology, we know that physical layout of an area can either flare up or diffuse aggression. For example, narrow passageways are known to be hot spots where dog fights start.

In this case, the layout made us very conscious of how we walked. And it was difficult to walk at all without stumbling onto the owners or the potentially nippy dog! We couldn't find more than a foot or so of clear floor space that wasn't filled with furniture or collectibles. Behind us, creating a narrow walkway by the door, were floor-to-ceiling glass shelves that were completely packed with decorative black and purple glassware. More glass shelves and even more unique glass collectibles occupied the facing wall, filling the entire living space with odd shadows.

The kitchen area was equally close, and it was a challenge to walk here as well. Only one item was large and this was the big-screen television, mounted midway up the wall in the adjoining living room. We also noticed a black wire dog crate wedged directly below the TV, and the owners told us this crate was for Smoky.

The television was playing and we got the impression that, just like in many homes we visit, it played most of the time. It was an older model and you could feel its bass vibrate in parts of the room- we assumed in the dog crate as well. The bathroom and bedroom doors remained closed at any time Smoky was free because of the cats, which Donna confined to the bedroom when he was out.

Donna told us that the dog and cats acted highly aggressive to each other and had never been able to be together since Smoky was a puppy. She also felt that there was no chance they *could* ever be together in future. And she asserted that, no matter how well we might train the dog, she was certain the cats would remain fighters, so she'd never leave the pets together.

When we initially spoke on the telephone, Donna reported that, even though Smoky never received more than one walk a day (only when the weather was acceptable), she did let him out several times a day to wander and relieve himself in a fenced yard. During our session we wanted to walk with Smoky to spend some time on neutral territory and, on the way, we passed through the "yard" she had referred to.

This "yard" was really just an extremely narrow twenty-foot long privacy fenced walkway with thin strips of grass on each side that also accommodated a large grill and patio furniture, so it barely offered any room for a dog of Smoky's size to run.

Despite the cramped conditions in the "yard"; as we got out into the fresh air, Smoky's tension started to dissipate. And his behavior improved more when we took him out of the closed space and started his walk. Donna complained that Smoky always lunged at people and dogs that suddenly passed on the street. She said, for this reason, her boyfriend, who had some physical problems, never walked the dog even though he stayed in the apartment with him all day.

On our walk, we showed Donna and her boyfriend how easily they could redirect Smoky from distractions on the street with techniques like stopping, turns and directional changes. Smoky did surprisingly well walking on the leash and not lunging at people and dogs that passed. Once she saw this progress, Donna agreed to consider walking him more often and longer. But she insisted that she'd only take Smoky for walks when she found the weather cool enough. And, even though it was the coldest season of year when we met her, she still found it too hot most of the time.

We often include realistic exercise suggestions as part of our recommendations for how to help dogs' behavior issues. In this case it became more apparent each minute how important lack of movement was to Smoky's diagnosis, and the young dog needed tremendously more exercise.

Smoky showed classic symptoms of a fearful and reactive dog. He was also a bit hand-shy, which was likely caused by physical corrections from the boyfriend. Smoky also was trembly, flinch and "afraid of shadows" but he acted less so when he practiced his obedience commands with us. He was also surprisingly quick to learn, and comply with, the "down" command, which is often difficult for defiant or dominant dogs. During the session we did observe him push on his owner for attention and Donna complained that he constantly annoyed her like this. She also told us Smoky had chewed up several rag rugs right in front of her in the kitchen, even though- on the rare occasions he was lose- he *hadn't harmed any other items in the house.*

Biting owners is not to be taken lightly. Even though Smoky's biting was not classically aggressive, it *was* frequent and it sometimes broke skin. Smoky's bites on the boyfriend seemed a bit more serious than those on Donna. But Donna did show multiple bruises on her legs from where Smoky liked to nip at her when she would put her feet up. And the dog, in a constant state of stress, was in definite emotional distress- the type that would likely lead to deepening problems. This dog was almost a lost soul- savable, but definitely on the brink. Every one of our senses told us this.

The problem was that, to save Smoky, and to save Donna and her boyfriend from further physical risk, we first had to convince them of what they were doing wrong. We knew that they had used some strong (perhaps violent) corrections modeled after what some popular trainers demonstrated on television; and this was a problem. But an additional problem was clear to us. This healthy, alert and intelligent young dog was getting no exercise, no sensory stimulation and barely any appropriate interaction with his owners.

The only time Smoky was allowed out of his crate, he was also allowed to climb up on a table by the window- which was the only light source in his environment, and his only source of seeing the world. And the second Smoky saw any living thing walk by the window, he raged at it. Perhaps he was so reactive because he had never been exposed to light, movement, people or dogs, etc. during the critical early months when puppies are open to proper socialization. This probably started with the original abusive owner who tried to dump him in the dumpster, and then the lack of socialization continued when he came to Donna's home.

Unlike a pup that had been free in his environment and taken out into the world by his owners to experience new stimuli positively and learn how to properly react, Smoky was shocked whenever he saw anything new. And he reacted by making pre-emptive strikes- puffing up his fur and lunging or barking, hoping that any scary or confusing new things would just go away and leave him alone.

Alone was all that Smoky was, hour after hour. As in many cases we encounter, the owners never told us in so many words that they crated excessively. But the schedule they reported told it all. They told us they crated Smoky seven nights a week throughout the entire night. He was also crated during the daytime during Donna's workdays so he wouldn't knock into the extensive collections of glass. And the couple crated Smoky immediately as punishment whenever he nipped, bit, barked or annoyed them when they tried to watch television- in other words, almost constantly during the evenings when Donna was home!

In the mornings, Donna got up at 6:30am yo free Smoky from the crate long enough to feed him and let him into the tiny back courtyard to relieve himself. Then she'd put him back into the crate so he wouldn't bother her while she got ready for work.

While Donna spent her workdays away, her boyfriend would stay home, usually lying on the couch watching television. He did not feel physically able to walk the dog at this time. But despite the fact that he could have physically done it, he also never opened the crate to allow the dog into the courtyard until Donna returned after 5:00 pm. Nor did he let Smoky out of the crate for any other reason during the days. He never brushed Smoky's abundant coat, never played with Smoky, never petted Smoky or reviewed any obedience commands with him. But the dog was able to stare directly at the gentleman for hours while *Judge Judy*, *The Price is Right*, and *Dr. Phil* boomed from the huge television over its head.

After 5:00 pm, *but only when the weather felt comfortable for her,* was when Donna might take Smoky for a short walk around the block on certain weekdays. But when they returned inside, if Smoky annoyed her or nipped at her, she and her boyfriend promptly dragged him back into his crate. And then bedtime in the home came early. This would start another cycle of more crating and isolation for the dog through the night. This amount of crating had been Smoky's life routine for almost two years and the dog's behavior was steadily getting worse. And the worse his behavior got, the more Donna and her boyfriend locked him in the crate.

Donna wished Smoky's nipping her ankles would stop. If it did, she said, she could allow him more freedom to be near her when she watched television at night.

But despite whether his behavior improved, Donna said she had no plans *ever in the dog's lifetime* to alter his schedule or living arrangements. For example, Donna said she was happy living where she was and she'd never consider renting a different apartment with a larger fenced yard. She also said that under no circumstances whatsoever would she ever stop crating Smoky every night and every day while she worked.

Working within these parameters, we advised Donna that it was imperative to increase Smoky's exercise and mental stimulation. So we set up a program of training and exercise that included leashed walks, interactive toys, daily brushing and obedience practice.

But, on several levels, this case did not have a happy ending. Donna would not, or could not, comply with our single biggest recommendation- to get this dog out of his cage and give him more stimuli and healthy interaction with living things! Years of solitary confinement were making the young dog nervy and snappy. And each time the people threw him back into the cage, or left him there for another dark afternoon with a blanket thrown over him to shut him up, he seemed to lose more of his moorings and self-control. There seemed to be only two directions the case could go. One choice was rehabilitation, which we felt offered good prospects for Smoky. But otherwise the situation would likely deteriorate further. And Smoky might reach the point where, if Donna or her boyfriend attempted any harsher corrections, his bites might turn serious.

Several months after terminating his training early because of concerns with spending more, Donna contacted us and told us that Smoky had a bad interaction with another dog they visited. Then not long after, she contacted us again to tell us what she felt was great news. On her own, she'd found an effective solution to Smoky's nipping her- an electric shock collar! Donna told us that when she shocked Smoky, it stopped his snapping every time. She reported that progress with the shock collar did not backslide or prove frustrating like with the many gentle interventions we had recommended for his nipping, and shocking Smoky didn't involve bad weather, inconvenience or expense, like some of our suggestions for giving him more exercise.

Along with a majority of gentle dog trainers, we generally caution owners against using electric shock collars, or "e-collars". In addition to hurting dogs, there's evidence that using an electric shock collar with certain fearful or potentially aggressive dogs can bring on worse symptoms. The problem for Donna and her boyfriend in the case of Smoky is the e-collar's tendency to *create* aggression, especially in susceptible dogs. In our conservative professional assessment *at the moment in time we last saw him*, we believed Smoky was *not* nipping to be violent, nor to attack, but only to act pushy and demand attention from his owner.

Intelligent dogs like Smoky can easily learn that the shock collar is only effective when they are wearing it and their owner is holding the remote. We feared that repeated painful electrical shocks to a dog that was already hand-shy due to inappropriate physical corrections by the boyfriend, combined with continued days and nights of crating, lack of movement and lack of stimuli over the course of many more years might someday explode at a moment when the people were not holding the remote! At that moment, this good-sized dog might truly, violently, attack.

Even if an attack like this never happened, continued excessive crating, combined with continued electric shocking, would likely make Smoky even more alienated, more nervous, crazier and less likely to deal correctly with novel stimuli. And we could only hope that something would change.

The irony is, this animal would have been thrown into a dumpster, where he would have died. Instead, Smoky was saved and will now live the majority of his life, probably for the next TEN to THIRTEEN YEARS in the conditions described.

And his sister? We found out that she was the dog he had met on a visit and attacked for no reason, even though she acted properly when she met him! His sister continues to live out of state and her existence is quite different than Smoky's. She is happy and generally well-balanced; she's free to run around on a large property and she doesn't show any signs of aggression to humans or dogs like her brother. No one can know exactly what caused the differences in behavior in the normal and abnormal siblings, but we do know their genetics are similar. And the main fact we learned about differences in their upbringing was that the sister was never crated.

Compare this to the amount of time Smoky was being crated by an owner who said that, no matter how bad things got, she would never consider re-homing him since it was her fate and destiny to save him. Rather than measuring the amount of time Smoky was caged in hours, it was easier to estimate the amount of time he was OUT of the crate. Unfortunately, on the frequent weekdays when the weather discouraged his owner from walking him, or on days when the walk was brief, we believe Smoky's amount of time out of the crate was not measured in hours, but in minutes!

Chapter 13: Housetraining

Housetraining is a simple, yet intense process that should take no longer than a few weeks under ideal circumstances, provided you start with a healthy normal dog with a healthy upbringing prior to his arrival at your home. For healthy normal puppies, the following are general principles of housetraining without crating:

(1) Learn the theory of housetraining (without crates) and plan out a general schedule before bringing your puppy home. Read this chapter and, if you want more information, read *Awesome Puppy*, our comprehensive training and activity puppy guide. Then try your local library. Rather than starting your research online, where crate-training information tends to pop up first, you can go to a library or bookstore, pull a large pile of books off the shelf and then search each index for "housetraining" or "puppy". Skim those sections before you buy to make sure any book you buy gives adequate information on how to housetrain without crates. You'll find much of the best information in older books, from the mid 1990's or before.

You can also ask members of older generations for advice on how they successfully housetrained their dogs. (Just don't try some of the mean corrections that used to be popular- like rubbing a pup's nose in his mess or hitting him with a rolled up newspaper.)

Plan for some flexible time to devote to your puppy while you housetrain him (for example, many people like to bring their new puppy home during summer vacation). And, if you must be away for long workdays while your pup's bladder is still maturing, you should arrange for a friend, relative or professional pet sitter to take him outside midday.

Like potty training a baby, the point of housetraining is to help the pup understand what is acceptable potty behavior while working around the challenge of bowels and bladder that are not fully developed.

Puppies of 8, 10 or 12 weeks are entirely different than young dogs of eight, ten or twelve months!!! So, even though some of the training techniques appear the same, an owner should never confuse physical housetraining issues in puppies with deliberate scent marking or any emotional/behavioral-based potty problems in mature dogs.

These days many owners obtain full-grown dogs from shelters or rescues or from Internet classifieds and then are shocked to find that many of these dogs aren't housetrained at all! We suspect the roots of this problem usually go back to dogs that were forced to spend their lives in crates, with no chance for walks. And crating more isn't a solution.

The problem of a full-grown dog that soils in the house is NOT due to immature bowels and bladder, like a young pup. But the problem may be due to lack of knowledge on the dog's part. So first, try the same principles of puppy housetraining. If the problem persists, however, there may be a medical or behavioral component (And the bathroom problem may be why the dog was abandoned or surrendered in the first place). Problems like this *can* be cured, but may require additional study and effort for the owner and/or consultation with a veterinarian or qualified trainer/behaviorist.

Sometimes dogs leave a shelter or rescue with house soiling issues because they were continuously forced to urinate or defecate in their crate or kennel at the facility without ever being walked. Ideally owners should make shelters and rescues aware that it is *not* okay to simply let dogs soil where they sleep in crates or cages at the facility and then adopt these dogs out to unsuspecting new owners who assume the dogs are housetrained! And the facilities that pass these dogs on without first training them properly, and/or revealing the truth, should be held accountable. The problem is not the dogs' fault. **Housetraining an adult dog is not something an average owner should have** to deal with unless they knew they were volunteering for it. If you are stuck with the problem, you will certainly want to do the best with your dog, but do not confuse these serious problems in adult dogs or older pups with simple puppy housetraining.

To cure older dogs and pups, you may need to use proper behavioral interventions. **At the same time we caution owners not to blame younger puppies' physically based elimination mistakes on emotional problems or attempts at dominance.** An 8-week old puppy that urinates on your floor is almost definitely doing it by accident, like a human baby would- because urine just slipped out of his immature bladder after sleeping, eating, drinking or playing and *not* because he wants to "mark territory" or dominate you.

Whenever a young puppy has an accident, you should first make sure that *you* did not make a mistake by leaving him too long. A young puppy can only hold their bowels, and especially their undeveloped bladder, for a short amount of time (no more than several hours for urine during the daytime for an 8-week old pup). And you should never expect a puppy under 6 months old to make it through an entire eight-hour plus workday without having to urinate. (Occasionally young pups *will* last this long, but they cannot be expected to consistently because their bodies are not fully mature.) consistently for that many consecutive hours.)

Puppy mill and pet shop crating has unfortunately created another unique problem. Pups are often left to soil themselves in crates with no alternative at the breeders, until they lose their natural instinct to keep their living space clean. Many new owners are completely shocked when they try to crate-train this new breed of puppies and find them lying in their own mess, day after day. The first step to rehabilitating pups like this that have had their natural instincts disrupted is to give up attempts at crate training, because they've already learned to soil in the crate. You will have a better chance with conventional housetraining. It may take longer than with a pup that did not come from a puppy mill, but eventually it should override these pups' background and produce good results.

Pups that come from pet shops/Internet/puppy mills are also many times more likely to come to you with diseases and parasites that cause elimination problems, and not every veterinarian may diagnose these diseases on the first visit. It helps to study all the diseases and parasites that can affect puppies in your veterinary manual. And then, if your pup shows any physical symptoms like loose, frequent or bloody stools, or abnormal frequency or straining when urinating, you should consult your veterinarian. If your pup continues to show symptoms, but your vet won't run tests, you should definitely seek a second opinion. **Almost every customer's dog that we've seen come from** a pet store or long distance via the Internet has been positive for some disease or internal parasite that affects bowels and bladder.

Even with healthy very young puppies, because of physical immaturity, the call of nature comes insistently. So you owe it to your pup to get him outside before that happens and he has an accident. We sometimes mention six months as an arbitrary cut-off because most pups of that age have already gained a good deal of physical mastery of bowels and bladder. But the youngest puppies- eight, ten or twelve weeks- cannot be expected to have that level of physical control. The good news is that with normal young puppies, housetraining can be accomplished in as little as several weeks. **You will still be taking the pup out quite frequently.** But each week and month he nears maturity also means that he can hold bowels and bladder longer. Different breeds reach bowel and bladder maturity at different rates but, sometime between six months and a year your puppy will likely physically mature into the same level of control as an adult dog.

(2) Crate-training is no panacea. It's simply a way to lock a puppy away when you don't have time to actually housetrain him. And it's no substitute for real housetraining where the puppy learns what his family wants. Crate training works only because dogs hold their bladders and bowels even though it hurts because they dread lying trapped in their own mess for hours. It also works because the pup can't move so this keeps his insides sluggish. Many owners also intentionally deprive their pups of water while crating them.

Crating doesn't make bowels or bladder mature quicker and it doesn't teach the pup to make good decisions. Teaching a pup to live all his hours in a crate simply delays when you'll have to start actual housetraining and it can make it harder when you finally try. This is because **it's difficult for a pup that's been crated all his life to learn that his owner's house in a larger sense is not a bathroom.** His whole world has become the crate and he holds bowels and bladder, not because he's learned proper toilet manners, but simply because he dreads sitting in his own mess in the tiny crate! And many puppies that are left too long physically can't hold it in any longer and so they do have accidents in their crate, which only makes them more confused.

Note that in both normal and abnormal dogs, crate training may keep urine and feces off your carpet, but it won't teach your dog not to eliminate in your home. When you leave your dog in a small enough crate, most puppies will hold bowels and bladder so as not to lie in their mess. This may get them used to holding their bowels and bladder for long periods (something they would have been able to do for increasing amounts of time anyway as their bowels and bladder matured). But it will not, usually, generalize to the house as a whole.

The irony is, if you own a normal healthy wonderful puppy that manages to successfully transition from not soiling his crate to not soiling anywhere in your home, the process may take months. But, as an alternative, as long as you were able to correct and redirect your dog kindly, yet properly, using the kind of regular housetraining techniques our parents did, you could have likely housetraining that same "good" puppy within weeks or even days without the intermediate step of crating!

In the case of "problem" dogs (puppy and adult) that were never housetrained in former homes or that suffer from serious emotional problems, crate-training still won't make housetraining any quicker.

We've seen owners hosing down seven or eight-month-old dogs every single weekday when they come home and let them out of their crates because the young dogs are completely covered in urine and feces. There's a good chance these dogs are ill. Or they require behavioral intervention for serious emotional problems. Or the owners could be crating them for far too long. But a scenario like this is certainly NEVER an acceptable outcome. Additional crating won't help such serious problems and hosing is traumatic for pups. It may not be great to find feces on your floor. But we'd feel much more horrified to find a poor *puppy* covered in feces!

It's even sadder that there's a third category of puppies. Some dogs could have easily been housetrained if the owners had done it using their house and tools like baby gates. But instead, their owners crated them as pups and they react unusually badly. One example is when a dog develops such severe separation anxiety in the cage that he works himself up into a panic and uncontrollably soils himself. Then the separation anxiety may persist even when the dog is released from the crate. Clinical separation anxiety, a serious disorder that often includes physical symptoms like uncontrollable voiding of the bowels, then becomes a much more difficult problem to cure.

(3) The basic principle of housetraining is to vigilantly watch over your young pup, take him out at the times he most needs to go and (kindly and swiftly) correct any mistakes until he understands that you want him to relieve himself outside.

Puppies are born with an innate instinct not to soil their dens where they live until they are weaned (one theory is that this was to keep predators from sniffing them out so they could stay protected.) This instinct has helped dogs learn not to soil their owner's homes for hundreds of years, as long as they are brought up to live in a house and view the *entire house* as their den/home- the place where they sleep.

Your puppy also does naturally want to please you (despite the theories of some prominent "positive" trainers to the contrary.) There is no need for debate about this. Since dogs are social/pack animals, being nice to the pack leader and supportive of the pack leader would always facilitate the wild dog or wolf's best interest, and we are not saying dogs have human-type concepts of guilt or obligation.

But it's a natural dog personality trait to want to win your approval by following your rules and doing what you want (this is why most of us love dogs so much as pets!) Dogs' tendency to try to please owners is in great contrast to other animals'. For example dogs are much more natural people pleasers than the rare green emerald tree boas with inch-long fangs that we used to raise. Our captive bred snakes were gorgeous and surprisingly gentle, but it just isn't their nature to enjoy loads of cuddling just because their owner does, or to bring you your slippers and give you kisses after a hard day! But this *is* your dog's nature.

Since your dog's nature is not to want to soil the house, the point of housetraining is to make him understand from the earliest that voiding in the house immensely displeases you, whereas you love him and are filled with joy whenever he goes potty in the yard! Your skill, timing and finesse, along with how much time you can spend with the puppy at first will determine how quickly you can teach him this. Repetition also aids learning so you will have to tolerate a few accidents that you can appropriately correct. Don't be upset about this. It's the whole point of housetraining, and a few accidents (*not* a hundred) are essential to making the puppy understand the difference between desirable and undesirable behavior much more quickly.

Very young puppies are immature like babies and they *physically* can't hold their bowels or bladder very long. But they are capable of learning as long as you make what you want clear without inducing pain or fear. So much of getting housetraining right depends upon your sensitivity, good timing, and reasonableness.

The One-Hour Rule: Some experts estimate that young pups can hold their bladders one-hour for every month of life and most healthy dogs can even comfortably "hold it" a bit longer than this, especially overnight. The youngest puppies usually need one walk in the middle of the night (and, like human babies, they will cry to let you know). One late-night walk like this is usually sufficient for young puppies, and older pups can usually make it through an entire night without problems. But the one month/one hour "rule" is a decent rule of thumb that can help people stay sensitive to their puppies' physical limits.

(4) Owners should set up a schedule and take your young pup outside frequently at times when pups commonly need to relieve bladder and bowels. The most common times are after sleeping, playing, eating or drinking. You should also learn to recognize your pup's unique signals that he feels a pressing need to go *before* he starts to void. Some pups very clearly let their owners know their needs in their unique ways: including barking, pacing, turning in circles, sniffing, scratching, going to corners or staring fixedly. Other pups seem a bit harder to read, but all give some indication. We've also helped some of our customers teach their pups to ring a bell at the front door whenever they need to go. (See instructions in our book *Awesome Puppy*.)

(You'll slso find detailed information on how to set up a potty schedule for your pup in many housetraining and puppy books. Just any ignore instructions for crating and instead use your own good judgment to substitute humane more humane, yet equally safe, containment alternatives.)

(5) Throughout the day, at your pup's scheduled potty times, and whenever he gives signals that he needs to go, immediately walk him outside, on a leash, so he can relieve himself in a designated spot. As you wait for the pup to eliminate, don't walk him around to see the sights, and don't give him any privileges or let him lead you by pulling. Just wait. When he starts voiding in the designated spot, say a verbal command like, "Go potty" to establish a connection to the behavior.

Then reward the pup with lavish praise, a play session off leash (if it's safe) or a pleasant leisurely walk.

(Some people successfully use treats as a reward for eliminating outdoors. Generally, we don't suggest this because it confuses some dogs. But it works well with others, so it's a personal choice.) Just use the method you feel most comfortable with so your puppy makes the connection that you're ecstatically happy whenever he relieves himself in the right spot outside.

And *never* reward your pup with a pleasure walk until he finishes eliminating where you want him to. Outwait him, or take him back inside.

If you give in to your puppy when he acts stubborn, this will reinforce bad behavior. The puppy may learn to make you take him on increasingly longer walks before he'll urinate or defecate, eventually holding your behavior "ransom" with power he has to withhold his urine and feces. Rather than getting frustrated and taking your anger out on the pup, you should simply outsmart him by making him understand that the only way he'll get free time to play or even a leisurely long walk is once he "earns" it by "going potty" on command while on leash.

Leashed walks on your street are good to teach your young pup how to walk with you and to expose him to the larger world. But never risk walking a very young pup with undeveloped immunity in busy areas where he may contact the feces of other dogs. Make sure he has all his shots first, and ask your veterinarian for specific recommendations on when or where it's safe to walk the pup. (If you do not have a clean area outside your yard, you can still walk your dog on leash to practice walking with you- just do it inside your yard or another safe clean area until your vet says it's safe to venture further.)

(6) If you know your pup has just gotten through sleeping, eating, drinking, stress, excited play, or any combination of these factors, then you he's "full" and has to go. So don't budge from his designated potty spot until he goes! **If you get tired after a while, bring him inside, but watch him even more closely because you know he's "full".** If you're unable to watch him at this time, you can humanely contain him, for example, in a spacious playpen or a small blank room. Then try taking him out again in fifteen or twenty minutes. If he tries squatting indoors again before twenty minutes is up, interrupt him with methods described in #8 below (for example, sudden sound) and then *immediately* take him outside.

Your success at housetraining and the speed that you can accomplish it depend upon how intently you watch your puppy, how well you read his signals and the precision of your timing. This is intense work and, at times you suspect the puppy may void, you must watch him diligently and *swiftly* get him outside. The good news is, if you start with a normal healthy puppy from a good start in life, your perfection at watching and catching the puppy will pay off and housetraining will be complete in just a few weeks. If you are really great at the skill, you may housetrain your normal healthy pup in just a few days.

(7) Don't hate your young pup for having potty accidents in the home, and never physically abuse him. Never shake a puppy by the scruff, hit, kick or throw him or hit or poke at him with household objects. Attacks like these for housetraining accidents could seriously injure a puppy, causing lifelong physical or emotional damage. And don't continue to "punish" a puppy hours after he has a bathroom accident by making him feel you hate him or locking him up away from the family for extended periods as punishment. Always remain calm and stick to housetraining protocol using reasonable, timely and consistent corrections that don't hurt the dog as described next in this list. This is the best way to get good results.

Being dogs, pups *do* want to please their owners. And canines do have a natural instinct not to soil their "den" (in this case, the house). But it's up to owners to teach young pups to make the connection of where it's appropriate to potty. Some owners mistakenly believe pups should have inborn moral guilt about soiling the home. But this is untrue and unfair- it's just not the nature of dogs to feel embarrassed about bodily functions.

Owners who physically punish their pups for soiling, hold grudges against their pups or treat them as "evil" because of potty accidents could cause lifelong emotional or behavioral damage. Instead, simply stay alert and consistent, treat housetraining as teaching moment and allow young pups ample opportunities to void outdoors while bowels and bladder mature.

Crating a Pup Can't Cure Bladder Infections, Worms or Disease: Are you having problems housetraining your young puppy, and does he need to urinate very frequently; does he strain, have strong smelling urine and/or run a fever? Are your puppy's bowel accidents diarrhea, watery, loose, unusually smelly or blood-tinged or do they contain strange items that look like worms or segments of worms? Is the pup unusually thin and/or bloated? And does he vomit or have poor appetite? These are all signs of physical disease- and you cannot effectively housetrain until these conditions are cleared up.

If you purchased your puppy from a pet shop and the shop gave you a coupon for a free initial vet care as part of your package, we advise you to be highly cautious. Don't let the veterinarian brush your concerns aside with a cursory exam with no diagnostic testing. Although it may cost more at first, if you ignore the free offer and instead immediately take your puppy to the best veterinarian in town, you may be able to save your dog unnecessary pain and save yourself huge expense in future. And, if your pup shows symptoms, make sure whatever vet you visit orders proper screening tests for bladder/kidney infections, intestinal parasites and other disease.

Unfortunately, as many as 90% of pet shop dogs are likely to come from negligent puppy mill breeders, and many of these puppies come diseased! Very many puppies die in transit, and many others die in the back rooms of the pet stores. Other pups are pumped with antibiotics to mask symptoms. In our home state of Florida, the law says that once a person purchases a pup, they cannot return it to the pet shop even if it's sick and they can't get their money refunded even if the pup dies within hours of leaving the store! This happens all too frequently. Unfortunately, by buying a puppy from a pet shop or having one shipped to you over the Internet, you virtually guarantee excessive vet bills for the life of your dog.

Once you have a pup from this background (or a pup with unknown history) spending a little more money upfront for comprehensive veterinary testing often reveals bladder infections or intestinal disease or parasites. If these problems are found and treated, it can save the pup from more serious illness and save you much more costly vet bills later on. And veterinary treatment for the underlying problem will also prevent unnecessary frustration in housetraining BECAUSE YOU CANNOT PHYSICALLY HOUSETRAIN A SICK PUP!

(8) **How to correct accidents in your house:**

It's best if you can get your puppy outside the moment he feels a pressing need to evacuate but before he loses control. If, however, he starts having an accident and you catch him in the act, you can make it a priceless learning experience.

Whenever a family member catches the puppy squatting, immediately interrupt him with a loud noise, like hard hand clapping. Or you can make a sharp "eh-eh!" noise or shake ten pennies inside a taped-up soda can behind your back. Noise aversion the second a pup starts to void tends to contract their sphincter muscles and stop elimination momentarily. And it will also mark the inappropriate voiding as the behavior that caused the unpleasant sound.

Use this moment to immediately take hold of the pup. (But never call him to you in an unpleasant situation like this, or he'll learn not to want to respond to the "come" command later in life.) **Quickly lift the pup or lead him away mid-accident, grab your leash and immediately rush him out to the yard, stopping at the area you have designated for elimination.** Move fast! If you forget to leave keys, shoes and leash right by the door, you won't be able to get him outside fast enough and you'll miss the critical moment for learning.

(9) **Once the pup is outside on leash in the designated spot, give the command for elimination you have chosen and then wait. And if he now urinates or defecates, immediately offer lots of praise and/or a reward like a nice little walk.** (In contrast, if the weather's unpleasant, you can allow him back *inside* as his reward.)

You should consistently associate some negative stimulus, like a sudden noise, with your puppy's bathroom accidents when you catch him in the act. But never physically punish your pup, even if you do catch him. And only correct once when you catch him.

Do not continue to yell at him or act mean for an hour afterward. **You want him to associate negative feedback only with one thing- the bathroom accident in the house.** Once he has done something good, like relieved himself in the appropriate place outdoors, it should be time for praise and pleasantry again.

You should never make your little puppy feel you hate him, or that you are rejecting him. Make it clear that you are only negative about the bathroom accidents, and don't keep snapping and snarling at your pup all day long. You want your puppy to grow up confident, and bickering in the family about the bathroom accidents can wear the puppy down and have a negative impact on his future personality.

(10) Once your dog has relieved himself indoors, if he left a wet spot or half a bowel movement, it's important to come back in and clean up the accident with a cleanser that neutralizes dogs' pheremones. (If you don't use a special enzymatic cleanser like this, the pup can still smell the accident and may feel compelled to go there again. And cleaners like ammonia can make the situation worse.) You should also clean up from any accidents from other dogs in the household. Dogs can smell where other dogs have marked and sometimes the scent sinks through layers of carpet and underflooring. A black light will help you find residue from past accidents. And in cases of long-term housetraining problems you may do some detective work and find out the problem is not just the new pup; rather the problem is multiple dogs in the household marking over each other for years. (This can be a serious problem. And a home that adult dogs are currently using as a bathroom is not a place to bring a new puppy, because you will never be able to housetrain him until that problem is completely solved.)

Scent can also work in your favor. Try carrying a bowel movement, a urine-soaked paper towel or a wet wee-wee pad out to the designated spot where you want your pup to relieve himself. The scent of the waste will help express that this is the "bathroom" you want him to use.

(11) Containment during housetraining:

Since you know your young pup's bowels and bladder are not fully developed during housetraining, you must expect some accidents. In order to protect your home, you can safely and humanely control the pup's environment when you can't supervise, but there's never a need to confine him cruelly. When your pup is very young, start out with a comfortable yet relatively small space. As he achieves success, you will gradually expand the area he's loose in. Containing pup's in a safe, yet sufficiently spacious and stimulating area, whenever you cannot watch them cuts down on accidents. And it also keeps pups safe from household hazards during teething.

The difference between crate-training and humane containment is that you humanely contain a pup: 1) only for short periods, 2) only when necessary, 3) only in safe and comfortable rooms or areas so he can move around and access varied stimuli necessary for ideal canine development and 4) and only where he can see and be near his humans when they are home.

You should never cage your pup for long periods with nothing to do during the critical months of his development, or you will be restricting the development of his mind, his senses and his personality and emotions. Ideally, the area your pup stays in when you're away should provide space for him to wander and play and access to safe toys, safe bedding and fresh water.

We suggest gating off a nice, totally dog-proofed, area with easily cleaned flooring. Young puppies (especially those under four months) can only hold their bladders several hours at a time. So until his bladder matures, if you cannot come home to give your young pup a midday potty break, it's best to ask a trusted friend to do it or hire a reliable dog walker.

If getting someone to take the pup out midday is not possible, however, you may have to leave papers, "doggie grass" or wee-wee pads in your pup's room. Some people say that giving your puppy a wee-wee pad will irreparably confuse him. But sometimes there's no choice. We think it's cruel to physically force a young pup to hold his bladder/bowels in a tiny crate just because he dreads lying in his own mess. If you give your young puppy a spacious room to stay in and you're away too long, he will likely soil on the pad in a corner you designate. And while this may confuse him a bit, it's not likely to ruin housetraining and it's just humane. (As the pup matures and gets accustomed, you can decrease the number of wee-wee pads and eventually eliminate them entirely. And newly popular doggie grass for indoors may be another solution since using it may generalize better to the outdoors.)

Chapter 6 describes how today's popular "open floor plans" have made it difficult to carve out a designated space for a puppy. Kitchens (with hazards taken up from the floor) used to be a great spot for puppy containment, but it's becoming increasingly harder to close them off securely in open modern floor plans. Pet catalogs do offer a selection of extra wide and tall furniture-quality gates. A dining room with hard flooring is another option for a puppy's area, or you might be able to use your home office space if you can move all office hazards like computer connections to another area temporarily.

Some bathrooms can also be big and comfortable for pups as long as they are large enough and well ventilated. Make sure the toilet is shut and all hazards like cleaners are removed. For example, a couple we worked with used their beautiful spa-size upstairs bath with a baby gate in the doorway. This was a great spot where their Shih-tzu puppy could watch them while they slept; with no risk for bathroom accidents on carpet or falling down stairs during the night.

You should be creative in choosing areas for safely containing your puppy when you need to, and plan and buy supplies like baby gates, wee-wee pads and exercise pens *before* you get your pup home. Start by keeping the pup in a relatively small and completely safe space while you are away. And then increase his free space based upon his progress and your lifestyle and convenience. You can always keep certain rooms with hazards or valuables closed while you are away (this might include workrooms, offices/studios, kids' rooms with unsecured toys or formal living rooms). But eventually you should be able to offer your dog full range of most of the house, as long as he's stopped teething and you're confident he won't hurt himself.

Never house your puppy in a garage, or in a crate outside, especially when it is very hot or cold! This can be deadly or make your pup very sick! Laundry rooms can sometimes be fine. But make sure they are adequately ventilated and not airless, that they are lighted and that there are no chemicals, detergents or bleach left around.

In every room, as you "dog-proof" to remove hazards, always assume that pups can jump, climb and pull things down from much higher surfaces than you could imagine. Rather than placing things higher, completely remove any real hazard- or prized valuables- completely from the area while your puppy may still be teething.

There is one condition when we believe owners can safely use a crate for puppy containment during housetraining and teething with no ill effects and this is if you need to use an extra large crate to temporary leave a tiny toy breed puppy. (A Chihuahua puppy in Great Dane crate, for example.)

One of our dog-devoted retired customers did this with his 2-pound feisty Yorkie mix pup when he left the house for doctors' appointments, and this was the only time he ever crated. In his large home filled with family heirlooms, he legitimately feared that if he left the tiny, extremely curious puppy total freedom, she might hide where he couldn't find her. And he happened to have an extra large crate (the pet shop had pressured him into buying a crate, so he'd bought the largest available). So the crate was Doberman-sized, and the teacup-sized Yorkie had plenty of room to run around and enjoy herself with her toys inside it. This caused her no stress, because her doting "parent" was never away for more than a few hours once a week.

If you already happen to own an extra-large crate and you don't have any safer or more comfortable alternative, you could use it to contain a tiny toy breed pup for extremely short periods during housetraining and teething. Just make sure the pup can't catch his head in the bars, and provide safe toys and water that won't tip over and maintain a comfortable temperature. And remember that this should only be a temporary alternative.

After this, if you choose to keep the crate in your home, you can leave the door open and just allow the older pup or mature dog to use it like a dog bed. And it's a good idea to have some safe means of containment for your pets during travel or emergencies. Remember that there is nothing *intrinsically* dangerous about the existence of a dog crate *unless* its existence tempts owners to use it too much, or use it improperly.

It may surprise you that, even though the authors are against the practice of Excessive Home Dog Crating, we don't advise leaving a young puppy full run of the house whenever you go away. But we always advocate being reasonable and safe and doing what's best for your dog. **Very young pups can sometimes be hazards to themselves when not supervised. We do NOT oppose reasonable temporary *containment* of the youngest puppies that might hurt themselves and that require frequent sleep and rest. But we do oppose cruel and excessive *confinement* in a cramped cage for many hours- especially if a pup is separated from owners and denied water, toys, bedding and interaction with normal household stimuli like running, playing or looking out windows.**

Should you leave food or water?

If you leave a young puppy confined to an area when you go out, there's a good chance he'll have the occasional accident. Because this type of "accident" usually has a largely physical basis, some owners try to gain control by controlling when and how much they feed and water the pup. Controlling feedings is a good idea. Owners who schedule when they feed, and then get their young pup outside ten to forty minutes after each mealtime tend to have the greatest success controlling where their puppy has his bowel movements. And we recommend against leaving food for your pup or dog to eat from freely- both for bowel control and for behavioral reasons.

But we do advocate leaving pups free access to water. Just monitor your pup's intake and make sure it's reasonable, because excessive drinking can be a symptom of illness and it can create metabolic problems just like a lack of water can. Constant drinking will make your pup have to urinate much more frequently. And some nervous dogs (especially from puppy mill backgrounds) have been known to drink water compulsively, leading to health risks. Dogs also shouldn't drink a huge amount of water immediately after eating, which can increase the likelihood of life-threatening bloat. So check with your veterinarian for a recommendation of the right amount of water to give your pup. And always provide enough water to prevent dehydration.

Many trainers advocate leaving your pup no water when you leave him alone or when you leave him crated. We were shocked to recently hear that some veterinarians are also recommending this! **But we feel there's serious danger if an owner leaves the dog alone too long without water every day**, and it can become even more dangerous if unforeseen circumstances keep the owner from getting home on time and the pup must wait even longer. Potty accidents aren't fatal, but the long-term effects of dehydration in a tiny puppy could be. No matter how well withholding water may work to keep your developing little puppy from urinating too soon, we feel that the risk to his health and comfort is too great. Dehydration is a serious health risk to young pups and it can affect vital systems like the kidneys and the electrolyte balance, which in turn can affect the brain and moods.

We've also observed a "privation syndrome" where puppies are being left crated for so long that when the owners return the first thing their pup does is to madly consume a big bowel of water and then lick out the bowl. (See the story of Champ in Chapter 4). Dogs and puppies with this kind of water privation become so insistent on drinking when they get the chance that they appear feral in their postures. And they will prioritize desperate drinking even ahead of greeting owners, stretching their legs in the backyard, eating or even urinating or defecating. Since they consume so much water so fast, they are also likely to have accidents all over the house if the owners can't get them outside immediately. By withholding water all day, these dogs' owners are teaching them to spring on limited resources in an absolute frenzy, without using any self-restraint- and this habit then carries over to other areas of behavior.

We advise being generous, yet reasonable. Most puppies can be left with some water when owners go away. However, if your pup tends to drink too much, to keep him hydrated you can leave some ice cubes, a small water dish or a water bottle he can lick at.

When an Adult Dog Relieves Himself on Your Floor, This is Not a "Housetraining" Problem- it's a Real Problem

True "housetraining" accidents happen in young puppies because of a combination of immature bladder and bowels and an ignorance of the proper place to eliminate. Yet strangely these days, especially with dogs that have been crate-trained, we find owners still "housetraining" when dogs are 8 months, one year or even 18 months old- and still acting as though this is a normal "puppy" problem! The truth is, all healthy pups of six months, under ideal conditions of training and husbandry (not crating) should be completely housetrained. If your dog is this old and you allow him frequent enough opportunities to go outside and he is still voiding in the house, something is seriously wrong!

Older puppies or adult dogs may use a home as a bathroom because of illness or behavior problems, which include scent marking as part of a syndrome of inappropriate dominance and mistakes in husbandry or training. Crating may have caused these problems or it may prolong them. We really can't imagine how some dog owners live with constant "accidents" like this for so many months or years. Instead, owners should get the help they need, starting with thorough veterinary screening. **Housetraining should be no more than a mild annoyance for a few days or weeks. It should never become the most pivotal characteristic of your relationship with your dog.**

Alternatives to housetraining- It's all right to just say "no":

Before choosing to bring home a pup, all family members should learn the exact responsibilities involved in housetraining and then honestly assess their own personal abilities, schedule and tolerance for cleaning occasional accidents. If the family fears they cannot handle it, there's no reason to feel ashamed. Instead consider one of the alternatives: 1.) Purchase or adopt a dog or pup that's already housetrained not to mess in a home (*not* just "crate-trained"); 2.) Pay your responsible breeder to humanely housetrain your pup before he comes home with you or 3.) Choose an adult dog that's already perfectly housetrained.

Before **bringing home a puppy is the time to accept the truth that not all people are ideally suited to housetraining puppy-** *and they shouldn't have to be.* **You can still own and love a dog without having to go through the housetraining phase.** Even under ideal circumstances, young puppies are like human babies, and no owner can completely avoid accidents during housetraining. People feel differently about their homes and physical surroundings and this is a matter of personal choice. While almost all of us feel distaste if we step on a bowel or bladder accident in our living rooms, some people literally cannot emotionally handle this. Some people are just more squeamish. Others collect vulnerable prized possessions that they are deeply attached to, like pricey Persian rugs or white velvet sofas.

While no one really wants their home to be nasty, some people consider perfection in home décor a much more vital priority than others do. A "dog-friendly" home can still be attractive, but it requires greater flexibility in finishes, arrangements of breakables and ways to close off certain areas while allowing the dog(s) ample space. **Even though adult dogs need some allowances made, most normal adult dogs with good manners can live safely around even the most fancy décor. But young puppies will put your home at some risk no matter what you do.** If you feel that, with your particular décor or feelings about cleanliness, you can tolerate zero bowel or bladder accidents in the common areas of your home where the dog would live and socialize with family, then we feel you shouldn't risk bringing home a puppy that's not housetrained! Choosing a dog that's already housetrained is kinder for dog and family than having to cage a young puppy far from where owners do their daily living.

Other owners might feel they simply cannot deal with housetraining a pup if they have an extremely demanding work schedule or if they have physical problems that make it difficult to bend or to wake in the middle of the night. And this is perfectly fine. The time to honestly weigh all these concerns is *before* you pick up a puppy, when there's still time to say "no".

Chapter 14: Behavior Training- How to Train a Well-Behaved Puppy Without Crating

Includes:

Part A: Stopping Problems Before They Start By Setting Your Family Up for Success &

Part B: Training & Behavior-Shaping Principles for Great House Manners

Never choose a dog on impulse. When selecting your dog, a good general rule of thumb is to invest at least as much care, energy and research as you would when buying a home. This makes sense, since, statistically, an average family will be with their dog approximately twice as long as they'll stay in each home they buy. Individuals who select their dogs with the same amount of care they'd use selecting their home will enjoy the best relationships with their dogs, plus the best quality of life overall!

Part A: Stopping Problems Before They Start By Setting Your Family Up for Success

What is your dog's quality of life?

With awareness, you can decide to make your dog's quality of life whatever you want it to be. It can actually be difficult to objectively assess how good your dog's quality of life is compared to other dogs', or compared to how good it could be, since notions of quality of life are subjective. And what we value may be different than what a dog experiences as pleasurable or important. So one way to consider quality of life is to break it down, first considering whether your dog experiences any discomfort (this includes physical discomfort.This includes lack of exercise and movement; and mental discomfort, including emotional feelings like loneliness or anxiety). Then rate any discomfort on a scale of 0-100.

Next, rate your dog's current level of pleasure. Consider all the things that have given him pleasure in the past, and things that you're sure he'd enjoy, even if he's never done them. Then rate his current level of pleasure on a scale of 0-100. (Examples of pleasurable activities could include being petted, playing in the park or going for long walks.)

Now, subtract any score for discomfort from the pleasure score and you'll have an overall figure for your dog's happiness. Is as high as you think *any* dog's score could possibly be? And are there any simple things you could do to improve the score, and your dog's quality of life.

It's Easy to Have a Good Dog- Without Crating

If you feel bad because you still crate your dog, this chapter offers alternatives. All families need to do is provide a reasonable (not extraordinary) amount of care, attention and training for their dogs- nothing superhuman. Ask friends and relatives from older generations who still live happily with dogs free in their homes. Twenty years ago, adult dogs didn't commonly stay crated in homes while owners worked or slept at night. Owners wanted dogs free for many reasons. For example, most owners *wanted* their dogs to run from window to window to bark and discourage possible burglars or intruders. (People today seem to forget that a crated dog can't save your life or protect your home).

Twenty years ago most pups were quickly housetrained, usually in a few weeks or less- something that' become almost unheard of these days. And as soon as pups matured and their adult teeth came in at the biological end of the "teething" period, most lived freely with their families, showing overall respect for the owners and their possessions (just like Shaun, the Labrador John Grogan owned before Marley.) Good house manners like this should be considered the baseline and if your adult dog cannot safely be trusted to live in your home free of a crate, something is seriously wrong.

Sometimes owners' actions since bringing a dog home contribute to his behavior problems. Or they may unknowingly bring home a dog that has existing emotional/behavioral problems caused by genetic defects, puppy mill upbringing, abuse, neglect and/or time spent in shelters. Some problems may be too serious for the average family to solve with just common sense and the resources at hand, but canine problems *can* be solved with the right resources and effor. Excessive crating is never a long-term solution and it always makes existing problems worse.

The best way to raise the dog that you want is to always start from the positive and be clear what actions you want your dog to take at any given time. **Aim for the highest expectations.** Too often, owners only think about a long list of the behaviors they *don't* want form their dog. Yet considering what you *do* want changes everything. It's rarely too late to begin enjoying your dog in a way that fits with your particular lifestyle. But the best results come from planning for the positive ahead of time. For ideas, read this chapter, our book *Awesome Puppy* (which includes instructions for teaching all commands plus fun activities to shape canine manners) and other in-depth training books and DVD's that don't advocate crating (such as those in the Appendix-Recommended Reading).

This chapter covers some of the most effective hints for teaching house manners and shaping behavior that we recommend to our customers and that you may not find anywhere else. (The authors also offer distance consultation for families; presentations for groups and consultations and customized training materials for businesses.)

How to Live Happily with Your Dog or Pup without Crating. The Basics:

A.) Preventing Problems Before They Start By Setting Yourself Up for Success:

Dogs respond almost magically to training at any age. **However, your actions and decisions *before* bringing a dog home could have as big an impact on your happiness as everything you do after you get him combined.** So learning about dogs and making the right choices and plans ahead of time is the most important thing you can do to promote compatibility and happiness.

There are hundreds of unique dog breeds in the world, each bred to have unique attributes and temperaments. And over a hundred breeds are fairly common in America. Yet most people are only truly familiar with perhaps 20 breeds or less! Dogs at a local shelter may only represent an even smaller number of breeds. And, if you don't know even know certain breeds exist, there's no way for you to contact breeders or rescue societies. Even many popular breed books on bookstore shelves do dog shoppers a disservice by just showing giant photos of a very limited number of breeds.

The burden of research is up to you. Before any family buys or adopts a dog, we recommend that they read several books that include **extensive descriptions of at least 100 different breeds, including detailed descriptions of their temperament.**

(1). **The first thing to do before bringing home a dog is to honestly ask yourself exactly what kind of dog you want. Are you looking for a dog to play active outdoor games with? To guard your home? To be obedient? To take to public places and show off to friends? Or just to cuddle? Not every breed is equally good at all these tasks. Breeds have been created for different tasks, so your honest answers about your lifestyle and priorities will determine which breed, or mix of breeds, is best for you.** But if you make an error, even for the noblest reasons, your family and your dog can suffer decreased quality of life for years.

Excessively high energy level is one of the biggest problems for average families who don't intend to use their dogs for work. Another common problem is active breeds that prove too large for average suburban families with small yards to handle and exercise. And the worst problems usually occur when large size and high energy combine. Of course, variables like a dog's individual personality, health, emotional stability and prior upbringing make a difference in what a good pet he will be. But families should never let well-meaning dog professionals convince you that breed is completely immaterial. If you make this mistake you may miss out on the single biggest predictor of your dog's temperament, energy level and suitability for your particular lifestyle.

Lately, it's "politically correct" to think that all breeds are the same. And certain breeds (notably Pit Bulls) have gotten an undeserved bad reputation just because of some horribly irresponsible owners; so potential adopters (and policy-makers) should always keep open minds. But families can have serious problems if they ignore breed (and energy level) totally and rescue a dog they can't provide with enough exercise or a suitable lifestyle. It's even worse if they start crating the young dog constantly because they feel they can't control it, and problems can become worse as you add dogs to a household.

Of course, dog lovers want to help dogs in any way they can. But volunteering at a shelter, giving a cash donation or fostering a dog is a better way to help than bringing the wrong dog into a home that is the wrong fit and depriving him of the chance to find the right home.

"High-Energy Dog" and "High-Energy Person" Don't Mean the Same Thing!

All dogs have different energy levels. According to Tracy Libby, author of the very useful book, *High Energy Dogs* mentioned in the Bibliography and Appendix there are specific ways to recognize if a dog is high energy, including, if he:

"comes from strong working lines that were bred to do a specific job, such as herding, retrieving, going to ground, guarding and so forth... Is always raring to go, be it working or playing... Is constantly up for any activity that involves movement, be it running, playing, swimming, and so forth... Requires two or more hours of physical exercise daily to take the edge off but could continue for several more hours... Is easily overstimulated to the point of losing control."

If this sounds like your dog it's not surprising because, according to the book, high-energy breeds make up 50% percent of AKC registrations today, while low energy breeds make up only 7%! In the book, Ms. Libby includes American Staffordshire Terriers, Australian Shepherds, Border Collies, German Shepherd Dogs, Siberian Huskies, Golden Retrievers, Jack Russell Terriers and Labrador Retrievers (America's favorite breed, and the breed we get the most calls on) on a list of 13 high-energy breeds. These are also some of the breeds and mixes frequently seen in shelters.

Owners often mistakenly select a dog based on semantics. Since they are physically fit, they assume they're best matched with a dog labeled "high energy". But the truth is that high-energy dogs usually only fit well with owners who can consistently provide them with two or more hours of extreme physical exercise every day. Even if an owner is fit, he or she may feel tired after long workdays. And many popular sports such as bodybuilding, yoga, dancing, mountain climbing, surfing, skiing or kayaking leave no place for dogs. The same is true if the children in the family constantly go to soccer, baseball or basketball practices and games. Your kids may be highly active, but there's no way to include the dog. Often, while kids participate in sports, their high-energy dogs sit crated at home.

Recently, even celebrity television dog trainer Cesar Millan, perhaps the world's biggest advocate for walking and running with dogs, has started to recommend that the best fit for most average families is not a true high-energy dog, but rather a *medium* energy dog.

Obviously, the best time to make a decision about ideal energy level is *before* you select a dog. But if you already own a problem dog, once you look at his true energy level, you may realize some of his behavior problems are simply the result of a frustrated need for physical activity. The only solution for an owner at this point is to either re-home the dog (not usually the favored option) or to get creative to provide more activity. (You can find hundreds of realistic activities to do with dogs that fit every lifestyle- even for owners who are busy or who are not athletes- in our comprehensive activity book *The Cure for Useless Dog Syndrome* available in print and navigable e-book versions.)

The absolute worst thing owners can do with a high-energy dog that isn't getting enough exercise is to restrict his movement more. Yet this is exactly what many families end up doing. Crating a dog that needs this much movement so that he cannot even wander around, play or stretch his legs adds immeasurably to the exercise deficit and the frustration level every hour he is caged. If you adopted a dog like this when he was already three years old and a previous owner has already caged him every day of his life, don't be surprised if he behaves badly when you get him home! The good news is that in some cases, generous amounts of healthy exercise may be all that's needed to start a problem dog on the road to healing.

(2). Once you've decided on breed, you should always obtain the best dog from the best local breeder or facility. Ideally, before bringing home a puppy, you should meet the puppy, the littermates and the parents and physically observe that the pups have been kindly and actively socialized in a house around people (and not crated or kenneled). As we have discussed in former chapters, pet shops that sell dogs from puppy mills will always lie when you ask what kind of breeder your pup came from. And, while most reputable breeders do have websites, **the Internet makes it infinitely easier for bad or criminal breeders to sell to the public by shipping pups cross-country. So, *unless you can physically travel there*, it's safest to simply write off kennels or rescues from other states**. And avoid shipping, which is extremely traumatic to pups, and can leave the door open to severe lifetime problems. **(Also, having a pup shipped to you without meeting it almost always means the wrong choice of dog.)**

Investigate your breeder. It's best if they breed to show standards (even if your dog is pet quality) and they should share extensive information and offer health guarantees that can save you much money and grief later on. A responsible breeder will happily answer all your questions and they'll also ask you probing questions to make sure your home is right for the pup. They'll also act patient, pleasant and articulate when speaking to you in person and over the telephone, and won't just make a good impression online, where anyone can fake civility and knowledge.

Before looking at dogs, learn the standard temperament tests for puppies. When you meet the puppies, test them and then don't compromise about the results. To avoid potentially serious behavior issues later on, NEVER buy or adopt ANY dog or puppy that shows negative reactions towards people, especially any growling, snapping or aggression.

Also reject puppies (or dogs) that fight or squirm when held; shrink, bolt or flinch away when touched; ignore people, look through or around them; or constantly turn away from people to have rowdy fun with toys or other dogs- these animals are giving early warning signs not to bring them home. Any of these behaviors can be normal in puppies to some degree, but if you sense at first meeting that a certain pup is just not reacting to you the way it should, listen to your intuition.

Also, NEVER purchase any puppy form a litter where ANY pup seems weak, listless or "sickly" in any way. The pups could be seriously ill. And some conditions can affect adult mental functioning and behavior years after treatment, so pups like this should only go to homes with owners who are experienced in helping special needs dogs.

If you have any bad feelings at all or any doubts about anything, we suggest you just walk away, no matter where you are in the process of buying or adopting a dog. And listen to any family member, especially a child, who indicates they have an intuitive bad feeling. Instinct is there to caution you for a reason.

There are rare instances where families have gotten lucky choosing a dog impulsively. But, most often, impatient or impulsive decisions cause tremendous problems later on. Commonly, customers whose dogs have the most serious problems tell us they had "odd" doubts about the pup or the breeder and yet persisted...

(3). Every family member must be in absolute agreement that they want a dog and they must prepare to interact with it and and take responsibility. Before deciding to bring home a dog, we recommend that the whole family discuss it in a "safe" non-judgmental manner. For example, the family could cast anonymous ballots on whether they want a dog. This is a case where the "no's" should win out with total veto power without any further argument or discussion. **Even if one family member does not want a dog, this is reason enough not to get one.**

In addition, the family should realistically check their schedule before looking at dogs. Rather than just saying, "I'll walk the dog every evening," the particular family member who is taking this responsibility should write down the time for this dog walk in their appointment book(s) for as long as they plan to have the dog. It's easy to assume that they have this time free. Yet when they actually pick up their day planner, smart phone or digital planner to note the dog walk times like any other appointment, they may realize that, more nights than not, they already have other scheduled commitments that interfere. Unless one of the other family members can find actual time slots open on their calendar, the truth is that the dog won't get walked. So the best time to find this out is before you bring him home.

Take a few hours to sketch out on paper or computer a schedule and a financial budget for your dog's lifetime that the whole family can agree with and now take note how any life changes will affect your lifestyle with the dog. Some modern families have such incredibly busy schedules these days that even elementary school children are stressed and lacking sleep. If a family starts to stress or squabble just attempting to pencil in time for the dog, or if you can't find money for his care in the projected budget without taking away from other household priorities, you may have trouble owning a dog right now.

Note: if you're not sure whether your schedule and finances will comfortably keep a dog in future, you could temporarily foster a dog for a rescue society. This also gives family members who are inexperienced or unsure an opportunity to see what it feels like to live with a dog, or a particular breed. You can let the rescue society know that you may be interested in adopting the dog after you've fostered him for a while, and they will most likely give your family first choice to adopt him.

Impatience on your part is a valuable clue to protect you from doing the wrong thing hurrying to get a (certain) dog. If you ever feel unwilling to endure the strain of researching ahead of time and instead feel like you must bring home a dog that second on impulse without planning, you are likely setting yourself, your family and your new dog up for disaster!

(4). Study up on how to train your dog in advance, and map out a general written plan for his first year of life, including time for training and outings to socialize him. It's easier to acquaint yourself early with the principles of gentle training so that, from the minute your dog arrives, you can be proactive (showing your dog the good things you want him to do), rather than reactive (constantly correcting mistakes and saying "no").

Search out training books that don't suggest harsh methods like choke collar corrections or crate-training. (Your local library and their online search may be the best resource. Also see the Bibliography and Appendix, Recommended Reading section, in this book. And read our new book *Awesome Puppy* which includes step by step training and a range of activities to positively shape canine personality.

Learn and rehearse the right procedure to introduce your new puppy to your home. Don't overwhelm him with too many stimuli or too much human attention on the first day. **What happens during your dog's first hours and days in your home will have a huge impact on his behavior in future years, and making small adjustments on his first day is a painless way to create the future behaviors you want.**

(5). Before you get a puppy, buy and study a detailed veterinary manual. It may feel disturbing to confront the variety of canine ailments and complexities required for the physical care of a dog. But this knowledge will help you prepare for costly medical "surprises". And preventative care can head off many problems. Also learn the cost of vet treatment to plan how you will pay for emergencies and your dog's old age.

If you haven't been exposed to the "dog world" in a couple of years, you should also visit upscale pet boutiques (which are an education in themselves) and acquaint yourself with the latest popular ideas in holistic veterinary care and nutrition, because this aspect of health and husbandry can also affect dogs' behavior.

"Dog Envy": You've got a wonderful dog and all the world can see it. You waited patiently, you chose the perfect dog for your lifestyle and you kindly shaped his behavior, with him living as a real family member. Your dog is beautiful or he's noticeably endearing- and the two of you exhibit such joy and ease whenever you're together that people sometimes approach you on the street and tell you they envy you. Usually this is meant as a good thing. But sometimes "dog envy" can turn toxic. Sometimes other people- friends, neighbors and even dog professionals- feel deeply disappointed in their relationships with their own dogs. An example is when dog professionals own unruly dogs and then spend all their time trying to control them through a combination of crating and intense physical methods. Rather than thinking of letting their dogs out of their crates and training more mindfully, people like this may lower their expectations and expect you to do the same.

So beware of people who approach your lovely and well-behaved dog with tense expressions, and give you dire warnings such as saying that, "you better crate that dog or he'll tear up your house or poop all over." When an owner who starts with a comfortable relationship with their dog gets scared into taking the advice to lock their beautiful dog in a crate- or use other needlessly harsh training methods- problems can begin. So if people ever approach you and tell you that your dog seems too good to be true, you can give them some friendly advice about how they can improve *their* dogs' behavior to be more like yours. But never let naysayers' toxicity ruin the lifestyle that's been working for you and your dog!

Part B- <u>Training Principles Based in Canine Psychology</u>: How to shape your dog into the great dog you want him to be:

If you teach your pup good house manners from the start, he'll easily learn good behavior for life and you won't feel you'll need to crate him to protect your home. These special tips make training easier than anything you may have learned before:

(1). Decide what you want your dog to do, not just what you *don't* want him to do. Always be proactive, rather than reactive. **In every situation, teach your dog positive activities that are incompatible with the activities you don't want him to do.** For example, if you teach your dog to sit to be petted whenever a guest comes in, he cannot at the same time jump on guests. And never give a pup attention unless he has all four feet on the floor. The theory of positive training is all about rewarding desired behaviors and extinguishing unwanted ones. In the case of "four on the floor" it's the owners' responsibility to stay consistent and keep children and visitors consistent as well. If you never pet, play with or talk to your 8-wk old Labrador puppy unless he has all four paws on the floor, it's almost guaranteed that he won't jump on you when he grows up and weighs 85 lbs

With thousands of "trials" throughout the day, the new desired response becomes almost a reflex, ingrained as a permanent part of your dog's personality.

(2). Positive training works remarkably well, and wanting to stay positive is no excuse to give up and crate your dog. The key to successful positive training is that owners must use 100% perfect timing and consistency in every single encounter with the dog.

We do not use crates.

In contrast, we're afraid that some dog trainers take a simplistic approach and confuse being a "positive" trainer with just being nice to dogs while running through fairly standard obedience commands. Unfortunately, this usually isn't enough to help families whose dogs have serious emotional/behavioral disorders, or history of trauma in their pasts, any more than a discussion with a friend would replace the services of a psychotherapist in a deeply disturbed human.

There are many "nice" dog trainers out there today who'd never violently correct a dog. And yet, seeking an "instant" solution to canine problems when they're in a customer's home and feel unsure what to do, they'll often simply lock the dog in a crate! Meanwhile, these trainers fail to demonstrate something vital to owners- how **complete consistency in frequent daily encounters will "softly", yet miraculously, improve the dog's behavior from the inside out. For positive reinforcement to work, a dog cannot be crated and constantly separated from owners. Instead, if the owners are able to follow through in everyday situations, the dog learns that all his negative behavior is ignored, while his positive behavior is always rewarded** with praise and attention. For learning like this to work, the dog must have ample opportunities to learn- and plentiful time to relate to his owners and practice.

(3 A). Always consider your dog's state of mind, because when you control the state of mind you control the dog. Calm is always the state of mind that you want. If you fail to control your dog's state of mind and try to push past it, you will face disaster. NEVER wait to try to influence the state of mind when the dog is already in a highly challenging situation. Instead, control the dog's state of mind and energy level many steps or stages before you meet the challenging stimulus or distraction. **If you have to put in a lot of energy reacting, things have already gone too far.**

Here's an example of how to train based on state of mind. Say you plan to walk your dog to the park, where usually the moment he sees other leashed dogs he reacts wildly. If you approach your front door and grab the leash and the dog starts jumping, how can you think his behavior will get *better* as you approach the park? Instead show your dog that you only reward calm behavior by closing the door, setting down the leash and waiting until he calms to open the door again. Or refocus him with some obedience commands. Wait until his heart rate is back to normal, and he refocuses on you.

Don't open that door and take your dog or puppy out for that adventure until he acts calm and waits for you to step out first. Some dogs progress quickly. Even if yours doesn't, it's still worth the wait. Then once your dog will wait patiently at the door, make sure he stays calm on the walk. If he pulls and flips around like a fish on the line when it's just the two of you, then the second he sees other dogs, he'll have no capacity to act calm, because he'll already be filled with adrenalin and his rational mind will be shut off. So stop the walk at any point that you have to. Even if it takes two more days of practice to get your dog to act calm and controlled on the walk, the day he is, he'll finally be in the proper state of mind to see the new dogs at the park.

(3B). No strain-no gain. Push for small increments of progress with each repetition, and with each day. You may have heard the bodybuilding saying "no pain- no gain", but we feel the concept of pushing that hard sets you up for unnecessary injury, so we've modified the saying to "no strain, no gain". The theory behind effective bodybuilding is to lift slightly heavier weights at each session, or challenge your body with slightly more repetitions at each session to keep your muscles growing and getting firmer. But you should never suddenly lift a weight so heavy that you injure yourself and set yourself all the way back. Likewise, with dogs and puppies, you should never attempt to push lessons too far, but you should bring the dog a little bit beyond his comfort zone with your guidance each day. **Always first achieve a small success and then build on that for more.**

In the example with the trip to the park, after your dog achieves a few successful walks down the block without acting crazy, he may do okay when he first sees another dog across the street. But then he may act wild if you attempt to move closer. If so, you should work at the closest distance that your dog still acts right, even if the strange dog can barely be seen. Stand there with your dog and practice some obedience in the presence of the other dog at a far distance. Then come back an hour later and approach a foot closer, watching your dog's body language. Get as close as you can with him behaving well. The next day, come back again and move a bit closer, as tolerated. If you practice carefully, and don't try for gains too soon, your dog will eventually stop overreacting and desensitize to the stimulus of the other dog as it loses its novelty, and he amasses repeated experiences staying calm in its presence.

Desensitization is an important concept in positive training, and introducing gradually more intense stimuli slowly, as tolerated, like this is known to also help fears, phobias and some cases of aggression. You can learn more by reading books written by expert behaviorists and scientists, such as the Nicole Wilde and Patricia McConnell books in the Appendix. But most families whose dogs have extreme fears or potentially dangerous aggression will be safest also enlisting the help of high-level trainer or behaviorist. And in everyday situations, once you learn to read your dog's body language and state of mind, you'll learn to refocus him to act more stable and alert before he ever "loses" it, and so you'll never experience full blown problems.

(4). Don't ruin life with your dog through low expectations. Yes, dogs and pups are animals, and you can't expect them to have manners like Emily Post. But family dogs are not grizzly bears on a rampage! Lately, people often make the mistake of expecting too much from their dogs in some areas, but far too little in others.

In the normal progression of life with a dog, housetraining your young puppy and getting him through teething (meaning when he actually loses and replaces baby teeth, and no longer) will be your biggest challenge. These few months also should be the only serious challenges in protecting your home and your pup's safety. So, at this age, you must dog-proof. Similar to "child-proofing", dog proofing will keep your pup, and your belongings, safe. Any time you expect to leave the puppy unattended, even for a minute, first check there's no dangerous object or chemical within his reach so he can't hurt himself. You may also want to protect your own valuables and breakables by moving them out of his way or simply closing a door.

If you own your home and own dogs, we suggest flooring other than carpet in common living areas. This one choice can improve quality of life tremendously for the next 10-15 years. If you miss the coziness of carpet, you can substitute non-precious area rugs. Renters may have to cover carpets during housetraining, gate their pup in non-carpeted areas when no one's supervising and/or use a good non-toxic stain and odor remover when the pup has occasional accidents. Normally housetraining should last a short time, so even renters with carpet can usually make it through without landlord problems.

Families should also take reasonable precautions during the few months when pups are teething. If you bring home a teething pup, it's unreasonable to leave your Persian carpets down- this would be a good time to mount a valuable Persian rug as a wall decoration instead. When you own a teething pup, you should also keep your low coffee table clear of: dark chocolate; Tiffany pearls; new laptops and Blackberries; leather wedding albums with no copies of the photos; children's favorite stuffed toys; costly Chanel pumps or bowls of hundreds of decorative glass marbles.

Unfortunately, we have been called in after families left out every one of these items with the expected consequences... This being said, we think it's even worse that someone has convinced most modern owners to give up all reasonable faith in their dogs. *House manners mean truly good manners in all of your house!* Yes, your dog is an animal, who will chew as a puppy because when his teeth pain him and who can't distinguish a designer label from a Goodwill castoff or discern kid's stuffed toys are any different from the trendy stuffed dog toys you buy at the pet store. But it *is* the nature of dogs to be man's best friend and to respect their owners- this is why we love them!

A young puppy, going through the overwhelming physical changes of housetraining and teething, cannot be expected to physically, mentally or emotionally show this kind of restraint because he is still immature. But a good adult dog will. We can now hear the howls of protest from other dog training experts. Many will say that our views are not politically correct, and that owners should no longer expect dogs to want to please man because that concept used to be a cornerstone of old-school compulsion training. But most dog owners should be able to recognize the correct balance in their gut.

A dog *should* act easy and fun to live with- around all family members and in every part of the home. Remember back when most of us grew up, whether in *Lassie* days, *Brady Bunch* days or even *Cosby Show* days- and you will remember that dogs that lived full time in the home were generally easy to live with and not horrendous problems. Yes, family dogs might have smelled doggy after a rain, or left some muddy pawprints in overexuberance to greet you or had one or two bathroom accidents in a lifetime when they were sick or left too long. But they did not trash your house like a gang of thieves!

If you don't remember this golden age of American dog ownership yourself, ask your parents and grandparents. In each dog's adult lifetime, their owners might remember a few minor incidents. But INDOOR DOGS (not all were!) DID HAVE GOOD HOUSE MANNERS IN GENERAL. AND YOUR FAMILY TODAY SHOULD EXPECT NO LESS. If 1.) you start with a normal, healthy dog from ideal background, and 2.) you give the dog a fair chance in life and shape his behavior, with reasonable kindness and consistency, and 3.) you provide the dog adequate exercise and sensory stimuli, you should NOT experience any serious problems like total trashing of your home from your dog during his adult life.

Some owners are not realistic and expect more manners from a dog than most *people* could deliver. **But if your ADULT dog always acts more like a marauding grizzly bear in your home than he acts like Lassie, something is seriously wrong. Rather than just locking the dog in a crate and hoping for change, you must get help.** (If you feel you can't deal with the dog's problems, rather than locking him up for life to control him, there's nothing wrong with giving him to a different owner who can provide the rehabilitation, training or additional exercise he needs.)

It is normal to initially have to work very hard at housetraining your young puppy- and this will likely include getting up once during the night like you would with a baby when your pup is very young. But you should not have to walk an adult dog every 15 minutes to prevent accidents unless the dog is sick! You should never expect daily bowel movements in the middle of your bed from adult dogs.

You should not have to expect your adult dog to roughly snatch food from your children or scratch or nip your children, drawing blood, or to mount on visitors so hard he leaves bruises. Dogs shouldn't jump on counters, or break through glass to jump out windows. A dog should not drag her adult owner on concrete, breaking her owner's arm on their morning walk!

These all happened in real cases that we were called to treat. But even if your dog is out of control like these true-life examples, you shouldn't be cruel and just stuff the animal in a cage and forget it. Crating will only make the problems worse (and excessive crating in the dogs' past may have caused the problems to begin with.)

Before you choose a dog, or if you ever want to see a great dog to restore your faith in the canine population- we recommend you attend a large AKC all-breed dog show. You should arrive early in the morning to see all the different breeds during breed judging, read the program and then wander around the entire show to get a look at the wide variety of breeds in different rings. Also, observe the behavior of the show dogs outside the rings and talk to some of their owners and handlers. You'll be amazed how placid, well behaved and reliable show dogs act under really stressful circumstances.

Some also "work" at home, whether herding livestock or visiting seniors as therapy dogs, and they often hold obedience titles as well. Meet a working therapy or assistance dog and ask the owner what tasks their dog accomplishes. There is nothing like these meetings to put your expectations back where they should be and provide clear goals for what you want your dog to accomplish.

(5). Make Obedience Training Real- and Relevant:

Why would anyone want to attend a group obedience training class with their puppy or young dog and learn five commands *without knowing what they are used for*? As trainers who specialize in helping all the unsuccessful "graduates" from other training programs, we often encounter owners who've have spent weeks teaching their dog a "down" command, yet have never used it in real life and have no clue what it's for. The important information their trainer probably failed to give them is that lying down *voluntarily* can calm a dog and help neutralize disobedience/defiance and aggressive feelings, and it's also incompatible with some problem behaviors like jumping on guests and excessive barking.

"Sit" is another great all-purpose command. The first benefit is that sitting is incompatible with so many problem behaviors like jumping on people or darting out the door. It's also one of the easiest commands to refocus a dog and get him looking to you for the next instruction, rather than starting some mischief. And it can even help outdoors with dogs that pull on leash.

We usually introduce commands to dogs at first by training with treats, but the overall goal is to create an obedient-minded dog. Treats are just there as a symbol to mark the behavior you want and to show good faith. But they should only be used intermittently and **you should always be asking your dog to perform obedience commands in real-life situations**. For example, ask him if to "sit" and "stay" patiently before leaping out of your car.

(6). Repetition aids success- Instead of one long formal obedience session out in some hot sunny field, we practice surprise moments of obedience frequently each day and around distractions. Whenever you have a minute, practice walking your pup perfectly on a lead or having him "stack" or pose like a show dog. **And teach your dog or pup to tolerate frustration with activities like learning to wait patiently to be handed a toy**. (This can be part of a game. Find detailed instructions in our book *Awesome Puppy*.)

If you, and everyone you expose your dog to, act consistent and give him and give him good feedback every time he acts appropriate for the REST OF HIS LIFE, this will deepen his good habits, while withholding reward, attention or privileges will extinguish bad behaviors. For example, you should only pet your dog when he's calm, never when he acts wild. You respond to your dog thousands of time each day, and each is a learning experience.

Since consistency and repetition are essential to learning, you must spend sufficient time interacting with your dog, especially when he's a young puppy. Consistency and repetition work with every dog. Building good habits and extinguishing behavior problems in a young puppy before they ever escalate is the easiest way to shape the perfect dog of your dreams. But if you lock a puppy away in a cage during his formative weeks and months, you'll miss out on thousands of opportunities to shape his behavior.

(7). Frequently introduce new stimuli. Between 5-20 weeks is the critical time for you to socialize your puppy to be comfortable around new people, animals, places and situations. At this age he'll be naturally open-minded (as discussed in detail in Chapter 3). So if you make all his encounters with new things positive- and don't introduce to too much at once- he'll simply accept the new things as natural and respond to new situations as a calm, happy and balanced adult dog.

Introducing your dog or pup to new things also helps behavior because it reduces boredom and frustration. And mental stimulation, just like physical exercise, drains excess energy that could make him behave wildly. So providing adequate stimuli is another building block for an all-around superior and more pleasant dog.

Other stimuli you probably want to introduce your pup to include: water, leaves, grass, trees, stairs, animals including cats, children, babies, elderly people, people in wheelchairs, bicycles, traffic on the street, places other than the family's home, staircases, surfaces that wobble, the veterinarian's office (just to say "hi" to staff at first and get some treats), riding properly in a car, separations from the owner and other dogs in the family, dogs of all ages and sizes (the puppy just needs to see them and react in friendly fashion- the dogs do not actually have to touch), sudden or strange noises, novel smells, sounds and toys. The more novel stimuli you properly introduce your puppy to, the more self-confident he will be when he grows up and the more he will trust you. You will also build his senses, his balance and coordination and his mind- so that he will be more intelligent than if he had not encountered so many new things to think about during his critical development as a pup. (See the research studies mentioned in Chapter 3.) Also see our book *Awesome Puppy* for lists of hundreds of fun new stimuli to introduce your puppy to.

(8). **Start training and shaping your pup's behavior immediately, the first day you bring him home.** Never underestimate what your dog can do. Even though puppies have short attention spans and tire easily, just like human children, even an 8-week old pup is old enough to start learning basic obedience commands. Pups can also learn the "Look" command, where the pup focuses on the owner's eyes and ignores distractions and the "Come" command, which can save his life. Most young puppies can learn the names of family members and how to play simple games. And **the first day your pup comes home is the time to start gently teaching him that he'll always be rewarded for good behaviors (like sitting patiently to wait for your attention) and always be ignored or denied real-life rewards for bad behaviors like jumping or nipping.** If you don't start actively teaching your dog the behaviors you want from the moment he comes to you, he *will* start learning anyway because dogs are remarkably intelligent. But, left to his own devices, rather than learning the skills you want, your puppy will likely start learning bad habits that you do *not* want.

(9). **Vital Training tip. Start teaching your puppy to come to you from the day you get him home.** This is one of the most important commands, both for safety and for dog/owner bonding, and it builds the groundwork for an obedient and respectful dog. The only way you can make your dog come to you is if he always wants to come to you and always associates it with good things. NEVER call your pup to you for something unpleasant or something he doesn't like. (For example, calling "come" to interrupt a potty accident.) Instead, call your puppy to you frequently and unexpectedly and reward him with lots of praise and occasional food treats.

(10). Utilize the leash when training a young puppy. We aren't fans of using a leash for rough collar corrections, which can hurt a young puppy. But, for your dog to behave his best around people you *should* get him accustomed to being linked to you, with you leading the way, starting when you first get him home. Some of the greatest behavior disasters happen when owners never put a collar and leash on their dog until he's 90 lbs and he goes ballistic at the veterinarian's office.

For best results with the collar and leash, first desensitize your puppy to the collar first and then the leash by repeatedly showing the items to him and offering treats. When he's comfortable near the new item, next touch it to him and give him treats. Then put it on him loosely and give him treats. Gradually work up to where the puppy acts comfortable wearing the collar and leash.

Next teach your pup to walk beside or behind you (not in front) on your walks. Doing it this way keeps leadership where it belongs, and teaches your puppy to look to you to make decisions for him. Learning to take your lead on leash will also generalize to obedient reactions in other areas of your relationship. And the worst problem dogs in other areas are also those that don't show respect on leash. **Even if your dog gets exercise in other ways, some daily leash walking is essential for dog/owner bonding.**

Pups under 16 wks are naturally wired to want to follow you, so keeping the pup controlled on the leash should be easy at this age. But if your pup or dog tries to pull ahead, use body language, turns, stopping, slowing down and speeding up to keep him guessing, so he'll always have to pay attention and follow you. **Never pull hard on a collar,** especially if your pup is young, frail or wearing a collar, as opposed to a harness. **With small breeds, you may want to use a harness, and never use a choke or prong collar on a pup under 6 months- these could seriously injure him.** (See detailed instructions for leash walking in our book *Awesome Puppy*).

If the pup already came to you with bad leash walking behaviors such as excessive pulling, rolling, backing away or biting the leash, you may want to read additional information on leash walking theory, consult videos that demonstrate gentle methods or call in a professional who uses kind teaching techniques.

(11). Every canine behavior problem happens for a reason, and the most successful owners can stay cool- headed enough to figure out what that reason is without becoming upset or hopeless. Dogs don't always think the way humans do. Sometimes canine behavior theory seems counterintuitive; other times problems are physically-based. For example, a hormone imbalance can make a dog hyper, or a painful tooth can make him chew on objects. And dogs can also be idiosyncratic in personal preferences- some dogs won't work for treats but they will respond if you offer to throw their favorite ball.

Whatever your dog's problems, other families have experienced similar challenges. So **never feel embarrassed.** And don't let anyone convince you that you can't find positive solutions.

(12). Lead Your Dog. This training principle of ours is based on the science of physics and the nature of dogs. Too often owners try to confront dogs' negative behavior head on, rather than simply leading the dog in an alternate behavior that is easier and more natural- following the leader.

The best time to teach your dog to happily follow you and look to you for guidance in all situations is when he's a pup under 16 weeks. One technique that allows you to supervise him to prevent teething or restroom accidents is called the "Umbilical Cord"- just hook the pup's leash to you so he must follow you as you move around the house going about your daily business.

Sometimes pet store or puppy mill pups have never been properly socialized to humans so owners will feel the pup is "different", "independent" or, "doesn't seem to care". But sometimes using the "umbilical" technique will help these pups literally feel more "connected" to humans and change their attitude for the better.

Another way to lay the groundwork for your dog to walk nicely with you outside rather than pulling ahead is to first practice leash walking indoors, teaching him to follow you around the house and look up at you for direction. Start by holding a treat at your side and luring the dog or pup to follow close at your (left) side in "heel" position. Later, phase out the treats. It's in a dog's nature to enjoy following, and you will find that **it's a fun challenge to see how long you can keep your dog walking beside you around obstacles in the house with no leash on. The better your dog does this when you practice, the more likely he'll walk properly outside.** (The skill of following an owner also helps with many sports and activities, including agility and some of the games described in our activity book, *The Cure for Useless Dog Syndrome*, including "Walk the Line", "Follow the Leader" and "Dancing Dog". (Also see more information about "Follow the Leader" in our puppy guide, *Awesome Puppy*.)

If your dog runs away, remember that *it's is a dog's natural inclination to follow:*

So don't chase after him wildly, attempting to grab him or you'll only make him dash away just out of your reach. Instead, *if you can keep a cool head and run in the opposite direction, making it look energetic and fun, your dog will likely want to follow you.*

The principle of making your dog follow you also helps in other situations, and it's a good way to remove bad energy without confronting a surly dog head-on. For example, if your dog lies down on your couch and you don't want him there, try the easiest solution first. Call him to you from across the room rather than pulling on his collar and getting into a physical struggle, which could make a stubborn dog snappy.

Using dogs' natural tendency to follow helps many problems in many ways.

Pulling: If your dog pulls straight forward on a leash, instead of pulling back and straining yourself, try moving deftly to one side, then turning, speeding up and jogging in the opposite direction. The dog will likely hurry back to your side and concentrate on following you. And whenever he does something you don't want him to do, don't scream, pull back hard with leash or collar or flail at him with your hands (which can create highly negative consequences). Instead, take a step back, make a few repetitive kissing or clicking sounds and tap on your leg to lure him to follow after you and he'll forget the bad behavior. (This won't help if your dog is already "red-zone" or aggressive, but it can stop at most negative behaviors long before they become real problems.

When you're proactive and move your energy forward in the direction you want, you can usually get your dog to follow. And this principal also helps less powerful family members, such as children and the elderly, control large dogs without physical force.

(13). Teaching the "Drop It" and "Leave It" commands.

Your puppy may pick up and try to swallow items that could kill him, so it's important to teach him to drop items, or not pick them up, on your command. As you may know, struggling to wrestle items out of your pup's mouth usually will only stimulate his natural "prey drive" and teach him to hold on tighter. And dogs are strong. So the laws of physics may be in his favor and you may not be able to pull a dangerous item out of a strong non-cooperative dog's mouth. But, **by training ahead of time, you can easily teach your puppy or dog how to "leave" or turn away from a forbidden item (like human food, children's toys, cell phones, medication, dangerous plants or reptiles) after he fixates on it, but before he grabs it.**

The basic instructions for teaching the "leave it" command start with you setting out a toy or other item that you know the pup wants to grab. Then instruct him to "leave it" while being ready to cover it with your hand or foot if he lunges for it. The second he backs off, leaves the item alone, or looks into your eyes, say "good leave it" and reward him with an even better item, like a dog treat. Practice frequently, working up to more challenging situations. Eventually, your dog should be able to turn away from even the most tempting items (like a squirrel running past him) on your command.

You should also teach your pup to drop items he takes in his mouth. To teach "drop it" first allow your dog to hold an item he enjoys (like a toy) in his mouth. Then offer a second, higher value item (like a treat) and say, "drop it". As soon as the dog drops the first item, reward him with the treat. Practice frequently, and gradually phase out treats except for rewarding the "best" performances of this command. And remember, when practicing, to always use a higher value item to distract your dog from a lower value one.

Next practice with real-world situations like if the dog grabs an acorn outside. Once he's performing perfectly each time you practice, he will be more likely to "leave" or "drop" a highly dangerous item, like a poisonous snake, if you ever encounter one. You should always keep hazards away from your pup, but training "Drop it" and "Leave it" can give you more control if he ever takes something undesirable in his mouth. (How to train the "Drop It" and "Leave It" commands is explained in more detail in our books *The Cure for Useless Dog Syndrome* and *Awesome Puppy*.)

Exercise and Energy Level- the "Missing Piece"

Your dog's natural energy level, and whether you provide for that energy level, will have an enormous impact on your dog's, and your family's, quality of life. To view the topic theoretically, consider bringing home a horse, rather than a dog and having to provide for its natural needs. If your pre-teen desperately wanted a horse for Christmas, you'd likely treat it as a serious decision. And one of the reasons is that most of us know horses physically need a lot room to run.

Since horses are grazing animals whose nature is to travel long distances each day in herds, your horse reasonably needs a certain amount of space just to stretch its legs and daily physical movement is absolutely necessary for horses to keep healthy. In extreme cases, horses can die from lack of movement, so daily exercise for a horse is a highly serious matter. Most people know this, so folks without horse experience and without large properties usually steer clear of owning horses.

For the sake of explanation, owners should consider dogs in exactly the same way. First take into account the fact that the wolves/ and wild canines are descended from are meat-eating animals that travel long distances each day, in packs, to track and hunt their prey. Running thirty miles a day over challenging terrain would be normal for a wolf, and it would also be comfortable for many of the higher-energy breeds today! The original canines that showed up hundreds of thousands of years ago to sit beside human campfires and garbage dumps were well equipped to run like this, even though they were starting to select less challenging ways of getting their food.

When humans first domesticated dogs, it was not as companions. Starting thousands of years ago, dogs were expected to work beside the humans that owned them. And humans in those days worked very hard. In order for a dog to earn his keep, he was expected to help his owners with extreme physical demands.

Throughout history, man has trained dogs to herd and guard large flocks of sheep and cattle. Farmers have also used dogs to keep herds of livestock moving while the men rode on horseback. Dogs would literally run most of the day while working. Then they'd take short intervals of rest to lie down in the shade, or they might lie down beside their owner whenever they both could grab a moment's rest.Other dogs were bred for hunting tasks that kept them moving, under exhausting conditions, all day long. Terriers chased prey like rabbits and pests like rats through tunnels in the earth, while Sighthounds chased after swift game like deer. Dogs like beagles and foxhounds ran out in a pack chasing game while hunters on horses followed. And retrievers ran long distances, sometimes swimming or slogging through swampy water that the humans could not get through, in order to retrieve shot game.

Over the years, man bred different breeds to serve widely varying functions and their appearance reflects this. When humans first took in dogs, it was likely not because of sentiment, but because they helped people do their work and survive while fighting a harsh environment. The more energy their dogs had, the better, because any energy expended helped the owner's family survive and advance under conditions where neighbors without dogs might perish.

Some breeds possessed a great deal of muscle and were naturally athletic with long legs made for running. Other breeds possessed features like extremely powerful jaws, muscular necks and overall strength that helped them latch on and not let go. These dogs were bred for fighting and killing, usually other canines like wolves that might menace livestock, and sometimes even bears! Other breeds of dogs were developed to be strong enough to pull carts or sleds.

For many centuries it was a sign of material success to have a strong energetic dog that was useful doing its job. Only in the 1800's did some European nobility start showing off dogs that weren't bred to work- an indication that they had so much leisure that even their dogs could have leisure. (It was rumored that Marie Antionette's lapdog wore real gemstone jewelry!) Generally these dogs bred mainly as companions, "lapdogs" or "toys" were the toy breeds. These were small passive dogs, not to be confused with the small working terriers that have an entirely different temperament.

Many of the terriers, although they are as small as some toy breeds, are really livewire action-packed working dogs that feel most content when running around, hunting or focusing on a task. And even some tiny dogs classed as toys, like Chihuahuas, have extremely spunky temperaments and a strong need to assert themselves and live on the ground like "real" dogs.

In contrast, true toy or lapdog breeds are characterized by noticeably sweet temperament, geared towards getting owners' attention; along with high pack drive (which manifests by these dogs enjoying being close with their humans), relatively low prey drive (the desire to chase after moving animals or items) and extremely low energy and exercise needs on the continuum of dog breeds (even to the point of appearing sleepy or sluggish).

On the other end of the spectrum, some giant breeds are relatively low energy and, although many people assume differently, not all extremely large and giant breeds have high exercise needs. As long as some of these dogs get to go outside on regular walks, they are content to spend most of their day lying by their owner's side inside the home- and you won't catch an adult dog of a low-energy giant breed running around the house just out of exuberance. This is not in their nature or their genetic makeup. So sometimes the giant breeds with the lowest energy levels can be a good match for less athletic families, as long as the family can provide these large dogs reasonable space and care.

But, **ironically, many of the most popular breeds in the 30-100 lb. size that families bring home today-even to condos- are also the highest energy**.

Perhaps no one wants to be the first to declare, "I want to own an extremely low energy breed; the less energy, the better," because they think it would embarrass them or make them feel lazy. But the truth is that most people today are not in Olympic physical shape. And, even though many of us wish we could exercise a lot in the great outdoors, opportunities and free time are limited. Remember that dogs are by nature more physically active than people. So what would be considered a low energy dog doesn't equate with an inactive human owner. **A low energy dog is actually a good match with an "average" owner.**

People also make a mistake thinking that, because they're an "active" person who goes to the gym or enjoys sports, an extremely high-energy dog would be a good match for them. The problem is that many people cannot take their dog to most of the places where they are active (the gym, the tennis courts, the dance club or scuba on vacation). **An owner should be realistic about whether they can provide their extremely high energy breed the equivalent of at least two hours of full speed running every day, plus at least 45 minutes of brisk on-leash walking, ideally broken into two sessions, for dog/owner bonding purposes.**

Many prospective owners think they need an extremely active dog to keep up with their active kids. But, first, they should consider their children's schedules. These days, some elementary schoolers are completely booked with sports and activities- and the dog can't be involved in these.

The other thing to consider is the fact that "active" is not a synonym for "rough" or "rowdy", and this cuts both ways. Dog and kids should always respect each other, no matter how actively they play. Unless parents actually fear that their kids' inappropriate play will hurt a dog, a MEDIUM-energy dog is usually the best fit for a household with kids unless the kids are extremely active teenagers. **Average "active" kids who simply like to play often can't handle a large, extremely high-energy dog or puppy, especially if the dog has been cooped up in a crate all week, and then let loose around their playset on the weekend!** Remember that some of these large working or sporting breeds were originally bred to run thirty to fifty miles a day, or to kill animals as large as bulls or bears.

There *are* ideal owners out there for the super high-energy dogs. These would include working farm or ranch families where the dog will get a real job to do. Or an extremely high energy two-year old dog might find the perfect match in a twenty-eight year old fitness enthusiast who runs with him every day; or a family with teenage boys who alternate soccer and Frisbee games with the dog with hiking and biking long distance; or an active woman whose dogs compete for agility titles and practice their skills every day!

Even an active senior could work out well with an active dog, provided that person really knows the breed. For example, a 74-year old Jack Russell enthusiast with a fenced property of several acres could allow his dog to run along beside him sniffing around while he takes daily walks (as long as he impeccably trains the dog to obey a recall command above its own prey drive!) Since a dog like a Jack Russell Terrier is incredibly high energy, but physically small, a large property isn't even essential. As long as the educated owner provided him tasks to do- like "helping" in the garden by fetching things, or running a small agility course, everyone could stay healthy and happy.

For the happiest scenario, owners who are athletic, outdoor people themselves and who truly value athleticism as a way of life make the best match with the super high-energy dogs. But statistics on dog ownership in the real world don't quite play out this way. In fact, two of the most-owned breeds in this country today are also among the most high-energy we can think of- and both these breeds are also large and extremely powerful.

One of these, Labrador Retrievers (now popularly being bred larger than in the past, with 90lbs not uncommon) also make up a huge proportion of the problem behavior cases we are called in on- far exceeding the breed's relative popularity. Frequently, when we're called to treat a Lab that jumps on kids and acts completely out of control in the home, we're told the family sought out the breed because they're supposed to be great with children.

Often, the problem is a disconnect with owners not understanding that this particular breed was designed to run and retrieve. These owners may have seen some examples of the breed that are extremely old, overweight and sluggish and they thought this seemed charming and wanted their young dog to act this way. But this is actually very unhealthy! **Trying to exercise a large healthy young retrieving breed with just two fifteen-minute walks a day is not enough for his health or his sanity. And it won't give him a chance to manifest as the nice, balanced dog he possibly could be with the proper exercise.**

If you already own and love your high-energy dog, just having the wisdom of hindsight is not enough for a do-over. Next time, you may choose to buy or adopt a lower energy breed. **But, for now, there are things you can do to increase your dog's physical exercise, and, in some cases, this alone is enough to stop behavior problems and to get dog and owner bonding properly for the first time in years.** Of course, problems like aggression always require qualified, high-level professional assistance. But just giving a dog the right amount of exercise for his breed usually improves most other common problems and it's an easy low-cost solution.

Even increasing the duration and length of walks, using more challenging terrain or playing games with your dog in the back yard can help. And you can try more ambitious exercise if you are interested. (Our book *The Cure for Useless Dog Syndrome* gives exercise alternatives for owners ranging from the highly active to those who have difficulty walking and bending.)

You can always get creative. Dogs with high-energy needs can sometimes swim or run on treadmills, or you can hire a dog walker/dog runner to exercise your dog. In some cases (but not all) doggie day care can help provide the exercise your dog needs without creating other problems. But you must be EXTREMELY careful selecting and investigating a facility to make sure it's beneficial and there's no chance that attendance could injure your dog or teach him bad habits (like acting "pushy" or soiling indoors). And always check first with your dog's veterinarian to clear him medically before starting him on any exercise program.

Try increasing physical activity overall and see whether this helps. Of course, crating is a vicious cycle. As we saw in the case of Bouncy the Labradoodle, by keeping a highly physical animal immobile all day, the dog will only be act more antsy and crazy when he gets the chance to run around at the time you can least tolerate this- when you're tired after a hard day at work. Plan in advance so this situation never happens. **If you give your dog regular intense exercise each day, the "craziness" or "wildness" that made you feel you had to crate him may vanish!**

See the Appendix (Recommended Reading) for our abbreviated suggested reading list. And consult our book *Awesome Puppy* for psychological dog training principles, step-by-step instructions for all the basic obedience commands and easy creative activities for fun, exercise and learning, which work both for pups and adult dogs. Also see our comprehensive activity book *The Cure for Useless Dog Syndrome* for hundreds of options for busy families and for dogs and owners with different lifestyles and challenges

Chapter 15- Hope for Excessively Crated Dogs; and the Rehabilitation of Bridget, "the dog that was afraid of light"

What if you want to save a dog that's already been Excessively Crated? Is there hope for such dogs? And can they ever be good family dogs?

These questions will increasingly confront concerned owners as more dogs and pups come into their homes from puppy mills, shelters and rescues. Just as they would with an adopted or foster child, adoptive parents of an abused or overcrated dog will want to combat any bad influences from the dog's past to gently and kindly shape new behaviors. For example, some of the national humane organizations' websites offer specific information to help new owners rehabilitate puppy mill survivors. Most dogs that have been excessively crated by either by former owners or by puppy mill breeders will show some behavioral symptoms, but dogs have tremendous ability to change when they are shown patience and consistency.

Positive training- based on rewarding good behaviors and withholding reward or attention for negative behaviors- works surprisingly quickly to extinguish behavior problems. And, as long as owners don't let disappointment turn into resentment, they can start shaping huge changes in their dog's behavior. These new owners may never be able to make a dog that has been excessively crated for prolonged periods early in his life exactly the dog he could have been with ideal husbandry from the start. But even a dog that was neglected or deprived of early socialization can still become a wonderful companion that meets or exceeds your initial expectations.

The exception is one class of behavioral disorder that often does not respond perfectly, or even adequately, to home treatment with positive training- and these are some cases of serious aggression towards humans. Often, when police and humane officials raid a puppy mill some of the dogs simply cannot be rehabilitated and must be euthanized. Some of these hopeless cases suffer from physical illnesses that don't respond to treatment. Others have suffered lack of socialization to the point that they simply cannot be integrated as pets for humans, even after intense efforts by shelters and rescues.

But, of all the thousands upon thousands of dogs that have suffered even the most horrendous confinement, these hopeless cases remain the exceptions. **No matter how extremely dogs have been abused by excessive crating, tethering or other bad treatment the majority of them *can* be rehabilitated.** And, for most, it happens surprisingly quickly.

We urge concerned dog lovers to know exactly what they are getting into before they start teaching a dog that has been excessively crated how to live properly free in their home. (Adopters who don't know their dog's history are safest assuming he *was* excessively crated at some point, especially if he shows a number of the symptoms described in Chapter 1.)

All dogs need some training and shaping. But establishing structure and clear goals and expectations in the new home is especially important with dogs that lack positive and diverse experiences in their past. And all these facts about rehabilitation are equally true if you were the one who crated your dog too much at first. **Once your dog is released from excessive confinement in the crate, he will enjoy relating to the world in a different light. But he will also have to learn new responsibilities.**

Some of the concepts of training according to canine psychology (see Chapter 14) may seem counterintuitive at first, and it may seem difficult initially to even get your dog to focus. If reading, researching and practicing behavior shaping on your own doesn't seem to be enough, you may benefit from some help from a professional. (Ideally, choose an applied animal behaviorist with an advanced degree or a high-level dog trainer who does not believe in crating).

Once your family has insight into what caused a dog's problems and once you take an active role in making changes, the emotional scars and behavioral quirks left as a result of excessive crating usually start to fade away. Given a little extra help to catch up, most dogs that have suffered excessive crating can soon resemble other dogs that had more healthy stimulation early in life.

This is what happened in the true story of Bridget, a case we worked with that deeply affected us. With Bridget, a mature couple with demanding careers and unrealistic expectations adopted a large, intelligent high-energy breed dog that they didn't have time or skills to work with sufficiently. Instead of spending more time engaging with the dog, they then intensified the young dog's relatively minor behavior problems by following the advice of several dog trainers and crating her excessively.

By the time we were called in, some of the problems were serious. But when we met Bridget halfway she was able to change, and so were her owners. Bridget's behavior improved in many ways when she was released from her crate and trusted by people, first in our home and then in her owners'. And this dog that used to demonstrate serious "autistic-type" symptoms of being unable to connect with humans became able to show an incredibly loving side, happily engage with humans at home and in public and, for the first time in a year and a half, meet people's eyes.

The True Case Study of Bridget:

This is a story that will make some people very upset, wondering how this could have happened to such a beautiful dog. But others will see a positive side to the story- the fact that, with good education, the owners and dog began the long road to recovery.

Bridget was a female German Shepherd Dog that a mature dog-loving couple bought from a good German kennel because they wanted the best. We first met Bridget when she was 1½ years old. We were called to treat her because, despite the fact the owners had worked with several other trainers, spending thousands, Bridget still jumped on them uncontrollably, bit at their hands and bodies and never listened to them or looked to them for feedback.

She also constantly played too rough with the several small rescue dogs that lived in the house with her. Sometimes she got much too aggressive during "scuffles" with them- a behavior that had the potential to turn quite dangerous. Bridget also lunged aggressively at any dog or cat she saw on the street, sometimes pulling her owner off her feet. (In fact, she once dislocated the owners' shoulder and scraped the woman's whole arm bloody while dragging her along the pavement of the driveway chasing a cat! And this was after one of her former trainers prescribed a prong collar for Bridget to wear on walks- a painful and counterproductive device that obviously wasn't doing enough.)

The owners already owned their small dogs at the time they decided to invest in the young German Shepherd. The husband's parents had owned a German Shepherd when he was young and, for very many years, he'd craved one of his own. So the couple did their homework to find a breeder with a good reputation and they had the breeder send them a 6-month old puppy, thinking that they would enjoy playing with her whenever they had time free from their busy professional schedules and long commutes.

Briefly, it seemed like a match made in Heaven. Then reality started to set in when they noticed that the new puppy had a lot of energy and liked to play rough with their small dogs. At first the owners didn't try to separate the dogs, even when they "played rough". But then Bridget began roughly jumping on the owners in her overexcitement- whenever they got home, or whenever they picked up her leash. After enduring the German Shepherd pup that was growing larger every day jumping on them whenever she got overexcited, they decided they needed a professional dog trainer to come in and work with her.

But this is where more serious problems started. The first dog trainer they hired came to their home and worked with the puppy that was already perfectly housetrained. But she told the couple that, since Bridget had too much energy for their household, they should buy a crate and leave her in it whenever they couldn't watch her. (And she never mentioned providing Bridget more exercise, toys or mental stimulation.) At this time, the husband was away from home over 12 hours each weekday between work and commute, and the wife was gone almost 14 hours at a time. So the trainer left the owners with a dog that spent 10 hours or more at time in the crate every weekday. Bridget now acted even wilder whenever she was finally let out to be free in the house with the family. She also started pulling hard on a leash and growling menacingly at the small dogs.

So the owners, wanting the problems to change and to finally have the dog they dreamed of, decided to call in another professional dog-trainer. This harder-edged trainer confidently asserted that she could solve all the problems. She started by telling the owners that they were letting the dog get away with too much. She told the couple that Bridget needed to be left in the dog crate all the time other than when they were walked her or worked with her on obedience. So now the young dog that had been spending 10 to 12 hours each day in a cage became a dog that spent 20 to 22 hours a day in a cage and even had to eat her meals there!

At first, after this second trainer left, it seemed like Bridget didn't give her owners as much trouble on walks. But, as time went by, the walking got harder to control. Now her female owner couldn't hold her when Bridget saw other dogs and reacted aggressively. Whenever the owners got home and opened the cage Bridget jumped on them worse than ever, and she started barking aggressively at any sound outside. She also began having bladder accidents in the house, and her rough play with the small dogs turned into real fighting. The owners knew they had lost all control over their 80-pound German Shepherd and they needed real help.

This is where the authors entered the picture. We spoke to the owners about their young dog and started to suspect that this might be a long rehab. As we stood in the kitchen getting a quick history, the dog sat in her crate in a shadowed hallway. It was six o'clock in the evening and our questions quickly revealed that, on that day, Bridget had been crated since 7:00 in the morning, just like she was every weekday. The only time the dog had been out of the crate on this day was when the owners had gotten home an hour earlier and briefly allowed her onto the back patio to urinate. Then they had immediately locked her back in her crate just like the last trainer had told them to do.

After briefly observing the German Shepherd in the crate and not observing any overt signs of human aggression, we asked the owners to please let her out for us to see how she reacted with the family and trainers in the house. The young dog came out of the crate like she was shot out of a cannon! Running in the house frantically, at first she didn't stop to see where the owners were, but just moved like she needed to stretch her body so badly that she might collide with the walls.

Then, after a moment or two she slowed down enough to notice that there were new people in the home. She ran up to us and tried to jump up to get our attention. But at the same time, we also noticed that she tried to keep some distance and she flinched if she got too close to us, as if she feared we might hurt her.

During the first session we were able to use positive training techniques of ignoring unwanted behavior and desensitization to triggers to extinguish the worst of Bridget's biggest presenting problem- her violent jumping on people. The couple of times she jumped on us before the behavior was extinguished were not pleasant. But the speed with which she responded to gentle interventions made it clear she was redeemable.

After just a few moments of jumping around, Bridget realized that the more she jumped the more we ignored her, so next she turned her attention to the owners and tried the same jumping tricks on them. At first they wanted to yell at Bridget. But instead we suggested they simply turn away from her, ignore her and continue conversing with us.

Finally Bridget got the point and she stopped jumping, settled down and sat there waiting patiently for the people to relate to her. We were pleased, and the owners were ecstatic, and everybody took turns rewarding Bridget with lots of calm praise and petting. At first she acted tentative and a little jumpy. She didn't seem used to ever getting praise, because she'd obviously spent so many other evenings like this simply struggling with her owners. But within a short time she really seemed to start to enjoy the gentle petting.

During this first session, we started rehabilitating Bridget by teaching her that if she calmed down, waited and acted properly, people would notice her. And Bridget began to realize that she didn't have to jump on people to get them to pet her- all she had to do was act calm and wait. At that moment Bridget made a huge stride in learning how to spend her life cooperating with the family she loved rather than spending all her time in a crate, just looking out at people. Bad advice from two unkind dog trainers had created much of this excitable young dog's problems. And now her family was starting on the road to recovery.

At first things seemed fine because Bridget began acting calmer and not jumping, and now she stayed calm enough that her owner could comfortably leash her for walks. But Bridget still didn't really know how to live with the family, and they still had problems controlling her when she was free with the smaller dogs. At our advice, the owners agreed to drop the other trainer's plan and they now crated Bridget less and allowed her free in the house whenever they were home. But, even though she had more freedom than before, they were still caging her all night every night and 12-14 hours at a stretch every weekday.

Things were improving, but Bridget was still not a totally normal dog. The owners had never socialized her- they'd never brought her around strange people or dogs in any public places, and they had no idea how to. And, even though Bridget was now readily obeying obedience commands and no longer jumping on them like a wild animal, she still couldn't focus on them deeply enough to actually look in their eyes. This was not normal- a German Shepherd of Bridget's age should be highly confident, rather than acting haunted by personal demons.

We suspected her previous dog trainers might have had some part in her fears and quirks. For example, we discovered that Bridget flinched at people's quick movements- especially women's- and sometimes submissively urinated because the last female dog trainer used to violently knee her in the chest whenever she jumped. Also dogs should not compulsively chew on rocks- but this was another "small" problem of Bridget's that the owners remembered to mention after some of the more troubling presenting problems had eased. They told us that whenever Bridget was outside where she could get to them, she used to compulsively pick up rocks the size of dinner rolls and chew on them violently, running away and refusing to drop them. The owners described this behavior as completely compulsive and unstoppable. And, when we looked inside young Bridget's mouth, we found that she had already broken off pieces of several teeth.

We wanted to help Bridget as much as we could, and we wondered if she could spend even less hours crated whether this might improve her emotional balance. And then we got an opportunity to spend several weeks with Bridget and the other small dogs in the pack when her owners asked us to board them in our home while they went on vacation.

The first thing that shocked us when we got Bridget home was that she literally seemed to have no idea how to exist outside of her crate! As soon as we took her out of the vehicle, we also took her out of her crate that we had carried with us for transport. But then she didn't seem to understand what to do. Instead of curiously exploring our home along with the other dogs, Bridget acted so panicked to be out of her crate that she immediately started scratching to get back into it! We hadn't even thought of this- the only reason we had taken the crate from the owners was to safely transport her. We never expected Bridget to be staying in it in our house so, without thinking, we'd closed the door, locking her out.

Now we had to lure the panicked young dog over to us so she could see that nothing was going to hurt her when she was out of the crate. After 5 or 10 minutes the poor dog calmed and started wandering around the living room, and next she gradually ventured into other parts of the house with us.

After Bridget calmed, we opened up her crate door for her again. This way she had an option of choosing to retreat back into the crate or staying out with the family and trusting that we would be there for her, which is what we hoped she would do. Things worked out well and Bridget chose to stay free in the living area with the family for a nice evening.

But then a sudden glare of distant car headlights shone through our large uncurtained front window and Bridget went into another bout of panic when she saw this new stimulus. She immediately tried to run back to her crate- the place she obviously associated with hiding from all the things in the world that frightened her. The problem is that a full-grown German Shepherd is meant to be curious and bold- and not to fear everyday stimuli like light through a window. Since we did not want to reinforce the behavior of Bridget running to her crate whenever she was a bad state of mind, and since we wanted to desensitize her to the light until she would be unbothered, we called her to our side. Next we pointed out what had made the light come through the window- just a car pausing on the street...

Bridget now learned about windows in a home for the first time! This was because, in her owners' house, her crate had been kept in a dark corner of an unused windowless foyer, and so she'd grown up totally unaccustomed to many types of light. And now, at 1½ years of age, in our home, Bridget finally learned the function of windows. Each time she saw an unfamiliar light or heard an unfamiliar sound outside now, rather than immediately running back to her crate, she'd hurry to the front window to check things out (totally normal behavior for a dog). Then she'd run up to us in good spirits each time, as if to proudly announce that she'd found out something new in the world that she wanted to show us!

So this is how Bridget's first hours in our home progressed until it was time for dinner. As Bridget saw us getting the meal ready for the other dogs, she shocked us again by hurrying into her crate. This was because she had been fed in a cage for most of her life! But we didn't plan to offer dinner behind bars, because we didn't feel this was proper hospitality to a respected guest. Instead, we fed the other dogs in their places and then put Bridget's food bowl down in an area of the kitchen we had designated for her.

It took a few moments of waiting in the crate until Bridget realized we didn't require her to be locked up to be fed. So she slowly emerged from the crate and walked over to her food bowl. At first she picked little bits of food out of her bowl in the kitchen, but then reentered the crate to eat each one. It took four days for Bridget to learn that (as long as she waited patiently to be served like any guest would) she was completely welcome to eat in the kitchen with us humans and the rest of her canine family.

Next, on that first night with us, it was bedtime for our family and our canine guests. And, again, Bridget thought it was time to head back to her crate even after comfortably spending the evening lying near us like any normal family dog. But when Bridget observed that we went nowhere near the crate and did nothing to force her to sleep in it, she finally followed us into our bedroom with the other dogs as we shut out lights in the living areas.

This would be the first night Bridget would spend in a house out of a crate in the past year. We felt certain we could trust her with our possessions- and with not hurting herself- because we'd already observed her loose in the house for hours and she'd had no problems with proper manners. At first Bridget seemed a little confused about what to do loose in the bedroom instead of locked up in a box. But, in not much time at all, she placed herself on the floor by side of our bed and fell deeply asleep. And that is exactly where we found her when we woke in the morning.

The next day of rehabilitation was the start of Bridget's learning how to conduct herself out in the big beautiful world that she had been deprived of during her months in the cage. Bridget's first few days as our guest included plenty of anxiety and challenges along with the excitement of investigating the special places we brought her. And starting on her first morning with us, she began to realize that a beautiful young German Shepherd's place in this world was by the side of the people she cared for and not caged all day in a dark corner.

Change sometimes comes slowly and (as scientific theory discussed in previous chapters demonstrates) dogs that have been crated to an extreme degree sometimes experience anxiety when first introduced to the world at large. And Bridget sometimes experienced flashback moments when she acted as though she feared she couldn't make us happy unless she ran to the cage. So, we gave her free choice and left the crate with the door sitting open, but we never rewarded her with attention when she went in. This was enough to make her leave the crate fairly quickly. And she'd come to us with a shy doggie smile as if she was saying, "Thank you for wanting me by you instead of in there."

When we first took Bridget for a long walk on our street, she showed her appreciation for the increased trust we'd put in her by walking relatively calmly at our side rather than pulling like she'd always done when with her owners. Walking properly with humans seemed easier for Bridget now that she'd learned the habit of looking to us for feedback in the house. Now she transferred that skill to walks outdoors and frequently "checked in" while we walked. She also learned to anticipate a fun game of Fetch in the yard as a reward after each successful walk with no lunging or pulling.

Each time we took Bridget on a walk, we ventured a little bit farther away from the familiarity of home, and we started to introduce her to places where cars passed and then to areas where she'd pass other leashed dogs. At first Bridget responded to these stimuli by barking and acting afraid- just like she was known to do at home. To help her with these reactions, we'd ask her to "sit" and then wait until she could calm down in the presence of the new stimulus.

Bridget became increasingly comfortable with new stimuli on the street. But all the hours inside a cage when she was growing up had obviously robbed Bridget of experience with many stimuli a dog would usually have to face in life. So at first we had to teach her how not to panic each time she saw new things.

When Bridget finally showed pleasure walking in the neighborhood without any fear reactions it was time for us to take her farther out into the world, to all the places she'd never been in the time she'd lived in the crate. So our next step was to bring Bridget into an uncrowded pet store. We were pleased to see our hard work pay off. Bridget calmly walked through the pet store, seeming to enjoy her first experience looking at all the new toys and treats. She even looked for attention from the store's employees.

When store employees walked up and asked if they could pet her or give a treat, Bridget surprised everyone and she sat politely without anyone having to ask. We practiced this a few times and Bridget did well each time. (Interestingly, in the shop we noticed that every time Bridget passed a display of dog crates, she gave them a wide berth in the same way she'd now started to avoid the crate in the house.)

Overall Bridget, who had been deemed hopeless by the family and two previous trainers, was now manifesting like a nice normal family dog- a pleasure to be around. We were even leaving her free in our home with the rest of her pack whenever we'd leave for a few hours and she acted perfectly with the dogs and disturbed not a single item. Bridget showed perfect house manners, just as if she was a dog that we had raised in the home with us rather than one that had been crated as much as 22 hours a day since puppyhood.

But there are always setbacks in cases of rehabilitation on the way to further progress. Bridget's came after we had worked with her for over a week. She had been doing so well with everything else that we decided to bring her to a public riverside park where we'd already brought the smaller dogs a few times. At first everything went well with Bridget walking around the park with us in mannerly and relaxed fashion. So then we decided to try leading her out on a small boardwalk over the water- another new stimulus.

She appeared to do okay at first, but then we reached the point of no return. It wasn't until Bridget found herself in the middle of the boardwalk out over the water that she realized she was no longer on flat land! And we quickly figured out that water was just another element that she had never been introduced to because of the months of her life she spent locked in the crate. The poor dog that had been walking happily one moment suddenly started shaking like a leaf on a tree during a hurricane!

Eighty-five pound Bridget froze in place and started to crouch as close to the boardwalk as she could get. Old fears caused by living in a crate rather than the real world for a year of her life were coming back again. And the German Shepherd that had been transforming into a proud dog through the week of rehabilitation now looked like a child curling herself into a ball to make herself seem as small as possible.

We took the time to lead Bridget out of her sudden panic by making her understand that it was safe for her to walk with us on the new surface. When Bridget first dug her claws into the wooden boardwalk, it felt like we had a 300-pound anchor on a leash rather than the graceful dog we'd a few moments before. But finally she let her panic dissipate and trusted the fact that we'd never done her wrong before and she resumed walking over gently the lapping water with confidence- another obstacle conquered.

When we got back to the grass we decided to stop under a shelter to give Bridget a moment to totally relax. But we had miscalculated. As the three of us rested in the now darkened park looking over the river, a dog approached, seemingly out of nowhere. And his owners made a common mistake. Rather than asking permission for the dogs to play together (which we would have denied at this point in Bridget's rehabilitation) they deliberately released the full length of their dog's extend-a-lead and they sent him running right towards Bridget.

And Bridget reacted by barking and lunging aggressively. All the stress she'd just gone through on the boardwalk now came out redirected in her nasty display. We had to show Bridget this was unacceptable. So, after holding her back so she couldn't get near the dog and apologizing to the couple, we immediately terminated her special outing with us and completely denied her attention on the trip home. This was enough to make Bridget understand that bad behavior would always make her lose privileges and attention she valued- no harsher correction was necessary. And over the course of the next week we planned to resume outings for Bridget. But we would just be more careful and not have her encounter more than one stress-inducing stimulus at a time.

The underlying problem was that Bridget had not been socialized to stimuli like new dogs during her critical socialization period before 20 weeks- and she'd never seen a boardwalk, she'd never seen water and never seen even seen a park. A dog that didn't get the socialization they needed like this when they were young might panic at any new stimulus. The more you can find out about the dog's past, the better. And then, no matter how much patience it requires, you should carefully help the dog work through its issues, always taking it in "baby steps" in order to stay completely safe.

In this case, we made a point of bringing Bridget back to the same park, and other public venues, several times in the next few days under careful supervision. And, with more exposure, she was able to easily conquer the fears that gripped her that first evening. On subsequent visits to the park, Bridget walked on the boardwalk as gracefully as she did on the flat land. She acted calm and confident around a variety of people in a variety of situations- including joggers, moms with strollers and kids running and playing.

She became just as easy to walk as the small dogs in her pack, even around distractions, so we could finally bring them all out together as a group, which improved her feeling of bonding with them. And, even though her two weeks with us weren't enough to eliminate all the overexcitement when she suddenly encountered strange dogs, Bridget now acted like she *wanted* to meet the dogs, rather than wanting to scare them away. Another unexpected bonus was being able to save the rest of Bridget's beautiful teeth, because we were easily able to stop her rock-eating compulsion.

Her owners returned from vacation to find what they believed was a different group of dogs. All were calm and patient, but what made the biggest impact was that they now had a German Shepherd that acted calm and focused. She listened to them when they gave her commands, and she easily stayed in the same room with the little dogs with no sign of aggression. But the couple still had a lot to learn about the dogs. And they were now willing to work with our suggestions to work towards a new life crate-free life.

A few months later, the couple demonstrated how they were now living crate-free with their dogs and how the dogs were calmer than they ever had been- especially Bridget. All her fears, over-excitement, jumping on people and aggression were now a thing of the past. And Bridget was now a visibly happy and well-balanced dog living free in their home.

The last time we visited Bridget, the thing that amazed us most of all was how she now seemed to enjoy bonding and communicating with her owners. She'd look to them for guidance; she'd show how much she enjoyed their petting. Physically, Bridget looked like a different dog. And, no longer afraid and jumpy, she had learned to do something she never used to do- she now looked humans directly in the eyes. Her owners were happy to see how differently they could bond with their dog. And, for us, gazing into Bridget's beautiful- and now fearless- eyes seemed to make everything worth it.

Chapter 16: How We Can Free the Dogs

Have you ever heard that saying that, if you are not part of the solution, then you are part of the problem? One night coming home late on a cold night on a back road near Savannah, Georgia, we encountered a ghostly creature lying at the side of the road, attempting to lift her head- a medium-sized abandoned white dog so skeletal that her breed could not even be identified. She had been hit by a car that had left her there and, as Ray sat with her waiting for the sheriff's car to arrive, he gave her the comfort to help her find her way to another, better world. She looked into his eyes and, despite all this human world had done to her, she still seemed to take comfort in his presence.

There was no hope for this dog with the extent of her injuries and she expired in minutes; but the car that had hit her and sped off had only been the last of her suffering. The dog showed months upon months of starvation and probably weighed half her healthy weight. How could her owners have abandoned her? There were houses all around and she was a friendly dog. So how could so many people have turned away from her for so long? And how could that last driver have hit her and not even stopped?

Emma remembers being a girl of six years old and standing beside her mother collecting change to support the SPCA outside local supermarkets. And, as a couple, we've frequently taken in stray dogs and cats and rescued injured wild animals that could not have survived without our help. How could we turn away? It only makes sense to us to want to save animals, especially when they are the victims of other people's cruelty.

One the nicest things we encounter in our line of work is the chance to meet many people who also care about animals- dogs in particular- and who are willing to heroically help dogs whatever the personal cost to them. Each time we're appalled at the cruelty men afflict on dogs, we're equally amazed at other people's kindness, generosity and the tremendous effort certain individuals devote to helping dogs in distress.

Both the authors have grown up adopting dogs from "kill" shelters, saving them on the eve of euthanasia, and taking in stray dogs and cats. We've also trained dogs in customers' homes as a way to help dogs by acting like translators between the human and canine worlds. We love to improve the communication between dogs and their owners and to show owners how easy it is to offer dogs a more stimulating environment. And we specialize in helping dogs with backgrounds of serious abuse to find freedom from constant fear and emotional illness.

Unfortunately, though we thought we'd heard it all when it came to abuse of dogs, when we began training dogs professionally we were shocked again, more deeply than ever. There are so many animal causes we want to support in a world where dogs and cats are still abandoned on streets, put to death in shelters and abused in shocking fashion around the globe. But since we first must provide our help where we feel it's most critical, one fact immediately stands out. **WE BELIEVE THE BIGGEST AND MOST EASILY PREVENTABLE ABUSE TO THE LARGEST NUMBER OF DOGS TODAY IS HAPPENING IN AMERICAN LIVING ROOMS IN THE NAME OF LOVE! AND THAT ABUSE IS EXCESSIVE HOME DOG CRATING!**

One troubling fact about Excessive Home Dog Crating is that the distinction between "good guys" and "bad guys" isn't always clear. The authors have supported many dog charities and worked beside other hardworking and outspoken volunteers. These people help dogs in many wonderful ways. But if people who work with dogs in any capacity instruct the public that dogs should be crated for life, this can hurt dogs needlessly and limit families' satisfaction with their dogs.

Caging in shelters, on a temporary basis to save dogs' lives, isn't the same as needless lifetime crating in private homes. The authors don't oppose temporary crating in a rescue shelter if it's truly the only alternative to save a dog's life in the immediate

sense. If, however, the dog must stay in a shelter or rescue facility for longer periods, we feel the animal should be given a spacious indoor/outdoor run or kennel (*never a crate*), plus frequent visits, play, leashed walks and exercise with humans. And we believe that any shelter that keeps dogs long-term should maintain transparency to the public to demonstrate active & frequent attempts to place each dog in an adoptive home, as well as providing records on how many hours/days/years each dog has spent in a cage.

If a dog is deemed unadoptable (for reasons such as age, temperament or chronic physical conditions) leaving him for years in a tiny cage is not a humane solution. No-kill shelters that know a particular dog won't be adopted in a timely fashion should attempt to place him in a safe foster home, or at least provide him a spacious enclosure, adequate stimuli and exercise.

We also believe shelters or rescues that benefit from public funding, tax breaks or free publicity or venues for events shouldn't be allowed to indoctrinate potential adopters that lifetime crating is the only alternative to raise adopted dogs. If a non-profit chooses to educate potential adopters about crate training, they should also be required to explain the dangers and drawbacks of crating and describe alternatives for housing and training dogs without crates.

Not everybody who crates dogs really believes in it. How the "Bell Curve" can sway public opinion:

When the authors look at sociological theories, we find the Bell Curve model used in statistics the most useful scale to describe the range of people's attitudes about Home Dog Crating across our population. Unlike clear-cut cases of dog abuse, where it's easy to see a villain, attitudes about crating dogs in our society seem to range from extremely kind to surprisingly callous and cruel. But most Americans, most likely sixty percent or so, or approximately the norm in the Bell Curve representation, seem to range somewhere in the middle and tend to keep their views in line with their contemporaries.

Years ago, when we grew up, most of this sixty percentile didn't crate dogs in their homes day and night for life. Most of our peers had never heard of the practice and most people's reaction at viewing a dog in a tiny cage was immediately negative.

Even back then, we know certain individuals disliked animals and they preferred to cage dogs all the time just because it made the dogs helpless, and eliminated the need for them to devote any significant time or effort. At that time, we believe people who crated because they cared nothing about dogs, along with the worst of the abusers (like dog fighters or puppy-mill breeders) existed only in the bottom one percent of the population which, in the Bell Curve model, is two standard deviations from the norm).

But today, unfortunately, we suspect that statistics have changed. With the anonymity of the Internet, along with increases in puppy-mill breeding and dog fighting (now increasingly promoted and organized online) we think much more than just the bottom one percent of the population are making dogs suffer. We suspect that currently as much as 20% of the population (or approximately one standard deviation in the Bell Cure model) of people with dogs are now either abusing the dogs they own or breed for profit, or abusively crating dogs at home.

These 20% of deliberately abusive craters are *not* the majority of dog owners that we speak to in this book to offer positive suggestions for change. This 20% overcrates, tethers dogs, fights dogs, denies dogs medical care, sells sick dogs to customers or abuses dogs in other ways just for their own comfort, enjoyment or monetary gain. These people do not know or care if an animal feels physical or emotional pain when caged and many of them argue that dogs aren't capable of feeling anything at all.

Unfortunately, these people have their own strong agenda to maintain lax legal enforcement about crating. For example, those who breed dogs to fight them couldn't do it with more interference, and puppy mill reform laws could cost an estimated 10,000 puppy mill breeders billions of dollars. Corporate sponsored lobbyists with large amounts of money have swayed the laws in their favor on many other issues. And it now appears that 20% of owners, including puppy mill breeders, are fighting aggressively for the right to cage dogs.

This message has gained widespread acceptance in the dog industry, and now it's finding greater acceptance in America at large. And now private dog owners in the norm, the majority, or approximately 60% of the population according to the Bell Curve, have started crating. We estimate that today, in addition to the 20% of dog owners (like puppy mill breeders or dog fighters) who cage dogs for darker motives, as many as 60% of average American dog owners crate their pet dogs and pups and believe that crating is okay.

These are the same people sixty percent of people, only a few years ago, acted as though they found crating unacceptable. They also found excessive *kenneling* of dogs unacceptable and most of them still do. This is why so many of us still cry when we watch those ASPCA commercials that show dogs behind the bars of shelters. But in the past decade or so, many average people who used to feel bad at the notion of locking dogs in cages or kennels were finally "won over" when someone sold them a crate. Others didn't change their minds until a trusted friend or relative talked them into it. Still others didn't "cave" until their trainer, breeder or veterinarian recommended crating, or until they watched a trainer do it on television or read that "dogs love crates" on the Internet or at a bookstore.

Other dog owners were told by the shelter or rescue that they adopted their dogs from that they must crate, with the implication that they'd be negligent if they didn't. And many dog professionals started out against Home Dog Crating until they read they had to do it in a training book, or until they learned about from a seminar, another trainer or a room full of their peers...

When we combine the 20% of dog owners who crate or confine dogs for deliberately evil reasons with the 60% who do it thinking it's okay, this leaves only 20% of dog owners who don't crate and are against the practice. This includes some families that have never even heard of Home Dog Crating; and others that find the notion appalling. Others families turned against crating after some dog "professional" forced them to try it and they noticed their dog's distress. **These people who already believe crating is cruel can connect with their friends and neighbors and act as role models once they learn the extent of the societal problem**.

We also need the help and support of all those people in the 60% of the population to help dogs, even if they are currently crating. The majority of folks are genuinely good people, who feel kindness and caring towards dogs and likely considered crating because of problems with their dogs in today's hectic world.

Most people then made the final decision to crate because experts told them it was right, yet they may have always still harbored lingering doubts about crating. So some owners dealt with those guilty feelings by lavishing their dog or pup with extra attention or activities whenever he came out of the crate. And some parents have felt heartbroken every time their children complained that they hated to see the dog locked up, even while they tried not to break the "rules" "professionals" gave them (as in the story of Champ in Chapter 4.)

The reason so many owners felt some instinctive emotional guilt about crating was that the "facts" they were told about the benefits of crating were *never* **really facts**. In a similar example, for decades, the media in this country, supporting the profit motive of rich tobacco companies, convinced a generation that it was healthy and cool, manly and/or sophisticated to smoke cigarettes. Many people can still remember television commercials advertising cigarettes years ago, yet today the majority of people understand that graphic television commercials that warn of the *dangers* of smoking make more sense.

Other myths have also been perpetrated on the well-meaning American public over the years, usually by big money interests that use the media to spread their message.

It's not that we're naïve. The reason it's so easy for special interests to deceive the American public is that most of us are well-meaning and don't suspect devious motives because *we're* not devious! We also tend to assume that, if something is truly dangerous, our government will protect us from it. But this isn't always true.

An interesting fact that we notice whenever we try to research Excessive Home Dog Crating on the Internet is the number of poisonous personal rants supporting crating and attempting to mock and injure anyone who doesn't support it. We also notice that nice people who care about dogs devote a lot of time to arguing with these angry, defensive and largely illogical people online. But our view is simple. **Each of us must look within our own conscience for the specific number of hours, days and years that we consider excessive or cruel to leave your pet dog in a crate in your home. Next, we urge you to look out into society and truly face how many people are crating their dogs more than that.**

We urge the 20% of people who already feel strongly against crating (including kids and teens) to reach out to your friends and neighbors in the 60 percentile to either get them to stop crating, or to convince them to crate much less, which also improves dogs' quality of life.

You may feel initially very saddened when you discover how many people close to you are caging dogs for surprisingly long periods of time in their homes. But remember the majority of friends, relatives, neighbors and coworkers are not the "enemy". They are likely also dog lovers who simply followed wrong information. And the biggest motivator to change their minds is their caring for their dog and the example of you, a good friend they can trust, who can give them good reasons why crating is not necessary and how it harms dogs.

The people who are currently in the 60th percentile of the population- who love dogs, but are currently crating to some extent- can also help. Even if you're concerned that you may not be able to handle your dog out of the crate full-time right now, we advise you to go with your heart and forget about all the wrong information you were given. Read up on safe alternatives to crating (including the detailed housetraining and behavioral tips in Chapters 13 and 14, and in our book *Awesome Puppy*.) And then slowly **work up to less and less hours that your dog has to spend in the crate.** When you do this properly (with the right professional support if necessary) you'll learn that healthy dogs are capable of great house manners and there are even kind- but still safe-alternatives for living with "problem" dogs.

This chapter is also for dog professionals and business owners to change how they educate customers. Start by reading the research in this book and then do your own extensive research. And then go with your own heart no matter how learned about crate training, or how many of your peers or superiors pressured you to use crates to train your customers' dogs.

Professionals like dog trainers need to make sure that well-meaning advice they've given about crating isn't being misused. (For example, in the case in Chapter 11 where a young woman left her dog to die mummified in a crate; or in the many cases where young puppies are left up to 14 hours at a time with no water!) **Whenever a dog professional hands a customer a small dog cage, they should be just as sure that person will use it humanely and safely as if they handed the person a gun.**

This applies to the dog trainers and vet techs next door. It also applies to the best-known, best-respected television celebrity dog trainers in America- starting with Cesar Millan and Victoria Stillwell. If you're an expert and your heart and your initial philosophy told you that dogs require freedom or that they should be members of a family in every way, now is the time to speak out- even if it means going against sponsors, producers, organizations or thousands of peers in the field. **If you are truly an expert and if you feel there's any chance your viewers (or readers, or students) misunderstood your policy and they are excessively crating their dogs because of it, now is the time to clarify your exact position with a formal policy statement about crating.** You have the chance to reach thousands- even millions- of dog owners through your shows, your teachings and/or your writings, and to save many dogs from unnecessary suffering caused by misunderstanding while helping families to enjoy better quality of life with their dogs.

Eventually, we want it to become a "no-brainer" that **caging pet dogs for almost every waking and sleeping hour of their entire lives is similarly cruel to keeping dogs in puppy mills.**

Many of the younger generation- teens, college students, even tweens and school-age children can sometimes see the clearest. If you're a younger person and you think excessively crating pet dogs makes no sense, now is your time to speak out. Hopefully, your generation will be the generation that put an end to the practice of Excessive Home Dog Crating!

In the remainder of this chapter we provide a specific list of how anyone who wants to help dogs can use their efforts and their voices to stop Excessive Crating. Many of the ideas require very little effort. In just a few minutes you can use your home computer, smart phone or mobile device to improve, or even save, the lives of many dogs. Other ideas are as simple as choosing certain products when you shop, or choosing certain replies to complements you receive on your dog.

We also have some advice for the 20% percent of people who have recently seized the reins of power and the viral capacity of the Internet to put so many dogs in crates with no thoughts for the feelings of the animals. If your advocacy of caging dogs starts in your personal living room, we sincerely hope you will try something else. Give your dog and your family a chance and allow your dog a little more time to be free- perhaps when the family is there to supervise. Start there and be reasonable. **Lessen the number of hours your dog or pup spends in the cage, at least so it's not more than you yourself find ideal. You can also make your dog more comfortable by using a larger cage, placing the cage in a more comfortable climate-controlled space or coming home to walk your dog midday. At least try to meet your dog halfway and see how life can change for the better in your own home.**

For those of you who continue to vehemently advocate crating theory through your writings and teachings, we think that the climate around you is going to change, just like if you made your fortune manufacturing toxic chemicals at this time when so many people are embracing green living and protecting our environment. Today many of the biggest companies have already seen the light and started manufacturing "green" formulations of their products and giving back to the planet so that their customers will respect them and they won't go out of business. The same may be true for professionals who make money caging dogs or advocating crating dogs.

If, after reading this book, you still *truly* feel that dogs do not feel physical or emotional pain when caged and you treat them accordingly, your customers may soon reject your ideas and your services along with the currently popular notion that, "dogs love crates". Even if your conscience doesn't stop your inhumane treatment of dogs, social pressure and loss of business revenue can eventually stop it.

Every day now, in multiple states, laws are changing against puppy mills (the latest is the anti-puppy mill ballot initiative, "Proposition B" that recently passed in the state of Missouri, known as our nation's puppy mill capitol.) And in many foreign countries, dog owners don't tend to think of indoor crating as an option for housing and training dogs. Most owners in countries like Australia have never even heard of crating.

As a new breed of progressive dog professionals starts to promote more effective and pleasant alternatives to Excessive Home Dog Crating, they'll provide better conditions for dogs at their businesses and sell better advice to the public, and their customers will appreciate them for this. And the "professionals" who continue to prescribe locking dogs in crates as the only alternative to train or house them will eventually find they won't get as much business as their kinder, more hardworking and more innovative competitors.

We see no purpose in devoting this book, or our Internet presence in any form, to infinitely debating whether dogs are "den animals" or whether "dogs love crates". Instead, we believe in the power of capitalism. And we hope the choices of 80% of dog owners who'd prefer their dogs to live more comfortably will eventually convince dog professionals to stop promoting Excessive Crating. As dog owners become more empowered, a "solution" like caging will not be enough for them. They'll demand better expertise and better service for their dogs and they'll easily put people who don't really care for dogs out of business.

A new era of more caring and effective dog businesses will emerge, taking the place of those who "trained" dogs by caging. These new professionals will be skilled at providing busy families (like Bouncy's in Chapter 6, Champ's in Chapter 4 or Bridget's in Chapter 15) the kind of excellent service they really need- so that dogs can live comfortably- and politely- in every part of their families' homes while providing the joy they were meant to!

And for all of you who want to save dogs from the distress of Excessive Crating, here are easy steps you can take, starting right in your own neighborhood or at your own desk:

HOW DOG LOVERS CAN SAVE DOGS FROM ABUSIVE CRATING RIGHT NOW:

1. **Offer yourself and your well-adjusted dog as role models. Whenever anyone approaches you to compliment your dog, mention that you don't crate** and your dog lives free in your home. These days, many people assume differently, so this one fact can change lives if you make it a point to always tell people.

2. *Nicely* **find out how much people close to you (friends, relatives, neighbors) crate their dogs.** Then if you find out a person crates their dog excessively because they're misinformed, afraid or stressed, you can educate them about the facts and steer them in the direction of resources that can help.

3. **In situations where it feels comfortable, you can also tell strangers why Excessive Home Dog Crating is unhealthy for them and for their dog. But we recommend that you be careful and never directly confront an angry, cruel or closed-minded stranger.**

4. Stop Puppy Mills! Early experiences at puppy mill breeders can start the cycle of Excessive Crating and your young puppy may have suffered terrible abuses before he came to your home. Currently millions of dogs are caged in these large-scale breeding facilities under shockingly abusive conditions, and the pups are sold in pet stores and over the Internet with their origins disguised. You can easily find information about anti-puppy mill efforts on line and if you wish. You can donate or volunteer your time to help organizations whose policies you agree with overall.

Also, if you decide to obtain a pup, start by choosing a reputable local breeder. (Dogs that are truly AKC registered are a good sign, but make sure the breeder doesn't fake the registration or use other bogus registries.) Even if you choose to buy a dog out of state, visit the property to observe the conditions where the dogs are kept and meet parents and littermates. And avoid buying from pet stores unless you are one-hundred percent sure that the pups have come from reputable breeders. (One estimate is that 95% of pet store pups currently come from puppy mills.) Another choice is to adopt a young pup or a grown dog from a reputable shelter, rescue or breed rescue society that keeps dogs in humane, enriched environments, such as foster homes.

And add your voice to the cause against puppy mills by contacting your legislators. Unfortunately, even though a few state laws against puppy mills have recently passed, some face legal challenges while others aren't being adequately enforced. The majority of people who care about dogs are horrified by puppy mills, but many more of us must make our feelings known in order to overcome powerful lobbies that are profiting from animals' suffering. There are many good online resources that you can visit to follow the headlines, read the stories of puppy mill survivors and help this important cause.

5. Never spend your money at dog businesses that excessively crate dogs at their facility or pressure you to excessively crate your dog at home; and patronize dog businesses that use and teach training methods other than crating. Explain to the dog trainer, groomer, veterinarian or rescue shelter representative that you don't like their policy on crating, and always speak directly to the business owner or person in charge, since it's possible that someone on their staff is giving out unreasonable advice about crating without their approval.

6. Spread the message that "Dogs Hate Crates" online. Using the Internet you can easily help this important cause, reach large numbers of people and improve life for huge numbers of dogs. Unfortunately, the Internet has been a great driver of the dog crating trend and people who aggressively promote crating have already glutted

Cyberspace with their non-scientific postings and rants. Rather than wasting time in endless online arguments with dog abusers who aggressively defend their callous treatment of dogs in chat rooms and online communities, computer-savvy people can make more of a difference by optimizing information about the dangers of Excessive Crating. It's vital to make scientific facts, case studies and true stories accessible on search engines so if people search for "cruel crating" online, they can easily find information other than thousands of postings, articles and websites telling them why crating is great.

Novice dog owners also need easy online access to information and help for behavioral training and housetraining puppies without crates. Because, at this time, parts of the dog community are controlling information so many new dog owners aren't aware that options exist. The Internet is about freedom of information and everyone should have a fair choice. So if you are talented at blogging, posting video on YouTube or connecting with others through social media, you can use these skills to reach many people and, in turn, help very many dogs.

7. **Young people should find your voice, and use whatever technology you are most comfortable with to save dogs from Excessive Crating.** Many young people today are volunteering to help dogs at shelters and rescues. And **you can do even more by connecting with your peers to let them know how dogs are suffering cruelly crated in homes right now.** Scenarios like the reconstructed ones in this book (Boxy and Champ) as well as the real cases (Smoky, Patton and Bridget) are happening in people's homes right now. *Your generation will be shaping the world from this point on and you do not need to tolerate this.* So speak out! Age should not be a barrier and technology today allows the voice of everyone who cares about dogs to be heard as easily as accessing a computer or smart phone to get the message out.

8. **Use your money and your donations to support the cause of stopping abusive home crating.** Donate to agencies that break up puppy mills, or rescues that allow dogs to live as members of the family in uncrowded foster homes. Always check that your donations don't go to shelters or rescues that keep dogs in cruel conditions or instruct or bully potential adopters to crate dogs excessively! If you visit and find that a shelter or rescue isn't taking care of dogs right or isn't making humane decisions about their care, withhold your donations and instead contribute to a more humane organization. Then use the media (including local newspapers, newsletters, the Internet and electronic media) to get the message to other potential donors and animal policy makers.

Money matters a great deal to non-profit organizations. Even small donations count. And donations in the thousands or tens of thousands are probably more important to most shelters' overall mission than pushing adoptive families to crate the dogs they take home. The board of directors (as opposed to the person at the shelter – usually a trainer or "behaviorist" who *made* the crating policy) will likely recognize this.

Boards of directors usually consist of "laymen" with business and financial links to their communities. They care about how the public feels and are more likely than some dog "experts" to follow common sense about issues like crating.

Most shelters can't completely keep dogs out of kennels or crates because, to save lives, they may need to cage dogs *temporarily* while the dogs await return to their owners or adoption. But there is *no* need for shelters to "educate" the public, as many shelters do today, that a lifelong existence in a tiny cage is how every dog should live *after* they are adopted.

If you're considering making a donation, first visit any shelter or rescue in person to view where animals are housed rather than just viewing the animals online or at pet store adoption events. Withhold donations from shelters or rescues that crate or cage dogs long-term without adequate food, water, cleanliness, heat, cooling, exercise and interaction with people. And spread the word about substandard conditions you have witnessed at any non-profit. **Even the nicest website and/or general popularity in a community can actually conceal shelters that house animals cruelly.**

Make Life Better for Your Dog- Even in a Crate:

You can make your dog's time in his crate more humane, even if you're not yet ready to transition him out completely, just by rejecting some "accepted wisdom" about crate training.

For example, **increasing the size of a crate always makes dogs more comfortable** -the larger, the better.

Another way to make crating less uncomfortable is by keeping your dog hydrated. Even though water dishes may tip, and a crated dog could overdrink out of boredom, **leaving a caged dog or pup no water is cruel and a risk to health!** To prevent overdrinking or dishes tipping some options are to leave ice cubes that take a while to melt or to use a travel type water bottle suspended on the outside of the cage. This way the dog can lick each time he needs water drink, yet not drink too quickly.

You can also allow a dog to have a safe toy in the crate *as long as it's not an item he can chew up out of frustration and hurt himself* with. Try giving him a special interactive toy he only gets while crated, and change out toys frequently to keep it interesting. Used with caution, bedding can also make adult and senior dogs more comfortable- but avoid any type of bedding the dog could ingest and hurt himself with, and avoid bedding with teething pups.

Always keep your house reasonably climate controlled for your crated dog. Since your crated dog cannot move around, he cannot take steps to cool himself (like lying near the breeze from a window) or warm himself (running around playing, or curling up on carpet.) Leave the crate in a well-ventilated area, but never in a direct draft. And **NEVER leave a crate in strong sun (like on an enclosed sun porch) or in an unventilated area with lingering fumes (like most garages).** Leaving crates in areas like these is actually a common practice, but it's extremely dangerous and can cause dogs and pups a great deal of needless suffering.

Seeing people as much as possible is important for developing pups. If you tend to keep your dog or pup crated when people are home, try to leave him in an area where he's near the family, rather than isolating the crate in a hallway, garage or laundry room where he cannot see or hear his humans.

Ultimately, we suggest owners find an alternative to a crate that allows their dog more space, more stimuli and more socialization with people. But, for the moment, just these few changes can eliminate a lot of stress and discomfort.

9. Support businesses and organizations that don't crate and that advocate against crating. Unfortunately, in the climate of the dog industry today, a business takes a risk speaking out openly against Excessive Home Dog Crating to their colleagues.

So, whenever you encounter dog professionals like veterinarians, trainers, groomers, breeders and retail shop owners who don't overcrate or advise customers to do it, support them with your patronage, your personal recommendations and favorable reviews on Internet sites. **A large number of dog owners with a large amount of disposable income are against crating dogs.** And, once they speak up, financial motives will persuade many dog businesses to amend their policies.

10. Buy products and books from individuals who are against Excessive Home Dog Crating. For example, buy this book and urge friends to buy it, as well as our activity book *The Cure for Useless Dog Syndrome* and our comprehensive puppy activity and training book *Awesome Puppy*. Buy all your training books, CD's and DVD's from dog trainers who do not teach owners to crate (see more books in the Appendix, Recommended Reading).

Avoid buying anything from individuals who promote home crating! Since so many books on dog subjects today include support of crating, before buying we suggest you first scan through the book in a bookstore or library. The easiest way to find the author's policy is to look in the "housetraining" section, although mention of crates, cages or confinement may be in other locations and you may have to check the index. If a book seems interesting, but you're disturbed because it includes crating advice, let the author or publisher know via email or online reviews.

Unfortunately many pet stores associates now pressure customers to buy crates whether the customers ask for this advice or not. At small, locally-owned stores, customers expressing they don't like this could make big changes. And customers of many upscale pet boutiques could probably convince the owners to stop selling rows of wire cages next to all their holistic health and luxury items for dogs. Managers of local branches of chain pet stores may have less say over what merchandise they carry, but they can tell their employees to stop pushing crates on customers without warning them of the risks.

11. **Product manufacturers**- including those that currently manufacture crates should explore new directions. The needs of dog owners are changing and, from our perspective, we see that as the dawning of a new era. **This is a great opportunity for manufacturers to design more humane alternative to crates that would safely give dogs freedom in private homes while adequately protecting possessions.**

One type of product that immediately comes to mind would be New-World baby gates- furniture quality, sturdy, convenient to open and large enough to stretch across vast Great Rooms. For example, some good choices we've already seen include: a gate that also converts to a spacious exercise pen; quality wood dividers that span entire rooms and a clear Plexiglass gate. Solutions like these keep teething puppies, and pups in need of housetraining, safely contained in more spacious and humane conditions than cages, and allow them to move around to stimulate their developing bodies and minds. **And, unlike traditional ugly wire cages, room dividers can be designed to attractively blend with home décor.**

Crates in themselves are not evil. They only become abusive when an owner crates their dog excessively. Thus, **rather than recommending that crates no longer be manufactured, we recommend that all dog crates come with a warning label describing safe usage and advising of specific dangers from irresponsible usage, similar to labels on other household products or on cigarettes.** This warning label could include limits on the number of hours dogs can be humanely crated and a chart for minimum square footage to allow different size pet dogs sufficient room.

As public awareness against excessive crating builds, if companies that sell crates want to stay profitable they would have to change their product- and this opens opportunities for creative marketing. In Chapter 6, we talk about problems with dogs and open floor plans. Instead of *crates*, these companies could start manufacturing better *gates,* play areas and runs-much larger and more adaptable enclosures.

These new enclosures could be customized for individual homes with expanded features to improve dogs' quality of life, and they could be designed to provide increased stimulation and opportunities for interaction with family. **Innovative products like this could sell at much higher prices than regular crates because there is a huge demand**.

We feel the problem with Excessive Dog Crating has been more about inhumane ideas from trainers and experts on how to use enclosures, and the lack of government regulation and prosecution in cases of animal cruelty, rather than the existence of enclosures themselves. As public opinion changes, there will be vast moneymaking opportunities for producing more humane barriers to customize space and accommodate owners and dogs.

Families would welcome humane aids for housetraining for when they can't get home to let pups out midday. Ideas like the newly popular patches of fake "grass" are just a beginning. Housetraining is one area open to tremendous innovation and profit for the industry and inventors should experiment with new technologies. (For example, we see no reason why a fully functioning indoor "toilet" for dogs couldn't be a real possibility...)

We also like innovative training aids and toys to help exercise dogs and reduce boredom. These range from automatic ball launchers, to doggie treadmills to complex interactive toys and puzzles that keep dogs' minds occupied. Today, many owners are buying products like these, and a good number of gentle dog trainers are recommending them. If more companies design more innovative products like this, we predict a vast market that could be much more lucrative than the sale of crates.

12. Dog Trainers and other dog professionals who don't believe in Excessive Home Dog Crating have unique opportunities to reach the public. If you are a dog trainer, speak out against Excessive Crating in group classes, individual sessions, on your website and at events where you speak. Also mention alternatives to crating in any free literature you distribute. **People constantly ask dog trainers questions at cocktail parties. So share your views on the drawbacks of crate-training with anyone who asks you about dogs-**

whether it's people you meet at the grocery store, customers, peers or shelters, rescues or dog businesses.

There's power in numbers. So dialogue and network with other trainers and professionals who believe Dogs Hate Crates, and build new professional associations. The tide will change tremendously when organizations and individual trainers who offer kinder alternatives than crating gain significant web exposure. **And trainers who are members of large professional organizations like the APDT should pressure these organizations to issue official position statements on the dangers of Excessive Crating.**

13. Society needs more talented and truly positive dog trainers who can find humane solutions to canine behavior problems without crating; and it's possible for trainers like this to get started working right now.

For trainers who are already working, this is the perfect opportunity to distinguish yourself from the crowd and appeal to a new generation of customers who want the absolute best for their dogs. If you are a trainer who does not teach crating as a behavior training or housetraining technique, you should advertise and publicize this. While your policy may not be popular with your peers at first, it should soon pay off amongst customers who will thank you for it and choose you because of it.

Even if you're a dog trainer who *has* been recommending crating, you can try other techniques in combination with less crate time and see how this works. And, before instructing your customers to crate, always tell them about the alternatives and ask them if this is what they prefer to do. Many experienced trainers have already shifted from old-school compulsion techniques like collar-yanking and newspaper hitting to positive methods, and they've seen their results improve and their incomes grow. So we predict it will be the same for dog trainers who offer new training methods to replace crate training. And, in the near future, customers will start to turn away from trainers who still advocate crating.

We believe **that families should be given a real choice. And we'd like to see fair competition where dog trainers are economically rewarded based on their talent, knowledge, compatibility with families and, most of all, their kindness and connection with dogs.** During the past two decades, a career field that was very small suddenly became glutted with intense competition due to many factors discussed at length in this book. But we feel society now needs even more trainers entering the field, who will popularize progressive training methods that don't include caging dogs.

If you want to work as an effective dog trainer and canine behavior specialist, *in addition to an innate talent that cannot be taught, you need to learn a vast amount of information and have a vast amount of practice.* But you should never let anyone tell you (no matter their credentials) that they're the lone authority on how you can get the proper education/practice. Instead, research what's legally required to start your business and then educate yourself according to your own conscience. Or observe and imitate an experienced dog trainer who seems to get "magical" results with methods you personally witness to be kind. But trust your internal compass and *never* compromise your ethics when training dogs, whether you're an established or celebrity trainer or whether you're training your first dog.

Dog businesses of every kind are one of the fastest growing, recession proof segments of the economy (as described in detail in Chapter 10). **We see dog owners willing to pay extremely generously for people who truly love and respect dogs, yet this level of service is still lacking in many areas.** So, even if you do not wish to train dogs, there are vast opportunities for people to offer all kinds of dog-related services and products- whether you are grooming dogs, pet sitting or opening a dog boutique or doggie day care facility. And we hope all the new people that enter the pet business will be truly progressive and humane, and abolish all the abuses of years past. In the new world of pet care there should simply be no need- and no paying market- for places like puppy mills, practices like excessive crating or any cruel training or husbandry technique.

14. If you observe cruel, abusive or excessive crating or other criminal offenses against animals, report it.

If you know of a puppy mill or kennel that breeds and/or houses dogs under abusive conditions, you can report it to the Humane Society of the United States Wilde Task Force Reporting HotLine, by calling 1-877-MILL-TIP, or report it online in the puppy mill section of the HSUS website. You can also fill out a Pet Seller Complaint form if you purchased a sick puppy from a pet shop. In cases of pet stores, breeders, etc. the HSUS also advises that, "if there appears to be cruelty or neglect (unsanitary conditions, sick animals, lack of food water, shelter, etc.)" you should also contact a "local animal control agency, humane society or animal shelter... If none of these exists in the area, call the police, sheriff or health department..."

Many private cases of crating, such as in your neighbors' living room, may involve a difference of opinion as to whether the conditions are legally dog abuse or just a different style of husbandry, and even many cases of obviously excessive Home Dog Crating aren't considered illegal under current laws. But many obvious and extreme crimes against dogs continue undisturbed in communities because authorities don't know what's happening. Sometimes this includes large-scale puppy mills that cruelly cage, neglect and abuse hundreds of dogs and puppies. But it also includes private "backyard" breeders who keep small numbers of dogs under similar conditions; owners who tether (or chain) dogs outside in violation of local laws without access to water, shade or shelter from the cold, often with the intent of fighting them; and owners who abandon their homes long term, leaving their dogs indoors, abandoned, locked in crates without food or water- a situation when dogs often die. Other abuses include overcrowded properties where dogs are denied proper care hidden under the guise of no-kill rescues; animal "hoarders" who keep tens or hundreds of animals under terrible conditions; and abusive, overcrowded or filthy boarding or kennel facilities.

15. Don't assume every "charitable" dog organization, shelter or rescue actually helps dogs just because it's non-profit. This may seem painful to dog lovers, but it's a fact communities can no longer ignore.

For example the "back room" of one private no-kill Florida shelter was actually a cramped, darkly shadowed corridor with no air conditioning. Here, frenzied cage-crazed-dogs continuously spun, barked and snapped in their small cages. And, although all were still listed for adoption online, some had lived in the inhospitable environment for months- and years- until they developed serious behavior problems, including aggression. Potential adopters and donors were never allowed to see the dogs in their day-to-day housing, where conditions were not technically illegal, but would give most dog lovers nightmares. Instead the public had to meet the dogs online, one at a time in the lobby or on weekends at pet store adoption events.

Another shelter in a remote location in a nearby county also brought their dogs to adoption events at chain pet stores, even though the majority of dogs that resided there for months and years had become either cage or food aggressive. The physical conditions at this shelter seemed more humane than at the first because at least the dogs had light and more spacious runs. Yet these dogs also had no air conditioning during Florida summers, and the odor in the kennel was sickening. Unlike at the other shelter, where a large number of staff did nothing to improve conditions for a small number of animals, at this facility only two overworked staff people struggled to care for a large number of dogs and cats. The dogs got little outdoor yard time and almost no leashed walks, socializing or training and this increased behavior issues, especially for some of the dogs that had resided there for years. Eventually, this shelter was shut down in a raid by the county, and all the animals were placed in other facilities for rehabilitation.

These days it's common to hear about shocking abuses by shelters and rescues all around the country and this is one way dog lovers must be discerning. Even fun "yappy hours" and dog social events in the name of charity don't always support dogs in the manner cash donors might expect. For example, we felt good about the pricey meal we purchased to support a breed rescue at a local event- until we personally met the director of the rescue. She boasted to us how she housed this sweet, sensitive small breed full-time in crates. And the otherwise placid little dogs in her care cringed every time she waved her hands!

Many dog lovers would cringe as well, realizing that this director was keeping dogs in her care long-term and making them less adoptable, rather than more so. But, **unfortunately the extent that dogs are crated, and the lifestyle they lead while in care rarely gets mentioned by most non-profits, shelters and rescues. Dogs (like the ones in this example) may not leave a rescue for years and may live in small crates the entire time.** Yet people who donate usually assume that people involved in dog charities or volunteerism are kind to dogs in every way, so they rarely ask about how dogs are housed.

Of course many individuals who run non-profits *are* **amazingly kind. Some heroically run rescues out of their own homes and their own pockets. Small, volunteer-run rescues often place a greater proportion of dogs than many of the bigger private community shelters- and they place them in better homes. We think volunteers who run truly humane rescues deserve all the monetary help they can get- much more help than many are getting now! Very many shelters and rescues are still operating for the right reasons and are truly helping dogs. And we also do not consider it abusive when a shelter keeps a dog in a cage temporarily to save his life.**

But we believe that any shelter or rescue that collects charitable donations and/or benefits financially in any way from its non-profit status should have to provide total transparency to the public.

Dogs living in shelters and rescues should never have to live in conditions as abusive as or worse than those they were taken from! But, tragically, because there's so little oversight on shelters and rescues, many not-for-profits with dangerous or inhumane practices continue to use and abuse dogs under the guise of helping them.

In some facilities, the front rooms and break rooms where large numbers of staff sit happily gossiping may be kept comfortable and attractive, while the indoor kennels where the dogs live are unheated in winter and lack air conditioning in southern states where summer "real-feel" heat indices often exceed 110 degrees! For many shelters, it's common for the public to only see their dogs at adoption at events at large chain pet stores. So often potential adopters have no notion what the dogs have gone through during their time in "rescue".

And it's particularly sad when a dog that has endured many months in a cramped cage in rescue to finally find a caring new home- only to have personnel from the shelter or rescue instruct the new adopter to crate him for the rest of his life. *No* dog benefits from crating. And, if the shelter believes a particular dog isn't safe in a family home out of a crate- then that dog isn't safe to go to your home at all.

New adopters should make their own choices for how to house your adopted dog and ignore any advice that doesn't feel right to you.

Whether to crate or not is a personal decision but, **if you ever witness clearly criminal abuses at a shelter or rescue in your community, you can report this to a national organization like the Humane Society of the United States (HSUS); American Society for the Prevention of Cruelty to Animals (ASPCA), or People for the Ethical Treatment of Animals (PETA).** These are *true* national organizations. Local shelters that use the words "Humane Society" or "SPCA" in their names may have no affiliation with these national humane organizations.

In your local community, if there isn't a specific agency to deal with animal abuse, you can inform your local sheriff's department about abuse you've witnessed at a shelter, rescue or boarding facility. Many communities have designated agencies to handle complaints of animal mistreatment. **However, in some communities, the animal rescue organization or humane society that you would ordinarily report animal abuse to might be the same organization that runs the shelter you wish to complain about!**

For this reason, before making a formal complaint about animal abuse at a shelter or rescue you should first use careful judgment about who to contact, and/or first ask one of the national humane organizations for general advice before making phone calls. If no one else helps with a complaint of abuse at a local shelter, concerned citizens can always contact the media.

Please Note: The use of a crate alone, *unless* it's extraordinarily crowded, lengthy, neglectful, unsanitary or dangerous in some other fashion, is *not* enough to constitute legal animal abuse in most situations. If the only problem you notice is simply that the shelter or rescue uses crates (or small cages) or advocates home crating to their adopters, then you can follow some of the other steps mentioned above (especially those for donors) to motivate the organization to find a better way. The goal is to put the bad shelters and rescues out of business while gaining more support for the truly humane ones.

16. Publish. Even if you're not an "expert", you can write about your own experiences and problems resulting from Excessive Home Dog Crating. You can publish anti-crating blogs on the Web or mention the issue on social networking sites, and, if you are interested in, or experienced at, writing professionally, you can submit articles to magazines and newspapers or even publish books. Research the problems with home crating and then publish in the most prominent way that is possible for you.

People can also help dogs by publishing written or online "crate-free" directories for all types of resources (including dog trainers who don't crate, groomers that don't crate, pet sitters that will walk pups midday as an alternative to crating and rescues that use crate-free foster homes).

Excessive Home Dog Crating is one of the most serious problems affecting animals today, yet most of the literature published opens the doors for owners to do it, which perpetuates the problem. And meanwhile, many of the most concerned pet owners who would be willing to help don't even know about the problem. So write about your concerns about Excessive Crating, both in puppy mills and private homes, whenever and wherever you can.

Also, write personal reviews online for books that you have read. If you bought a book by a well-known dog expert and you're disappointed that the only solution they offered for housetraining or behavior problems was the crate, let the author, publisher and the world know your opinion. Also comment on magazine, newspaper and online articles about crating dogs to let people know that there *are* alternatives.

17. Distribute and post anti-crating materials. For example, at the time of publication, PETA was offering free posters and flyers against crating online, available to download. Or you can design your own. Post anti-crating designs, slogans and materials online and wherever you can at pet-oriented locations. You can even sell items like anti-crating T-shirts or bumper stickers for profit. Young people can do this, too. Creating trendy materials that are eye-catching for kids and teens is also a great way to show your creativity while making sure dogs live better in the next generation. The more you spread the word, the more you'll help dogs.

18. Journalists/media: Talented and curious journalists need to investigate and expose the problem of Excessive Home Dog Crating, along with the scope of the puppy mill problem. We hope that leaders in investigative reporting and journalism will start to look into the well covered up subject of Excessive Home Dog Crating as a result of this book's publication, and at the urging of many people who care about dogs. This cause needs all the help it can get. Media personalities have recently gained tremendous attention for dog causes, and we hope that this book will shine just a little light on the secret of cruel and excessive crating hidden behind suburban doors.

19. Scientists, veterinarians and researchers can help by publishing more research that proves the ill effects of crating on dogs. Society needs creative and flexible scientists who can do research the effects of confinement without causing dogs further pain. (For example, by applying pertinent data on laboratory dogs' reactions during studies that were done for other purposes without the need to cage dogs further- or by compiling long-term reports on dogs that were excessively confined and/or separated from people during puppyhood.) The public also needs veterinarians' case studies that document behavioral/emotional and physical ill effects of Excessive Home Dog Crating. If enough professionals publicize this type of information, it could help put an end to abusive crating, just like demonstrating the link between smoking and lung cancer has changed public behavior.

20. Organize fun dog events to raise awareness and support the cause of freeing dogs from Excessive Home Crating. These events can be just like the big street party-style events held by local shelters, with games, contests, food, treats, demonstrations and kids' events (some basic ideas are described in the family games section of our book *The Cure for Useless Dog Syndrome*). Or hold smaller, "yappy-hour" style parties, perhaps at restaurants or private homes. Children and teens can also organize charitable events. You could establish your own animal charity with the money you raise or donate the proceeds of your events to existing organizations that rehabilitate animals in a truly humane fashion. Check any organization's policy before you donate. You may wish to support local shelters or rescues that don't advocate crate training for behavioral purposes; to animal rights organizations with positive policies or to organizations that save dogs from puppy mills and other abuses. Whatever animal charity you will be supporting, let the local press know all the specifics on your event(s). Local newspapers will usually give you a free listing, and your event may also be featured with a full-length article.

21. Get at the truth by asking the right questions. We can't fight the problem of Excessive Home Dog Crating until we know how widespread it is. The knowledge that privately owned dogs like "Boxy" in the prologue are suffering in cages in individual homes just like dogs suffer in puppy mills or the county pound may deeply upset people who love dogs. But we can't make changes until we reveal the shrouded truth, and the best way to get the truth is by asking without judgment.

Whether you're a professional or simply a concerned individual, you can amass your own statistics about the extent of Excessive Home Dog Crating in your community by asking people you know non-judgmental questions. **You may find quite a few people in your own social circle crating dogs 18 hours a day or more**. By providing advice, but not appearing condemnatory, you may be able to help. Even if your acquaintances don't stop crating entirely, every additional hour of freedom is good for their dogs.

Right now the Internet and online communities are fueling Excessive Crating. But meanwhile many other dog lovers aren't even aware there's a problem. **Tell your personal stories online to spread awareness**. (And also give us feedback through social media.)

22. Talk to people about why you don't crate, including your own circle of acquaintances and also people you meet at dog events or online communities. You may find like-minded people who are against abusive crating; and this is a way to build a strong network and build momentum. Also, **the fact that you stand against crating can leave a powerful impression on people**- employees and coworkers; neighbors, parents at your children's school or families you worship with. If people know you, trust you and admire you, they'll value your opinion. Remember that many people excessively cage their dogs just because of pressure from acquaintances or people who work with dogs; yet meanwhile they're open for better options. Once they realize that nice people they know (like you) *don't* crate, they're likely to see the subject in a different light.

23. You can help dogs in trouble even if you don't own a dog: The fact that Americans tend to cherish our pets is part of our notion of "quality of life" and you don't have to be a dog owner to be a dog lover who feels it's important for animals to live in humane conditions. Even if you don't own a dog right now- make your feelings known to abolish cruelties against dogs- both in puppy mills and private homes.

Why not ask your kids for advice? The likelihood is that your children's intuition already tells them that crating or caging family dogs isn't right. And most kids won't hesitate to speak out about it! The reaction of the little boy in the story of Champ is based on children's reactions that we encounter all the time. Of course, parents must always make decisions for their children based on what is safe. *And in certain situations, notably with aggressive dogs, a dog cannot be immediately released around children until the animal's behavioral symptoms are treated.* But these cases are the exception.

As long as you know your dog or puppy is safe around your kids, if the kids keep telling you that it's mean to keep him locked up, why not refrain from arguing with them and try a more humane way of housing or containing him? Instead of just repeating pro-crating "facts" to your children that you heard from acquaintances, dog trainers or over the Internet, why not take a breath and let the kids talk? Ask them why they think crating is cruel or why they think the dog or puppy should have more freedom. Children, especially young children, often have amazingly clear logic unclouded by popular societal trends and prejudices. So why not take some time to sit down together and really listen? You may learn more about your dogs from your childrens' insights than from all the professional "dog people" out there!

Appendix- Recommended Reading

We complied this list as an overview of dog training, dog psychology and dog behavior books (plus one DVD and one website). These books range from in-depth scientific research and canine behavioral theory to lighthearted activities. We've attempted to include authors who use gentle methods and don't support crating, but we ask readers to disregard crating references if they find any. There are many other valuable dog training books and resources. But, since crating information is so ubiquitous, we prefer that readers screen materials on depth on their own.

Also, follow the authors, Ray & Emma Lincoln online for the upcoming release of our books *Awesome Puppy, Dog In a Box,* and a book that will include step-by-step instructions for training house manners and obedience commands.

Coren, Stanley. *How dogs think: understanding the canine mind.* New York: Free Press, 2004.

Delmar, Diana. *The guilt-free dog owner's guide: caring for a dog when you're short on time and space.* Pownal, Vt.: Storey Communications, 1990.

Diamond Davis, Kathy, *Therapy Dogs: Training Your Dog to Help Others*. Dogwise Publishing. (includes good general training info.; Also the author of *Responsible Dog Ownership*.)

Fennell, Jan, and Monty Roberts. *The dog listener: a noted expert tells you how to communicate with your dog for willing cooperation.* New York, NY: HarperResource, 2000.

Frost, April, and Rondi Lightmark. *Beyond obedience: training with awareness for you and your dog.* New York: Harmony Books, 1998.

Langbehn, Jenny, and Pat Doyle. *97 ways to make a dog smile* . New York: Workman Pub., 2003. (Simple, lighthearted activities to have fun & bond)

Libby, Tracy. *High-energy dogs: a practical guide to living with energetic and driven canines.* Neptune City, NJ: T.F.H. Publications, 2009. Print.

Lindsay, Steven R.. *Handbook of applied dog behavior and training* . Ames: Iowa State University Press, 2000-2001. Print. (the definitive in-depth scientific guide. Vols. 1 and 2 are cited frequently in this book. Also vol. 3. This book is often used in college curricula)

McConnell, Patricia B.. *For the love of a dog: understanding emotion in you and your best friend*. New York: Ballantine Books, 2006. Print. (includes photos of dogs' expressions; we also recommend the other books & video materials by this compassionate dog behavior expert)

Weston, David, and Ruth Weston. *Dog problems - the gentle modern cure* . Flemington, Vic: Hyland House, 2005. Print.

Wilde, Nicole, Help for Your Fearful Dog: A Step-by-Step Guide to Helping Your Dog Conquer His Fears, Phantom Publishing; 2006. Print

DVD: 15 Easy & Fun Tricks to Teach Your Dog, Claire Arrowsmith, Nylabone Library (no cruel methods; fun and lighthearted)

Dog Breed Info.com (our favorite website for breed personality info. Avoid the link for crating!)

Bibliography:

(Pro-crating) Andersen, Jodi. *The Latchkey Dog.* Harper Collins, 2002. Print
Beaver, Bonnie V. G.. *The veterinarian's encyclopedia of animal behavior* . Ames: Iowa State University Press, 1994. Print.

Beck, Alan M., and Aaron Honori Katcher. *Between pets and people: the importance of animal companionship.* New York: Putnam, 1983. Print.

Becker, Marty, and Danelle Morton. *The healing power of pets: harnessing the amazing ability of pets to make and keep people happy and healthy.* New York: Hyperion, 2002. Print.

Budiansky, Stephen. *The truth about dogs: an inquiry into the ancestry, social conventions, mental habits, and moral fiber of Canis familiaris.* New York: Viking, 2000. Print.

Coren, Stanley. *How dogs think: understanding the canine mind.* New York: Free Press, 2004. Print.

Delmar, Diana. *The guilt-free dog owner's guide: caring for a dog when you're short on time and space.* Pownal, Vt.: Storey Communications, 1990. Print.

(Pro-crating) Donaldson, Jean. *The Culture Clash.* James & Kenneth Publishers, 1996. Print.
Eckstein, Warren, and Fay Eckstein. *Understanding your pet: the Eckstein method of pet therapy and behavior training.* New York: H. Holt, 1985. Print.

Eckstein, Warren, and Andrea Eckstein. *How to get your dog to do what you want: a loving approach to unleashing your dog's astonishing potential.* New York: F. Columbine, 1994. Print.

Fennell, Jan, and Monty Roberts. *The dog listener: a noted expert tells you how to communicate with your dog for willing cooperation.* New York, NY: HarperResource, 2000. Print.

Festinger, Leon. *Cognitive dissonance / Leon Festinger* . Des Moines, Iowa: Communications Data Services, 1962. Print.

Fogle, Bruce. *K.I.S.S guide to living with a dog* . New York: Dorling Kindersley, 2000. Print.

Fox, Michael W.. *Understanding your pet: pet care and humane concerns.* New York : Coward, Mccann & Geoghegan, 1978. Print.

Fox, Michael W.. *Superdog: raising the perfect canine companion*. New York: Howell Book House, 1990. Print.

Frost, April, and Rondi Lightmark. *Beyond obedience: training with awareness for you and your dog*. New York: Harmony Books, 1998. Print.

Gallagher, Winifred. *House thinking: a room-by-room look at how we live*. New York: HarperCollins, 2006. Print.

(Pro-crating) Geller, Tamar. *The Loved Dog*. Simon Spotlight Entertainment, 2007. Print
Grogan, John. *Marley & me: life and love with the world's worst dog*. New York: Morrow, 2005. Print.

Horwitz, Debra F. & Jacqueline C. Nelson, *Blackwell's Five-Minute Veterinary Consult Clinical Companion*, Blackwell Publishing, Print

Horowitz, Alexandra. *Inside of a dog: what dogs see, smell, and know*. New York: Scribner, 2009. Print.

Jackson, Maggie. *Distracted: the erosion of attention and the coming Dark Age*. Amherst, N.Y.: Prometheus Books, 2008. Print.

Jessup, Diane. *The working pit bull* . Neptune City, N.J.: T.F.H., 1995. Print.

Jessup, Diane. *The dog who spoke with gods*. New York: St. Martin's Press, 2001. Print.

Libby, Tracy. *High-energy dogs: a practical guide to living with energetic and driven canines*. Neptune City, NJ: T.F.H. Publications, 2009. Print.

Lindsay, Steven R.. *Handbook of applied dog behavior and training* . Ames: Iowa State University Press, 20002001. Print.

Lobprise, Heidi B.. *Blackwell's five minute veterinary consult clinical companion: small animal dentistry*. Ames, Iowa: Blackwell Pub., 2007. Print.

Loeb, Paul, and Suzanne Hlavacek. *Smarter than you think: a revolutionary approach to teaching and understanding your dog in just a few hours*. New York: Pocket Books, 1997. Print.

(Pro-crating) McClennan, Bardi. *Dogs & Kids; Parenting Tips*. Howell Books, 1993. Print
McConnell, Patricia B.. *For the love of a dog: understanding emotion in you and your best friend*. New York: Ballantine Books, 2006. Print.

Mech, L. David. *The wolf: the ecology and behavior of an endangered species,*. [1st ed. Garden City, N.Y.: Published for the American Museum of Natural History by the Natural History Press, 1970. Print.

Millan, Cesar, and Melissa Jo. Peltier. *A member of the family: Cesar Millan's guide to a lifetime of fulfillment with your dog.* New York: Harmony Books, 2008. Print.

Schaffer, Michael. *One nation under dog: adventures in the new world of prozac-popping puppies, dog-park politics, and organic pet food.* New York: Henry Holt, 2009. Print.

Tennant, Colin. *21 days to train your dog* . Richmond Hill, Ont.: Firefly Books, 2004. Print.

Weston, David, and Ruth Weston. *Dog problems - the gentle modern cure* . Flemington, Vic: Hyland House, 2005. Print.

Magazine/Journal Articles:
"Sensory, Emotional and Social Development of the Young Dog", *The Bulletin for Veterinary Clinical Ethology,* Vol. 2, n1-2, pp 6-29, 1994, Brussels

"Scandal of America's Puppy Mills", Michael Ecenberger, *Reader's Digest,* Feb, 1999

"Operation Rescue", Barry Yeomen, O; *The Oprah Magazine,* June 2009

"What I Know for Sure", Oprah Winfrey, O; *The Oprah Magazine,* June 2009

Dog World, May 2009
Wendy Bedwell Wilson (Statistics about global pet food sales)

"The Making of Dog-dogs and People-Dogs"
Ed. Bailey, *Gundog Magazine,* 1989

Veterinary Forum, November, 2008

"Eating Dogs, Cats Could Be Outlawed" *Global Times,* Jan 27, 2010

"Truth About Pet Trade: Extremely Sad Case in Mississippi" *The Daily Journal,* May 22, 2008

"SPCA raids 'horrific' LeHigh County kennel", Amy Worden, *Philadelphia Enquirer,* October 2, 2008

"Keeping Dogs Friendly", *Better Homes and Gardens*, May 2006

"Bel Air's well-bred pooches are in fact "factory farmed", Andrew Grumbel, *The Independent World*, Dec 13, 2007

Barker, Phil. "Cognitive Dissonance." *Beyond Intractability*. Eds. Guy Burgess and Heidi Burgess. Conflict Research Consortium, University of Colorado, Boulder. Posted: September 2003 <http://www.beyondintractability.org/essay/cognitive_dissonance/>.)

"Animal Agents searching Upper Milford Kennel on Suspicion of Cruelty", Dan Sheehan, the *Morning Call*, Oct 1, 2008,

Daniel Anderson and Heather Kirkorian, "Attention and Television" in *The Psychology of Entertainment"*, 2006

Interview with Elinor Ochs, See also Joseph Verrengia, "American Families' Plight: Lives Structured to a Fault", *Seattle Times*, March 20, 2005

Barbara Schnieder and N. Broege, in "Why Working Families Avoid Flexibility: The Costs of Overworking", paper presented at the Alfred P. Sloan International Conference, "Why Workplace Flexibility Matters" Chicago, May 17, 2006

Eulynn Shiu and Amanda Lenhart, "How Americans Use Instant Messaging", Washington, DC: Pew International & American Life Project, 2004

"U.S. Pet Ownership Statistics", December 30, 2009, The Humane Society of the United States

"The Rise of Dog Identity Politics", *John Homans, New York Magazine*, Feb 1, 2010

"Chesco Farmer charged with animal cruelty", Nancy Petersen, *Philadelphia Inquirer*, Fri. Jul 18, 2008

"Animal-cruelty convictions Stand; West Earl kennel operator looses appeal, 18 dogs seized in raid", Susan Lindt, *Intelligencer Journal*, May 31, 2008

"Wild dogs maul elderly couple on Georgia Road", Deseret News (Salt Lake City), Aug 19, 2009, by Kate Brumback, Associated Press

(Pro-crating) "Crate Craft", Stephanie Bossence, *Animal Wellness Magazine,* Oct/Nov 2008, Pg. 78

Court Documents:

State of Florida vs. Christine Dawn Abrams, Case No. 05-2008-CF-020434

Web References:

www.mainlinerescue.com

WolfCountry.net www.wolfcountry.net/information/Wolfpup.html

Barker, Phil. "Cognitive Dissonance." *Beyond Intractability*. Eds. Guy Burgess and Heidi Burgess. Conflict Research Consortium, University of Colorado, Boulder. Posted: September 2003 <www.beyondintractability.org/essay/cognitive_dissonance/>.

Puppy Gal's English Bulldog Medical Information, http://www.puppygal.com/english_bulldog_medical_crate_behavior_problems.html referring to: http://www.doglinks.co.nz/problems/barry_place/obsessive_compulsive_behavior.html

Champaign County Humane Society Pet Library Online; Home Alone? Basic Time Management for Your Dog http://www.cuhumane.org/topics/alone.html

PETA.org "Animal Rights Uncompromised: Crating Dogs"
Also: KP's blog; http://bloghelpinganimals.com/2008/03/but_he_loves_his_crate.php

"Pet Industry Continues to Defy Recession" ohmidog! Feb 9, 2010

"Dogs Rescued from W. Va. Puppy Mill on Road to New Lives", The Humane Society of the United States, Aug 25, 2008, www.humanesociety.org

"They Eat Dogs in China: Slaughter and Cruelty"!: "The Shocking and Inhumane Treatment of Dogs in Modern Day China"; "Dog Meat Industry in China"; "Dog Meat Factories in China", Squidoo.com

Vet Info.com "A Guide to Dog Anxiety Medication"

National Animal Interest Alliance (NAIA), "Are There Too Many Dogs and Cats?", by Norma Bennett Woolf

Reading Eagle.com, "Humane Society Officers Raid Maxatawny Township Kennel, Seize Dogs"), Sept 3, 2008
http://readingeagle.com/article.aspx?id=104525

Able2Know.com, "A Dog's Intelligence", Doug Gross, CNN Aug 8, 2009 (citing Stanley Coren, *The Intelligence of Dogs*)

"Harrison's son expected to recover", Associated Press, May 23, 2009;
http://.espn.go.com.nfl.news/story?id=4199432

American Pet Products Association, Industry Statistics & Trends, 2009/2010 National Pet Owner's Survey;
httpwww.americanpetproducts.org/press_industrytrends.asp

American Veterinary Medical Association (AVMA), Dog Bite Statistics, (avma.org)
http:/www.avma.org/press/story_ideas/dog_bites.asp

"Animal Planet Investigates: Petland", May 17, 2010
YouTube, "I'm Alive, Puppy Mill Documentary, Part 3, Pets of Bel Air: Peddling Puppy Mill Pups" (from LAPM, Locals Against Puppy Mills website)

Suite101.com; Oct 6, 2010, "Puppy Mill Cruelty Prevention Act, Missouri Proposition B", by Joy Butler

American Pet Products Association (APPA), Industry Statistics & Trends, (americanpetproducts.org),
http:/www.americanpetproducts.org/press_industrytrends.asp

Donald Hanson, Trends in Training- The Evolution of a Pet Care Professional, 2008, ABKA-19MAROB.doc

Yahoo! Answers, "What are the effects of long term crating?
http://anwers.yahoo.com/question/index?qid=20071224021148AA7G4PF

"Animal Cognition" online, study by Friederike Range from the University of Vienna in Austria (reported in *Veterinary Forum*, November 2008)

ASPCA Kids, "Animal Testing", http://www.aspca.org/aspcakids/real_issues/animal-testing.aspx

Bloomberg Businessweek, "The Pet Economy" by Diane Brady and Christopher Palmieri, Aug 6, 2007,
http://www.business.com/magazine/content/07-32/b40450001.htm

(Pro-crating) Wuda Face Shar-Pei- Crate Training, "Crate Training... Your Pet's Home" (information noted as provided by "Mid-West Homes for Pets"), http://homepaonline.com/wudaface/CRATETRN.HTM

(Pro-crating) Midwest Homes for Pets, "Why Crate Train", midwesthomesforpets.com/information/WhyCrateTrain.aspx

(Pro-crating) Terrific Pets.com, discussion board, training topics

(Pro-crating) DPCA Breeder's Education Website, "Safe Haven- the Ultimate Nap Zone", Aug. 16, 2009, http://www.dpca.org/BreedEd/crating_your_dpg.htm

About The Authors

Canine psychology specialists and authors of *The Cure for Useless Dog Syndrome*, husband and wife Ray & Emma Lincoln have had unique opportunities to observe dog behavior while treating complex canine issues in suburban environments. Long term advocates for environmental preservation and animal rescue, the authors learned that excessive crating is a poorly understood problem affecting a huge number of dogs, so they made it their personal mission to raise public awareness. *Dogs Hate Crates* combines months of research with the authors' previous education in psychology, philosophy, biology, animal behavior and social trends. Ray & Emma are wide-ranging travelers who now spend most of the year on Florida's East Coast.

Other Books by Ray & Emma Lincoln

The Cure for Useless Dog Syndrome
Awesome Puppy
Dog In a Box

Printed in Great Britain
by Amazon